CLAUDE JAY AND ALFONSO SALMERÓN

CLAUDE JAY
AND
ALFONSO SALMERÓN

Two Early Jesuits

William V. Bangert, S.J.

LOYOLA UNIVERSITY PRESS
Chicago 60657

© 1985 William V. Bangert, S.J.
All rights reserved
Printed in the United States of America

Loyola University Press
3441 North Ashland Avenue
Chicago, Illinois 60657

Book design by C. L. Tornatore

Library of Congress Cataloging in Publication Data

Bangert, William V.
Claude Jay and Alfonso Salmerón.
Bibliography: p. 437
Includes index.
1. LeJay, Claude, 1504–1552.   2. Salmerón, Alfonso,
1515–1585.   3. Jesuits—Biography.   I. Title.
BX3755.B36   1985   271′.53′022 [B]   85-186
ISBN 0-8294-0459-7

PIAE MEMORIAE
PARENTUM MEORUM
DILECTISSIMORUM

CONTENTS

ILLUSTRATIONS

Maps

Figures

PREFACE

At the foundation of the Society of Jesus in 1540 there were ten members: Ignatius Loyola, Francis Xavier, Pierre Favre, Simão Rodrigues, Diego Laynez, Alfonso Salmerón, Nicolás Bobadilla, Claude Jay, Paschase Broët, Jean Codure. Modern scholarly studies, in various languages, have been published on Loyola, Xavier, Favre, Rodrigues, and Laynez. Jay, Salmerón, Broët, Bobadilla, and Codure have not received their due. This volume is an effort to satisfy in part that debt.

Jay and Salmerón merit careful and reflective study because they were notably effective in bringing Ignatius's intuitions and aspirations to widespread areas of Europe. Ignatius, from 1537, when he arrived in Rome, until 1556, when he died there, rarely left the Eternal City. His excursions were few and only to nearby towns. Bologna, Faenza, Salzburg, Augsburg, Ingolstadt, and Vienna were among the towns never visited by Ignatius but in which his spiritual and cultural values were planted—and this by Jay and Salmerón. Without a close knowledge of these two men, any genuine understanding of the Jesuit contribution to the religious reform of the sixteenth century must remain truncated.

Claude Jay's achievements were distinguished. He exerted on Ignatius Loyola one of the greater influences to turn the Society of Jesus toward formal education as a Jesuit apostolate; he started the first Jesuit college in German-speaking lands; he was the apologist par excellence among the bishops of Bavaria and Austria for a program of educating learned and devout secular priests; he was Germany's regnant voice at the first period of the Council of Trent; and he developed a friendly rapport with German Protestants in a period of religious hostility.

Alfonso Salmerón's achievements also were notable. With his sixteen folio volumes of scriptural commentaries, he was among the first Jesuits to turn the Society toward the apostolate of publishing; for twenty years as provincial he directed one of the more important provinces of the early Society; he did yeoman's work in hammering out conciliar decrees through the three periods of the Council of Trent; and he was a leader in raising sacred oratory in Italy to a high level of dignity and elegance.

The last two lives of Claude Jay appeared within four years of each other, toward the close of the nineteenth century. Jean-M. Prat, S.J., published *Le Père Claude Le Jay: Un des Premièrs Compagnons de S. Ignace de Loyola* in 1874. Giuseppe Boero, S.J., issued his *Vita del Servo di Dio P. Claudio Iaia* in 1878. Prat's work is more ample and more fully researched than Boero's, which Boero himself acknowledges in the preface of his own volume. The last life of Salmerón, Boero's *Vita del Servo di Dio P. Alfonso Salmerone*, came out in 1880. Surely, after a century, the time has come to present fresh lives of Jay and Salmerón.

Since the publication of these biographies, important primary sources with extensive information about Jay and Salmerón have appeared. These include the 110 volumes of the *Monumenta Historica Societatis Jesu*; the *Concilium Tridentinum*, edited by Stephen Ehses and the Görres Gesellschaft; the *Acta Reformationis Catholicae Ecclesiam Germaniae Concernentia Saeculi XVI*, edited by Georg Pfeilschifter; and the *Beati Petri Canisii Societatis Jesu epistulae et acta*, edited by Otto Braunsberger, S.J. Even though outdated, the lives by Prat and Boero nevertheless still retain a value, limited though that value might be. They provide data from several older important works that are not readily available in the United States.

Among those older works which Prat cites are *Metropolis Salisburgensis* (1582) by Wiguleus Hund von u. zu Lauterbach; the *Viridarium Sanctorum* (1604–14) and the *Bavaria Sacra* (1628) by Matthäus Rader, S.J.; the *Historia Provinciae S.J.*

Germaniae Superioris (1727–29) by Ignaz Agricola, S.J.; the *Germania Sacra* (1727–55) by Marcus Hansiz, S.J.; the *Monumenta Vaticana historiam ecclesiasticam saeculi XVI illustrantia* (1861) by Hugo Laemmer. Among the works cited by Boero are *Portraits de héros* (1566) by Henri Pantaléon and the *Istoria della Compagnia di Giesù appartenente al Regno di Napoli* (1706–11) by Francesco Schinosi, S.J.

The specific quest of this volume is an understanding of those points at which Jay and Salmerón, as Jesuits, entered the highway of history that cuts through the sixteenth century. It is an effort to get a clearer and more precise view of those early meetings that took place between Europe and the new Society of Jesus. For the sake of clarity, this work is divided into two main parts, flanked by this introduction and a recapitulation. Part one is a study of Claude Jay as one personification of the initial meeting of Europe and the Society of Jesus. Part two is a study of Alfonso Salmerón under the same rubric. The recapitulation is a synthesis of what has gone before. Through parts one and two, the stalks of factual information are scattered widely over far-reaching fields; the conclusion gathers those stalks and binds them into sheaves. It is presented as a compendium of general headings under which are summarized those points at which the first Jesuits, especially Jay and Salmerón, moved into the European scene. A thread, therefore, laces all that follows into a unity. It is the inquiry into those junctures at which Jay and Salmerón, as members of the Society of Jesus, held their several rendezvous with European life.

The studies of Jay and Salmerón are deliberately detailed. They recount what the sources tell of their lives, day to day where possible, filled with preaching, advising bishops, conferring the sacraments, counselling penitents, guiding retreatants, and founding schools. Because the details can at times become tangled thickets, the reader may lose his or her sense of direction. To safeguard against this, several guideposts have been set in place. Each chapter has a brief introduction indicating the time and the major events to be covered, and ends with a brief conclusion summarizing the dominant features of the period just covered. Headings have been placed throughout the course of the narrative to alert the reader to the shifts in issues, persons, and tasks that occurred so often in the lives of those two men.

Two small cautions: one, Iñigo López de Loyola changed his name to Ignatius. The first recorded time that he used Ignatius was in August 1537; the last time he used Iñigo was in August 1546. In this volume the founder of the Society of Jesus appears as Iñigo up to his arrival in Rome in the fall of 1537. After that, he appears as Ignatius. And two, a number of quotations in foreign languages use incorrect grammar and spelling. This indicates the imperfect grasp some of the first Jesuits had of languages not their own. And it intimates how difficult at times was the work of translating.

Several Jesuits have given me much help in preparing this work for publication. Fr. Thomas H. Clancy and Fr. James J. Hennesey read the original text and made several suggestions for the betterment of its organization, style, and argument. Those suggestions I have tried to follow. Fr. Thomas M. McCoog prepared the index. Fr. Arthur C. Bender and Fr. Elmer J. Henderson proofread the galley sheets. Fr. Robert B. Clark handled the final editing and saw the work through the press. Their help was essential. I thank them all.

William V. Bangert, S.J.

Fordham University, The Bronx, New York
22 April 1985

PART I

CLAUDE JAY

CHAPTER I

SAVOY, PARIS, ROME, FAENZA
1504–1541

Introduction

This chapter opens with the probable year of Claude Jay's birth, 1504, and closes with 1541, the year Jay pronounced his vows as a Jesuit.

Jay, seemingly destined for a quiet life as a teacher in rural Savoy, went to Paris, met Ignatius Loyola, joined him and a group of his friends in founding the Society of Jesus, and so entered into one of the more powerful currents of the Catholic Reform of the sixteenth century.

Alpine Origins

In May 1521 a Swiss priest, Pierre Veillard, conducted a school in the Savoyard village of La Roche, which rested on the bank of a small stream that raced through the meadows and woods into the river Arve at Bonneville. Among Veillard's students were two Savoyard towheads, close friends, Claude Jay from Vulliets, and Pierre Favre from Villaret. Claude was then about seventeen years old; Pierre was fifteen.[1]

That same May, five hundred miles away, the troops of Francis I of France, on their way to aid the Navarrese in their rebellion against the rule of the Emperor Charles V, besieged Pamplona, a key town in the northern Spanish province of Navarre. On the twentieth of May, the cannon of the best artillerymen of Europe pounded the walls of the garrison. One of the defenders who fell, seriously wounded, was a Basque nobleman, Iñigo de Loyola. News of this military thrust by France through the Pyrenees probably never penetrated the valley of the river Arve, but the future of Claude and Pierre was tied to the litter in which the French carried Iñigo from the field of battle. Both were to be among his first nine companions in the founding of the Society of Jesus.

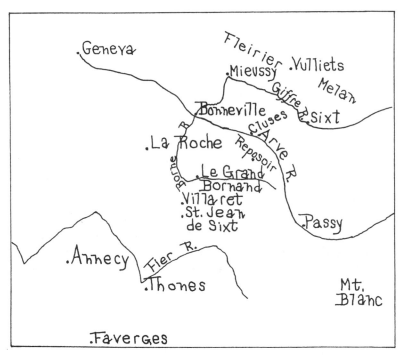

Homeland in Savoy of Claude Jay and Pierre Favre

High above the plain of Fleirier-Melan, through which winds the river Giffre, and looking across the soaring Alpine peaks lay a remote region known as Es-Gevallets. In the hamlet of Vulliets, known today as Vers les Jay, one of a half dozen similar hamlets

2

that clustered tightly together in Es-Gevallets, Claude spent his childhood with his sister Michelle and his brother Gervais. From his mountain house of wood and stone, set off against the rich apple orchards, Claude had a superb view of the southeast of Mount Blanc and its entourage of lesser peaks. Close by were the stables and hay lofts, the meadows and the cornfields. The large parish of Mieussy lay slightly to the west. About twenty miles still farther to the west was Geneva. And about twenty miles to the south was Villaret, the home of his friend Pierre Favre.[2]

Early Influences

Thirty years of living in this remote Alpine countryside left their mark on Jay's character. One dominant influence was the tightly knit form of family life. The six hamlets of Es-Gevallets formed an agricultural colony where a patriarchal kind of life was to be found. The twenty or so families were all related in one way or another, and many of their names, such as Briffoz, Chatellet, Delassait, Guebey, and Peyrasset, are still found in that part of Savoy. Claude's mother was of one of these families.[3] Claude's father, Gerard, was one of four sons of Rudolph Jay, who was possibly the first Jay to settle in Mieussy. One of these sons, Pierre, became a priest and in 1524 was the rector of the Chapel of Cinq Plaies in the church at Fleirier. Perhaps Claude began his formal schooling there under his uncle.[4] Tranquility of spirit, a natural openness, simplicity, quiet friendliness, and unassuming charm marked him through the years.

Then there was a strong religious influence. Claude's early years were in a world apart from the great international events of the age. From the hamlets of Savoy, little islands of venerable and revered customs, spread the popular devotions to the Five Wounds, the angels, and the saints.[5] The Carthusians took to the deep valleys and rugged mountains like the giant firs that dig deep into the Alpine soil. Close to Jay's home were the Charterhouses of Vallen and Melan. And not many miles away was the monastery of Reposoir, so loved by Pierre Favre, where Pierre's uncle, Dom Mermet Favre, was the prior.[6] This was the second influence in Jay's life. Piety and prayerfulness remained as constant traits of his character.

3

The strong religious sense of these mountain folk also permeated the school at La Roche, where Pierre Veillard was professor. There Claude received most of his education as he advanced through literary, philosophical, and theological studies. Veillard had come from Cluses to La Roche in 1517 or 1518. While at Cluses he published a small volume, *A Way to Write Letters* (*Modus Componendi Epistolas*), which he dedicated to the archbishop of Tarentaise, Claude de Chateauvieux.[7] For his theological lectures, Veillard used the *Sentences* of Peter the Lombard. Claude, when he was about sixteen, had already written out an abstract of the first book of the *Sentences*.[8] Pierre Favre recalled Veillard as a holy and fervent priest who breathed into the authors he taught a Christian spirit, "so that he turned them into teachers of the gospel" (*ut faceret evangelicos*).[9]

Veillard's teaching was a third influence in Claude's early life. Jay became what Johann Cochlaeus called Favre years later: a master of the affective life.[10] To the order and system that he learned from the method of Peter the Lombard, Jay brought a spirit of prayerful reflection that made theology more than an intellectual exercise. Impelled by the strong spiritual sense developed by his study, he wrote some dicta from Holy Scripture and the church fathers into his breviary: St. Luke's "Woe to you who love the first seats"; St. Augustine's "Unbecoming is it to have an appetite for high office, even if one fills it with credit"; St. Gregory the Great's "Let the strong in virtue take on the office of ruling only under constraint; let the unworthy go not near it even under compulsion"; St. Bernard's "Not everyone who is called to be a minister is chosen for the Kingdom, as is clear from the example of the reign of Saul and the priesthood of Judas."[11] Jay dug a single riverbed for the waters of piety and learning that flowed into his life.

Pierre Favre

Just as influential as the learning Claude received from Veillard was the friendship he formed with his younger fellow student Pierre Favre. Pierre, now a blessed in the calendar of the Catholic Church's saints, was to be the link between Claude and Iñigo de Loyola. A shepherd boy from Villaret in the delightful valley of the river Borne, at the age of seven Pierre had felt a special

4

attraction of God's grace to a life of holiness; and at twelve, when out in the fields one day tending his father's sheep, he had made a vow of chastity.[12] Within him there also burned a strong desire to grow in knowledge and learning, and it was this desire to go beyond what he had learned at La Roche that caused him at nineteen years of age to quit Savoy and to go north to the Aurora Borealis of Europe's intellectual world, the University of Paris.[13]

Whether Claude ever entertained the thought of going to Paris with Pierre is not known. He continued his studies in Savoy, and three years after Pierre had left he was ordained a priest at Geneva on 28 March 1528.[14] He offered his first solemn mass at Faverges. And it was at Faverges that this pleasant and pious man of medium height, blond hair, and grey eyes settled down to run a small college in the town.[15]

Five years passed before Jay and Favre met again. During these five years away from Savoy, Pierre had grown intellectually and spiritually. On 10 January 1529, after three years of philosophical studies, Pierre received his baccalaureate at the University of Paris, and on 15 March 1530, he received his licentiate, by which he was authorized to teach ''at Paris and anywhere else in the world.''[16] Pierre grew spiritually through the friendships he formed with two Basque gentlemen, Francisco de Jassu y Xavier and Iñigo López de Loyola. Francis Xavier, who was from Navarre and six days older than Favre, was a handsome, charming, slender man with black hair and dark brown eyes. He had come to Paris with tender memories of his devout mother kneeling with him before the family's large, graphic crucifix, and searing remembrances of the methodical destruction of his home by Cardinal Francisco Jiménes de Cisneros in reprisal for the Xaviers' rising against Spain on the death of King Ferdinand in 1516. Francis enrolled at the university at the same time as Favre. They became roommates at Collège Sainte-Barbe, fellow students, and dear friends.[17]

Iñigo López de Loyola

Iñigo was forty-two years old in 1533. He was born in the Basque province of Azpeitia in 1591, exquisitely trained as a courtier at the court of Ferdinand and Germaine de Foix; he was a gallant defender against invading French forces, a casualty in the siege of Pamplona in May 1521, and he experienced during a convalescence of eleven months at Loyola an interior conversion of heart and mind as he discovered in reading some medieval works of piety the immense majesty of God and the attractiveness of the person of Christ. During about a year of intense prayer and penance at Manresa, a little town about thirty miles from Barcelona, Iñigo experienced in turn deep desolation and high mystical exaltation; and he wrote the nucleus of a little manual that he called the *Spiritual Exercises*, a work which later became one of the masterpieces in the spiritual tradition of the Catholic Church. For a little less than five years before he arrived in Paris in 1528, Iñigo had studied at Barcelona and Alcalá—he was frustrated in his desire to study at Salamanca—in order to better equip himself for the service of Christ.[18]

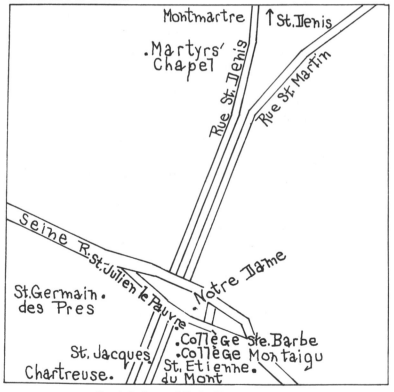

Sites in Paris especially familiar to the first Jesuits

In the fall of 1529, Iñigo transferred from Collège Montaigu, his first Parisian residence, to Collège Ste.-Barbe, where he became a roommate of Pierre Favre and Francis Xavier. Iñigo's tutor, Juan de Peña, asked Favre to coach Iñigo in philosophy.[19] At this time Pierre was experiencing deep interior desolation as relentless temptations to impurity, uncharitableness, and gluttony assailed him. He was prepared to flee to a desert place and eat nothing but herbs for the rest of his life, if only he could be freed from this cruel affliction. Indecision about his vocation, whether to marry, or be a doctor, or a monk, or a professor, only aggravated his distress. As the days of studying together passed by, the two men grew in love and respect for each other.

The day finally came when Pierre Favre opened wide the door of his soul to Iñigo and gave him full view of the grievous anguish and tribulations that he bore within. Without realizing it, Pierre had placed himself under the direction of one of the greatest spiritual masters in the history of the Church. Deftly and skillfully Iñigo went to work on loosening the shackles and releasing the fetters that had gripped Pierre's spirit. He told Pierre to make a general confession, showed him how to handle temptations, how to recognize the deceits of the evil spirit, how to control his tendencies to evil, and how to develop individual virtues. Quietly and gently, rays of peace and joy filled Pierre's soul.[20]

With interior tranquility came the discovery of his vocation. Iñigo told Pierre of his own personal resolve to follow Christ our Lord in poverty and apostolic zeal. Pierre determined to do the same, and in his own words, he and Iñigo became "one in will and desire." Thus in an obscure room in the large city of Paris, this union of Iñigo and Pierre formed the origin of a company of like-minded men who within a decade expanded and developed into the Society of Jesus. This then was the intellectual and spiritual background of Pierre Favre when he visited Claude Jay in 1533 and urged him to round out his studies at the University of Paris. For some reason or other—probably his obligations to the school at Faverges—Jay did not act immediately on Pierre's suggestion and therefore did not join him when he returned to Paris at the end of 1533.[21]

A Ceremony on Montmartre

When Favre arrived back at the university, he found that Iñigo had attracted a special group of friends who desired to share his spiritual ideals. All university students, they were, besides Xavier, the urbane but restless twenty-three year old Portuguese Simão Rodrigues, the gruff and impulsive twenty-four year old Castilian Nicolás Bobadilla, the brilliant and devout twenty-one year old Castilian Diego Laynez, and the candid and articulate nineteen year old Toledan Alfonso Salmerón. Two years later, in 1535, Iñigo confided to his nephew Beltrán that he was thinking of founding a *compañía*, a pious confraternity.[22] In Paris he had already set about gathering its members.

These students had serious discussions on how to refine and implement their ideals. They decided that they would dedicate themselves to apostolic labor as priests in imitation of the poor Christ, and they would initiate their common project by a pilgrimage to the Holy Land. Once at Jerusalem, they would decide by vote whether to remain there or return to Europe. If the majority should decide to return, or if it proved impossible to work in the Holy Land, or if they could not even get there, they would go to Rome and place themselves at the disposition of the pope. They reached this last resolve not so much to help the pope as to obtain the pope's help for themselves in determining the areas of the world in which they should labor. In their discussions they differed about what their mission should be once their commitments to the Holy Land had been fulfilled. Since, as Favre explained, the pope had a knowledge of the Church that was worldwide and that rose above regional and national concerns, he and his friends decided to seek the pope's aid in discovering more surely what was God's will for themselves.[23] By August 1534 all, save Xavier, had made the Spiritual Exercises. Favre, who was ordained on 30 May and offered his first mass on 22 July 1534, was the first of the group to become a priest. The seven then decided to ratify their resolutions in an intimate and private ceremony.[24]

On the morning of 15 August, the feast of the Assumption of the Blessed Virgin Mary, they left the Latin Quarter, crossed the Seine, and ascended the steep slope of Montmartre to the little Martyrs' Chapel, dedicated to St. Denis, St. Rusticus, and St.

Eleutherius, who, as tradition had it, suffered martyrdom at that spot. In the quiet and solitude of the crypt Favre offered mass. At the communion, as Favre held up the host before them, each pronounced his vows to be a man of poverty and chastity and to make a pilgrimage to the Holy Land. Favre then turned to the altar and pronounced his vows. This simple ceremony, quiet and unpretentious, brought the men profound joy of heart. After the mass they had a picnic at a fountain on the side of the hill. There they stayed the remainder of the day, enjoying the consolations they experienced. Forty-three years later Simão Rodrigues recalled: "These fathers vowed themselves to God with a genuine and unlimited spirit of dedication. They made their offering with a spontaneity, a surrender of self-will, a trust in the divine mercy, that whenever I think back on the occasion, as I have often done, I am filled with intense fervor, renewed with a growth of piety, overtaken by wonder unspeakable."[25]

This simple ceremony had a far-reaching significance. In many corners of Europe through the fifteenth century and the first part of the sixteenth century small springs began to break forth, and these eventually built up into the flood tide of Catholic reform. Forty years before this event, Cardinal Francisco Jiménes de Cisneros started his purification of the Franciscans in Spain; thirty-seven years before, in the city of Genoa, a lay woman named Catherine Fieschi inspired the formation of the Oratory of Divine Love; ten years before, Gaetano di Thiene and Gianpietro Carafa, members of the Roman Oratory of Divine Love, received papal approbation for the foundation of the Theatines; five years before, Matteo di Bassi drew up the rule for the Capuchins; four years before, Antonio Maria Zaccaria founded the Barnabites; and one year after, Angela Merici organized her Brescian group of women, the Ursulines, for the education of girls. Iñigo and his friends at Montmartre contributed to the rising tide of spiritual energy within the Catholic Church.

Jay at the University of Paris

About a month and a half after the ceremony at Montmartre, Jay arrived at Paris in October of 1534 and enrolled at Collège Ste.-Barbe.[26] Soon afterwards, under Favre's guidance, he went through the Spiritual Exercises for thirty days. During that period of intense prayer Jay heard Favre open up the treasure of meaning behind the terse and abrupt phrases of the Exercises with his soft voice, gentle eloquence, and delightfully winning manner.[27] (In the estimation of Iñigo, Favre was the retreat master par excellence among the early Jesuits). Jay was now thirty years of age and wholehearted in his desire to make a worthy retreat. He showed the measure of his generosity by a complete fast from food and drink for three days.[28] In his own interior spirit he lived the experience of Iñigo as he knelt before Christ crucified and asked himself: ''What have I done for Christ? What am I doing for Christ? What ought I to do for Christ?'', as he professed his earnest desire to follow Christ in poverty and humility, as he repeatedly begged the grace to know Christ more intimately, to love him more ardently, and to follow him much more closely.

The Spiritual Exercises revealed clearly to Jay the unseen bond that held Iñigo and his friends in such a close unity. Jay decided to enter that special circle, and on 15 August 1535, the first anniversary of the vows pronounced by Iñigo, Favre, and the others, Jay joined the group as they ascended Montmartre to the chapel of St. Denis. There he made for the first time, as the others renewed them, the promises to lead a life of poverty and chastity, and to go to the Holy Land.[29] Jay was Pierre Favre's first catch in the net that he would, in the years ahead, spread over northern Italy, the Rhineland, Bavaria, the Netherlands, the Iberian peninsula, and that would bring many young men of various nationalities to the Society of Jesus.

When Jay completed the Spiritual Exercises, he started his program of study to earn his academic degrees. On 6 March 1535 he stood for his licentiate examination. He made a mediocre showing, placing seventy-third in a list that normally numbered a hundred. During his philosophical studies, he also followed lectures in theology. In October 1536 he received the degree of master of arts.[30]

Jay pursued this program of studies during a period of intense intellectual ferment in the university. Old and new forms of thought, old and new scholarly preoccupations, old and new moral attitudes were locked in combat. The university had become the lists in which a momentous joust was taking place. Imbart de la Tour discerned in this intellectual struggle a major turning point in Europe's history. "No period was more complex, more intricate, more unsettled, yet at the same time none more fecund. It was during this period that the religious character of the sixteenth century was delineated. . . . The great epoch of the Renaissance was closed; a theological era was under way. Humanity in its reflection had learned from antiquity all that it could teach. Other problems, other predilections rose to the ascendancy: mankind's moral purpose, salvation, faith."[31]

Christian Humanism

This theological era lit one of the more intense intellectual flames of the age, whose light illumined the road taken by Iñigo and his friends. It was Christian Humanism, marked by a concentration of study on the Scriptures and the church fathers. It evoked at least three important reactions in Paris: conservative, progressive, and revolutionary.[32] Noël Beda, the intransigent repudiator of innovation, represented the negative and conservative response. Jacques Lefèvre d'Etaples (Faber Stapulensis), devout apostle of the interior life as delineated by Raymond Lull, Nicholas of Cusa, and Pseudo-Dionysius, and diligent searcher into the "coffers full of manuscripts of works on mysticism,"[33] embodied the positive and progressive response.[34] John Calvin, who also sought reform but by breaking with the traditional church, personified the revolutionary reaction.[35] When Jay arrived at the university, Beda, Lefèvre, and Calvin were still living, but no longer in Paris.

Jay's enrollment at Collège Ste.-Barbe guaranteed that he would feel the full impact of Lefèvre's brand of the new Christian Humanism. In 1534, the year Jay came to Paris, André de Gouvea, brilliant champion of a scripturally and patristically oriented theology, terminated a period of substituting as rector of the college for his uncle, Diogo de Gouvea.[36] André had broken with his uncle's educational conservatism and actively advanced a theology permeated with Scripture and the church fathers rather than the sophistries of authors like Pierre Tartaret and Durand de Saint-Pourçain.[37] Jay's earlier education in Savoy, marked by the piety of the Devotio Moderna and an intimacy with Scripture and the

11

church fathers, fitted congenially into this intellectual and spiritual atmosphere of Collège Ste.-Barbe, so deeply colored by the influence of Lefèvre d'Etaples.

Lefèvre, according to Beatus Rhenanus, one of his students, aimed at a union of wisdom and piety and eloquence. He sought a holiness, evangelical and pure, that harmonized with philosophy, envisaging a union of devotion and philosophical reflection, a union to be achieved by moving from the philosophy of Aristotle to Holy Scripture, the church fathers, and the mystics.[38] He taught a reading of the Scriptures that was guided by Cyprian, Hilary, Origen, Jerome, Augustine, Chrysostom, Athanasius, Nazianzen, John Damascene, and other fathers. "Once these studies have purified the mind and disciplined the senses", he insisted, "the generous mind may aspire to scale gradually the heights of contemplation, instructed by Nicholas of Cusa and the divine Dionysius and others like them."[39] In 1519, when he was about sixty-five years old, Lefèvre edited his last mystical work; and in 1520, his last patristic work. From then on he made the Gospels, which had long been the center of his religious life, the exclusive object of his scholarly endeavors. In 1522 he wrote:"To know nothing beyond the Gospels is to know all things."[40]

Iñigo, alert to the teachings of the past spiritual masters of the church, dipped sympathetically into this particular well of Christian Humanism.[41] In his Rules for Thinking with the Church, he praised what he called positive theology, a theology that moves in a notably spiritual ambience, shuns philosophical and speculative questions, and grounds itself in the data of Scripture and patrology.[42] With his composition of these rules, Iñigo became one of the first in history to use the term "positive theology."[43] He noted that "it is characteristic of the positive doctors, such as St. Augustine, St. Jerome, St. Gregory, and others, to rouse the affections so that we are moved to love and serve God our Lord in all things."[44]

Despite his respect for its spiritual orientation, Iñigo split with the Lefèvre brand of Christian Humanism. In it he detected an "adogmatic mysticism," and this he rejected, as indeed he repudiated the semirationalism of Erasmus.[45] Lefèvre condemned scholastic theology as "empty sophistry."[46] Iñigo endorsed it as an instrument of clear and precise understanding. In his Rules for

Thinking with the Church, Iñigo wrote that scholasticism merited praise and that "it is more characteristic of the scholastic doctors, such as St. Thomas, St. Bonaventure, the Master of the Sentences, and others, to define and state clearly, according to the needs of our times, the doctrines that are necessary for eternal salvation, and that help to refute and expose more efficaciously all errors and fallacies."[47] This was Iñigo's response to one of the more pressing needs of the day: logical, clear, precise thought.[48]

This response had profound significance because Iñigo was addressing an age that culminated "in a relativization of traditional, objective, doctrinal Christianity."[49] He met head-on the Middle Ages at its journey's end of "theological unclarity."[50] He went beyond Lefèvre and endorsed a synthesis of "two finalities or rather two genera or two forms of theology."[51] There were two needs in that day that demanded the attention of the theologian: humanism and heresy. Between them there were close ties.[52] Lefèvre addressed only the first. Iñigo addressed the first and the second. Lefèvre's response, for all its spiritual cast, was truncated and adogmatic. Iñigo's response, also spiritual in its intent, was in its quest for dogmatic precision more complete and therefore more rich.

Claude Jay, therefore, entered a circle of friends whose leader and inspirer conceived a synthesis of two "finalities of theology," spiritual and speculative, that Lefèvre put in opposition. This form of Christian Humanism intensified and carried forward the basic spiritual and intellectual formation that Jay had received from Père Veillard at La Roche. In later years, especially at the Council of Trent and at the universities of Ingolstadt and Vienna, Jay radiated the fervor and the intelligence of his earlier training. One of the fruits of his Paris years remains in his theological reflections; they can be found in a 342-page manuscript in the archives of the Jesuit Upper German Province.[53] The scriptural and patristic emphasis is strong. The chief tract within the manuscript, from page twenty-one to page seventy-one, is an introduction to Holy Scripture and a treatment of hermeneutics.[54] Besides theses refuting Luther, Calvin, and others, the manuscript contains many quotations from Scripture, the church fathers, canon law, and theologians such as Alexander of Hales, Thomas Aquinas, Bonaventure, Erasmus, Cochlaeus, von Eck, and others.[55] A thread of continuity, therefore, ran through Jay's life, from Savoy, where he was born, to Paris, where he met Iñigo, and on to Vienna, where he died. It was a thread of a religiously stamped Christian Humanism.

Learning and Devotion

Jay and the other members of Iñigo's group of friends caught the attention of several professors and students at Paris, men as diverse as Diogo de Gouvea, Jerónimo Nadal, and Pedro Ortiz, who would remember them in one way or another in the years ahead. One of the devotees of humanism who recalled them was a brilliant and eccentric Norman, Guillaume Postel, who recorded his impressions of them and described what he detected in their brand of theology. Postel recognized a union of *eruditio* and *pietas*, of learning and devotion, "a kind of theology, most fruitful, slanted toward meditation, founded more on affectivity than on intellect," a kind that he felt had come into being with the Ignatian group.[56] In this union of *eruditio* and *pietas*, of learning and devotion, Postel discerned an alliance of Manresa and Paris, an amalgam of the *Spiritual Exercises* and the Master of Arts degree. Two ceremonies symbolized this union: the religious one at Montmartre and the academic one at the university. Six years, therefore, before the Society of Jesus came into being and when the Iñiguistas had no thought of forming a religious order, two emblems, *eruditio* and *pietas*, were set in place that would characterize the Jesuit apostolate through the centuries.

Pierre Favre stands out among Iñigo's friends as the one who achieved this harmony in his own life in a striking way. In 1543 a twenty-two year old Dutchman, Peter Canisius, who was studying at the University of Cologne heard about Favre, who was then at Mainz, went to see him, made the Spiritual Exercises under his direction, and then wrote to his friends in Cologne:

> I have found the man whom I was seeking, if indeed he is a man and not rather an angel of the Lord. Never have I seen nor heard a more learned and more profound theologian, or a man of such striking and remarkable holiness. His paramount desire is to labor with Christ for the salvation of souls. No word of his, be it in private conversation or in friendly greeting, or even while at table, is not filled with God, and never does he become wearisome or irksome to his listeners, so eloquent is he.[57]

Claude Jay, so like Peter in temperament and personality, also forged in his life this attractive harmony of *eruditio et pietas*. And Peter Canisius bore witness to this, as he had done for Favre. Years later, in 1550, Peter wrote of Jay and his dealings with the Protestants at the Diet of Augsburg, describing the learning and charity with which he handled the Protestant objections: "Superb artist that he is in understanding and treating with people, Jay responded with the utmost modesty, uncovered the roots of perplexities, gave freedom from doubts, illuminated the truth—and in such a manner that both Catholics and Protestants were filled with admiration."[58] On a page of his theological notes, still in unedited form, Jay wrote: "Nothing is sweeter in this life, nothing so draws the spirit from the love of the world, nothing so fortifies the soul against allurements, nothing so moves and helps us to every good work and every toil, as the grace of holy contemplation.[59] Jay stamped the entirety of his life, as well as his approach to theology, with that *eruditio et pietas* that Guillaume Postel recognized as a hallmark of the men gathered about Iñigo de Loyola.

The Move to Italy

About five months after Jay first reached Paris in the fall of 1534, and about five months before he first pronounced the vows at Montmartre on 15 August 1535, Iñigo was forced to leave Paris. Because of distressing and prostrating sickness, doctors advised him to seek relief in his native Azpeitia. He placed Favre in charge of the group, planned to meet them in Venice in the early part of 1537, and left Paris in March or April 1535.

During the next year, 1536, Favre guided two other men through the Spiritual Exercises: Paschase Broët, a priest of stately bearing from Picardy, and Jean Codure, an innocent and delightful Provençal. Like Jay, they too elected to join the group of friends; and on 15 August 1536, they joined the companions at Montmartre in the ceremony of vows to follow Christ in poverty and chastity and to honor him by visiting the Holy Land.[60]

International diplomacy and war then forced Favre and his friends to change their plans. In 1536 Emperor Charles V and King Francis I again went to war as the frayed cords of the Paix des

Dames of 1529 snapped. As imperial and French armies maneuvered in Provence, national feeling in Paris rose against the Spaniards, and Favre's group decided to leave for Venice ahead of schedule. They left in two groups, about five days apart, during mid-November of 1536.[61]

For nearly two months, along mired highways and under constant rain in Champagne, on windswept roads in Alsace, through deep snows in Switzerland and the Alpine valleys, they pushed on to Venice. Rodrigues recalled that they "desired with the greatest eagerness to suffer such things for God's sake." On 8 January 1537 they reached Venice. And there they found Iñigo, whose plans had also been altered and who had been in Venice since December 1535.[62]

About six months remained before Iñigo and his friends could sail for the Holy Land, because the pilgrim ships normally did not leave Venice until June or July. They decided, therefore, to spend their time in the service of the sick. They went to the hospitals of the city, washed the patients, made beds, swept the buildings, and buried the dead. These volunteer helpers, all masters of arts, created a minor sensation in the opulent and sophisticated city, and people went to the hospitals to verify for themselves the unusual stories they had heard.[63]

In mid-March the group decided to go to Rome to request the pope's blessing on their projected pilgrimage and to obtain his approval for the ordination of those not yet in holy orders. Iñigo alone remained in Venice, because there were two important men then at Rome who had reservations about him: Dr. Pedro Ortiz, the emperor's special representative at the Holy See, and Gianpietro Carafa, who was made a cardinal only three months earlier.[64] In Paris Ortiz had seen Iñigo's impact on the students and became suspicious. In Venice, Carafa, superior of the Theatine community, spoke with Iñigo and resented his criticism of the Theatine concept of religious poverty.

The journey to Rome under the heavy spring rains in many ways equalled the trip from Paris to Venice in discomfort and distress. With the others, Jay crossed swollen streams, waded through water up to his chest, eased hunger with pinecones, and begged for bread.[65] Before they reached Rome an incident occurred which revealed in a spontaneous way the veneration Jay

16

felt for Iñigo. At one place Jay, utterly famished and terribly weakened, fell to the ground. He could not go a step farther and calling to God in prayer, he said ''Lord, through the merits of your servant Iñigo free me from this infirmity.'' Then and there strength returned to his exhausted body, and he was able to go on to Rome with his companions.[66] In the evening of Palm Sunday, 25 March, the group passed through the Porta del Popolo into the Eternal City.

At Rome, to the great surprise of them all, Ortiz cordially greeted Iñigo's friends and arranged a meeting for them with Pope Paul III. The audience was odd. The Farnese pope enjoyed listening to theological discussions while he ate. On 3 April, Easter Tuesday, he took his noon meal at the Castel Sant' Angelo. Around the pope's table stood cardinals, bishops, and theologians. Into this scene the Ignatian group was introduced.[67] A lively theological give-and-take was soon under way as the members of the papal entourage questioned the new arrivals. The masters of Paris did credit to their alma mater. The slight sixty-nine year old pope with his strong intellect and piercing eyes applauded and said he was delighted with their combination of learning and modesty, and he spontaneously granted their request for his approval of their projected pilgrimage and for the ordination of the nonpriests.[68]

A Temporary Diaspora

On June 24, in Venice, Vincenzo Nigusanti, bishop of Arbe, ordained six of the companions—Salmerón had to wait because of his youth. After their ordination the men postponed their first masses in order to prepare themselves more worthily. Again they worked in the hospitals. About mid-July they sensed that this labor was impeding the deep recollection that they desired, and so they chose by lot different places to which they would scatter and there spend three months in solitude, prayer, and penance. After forty days of this strict regime, they would do some preaching for the rest of the three months. Iñigo assigned the groups, pairing a man of one national background with another of a different national provenance. Vicenza was the destination of Savoyard Favre and the Spaniard Laynez, and Iñigo personally joined them. The French Broët and Spanish Bobadilla went to Verona. The Basque Xavier and Spanish Salmerón went to Monselice. The Provençal

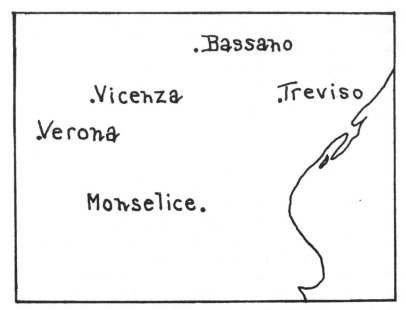

Towns of the dispersion of September–October 1537

Codure and Spanish Hozes went to Treviso. And the Savoyard Jay and Portuguese Rodrigues went to Bassano. They left Venice on 25 July.[69] At Bassano, in the hermitage of San Vito built outside the city walls, lived a pious, ignorant, and gaunt recluse named Antonio. Jay and Rodrigues followed Antonio's austere way of life, sleeping on planks, and driving a little donkey before them to carry the wine and wheat they had begged.[70]

Near the close of September, before the end of their planned three months of solitude, Iñigo summoned his friends to Vicenza, where he, Favre, and Laynez had created their own Thebaid in the windswept ruins of the abandoned Hieronymite monastery of San Pietro in Vivarolo. The reason for the abrupt change of plans was the formal entry on 13 September of Venice into the papal-imperial alliance against the Turks. Four months earlier, on 17 May, Suleiman had started westward with two hundred thousand troops. Throughout the summer there had been skirmishes between the Christian and Turkish fleets. When Venice finally entered the war, the sea-lanes of the Mediterranean became closed to pilgrims.[71] Iñigo and his friends therefore had to formulate fresh plans, and in late September they congregated at San Pietro in Vivarolo from

18

their various places of retreat. On dates unknown the newly ordained—save Iñigo and Rodrigues, who chose to delay even
longer—offered their first masses.[72]

Two Important Decisions

Despite the war on the Mediterranean, Iñigo and the others
still harbored hopes for a sailing the next year. Suleiman was
extending the olive branch to Venice, and the Venetians informed
Emperor Charles V of the Turkish peace feelers.[73] The pilgrimage
remained a strong possibility. With this happy prospect Iñigo and
his friends made two fresh decisions. The first, of long range
import, touched their identity as a group. Aware that their close
association with one another was attracting attention and that some
people were dubbing them Iñiguistas because Iñigo was their
leader, they decided, since Christ Jesus was the one to whom they
gave their deepest loyalty, and since he was the one who bound
them together in this special fellowship, to identify themselves as
the Society of Jesus.[74]

The second decision, of short range import, concerned their
occupation during the eight months or so that would elapse before
they could realistically expect to board ship for the Holy Land.
They decided, as they had done in July, to break into small groups,
to disperse, this time not to remote corners of solitude but rather
to university towns in northern and central Italy, and to seek
among the students there recruits for their Society, preach, counsel, administer the sacraments, and give the Spiritual Exercises.[75]
Iñigo, who planned to go to Rome with Favre and Laynez, was to
summon them to the Eternal City in the following spring, when
they would have to reassess the fluid situation. Iñigo assigned
Codure and Hozes to Padua, Broët and Salmerón to Siena, Xavier
and Bobadilla to Bologna, and Jay and Rodrigues to Ferrara.[76]

Ferrara of the Este Family

Jay and Rodrigues prepared for their work at Ferrara by a
further period of solitude with their hermit friend Antonio at Bassano.[77] Then they started south through the broad, fertile plain of
the Po, to the city of the Este family, which, after Medicean
Florence and papal Rome, was probably the most celebrated center

Towns of the dispersion of October 1537–1538

of all that was most beautiful and most despicable in the Renaissance. A short way to the right and across from the twelfth-century cathedral stood the focal point of Ferrara's cultural life, the famous Castello Estense "with its sombre moat, chained drawbridges, doleful dungeons, and unnumbered tragedies."[78] In that year Ferrara was a crossroads at which several diverse spiritual and cultural currents of the age converged.

Duke Ercole, son of Alfonso I and Lucrezia Borgia, incarnated one of those currents: the craftiness of the Renaissance prince amid the fickle and mercurial diplomacy of early modern Europe. When he succeeded his father in 1534, he inherited a diplomatic debacle. In 1528, when Alfonso tried to hammer out an alliance with France, Ercole married Princess Renée, daughter of Louis XII of France. Only a year later the alliance collapsed

20

when the king of France, the emperor, and the pope, by their treaties at Barcelona and Cambrai, isolated Ferrara. Princess Renée and her entourage became an awkward and irritating French presence at the Estense court.[79] Soon, however, after his father's death, Ercole took the initiative, and in 1535 broke the bond of isolation about him by forging a new alliance with the pope and the emperor against France. In April 1536 he imprisoned members of Renée's entourage.[80] Jay and Rodrigues arrived in Ferrara during this seesaw period in Ercole's diplomatic ventures.

Renée personalized another current: the incursion into Italy of the ideas of the Protestant Reformation. The most brilliant of the pleiad of intelligent women at the court of Francis I of France, and a religious woman of intense humanistic interests, she embraced the new transalpine religious and doctrinal movements that were penetrating all social classes in Italy, and harbored Protestant scholars and litterateurs at her court.[81] She appointed Madame de Soubise as her *gouvernante* and Clement Merot as her secretary. Lynn Jamet attended her. John Calvin, from whom she received spiritual direction, visited her. She corresponded, directly or indirectly, with Pier Paolo Vergerio, Camillo Renato, and Baldasarre Altieri.[82]

Renée's circle was neither the first nor sole Protestant presence in Ferrara. As early as 1521 the Vatican espied Lutheran ideas there. Protestants studied in the literary academies. The Sinapius brothers, Nascimbene Nascimbeni, and Francesco Porto held posts in the university. Protestants also served in Ercole's court.[83] In April 1536, as noted in the previous paragraph, Ercole jailed members of Renée's court. The immediate occasion was an incident at the ceremony of the adoration of the cross on Good Friday. One of Renée's court singers, Jehannet, refused to genuflect before the cross and stalked out of the church. Ercole, now committed to his anti-French alliance with the pope and the emperor, grasped this religious pretext to carry out his diplomatic design, and imprisoned Renée's French and Protestant circle.[84] The papal nuncio to France, Rodolfo Pio di Carpi, reported France's interpretation of the peculiar cast of Ercole's coup: an assault on French influence under the banner of Catholic orthodoxy. Georges d'Armagnac, bishop of Rodez, made the same judgment: "Political prisoners held captive on the pretext of their

[Protestant] faith.''[85] Jay and Rodrigues arrived in Ferrara at this point when the religious air was murky with diplomacy.

Vittoria Colonna, the marchesa of Pescara, personified still another current of the age: the intimate union of ardent piety and cultural aspiration. At this time this cultivated poetess was forty-five years old and was residing at the Este palace. She was a widow of twelve years, ever since her husband, Don Ferrante de Avalas, the marchese of Pescara, fell in the battle of Pavia in 1525. In the early 1530s she moved in the circle of intelligent women in and about Naples who embraced a Christian Humanism that was basically inspired by the biblical lectures of Juan Valdes. In her poems she combined her devotion and tender human feeling.[86] She came to know Reginald Pole, Gasparo Contarini, and others of that circle, and through them became absorbed in the reform of the Catholic Church. What Pole said she accepted as a message from God. She called Pole her Eliseus and Alvise Priuli his Giezi.[87] Since 8 May, six months before the arrival of Jay and Rodrigues in the city, she had been at the court of Ferrara. Duke Ercole had invited her in the hope that she might woo Renée from her Protestant beliefs.[88]

Bernard Ochino symbolized yet another current of the period: the strong impulse toward spiritual renewal within the church as realized in the new order of Capuchins. Ochino, future vicar general of the Capuchins, arrived in the city toward the end of November 1537 to preach the Advent sermons.[89] The gaunt, emaciated, austere friar, with his vibrant voice, mystical fervor, and direct and simple style that made him perhaps the most celebrated preacher then in Italy, received an enthusiastic welcome to Ferrara.[90] Vittoria Colonna, who had known Ochino since three years before in Rome, shared that enthusiasm.[91]

Jay and Rodrigues at Ferrara

At the height of this confluence of Renaissance splendor, Catholic reform, and Protestant penetration, humanism and religious ardor, Jay and Rodrigues appeared at Ferrara either in late October or early November 1537.[92] The weather could hardly have been worse. A cold penetrating fog lay about the buildings. Heavy rains deluged the streets. The two strangers went to the most poverty-stricken hospice of the city, an immense structure built of clay bricks, horribly damp, and open to every wind that swept across the city.[93] Rodrigues described the outrageous reception tendered them at the hospice.

> The care of the hospice was committed to a shrewish old woman who allowed no one to get into bed with any clothes on. Before she retired she insisted that each of the poor guests take off all his clothes, both outer and inner, in her presence, so that if any were found to be full of sores or showed other signs of disease, they could be shunted elsewhere. Those who were in good condition had to leave their clothes on the bench, at quite a distance from the bed, so as to allow no chance that the blankets and sheets be infected with lice. Then they got into bed. Our two brethren, to whom a single bed had been assigned, had to undress and stand naked before the eyes of this old woman. In this most difficult of situations they handled themselves with as delicate modesty as possible.[94]

This indignity was a wretched introduction to the brilliant city of the Este. But Jay and Rodrigues made this dreary hospice the starting point of their apostolic work. They began to teach their fellow guests Christian doctrine. The old custodian kept a sharp eye on them, noted that they ate little, and that they would get up after a brief sleep, light a lamp, put on their poor clothes, and spend hours in prayer. She told people what she saw, and soon the citizens of the town were talking about the two strangers. The gossip came to the ears of Vittoria Colonna. What especially aroused her interest was the talk about Jay and Rodrigues having hopes of going to the Holy Land. Vittoria herself had the same hope. One day she spoke to one of the two—Rodrigues does not say whether it was he or Jay—and confirmed what she had heard of their plans. Quietly she went off to the hospice and interviewed the caretaker. Garrulity was among the old woman's unattractive qualities, and she gave it full play as she depicted the edifying lives of her two guests. Vittoria rescued Jay and Rodrigues from the dank and drafty hospice and arranged that they be put up at another house for the poor, more commodious and where they could be sure of a room and some bread each night.[95]

Vittoria Colonna never reached the Holy Land. But this meeting with Jay and Rodrigues, her first with the Jesuits, turned her piety into fresh channels. "The first wave of the spiritual movement that Ignatius had stirred up had reached the soul of this great woman.''[96] She returned to Rome and became one of Ignatius's devoted helpers at the House of St. Martha that he founded for the care of fallen women.

In Ferrara, at the different piazzas of the city, Jay and Rodrigues gathered people together for instruction in their religion. They stressed the value of frequent holy communion. Ottaviano del Castello, the vicar general and administrator of the diocese in the absence of Cardinal Giovanni Salviati, dropped his initial reserve and invited them to dine with him.[97] He explained to his guests the reason for his original coolness and suspicion. ''Please forgive me that although officially obliged by reason of my office to foster worthy works, I never gave you a hand in your labors, nor ever encouraged your efforts with a sign of favor. But, really, my stance should not cause you surprise, since we are batted about by so many errors and so much maliciously concealed deceit these days that there is nothing so sacred and holy that it can escape the suspicions of even a prudent and balanced person.''[98] Del Castello voiced the uneasiness, the tension, and the suspicion that became part of the cultural and spiritual atmosphere in so many European cities and towns of the sixteenth century. Jay was to meet this state of affairs frequently in the years ahead.

Finally the court took notice of their presence in the city. Duke Ercole heard Jay and Rodrigues give their exhortations a number of times, and promised to defray all their expenses on their pilgrimage to Jerusalem. He confessed to Jay and received holy communion from him. Even though Jay and Rodrigues had gained entrée to the court, they continued to make the hospitals their favorite haunt.[99] Then, in the middle of March came a new development. At Padua, Diego Hozes, a Spaniard who had joined Ignatius at Venice and who had been working with Jean Codure, became ill and died. Rodrigues left Ferrara for Padua to take Hozes's place and Nicolás Bobadilla, who had been at Bologna with Xavier, quit Bologna to replace Rodrigues as Jay's companion.[100] Bobadilla's stay in Ferrara, however, was very brief, because not long after his arrival he and Jay received word from Ignatius to terminate their work there and go to Rome. Ignatius, who had been at Rome with Favre and Laynez since November 1537, had decided in the following spring to summon all his friends to the Eternal City.[101] Jay took leave of a profoundly grateful Duke Ercole, but he had not seen the last of Ferrara and its ruddy brick castello. Nine years later he would be back, only to experience a reception that was to prove how unpredictable a Renaissance prince could be.

The Ten Companions at Rome

By the end of April 1538, Ignatius and his friends were once more all together, this time in Rome, in a villa on the Pincio placed at their disposal by a generous patrician, Quirino Garzonio.[102] On 5 May Cardinal Gian Vincenzo Carafa gave them faculties to preach and hear confessions. This they did in several churches of the city. Jay worked at San Luigi dei Francesi.[103] However, the friendship of Garzonio and the approval of Carafa were offset by an outburst of opposition and libel that lasted several months.

The focal point of the trouble was the Augustinian friar, Agostino de Piemonte. Prior of Sant'Agostino in Pavia, a fine looking man of vibrant eloquence, the friar was the Lenten preacher of 1538 at the Augustinian church near Piazza Novara. Favre and Laynez heard him speak, detected Lutheran doctrine, and spoke to him in private. Fra Agostino refused to change his teaching. Without mentioning the friar by name, and with Ignatius's approval, four or five of the Society of Jesus began in May to preach against Agostino's doctrines.[104] Some men among Agostino's admirers inaugurated a smear campaign against their hero's critics. This Ignatius determined to fight. One calumny announced that Ignatius and his friends were wanted in several Italian cities on charges of heresy. In rebuttal, Ignatius presented several testimonials of approval from Siena, Bologna, and Ferrara. From the last city, Duke Ercole, recalling Jay's five months there, threw the weight of the house of Este behind Ignatius with a letter of praise of Jay and Bobadilla.[105] This he followed up with instructions to his Roman ambassador to give bond for the maligned men.[106] Ignatius's strategy worked, and on 18 November he capped his efforts by receiving an official document of vindication from the governor of Rome, Benedetto Conversini.[107]

Within a week after Conversini's decree of exoneration, Ignatius and his group made a momentous decision: to bind themselves in a profoundly personal way to the pope. The occasion

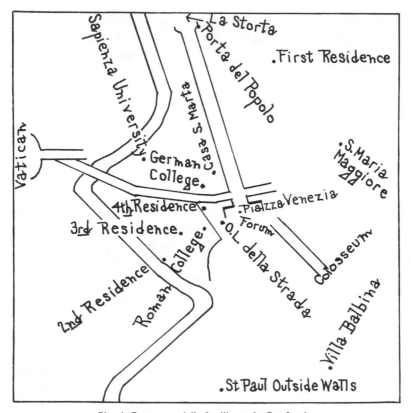

Sites in Rome especially familiar to the first Jesuits

for this decision was a casual remark by Pope Paul III. Four of the group were at the papal court, conducting one of their bimonthly theological discussions while the pontiff had his meal. Paul asked: "Why do you men have your heart so set on going to Jerusalem? Here in Italy you have a true Jerusalem if you are anxious to achieve some good in the church of God."[108] The four disputants brought back this remark to their friends. Reflection on it gave a new direction to their life. The war between Venice and the Turk made their vowed journey to the Holy Land an impossibility. In Paris, in 1534, when they had their quiet ceremony at Montmartre, they had decided that, if the trip to Jerusalem should be impracticable, they would place themselves at the disposition of the pope as a more sure way of discovering

26

God's will in regard to the area of the world in which they should labor. The pope's recent comment forced the issue. They therefore made their offer.

Ignatius later incorporated this bit of history in the *Constitutions of the Society of Jesus* when he wrote of the special vow of obedience to the pope in regard to missions that Jesuits pronounce in their solemn profession. "The intention of the fourth vow pertaining to the pope was not to designate a particular place but to have the members distributed throughout the various parts of the world. For those who first united to form the Society were from different provinces and realms and did not know into which regions they were to go, whether among the faithful or the unbelievers; and therefore, to avoid erring in the path of the Lord, they made that promise or vow in order that His Holiness might distribute them for greater glory to God."[109] This offer to Pope Paul III made a deep impression on Pierre Favre. In his spiritual diary he wrote: "This was a memorable blessing and the quasi foundation of the whole Society. . . . Therefore I shall ever feel, as indeed does each of the others, the obligation of giving thanks to Christ Jesus, head of the universal and Catholic Church, who through the voice of his vicar on earth deigned to show his pleasure in our serving him and his wish to use us even to eternity."[110] In that November of 1538, Ignatius and his friends defined another mark that would distinguish the future Society of Jesus: a readiness to move at the pope's bidding to any point in the world.

A month after this offer to the pope, a cold spell that lasted for months gripped Rome. From Christmas until the end of May, bitter cold, constant sleet, and driving rain brought to the city its worst winter in forty years. The crops of the previous fall had been poor. The extreme cold killed cattle and sheep. Corn, oil, and cheese became extravagantly expensive. Starving people poured into Rome from the countryside and died in the streets.[111] "No one," recorded Simão Rodrigues, "took care of these poor people; no one showed any friendliness. Nor was any to be found who was touched by the calamities of these miserable wretches.[112] Ignatius and his friends moved into this mass of frozen people. At night they went through the streets, guided the poor wretches they found back to their house, now a larger dwelling near the

Capitoline and the Church of Santa Maria in Aracoeli. There they washed them, fed them, and warmed them with the fire fed by the wood they themselves had gathered. Some four hundred they took care of in this way in their own house as well as about two thousand more in other sections of the city.[113] For Jay and his friends, this memorable experience, like their work in the hospitals of Venice, highlighted a characteristic of the early Jesuits: a penchant for the poor and the distressed.

Toward a New Religious Order

As 1538, the year 1539 was also a year of significant decision. And again it was the pope who gave the cue. In March 1539 Paul III, through Cardinal Gianpietro Carafa, directed Paschase Broët to go with another of the Ignatian group to Siena. There they would initiate a reform at the convent of Sant' Agnese, torn by a bitter struggle between two factions of Benedictine nuns, those of Sant' Agnese and those of San Prospero, who had been transferred to Sant' Agnese because of scandal.[114] This order brought Ignatius and his friends face to face with an ominous prospect: the breakup of their union, the gradual demolition of the arch of companionship which they had put together in Paris. Requests from various prelates and the plea of King Jāo III of Portugal, through Dr. Diogo de Gouvea, the former president of Collège Ste.-Barbe, for some of the group to go to the Indies underlined the imminent danger of dismemberment. This danger prompted them to consider even more thoroughly the nature of their vocation.[115]

Most likely as many as seventeen men participated in the discussions. Since their arrival at Rome, the original group of ten had received seven new companions, all Spaniards save one: Diego de Cáceres, the brothers Diego and Esteban Eguía, the brothers Antonio and Francisco de Strada, Antonio Araoz, and the Portuguese Bartolomeu Ferrão.[116] Systematically they arranged their discussions. They set up clearly defined issues. On these they prayed and reflected. In their meetings each presented his personal convictions. The minutes of the discussions, taken down by Antonio de Strada, reflected the earnest, simple, prayerful, and detached way in which they wrestled with the questions that would determine their future way of life.[117]

When Lent was almost over and the time was upon us when we must be divided and separated from one another . . . we decided to meet for several days before our separation and discuss among ourselves the subject of our vocation and manner of life. After several meetings we discovered ourselves, some of us being French, others Spaniards, others Savoyards, others Portuguese, to be split by differences of opinion on the question of our particular state in life. Yet in all of us there was one common mind and purpose, the seeking of God's good pleasure and his perfect will. . . . It was on the point of just what were the more expedient and fruitful means of achieving this divine will that our judgments were splintered. . . . Nor should anyone be surprised that this diversity should have existed among us, frail and weak as we are, when even the leaders and pillars of Holy Church, the Apostles, differed among themselves. . . . In view of this conflict of opinion that went nevertheless hand in hand with our intense desire of discovering some sort of *via media*, acceptable to all, we eventually reached the unanimous decision to give ourselves more fervently than usual to prayers, sacrifice and meditation. . . .

We therefore set to work and proposed to ourselves some *dubia* that merited carefully mature reflection and forethought. On these we thought, meditated, prayerfully pondered during the day. With a view to arriving at the truer judgment, tested and examined by the searching inquiries of several minds, at night each one presented to the group his personal opinion of what he judged the more expedient and proper.

On the first night that we met, this *dubium* was proposed: would it be better, now that we had offered and dedicated our life to Christ our Lord and to his true and legitimate vicar on earth to dispose of us as he willed, would it be better that we be so joined and bound into one body that no corporal division, no matter how great, would separate us one from another? That this point might be illustrated by an example: at this time the pontiff is sending two of us to the city of Siena. Should we be mindful of those two and they of us in a spirit of common understanding, or should we have no greater concern about them than we have for those who are not of the Society? At length we decided in the affirmative, that, inasmuch as the most clement and loving Lord had deigned to unite us, weak as we are and from such a variety of countries and backgrounds, we ought not break the God-given bond of unity but rather confirm and strengthen it with the passage of time.[118]

The issue that gave the most difficulty was whether the vow of obedience should be adopted as the means to preserve the unity they desired, since to add this vow to those of poverty and chastity meant effectively the creation of a new religious order. For about fifteen days they wrestled with this key problem. Finally they agreed that their Society of Jesus should become a canonically established religious community, contingent of course on papal approval. They underlined the solemnity of their decision by a private ceremony reminiscent of that at Montmartre on 15 August 1534. Again Pierre Favre was the celebrant of the mass. On 15 April Jay and ten of the others read the following formula at the communion of the mass:

> I . . . the undersigned, state in the presence of Almighty God and the most Blessed Virgin Mary and the entire heavenly court that, after prayer to God and after mature thought, I have freely arrived at the decision that it is more to God's praise and the Society's preservation that the vow of obedience be pronounced. Further, that I have deliberately offered myself, aside from any vow or other obligation, to enter the same Society, if the pope, God willing, should grant this confirmation. To the keeping of the memory of this decision, which I acknowledge is a gift of God, I now, with the same deliberation and despite my unworthiness, approach Holy Communion. The 15th of April, 1539.[119]

The First Sketch of the Institute

The discussions went on in orderly stages. On 3 May the group agreed on eleven other points, among which was the provision that each novice should spend three months in the Spiritual Exercises, in pilgrimage, and in service of the poor in hospitals or elsewhere. On 11 June they adopted three further clarifications, one of which determined that the general superior's term should be for life. By 24 June they resolved to forego choir, prescribed penances, and a distinctive habit, and to ratify formally their earlier desire to call their organization the Society of Jesus. "These discussions," they noted, "went off in peace and unity of spirit, and not without exacting vigils, prayer, and mental and bodily labor." At the bidding of his friends, Ignatius pulled together the results of the three months of meetings into a document of five chapters. It was known as the First Sketch of the Institute of the Society of Jesus (*Prima Societatis Jesu Instituti Summa*). In it Ignatius briefly sketched the basic characteristics of the Society of Jesus: its apostolic purpose in the propagation of the faith; its distinctive name; its practice of poverty through the gratuity of ministries; its special obedience by vow to the Holy See; the authority of the general; the omission of choral chant and music in religious ceremonies; the private recitation of the divine office; the exclusion of fixed penances.

Ignatius gave this formula to Cardinal Gasparo Contarini for submission to Pope Paul.

Ignatius made a shrewd move in asking Cardinal Contarini to present the document to the pope. Probably no one in the papal curia had ideas for church reform that so resonated with those of Ignatius. Contarini was then fifty-six years of age. Only five years earlier he had been a member of the Great Council of Venice. Then it was that Pope Paul, in reshaping the papal curia, nominated this distinguished layman a member of the college of cardinals. Paul recognized in Contarini the stamp of personal holiness, a holiness hammered out amid the swirl of an active civic life. Contarini's vision of holiness had crystallized in his early twenties when he formed a deep personal friendship with two unusual men. Tommaso Giustiniani, seven years older than Contarini, was his confessor. Vincenzo Quirini, four years Contarini's senior, became his alter ego. These two friends had together become intensely taken up with the spiritual renewal of the church, and this preoccupation began to shape Contarini's own thinking.[120]

Around 1512 Giustiniani and Quirini withdrew to the solitude of Sacro Eremo of Camaldoli. This move brought on a crisis in Contarini's life. It accentuated the attraction he felt for his friends. It also brought to the fore the strong pull he felt toward a life of charity in the public service of his countrymen. In 1513 the two hermits presented to Pope Leo X a plan for the spiritual renewal of the church. The breadth of their design absorbed Contarini. But the next year, 1514, Quirini died, and Giustiniani deflected his energies into the narrower channels of monastic reform. Contarini kept his eyes fixed on the ideal of Christian service in civil society. He went on to immerse himself in the busy world of the Renaissance as a diplomat, a political thinker, and a counselor in the Venetian government. With the demands of this activity he worked out a harmony with the exigencies of a vital Christian charity. Like Thomas More, whom he had met at least twice, he welded into an attractive unity a deep sense of religious devotion and an active civic life.[121]

When Contarini entered the college of cardinals, he pushed for the spiritual renewal of the Church. In a way, he became the spiritual legatee of the program presented to Leo X in 1513 by

Giustiniani and Quirini. This sensitivity to the inner depths of the Church's life alerted him to the reservoir of spiritual force he had found in Ignatius. Under Ignatius he had made the Spiritual Exercises in Venice. He became a warm admirer of his Basque director. He saw in the Ignatius of 1539 a man to carry out the aspirations of 1513 of his two eremetical friends of Sacro Eremo. He took Ignatius's document to Pope Paul in late June or early July of 1539.[122]

This First Sketch of the Institute crystallized tensions within the papal curia, and more than a year passed before the pope gave his formal and solemn approval. Paul first turned the document over to the Dominican Master of the Sacred Palace, Tommaso Badia. After two months, Badia judged the project to be a holy and pious one. On 2 September Contarini read to Paul the texts of Ignatius's First Sketch and of Badia's opinion. Paul, in a verbal expression of approval, commented that the Spirit of God was blowing there, and commissioned Cardinal Girolamo Ghinucci, the secretary for papal briefs, to draft the official document of approbation.[123] Here trouble began.

Ghinucci latched onto three items in the First Sketch of the Institute that especially troubled him: first, that the members of the Society of Jesus were to avoid the use of organs, music, and chant in the mass and other religious ceremonies; second, that the members were not to be obligated under pain of mortal sin to use distinctive penances such as fasts, disciplines, hairshirts, and other corporal austerities; and third, that the members were to make an additional vow of obedience to carry out whatever the pope should order for the propagation of the faith. Since choral chant of the office and fixed penances had been an integral part of the monastic tradition for centuries, Ghinucci feared that the first two items would seem to be concessions to the Lutherans, who had been strongly criticizing monastic practices. And he felt that the additional vow of obedience to the pope was superfluous.

Ghinucci articulated curial defensiveness in the face of change. Since his youth, when he served as secretary under Julius II and Leo X, he had always been closely associated with the papacy in various posts, including that of nuncio to the England of Henry VIII.[124] Prolonged association with the curial structures made him apprehensive in the face of the demonachization of religious life as envisaged by Ignatius. Contarini, on the other hand, contested Ghinucci's conservative stand. As has been seen, the Venetian cardinal spoke for openness to innovation and fresh idioms in the task of reform. He knew the modern world. In Ignatius's project he recognized an instrument to meet this modern world. Pope Paul was caught between the conflicting advice of two competent cardinals. To resolve the differences between Ghinucci and Contarini, he turned to another cardinal, Bartolomeo Guidiccioni.

Guidiccioni, seventy years old, personified in a forceful way one special facet of the Catholic Reform: the use of the winnowing fan among the religious orders. The orders had been almost universally tainted with scandal; they were frequently split by internal strife; they generated a spirit of dissension with the secular clergy. Guidiccioni felt that a sure medium of reform was to prohibit new orders and to reduce those currently existing to four: Dominicans, Franciscans, Cistercians, and Benedictines. Ignatius and his friends visited Guidiccioni in order to explain personally their aspirations. The cardinal received them ungraciously; he taunted them; he ridiculed their plans; he suggested that they were up to some mischief.[125]

Papal Approval of the Society of Jesus

To change the mind of Guidiccioni, Ignatius did two things: he promised God that he and his companions would offer three thousand masses; and he appealed to persons of influence who were acquainted with the work of his friends. Many testimonials came to Rome from the cities of northern Italy. One was from Ferrara. In December 1539 Jay received an encouraging letter from his friend Duke Ercole d'Este of Ferrara, informing him that he was commending the men of the Society of Jesus to his brother, Cardinal Ippolito d'Este.[126] Around 4 September, more than a year since he first saw the First Sketch of the Institute, Pope Paul commissioned Cardinals Guidiccioni, Contarini, and Rodolfo Pio de Carpi to come to a definitive conclusion about the Society of Jesus. Guidiccioni finally retreated a bit from his hard line. He was willing to see the Society approved if it were limited to sixty professed members. Paul accepted the compromise and on 27 September in the Palace of St. Mark signed the bull *Regimini Militantis Ecclesiae*, and so approved the Society of Jesus as a canonically established religious order in the Catholic Church.[127]

Significance of the New Religious Order

This bull incorporated an abbreviated and slightly altered version of the First Sketch of the Institute which, in this form, became known as the Formula of the Institute of the Society of Jesus. It had a fourfold significance: it sketched the Jesuit way of life for centuries to come; it announced a freshness of concept in the history of religious orders in the Church; it saved the religious order as a form of life within the Church; it reflected the turning point in the Church's history brought about by Pope Paul III.

The sketch of the Jesuit way of life: in the Formula of the Institute of the Society of Jesus, Ignatius wrote that anyone who desired to be a member of the Society of Jesus should "take care, as long as he lives, first of all to keep before his eyes God and then the nature of this Institute which he has embraced and which is, so to speak, a pathway to God."[128] From this document the thousands of Jesuits in the centuries to come received a life-long orientation. It was literally their pathway to God.

A freshness of concept in the history of religious orders in the Church: the new Society of Jesus explicitly set aside several of the forms of the older religious orders. Among the basic segments in the monastic structure were the lifelong residence in one house; the placement of decision making in matters of major concern in the community as a whole, assembled in chapter; the primary concern with liturgical prayer and the chanting in choir of the divine office; distinctive dress and regular penitential practices.[129] Changes came with the friars. The friars omitted some of these traditional forms; some they modified; still others they retained. Still further changes came with the clerks regular, those bodies of priests who lived in community and pronounced religious vows but who in their manner of life professed to follow the pattern set by "good clerics of the city or country." The first of this new genre of religious were the Theatines, approved by Pope Clement VII in 1524. The Clerks Regular of the Good Jesus

followed soon after. Then the Barnabites. All preceded the Society of Jesus, and moved toward what has been called the demonachization (*démonachisation*) of the religious life. But their
moves were limited. The Jesuits took the whip hand.[130] They
replaced the older forms mentioned above with detachment from
any particular apostolate, mobility, prompt availability to the
pope and the order's general, the private recitation of the divine
office, and penance accommodated to individual need.

The reclamation of the religious order as a form of life
within the Church: by its vitality and spiritual fibre, the Society
of Jesus appeared when the religious orders were threatened by
extinction. The document *A Deliberation on the Reform of the
Church (Consilium de emendanda ecclesia)*, the report in 1537
of nine influential churchmen deeply concerned with reform,
recommended that in view of the scandalous condition of so
many religious orders, the conventual orders be dissolved.[131]
Some prominent humanists, including Erasmus, deflated the
ideal of religious life by their sharply written and pervasive criticism.[132] Secular colleges and chantries, communities of secular
priests who were attached to a church or a chapel or a university,
multiplied in the fifteenth century.[133] Curial officials, of whom
Cardinal Guidiccioni was a vigorous member, aimed at reducing
the number of orders in the Church. In this climate so unsym-
pathetic to and even erosive of religious life, the Society of Jesus
"may be said to have preserved the religious order for the Church
militant."[134]

An expression of a new orientation in papal history: the
approbation of the Society of Jesus was one of several actions
that demonstrated the vigorous determination of the Farnese pope
to organize the Church's resources for reform.[135] He transformed
the college of cardinals by the appointment of such men as Marcello Cervini, Gianpietro Carafa, and Reginald Pole; he instituted
the commission that produced the report *De Emendanda Ecclesia*; he opened the Council of Trent; he approved Angela Merici's
community of Ursulines and the Barnabites of Antonio Maria
Zaccaria. Paul's approval of the Society of Jesus was part of the
pattern designed by his pontificate.

By the time Paul gave his approval, several of the Society
of Jesus had left Rome for various far-flung assignments. Even

before they terminated their discussions in June 1539, some were on the road. Soon after mid-April Broët, joined by Rodrigues, set out for Siena. On 20 June Favre and Laynez started for Parma. In March 1540 Xavier and Rodrigues, assigned to the Indies, started for the port of Lisbon in Portugal. Jay's turn came the same month with his assignment by Paul III to Bagnorea, the city of St. Bonaventure.[136]

Pastoral Work at Bagnorea and Brescia

Claude makes his debut in the *Monumenta Historica Societatis Jesu* with a letter of 3 April 1540 from Bagnorea. His second letter he sent from Brescia on 27 November 1540; his third from Faenza on 11 June 1541.[137] He worked in these three towns within the one year period, 1540–41, during which the rapidity of his changes set the pattern for his future highly flexible life, when one after the other orders were handed him that took him to Regensburg, Dillingen, Ingolstadt, Eichstätt, Salzburg, Worms, Trent, Bologna, Ferrara, and Vienna. Mobility, adaptability, and versatility, as distinctly Jesuit qualities, became ingrained into the innermost attitudes of this modest priest, who years before seemed to have been destined for the ordered and secluded life of an unknown school teacher in remote Savoy. Through the Spiritual Exercises under the direction of Pierre Favre, and later through the personal friendship of Ignatius, Jay learned the lesson of complete detachment from persons and places so absolutely essential to the Jesuit spirit of promptness and readiness to move to any place in the world where there is hope of God's greater glory.

Jay was about thirty-six years old when he received a papal order to go to Bagnorea, a tiny town resting at the foot of the Cimini Mountains and about fifty miles north of Rome. He left Rome on 17 March 1540 and arrived there two days later. Like so many Italian cities of the Renaissance, Bagnorea was torn by ruthless factions, for whom murder was a peculiarly apt and decisive way of expressing a variance in viewpoint. And, as usual, religious practice was severely undermined. The hotheads of Bagnorea immediately lifted their guard against the mild, fair complected, blond, grey eyed stranger who suddenly appeared in their midst.[138] Their reception was distinctively frigid.[139]

Centers of Claude Jay's Italian apostolate

Claude bided his time, quietly moving among the cautious citizens. Patiently he waited until Palm Sunday before he gave his first formal sermon. By that time the thaw had set in, and the aloofness and reserve of the Bagnorese melted under the warm rays of the Savoyard's sweetness and charity. A few years later, Peter Canisius made the observation that all Jay had to do was smile, and it became impossible for anyone to deny what he wanted.[140] With disarming simplicity the people of Bagnorea vied with each other in their spirit of repentance and their resolve to bury their hatreds and feuds.

Jay's only extant letter from Bagnorea deserves quotation, since it is a detailed portrayal of how modest and yet how effective was the Jesuit entry into the toil of the Catholic Reform. Claude's own feats at this little town were a specimen in its basic pastoral aspects of the work done by his companions in other quarters of Europe. He reported to Ignatius as follows:

> On Palm Sunday, after giving a kind of justification for my presence among them, I delivered my first sermon. I then kept at the work of preaching for several days. The result is that we have had first hand

37

experience of how our Lord will make the seed bring forth fruit once it has been sown. Each day my audience grew. With definite manifestations of humility, they came to confession, first the city's rulers and then the greater portion of the citizens. So great have been the crowds, which increase daily, that there is not enough time in the day to take care of them all. And at present I cannot get away from the church until the middle of the night.

What shall I say about those who, in addition to the city folk, came from the nearby farms, and of those, who, once having confessed but still not satisfied, return to confess again? Such are their numbers that on some mornings I discover that they have scaled the walls and are actually settled inside my house waiting to go to confession. Since I have not been able to take care of everybody before Easter, I began again immediately after the feast with the same procedure.

Then there were the enmities that have been broken down, enmities among the leading citizens, yes, even among some clerics and canons, which have their root in murder and other acts of violence that fed the spirit of discord. These men who had been nursing their feuds now humble themselves, embrace one another, confess their sins and go to holy communion, things some of them have not done for years. Then there are the children who attend the Church of St. Francis with their lively interest in learning the Commandments, the Creed and other rudiments of Christian doctrine. Not satisfied with what is taught them in common, some of them seek me out at my house in their desire to outpace the others.[141]

Jay's report from Bagnorea recorded two distinct features of this particular moment in the history of the Society of Jesus and the Catholic Reform: first, it showed—as indeed did similar reports from Favre, Laynez, Broët, and Salmerón—the pastoral and sacramental character of the early Jesuit apostolate; secondly, it revealed—as did many other sources—the decadent state of the Catholic clergy. As Jay told Ignatius: all that was needed was to sow the seed; God would bring forth the fruit. Today the memory of Jay is kept alive in Bagnorea by a statue of Our Lady called Jaiaro or Madonna di Jaio, set up near the house where he had lived.[142]

During most of that same year, 1540, the city of Brescia, nine miles from lovely Desenzano on fair Lake Garda, had heard the voice of a young Spanish Jesuit, not yet a priest, Francisco de Strada, whom Ignatius had met near Monte Cassino in 1538, and whose fiery eloquence had inspired over a hundred religious and priestly vocations among the Brescians.[143] Strada's achievement was all the more unusual because Brescia was among the first of the Italian cities, if not the very first, to receive Lutheran doctrine favorably.[144] In just the few days he spent in Brescia in April 1540, Pierre Favre detected the Lutheran influences.[145] In view of this situation, Ignatius felt that Strada should have the assistance of a trained theologian, and in the late fall of 1540 ordered Jay to Brescia. Sometime in November Jay arrived there.[146]

Jay's stay in Brescia was brief, only about four or five months. As in Bagnorea, his work there was distinctly pastoral. He preached frequently in the cathedral on the Creed and the Commandments. His audiences were large.[147] Jay felt gratified and expressed this on 27 November 1540 in a letter to Father Pietro Codacio: "Recommend me in prayer to our Lord, and give thanks to him for the love he bears for our Society, a thing I know from experience, having achieved in Brescia something more than I had first envisaged: the uprooting of cockle."[148] A summons from Ignatius in the spring of 1541 brought Jay back to Rome.

Election of the First Jesuit General Superior

An important moment had arrived in the Society's early history: the election of the first general.[149] Besides Ignatius, only five of the group were easily available: Laynez, Salmerón, Broët, Codure, and Jay. Favre, Rodrigues, and Xavier sent their votes by mail. Bobadilla, who was ill in Bisignano, did not send a vote. In early April the six at Rome began a period of three days' prayer. Then they balloted. Ignatius voted for the one, himself excluded, who received the majority of the votes. All the others voted for Ignatius.[150] Ignatius persuaded his friends to reconsider. After four more days of prayer, they again voted. Once more they unanimously chose Ignatius. Ignatius then took the matter to his confessor, the Franciscan Fra Teodoro. Fra Teodoro told him that to refuse would be to resist the Holy Spirit. On 19 April Ignatius accepted. Then on 22 April 1541, the five joined their superior general in a pilgrimage to St. Paul's Outside the Walls, where, in the chapel of the Holy Eucharist and Blessed Mary the Virgin, they all pronounced their vows as Jesuits.[151] This was the third memorable ceremony in which Jay participated in six years, the first in Paris in 1535 when, during Pierre Favre's mass, he pronounced for the first time the vows his friends were renewing, to be men of poverty and chastity and to labor in the Holy Land; the second at Rome in 1539, also during Pierre Favre's mass, when they all declared their willingness to vow obedience in a new religious order; and now this third, during Ignatius's mass, when they solemnly committed themselves to the canonically erected Society of Jesus.

Pastoral Work at Faenza

Very little time was left to Jay to be with his companions in Rome, for once more he received an assignment to northern Italy. In Faenza, an industrial center in the plain between the Adriatic and the Romagna, the bishop, Cardinal Rodolfo Pio de Carpi, was in need of help. He insisted that Jay be sent, and Ignatius acceded to his demand.[152] In early May 1541, Jay said farewell to Ignatius. It was the last time the two men saw each other. Jay arrived at Faenza on 21 May. For six months, until December, Jay preached, taught catechism, encouraged in private conversation the frequent reception of holy communion, visited the sick in the hospitals. At first the pulpit in the cathedral was reserved for the Servants of Mary, who were then holding a general chapter. But that situation prevailed for only about a month.[153]

Most of the early Jesuits had associated with their names, in one way or another, the formation of an organization of lay people dedicated to a deeper interior life and practical apostolic charity. At Faenza Jay set up a Sodality of Recipients of the Holy Eucharist (*Compagnia di Communicanti*). The members of this sodality received frequent holy communion, took care of the sick and the poor. The tone of the organization's spirit was set by a doctor and a lawyer, both prominent men, who, without fee, helped the poor in their medical and legal needs. Other sodalists collected alms for poverty-stricken families, others took care of abandoned orphans. Faenza, in Renaissance fashion, had its share of feuds. As at Bagnorea, Jay became a symbol of peace. Moving quietly and gently among the factions, he created a spirit of forgiveness and charity.[154]

Summary

Jay was about thirty-seven years old in 1541. The last six of these thirty-seven years, 1535–41, Jay spent in intimate contact with Ignatius and his friends as they groped step by step toward the discovery of their vocation in the founding of the Society of Jesus. With them he reflected the dominant mood of the Catholic Reform of the sixteenth century: the powerful desire to aid others toward eternal salvation by energetic works of charity. Jay and the other first Jesuits joined the company of the Theatines, Barnabites, Ursulines, and Capuchins in the great apostolic urge within the Church of that era, the key-note of which has been described as "activism in Grace."[155]

In the last two of these thirty-seven years, 1540–41, Jay exemplified a distinctively Jesuit modality of this apostolic impulse: the mobility of the Society's members. In quick succession Jay labored in Bagnorea, Brescia, and Faenza. With his companions he had written into the *Formula of the Institute* of the Society the readiness to move to any part of the globe for the helping of souls. What he had written he lived.

CHAPTER II

ITALY AND GERMANY
1541–1545

Introduction

This period begins in Italy with Jay's orders to leave Faenza in 1541 and concludes with his summons to the Council of Trent in 1545. For most of these four years Jay was in Germany. He came to know the bishops of Salzburg, Eichstätt, and Augsburg on personal terms. In a painful educational experience, he learned at first hand the German religious situation, and formed one of his deepest convictions: the best contribution the Society of Jesus could make to the vitally needed renewal of the Catholic Church in Germany was the foundation of Jesuit colleges at the universities.

A Plan for Catholic Renewal in Germany

While Jay was at work in Faenza, Bernardo Sanzio, bishop of Aquila and papal agent at the court of Charles V, penned a strongly worded document, the repercussions of which suddenly altered the course of Jay's life and brought him into the maze of German history. Dated 8 June 1541, the document was a precise resumé of the failure of the Colloquy of Regensburg (1540–41) and the weakness of the Catholic Church in Germany.[1] Sanzio added suggestions for a Catholic program. He called for men in whom were combined learning and holiness. "Since the Protestants," he wrote, "move freely in the cities and through the countryside, sowing everywhere their errors, their slanders, and lampoons, it is essential that His Holiness send into Germany learned and holy men, who, ready to sacrifice their lives for the faith, will also travel through the country in order to undeceive the people, strengthen them in their religious practice, and edify them by a holy life."[2]

Sanzio had the Jesuits in mind. Observing Pierre Favre at the Colloquy of Regensburg, he discerned in the Spiritual Exercises of Ignatius Loyola a new force in Catholic life.

> Means are at hand that Your Holiness could use to give the Church in this country the consolation of a restoration of its liberty and purity. I have in mind, for example, the Spiritual Exercises. I know from experience that these Exercises have achieved an immense amount of good here, among princes as well as subjects. Many of these, previously shaken in their faith, have been strengthened; others who gave up the faith have been led back. For this we are indebted to Master Pierre Favre, one of those who went to Parma with the cardinal of Sant' Angelo. It would be a good idea if two members of the Society of Master Ignatius, for example the Spaniard Diego Laynez, would be sent to Germany, where, I am convinced, they would gather the greatest kind of harvest.[3]

Sanzio's message eventually touched Jay at Faenza. At Rome Cardinal Gasparo Contarini drew up a plan, similar to Sanzio's that envisaged a roving mission of devout priests, carefully trained spiritually and intellectually, who would move from city to city strengthening Catholics and exposing Protestant error. Pope Paul adopted the proposal, appointed the veteran of German affairs Giovanni Morone, bishop of Modena, as nuncio, and assigned to him Robert Vauchop, the exiled archbishop of Armagh, and three Jesuits. The Jesuits selected by Ignatius were Favre, Bobadilla, and Jay.[4] The distance that two of the three Jesuits had to travel to get to Germany indicated the difficulty of obtaining qualified priests. Jay at Faenza was not very far away, but Bobadilla had to travel from Calabria and Favre from Spain.[5]

Robert Vauchop had known the Ignatian group since their student days in Paris. A Scots secular priest of the diocese of St.

Andrew, Vauchop had been a teacher of philosophy at Paris since 1526, and in 1531 received his licentiate in theology. Under Pierre Favre he made the Spiritual Exercises. In 1539 Pope Paul III named him administrator of the Irish archdiocese of Armagh, in which, however, he could not take up residence because of the break with Rome by King Henry VIII. At this time his sight became impaired. Despite this infirmity, he joined Jay and Bobadilla on this mission to Germany and Austria. Often this blind priest, who was soon to be consecrated archbishop of Armagh, labored side by side with the Jesuits.[6]

Beginnings of Jay's German Apostolate

Jay met Vauchop and Bobadilla at Bologna. The trio started north on 17 January 1542. They trudged through the Alps during the severe cold of late January and early February. The winter took its toll, and they had to stop at Innsbruck to recoup their energies. They arrived in Speyer on 9 February, the day that a diet of the empire opened.[7] The nuncio, Giovanni Morone, had arrived only the day before.[8] Won by the openness, candor and gentleness of Jay, he wrote to Cardinal Contarini on 21 May 1542: "Truly we have here an Israelite in whom there is neither guile nor duplicity."[9] Sixteen years later, when Morone was being hounded on charges of heresy by Pope Paul IV, Morone, desirous to show his love for the Society of Jesus, known for its orthodoxy, recalled that his confessor had been Pierre Favre, and that after Favre's death it was Claude Jay.[10]

Morone delineated the areas to be covered by his three Jesuit assistants. To Favre he assigned Speyer, Mainz, and the Rhineland. To Bobadilla he assigned Hungary, and to Jay Bavaria and the area washed by the Danube.[11] Jay made Regensburg his first stop. He arrived there in early April 1542. There his program was distinctly pastoral: a stress on preaching, hearing confessions, and conducting the Spiritual Exercises.[12]

Diffused through Regensburg's proud past were the memories of St. Boniface, who created the bishopric there in 739, and of the Irish monks whose Schottenkirche was consecrated in 1110. Every place Jay looked in that April of 1542, the monuments affirmed Regensburg's position in the Catholic tradition: the thirteenth century's St. Peter's Cathedral, the Alte Kapelle with origins in the ninth century, the Benedictine Abbey of St. Emmeram, grounded in the seventh century. But Regensburg, for centuries united in its faith, was now a city divided.

Regensburg received special attention in Sanzio's dispirited report of 1541. This city, as he saw it, was on the brink of apostasy from the Catholic church.[13] One key reason for this state of affairs was financial. The city government had heavy debts. To liquidate these, the city counsellors despoiled the cathedral, canonrics, convents, and monasteries. Litigation deepened animosities. The magistrates widened the gap between themselves and the Church by abetting the establishment of Lutheranism in the city. Apostate priests and monks, like Johann Forster of Nürnberg, immigrated from other towns. Two Catholic churches were placed at their convenience. These were practical steps taken by a city government that had been in correspondence with Wittenberg for almost twenty-five years. Matching the advances of the Lutherans among the burghers, the Anabaptists had made inroads among the handworkers. Regensburg was a city torn by religious dissension.[14]

Jay started his work quietly and modestly. He conferred privately with the bishop, Pankratius von Sinzenhofer, and the cathedral canons. Von Sinzenhofer urged Jay to give public instructions in the Catholic faith. On 18 April Jay wrote to Ignatius that he hoped to do this soon.[15] During Holy Week he heard confessions in Spanish and in French. He began to learn German. On Palm Sunday he gave holy communion to about two hundred, and to many more on Easter Sunday.[16]

Discouragement at Regensburg

Two months later, on 18 June, Jay again wrote Ignatius and described his quiet apostolate, in which he stressed personal contacts. Frequently he visited Bishop von Sinzenhofer and encouraged him to carry out the obligations of his office. From house to house he went, visiting lay people and religious, exhorting them and directing them in the Spiritual Exercises. He seized an opportunity to address the city senate.[17] Then a note of discouragement crept into his report. In some quarters he met apathy and incomprehension, about which he wrote the Jesuits in Rome: "Some listen but do not comprehend, others comprehend but are not moved. Some do not even want to listen."[18] Jay now had met something he had not experienced in Bagnorea, Brescia, or Faenza. His German education had begun. Regensburg brought him face to face with a massive rejection of the Catholic Church.

This rebuff went deeper than apathy. Jay also met outright hostility, danger to his person, even to the point of a threat against his life. This hostility arose from two sources: lax Catholics and Protestants. Many people, at least nominally Catholic, were wary about the idea of reform and the sacrifices that reform would demand. Whisperings and rumors bred an atmosphere of suspicion and distrust about Morone's mission and his three Jesuit aides.[19] The Protestants in Regensburg had a vigorous spokesman in a preacher who was a favorite with the town's senators. Jay challenged the teachings of this preacher.[20] Many in Regensburg turned against Jay and threatened him. He wrote Ignatius that his life was in great peril.[21] One day some of the Protestants threatened to toss him into the Danube. Jay rather casually replied: "One can go to heaven just as easily by water as by land."[22]

Jay's answer was not a crude show of bravado. It arose from an interior conviction that in the following of Christ the sure and fruitful way was the way of the cross, a conviction that brought him the precious gift of deep interior peace and consolation. He told Ignatius:

> As great as are our tribulations, much greater is the consolation given us through the goodness and mercy of God. So, I can say to the Lord: According to the multitude of sorrows in my heart, my comforts have given joy to my soul. We hope in our Lord that our coming here will not be in vain, although even now, as was the case when we first arrived, we are called upon to share the cross of Christ. I am convinced, therefore, because of the hardships, that our presence will with the divine favor be fruitful for the service of God our Lord. We ask you to keep us more and more in your fervent prayer.[23]

Through discouraging months Jay continued his efforts to strengthen the Catholics of Regensburg. On 25 September, at the request of the bishop and the chapter, he began a series of public instructions on Paul's Epistle to the Galatians. These, however, he could give only at irregular intervals because of the harvest time.[24] Many faithful Catholics found strength in his presence, but persistent hatred and the whisperings took their toll on his position in the city. In this war of attrition, some of the Catholics gradually deserted him.[25] Bishop von Sinzenhofer, glad to have Jay speak out, nevertheless held back from open cooperation. Jay began to lose his confidence in the wisdom of staying in Regensburg, and in August, 1542, suggested to Ignatius that he might achieve more elsewhere within the duchy of Bavaria. Four months after his arrival at Regensburg, he compared his own disheartening fortunes with the happy results Pierre Favre was then achieving at Speyer.[26]

Favre had arrived in Speyer from Spain on 14 April 1542. He too met a people antagonistic and suspicious, but within a few months he had captured the hearts of all.[27] Jay heard about his friend's notable success and on 27 August 1542 he wrote to Ignatius and made a discouraging comparison between what his friend had accomplished and what he felt was his own failure.[28] Jay was not exactly fair to himself, because Favre had the help of two other priests from Spain, Juan de Aragon and Alvaro Alfonso, as well as the support of the influential canon, Otto Truchsess von Waldburg. But at Regensburg, Pankratius von Sinzenhofer, anxious though he was to see Jay oppose the Protestants, nevertheless held back from a fearless and open backing of his work. In this disappointment Jay came to the same conclusion about the religious contest in Germany that Favre had earlier reached: the most effective way to make headway against the Lutheran movement was by the overpoweringly good example of Catholics leading devout, self-sacrificing, charitable lives.[29]

Crisis in Regensburg

Early in 1543 events moved toward a crisis. Pope Paul III had announced a jubilee. Many of the Catholics in Regensburg wanted the jubilee proclaimed in their city, and even anticipated their bishop's doing so by fasting, giving alms, and then receiving the sacraments of penance and Holy Eucharist.[30] The bishop hesitated. Jay went to von Sinzenhofer, reasoned with him, and finally persuaded him to proclaim the jubilee.[31] The Protestants were indignant. They were also conscious of their strength. Twice Ferdinand, the King of the Romans, ordered that the Protestant preacher who had turned so many against the Catholic Church and against Jay personally be denied the pulpit. The city's rulers ignored the royal orders.[32] Duke Wilhelm of Upper Bavaria

47

exacerbated the Protestants still more when he announced his unchanging fidelity to the Catholic Church: "I am solidly determined to suffer the loss of my realm, my family, even my life, rather than allow the people whom providence had entrusted to me to be drawn into the way of perdition by faithless imposters."[33] He determined to bring the people of Regensburg to their knees. Regensburg, in the very heart of Wilhelm's imperial estates, was a free city and so did not fall under his jurisdiction, but the duke girded the town with a legal cordon and forbade his subjects to have any commercial dealings with the Regensburgers.[34] This failed to curb the Protestants, and in March 1543 the senate took direct action against Jay and Robert Vauchop, who also was working in Bavaria.[35]

This action of the senate terminated Jay's work in Regensburg. On 11 March Vauchop left Regensburg for a trip that would take about two weeks. Two days later, on the thirteenth, the syndic of the city went to Jay and gave him two orders: first, that he write to Vauchop and inform him that the senate prohibited his return to Regensburg on the grounds of fomenting dissension among the priests and the citizens; and second, that he himself, because of his association with Vauchop, should leave the city within two days.[36] Jay protested, but in vain. He sought the advice of friends. One suggested that he leave Vauchop's belongings at the home of Father Salzenburch, a priest who had been host to the archbishop and Jay, that he cross the Steinerne Brücke to the suburb of Hoff, and there await developments. The civil administrator of Hoff, however, refused to tolerate Jay's presence even for a day without written commendation from the two dukes of Bavaria. Jay visited as many friends as he could. Some said goodbye with tears in their eyes. Jay then arranged that Vauchop's grain, oats, and wheat be left with Salzenburch, gathered up the archbishop's personal belongings to carry with him, turned the key to the house over to an old woman on whom he could depend, and started to Ingolstadt. "We judged it better," Jay dolefully explained to Girolamo Verallo, the apostolic nuncio to King Ferdinand, "to give way before the blind and senseless madness of the senate rather than uselessly to stir up a hornet's nest."[37] On 15 March 1543, he quit Regensburg. Two days later, Palm Sunday, he arrived at Ingolstadt.[38]

Widening Knowledge of Germany

The next two years and a half deepened Jay's education on the German scene. He lectured at a university, participated in a religious synod, attended an imperial diet, guided bishops through the Spiritual Exercises. All this activity was focused within the narrow area outlined by the three Bavarian towns of Dillingen, Ingolstadt, and Eichstätt, and the Austrian town of Salzburg. Jay shuttled back and forth between these places.[39] Save for Salzburg, which was about a hundred miles southeast of Ingolstadt, the other towns were clustered conveniently together, Dillingen being only fifty miles west of Ingolstadt, and Ingolstadt being only fifteen miles southeast of Eichstätt. These varied experiences gave him an intimate personal knowledge of the complex religious situation in Germany and a grasp of the current needs of the Catholic Church there.

During Jay's first weeks in Ingolstadt, the character of his work was for the most part the same as at Regensburg: the establishment of personal contacts with the Catholic population through the Spiritual Exercises, private counsel, and confession.[40] Three

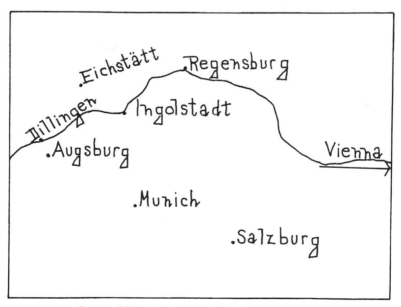

Centers of Claude Jay's apostolate in Germany and Austria

bishops vied with one another for the services of Jay: Otto Truchsess von Waldburg, soon to be appointed bishop of Augsburg, on 10 May 1543; Ernst von Bayern of Salzburg; and Moritz von Hutten of Eichstätt. Jay immediately won their hearts. Peter Canisius, who met Jay shortly after this, wrote Ignatius about the impression Jay was making in Germany. "Great is his facility in adapting himself to each and every one, in high or low station of life. His discretion is of such high calibre that it gives him the knack of handling any sort of temperament and the ability to win friends for himself in our Lord. Frequently many have been struck with amazement that this simplicity and modesty that they see in Father Jay should go hand in hand with the authority and widespread fame he enjoys. Seemingly there is no wish of his he cannot obtain just by a smile."[41]

Lecturer at the University of Ingolstadt

In the early summer of 1543, Jay began a series of lectures in theology at the University of Ingolstadt. The immediate occasion of Jay's lectures was the death on 10 February 1543 of the veteran, hard-hitting champion of the Catholic Church, Johannes Meier, usually known as Eck from his birthplace of Egg an der Günz.[42] Eck had been the last lingering light in the worthy intellectual tradition of Conrad Celtes, Jakob Loeher, Johann Turmeier, and Johannes Reuchlin at Ingolstadt.

Despite Eck's energetic leadership against Lutheranism, two developments at the university seriously clouded the expectations of those who had hoped that Ingolstadt would become for Catholics what Wittenberg was for the Protestants in the north. First, the quality of the Catholic professors deteriorated as no one of Eck's talents appeared. Second, an increasing number of Lutheran professors obtained chairs in various subjects, and used these as podiums for the spread of their religious ideas. Philip Appianus, professor of mathematics, brought his theorems and equations into the services of Lutheran theology.[43] The era of Protestant ascendency at Ingolstadt seemed at hand. Eck's death therefore left a yawning gap in the Catholic ranks.[44]

To meet this crisis Duke Wilhelm, his brother Ernst, and the Catholic doctors at the university urged Jay to take Eck's chair of theology. Jay held back. Although he had received the Master's degree at Paris, he had not earned a doctorate in theology. He also felt that he could achieve more for the Church with the freedom of a private priest than in the official capacity of a university professor. Robert Vauchop finally overcame his reluctance. Armed with his dignity as internuncio, Vauchop convinced Jay that the great need of the moment was to save the University of Ingolstadt for the Catholic Church.[45] So, early in the summer of 1543, a few months after Johannes Eck was placed in his tomb in the Liebfrauenkirche, Jay began his discourses in theology.

To follow Eck was a formidable undertaking. For over three decades Ingolstadt had heard the thunderous voice of the burly, animated Swabian; it had become used to his aggressive tactics, his relentless drive against the Protestants, and his vituperation that was the match of Luther's. Jay lectured on the Epistles of St. John. Clarity, depth, and firmness characterized his teaching. One annalist recorded that Jay "upheld the majesty of the chair of Eck."[46] Archbishop Robert Vauchop wrote from Ingolstadt to Cardinal Giovanni Morone on 6 February 1544: "Master Claude is a charming person and is well received here because of his lectures at the university. There is a widespread desire that he remain at the university, since his accomplishments are more than ordinary."[47]

But because of these very accomplishments Jay did not remain at Ingolstadt. In the spring of 1544, he received an order from Rome to report to the new bishop of Augsburg, Otto Truchsess von Waldburg, who was then residing in Dillingen. Truchsess had heard of Jay's achievements at Ingolstadt and, envisaging "an abundance of fruit in Germany" (*molti frutti nella Germania*), asked Cardinal Marcello Cervini on 22 March 1544, that Jay be placed at Truchsess's disposal.[48] Rome honored his request.

Friendship with Otto Truchsess von Walburg

Before Jay left Ingolstadt to join Truchsess, two new matters demanded his attention. First, the authorities at the university offered Jay a stipend for his lectures. Jay declined, explaining that the Jesuit way of life excludes the acceptance of recompense for apostolic work. And second, he received word that he was to make a brief diversion to Eichstätt. The bishop of that city, Moritz von Hutten, had obtained permission from Truchsess to have Jay stay with him for a short interval. Jay remained with von Hutten from Holy Thursday until 26 June.[49] He directed the bishop through the first week of the Spiritual Exercises, and in private conferences built up his sense of fortitude in the discharge of his obligations. When the time arrived for Jay to leave for Dillingen, he resolutely refused the money von Hutten offered him, but yielded to the bishop's insistence that he go horseback and in the company of two men as protection against the dangers of the highway. If von Hutten was the example of delicate courtesy to a guest, von Truchsess was no less so. Somewhere on the road Jay met a party from Dillingen bringing a horse, which the bishop of Augsburg was sending ahead for him. Truchsess was anxious that Jay get to Dillingen without waste of time. What he wanted especially was to make the Spiritual Exercises.[50] Not that the Exercises were for him some unknown wonder, for he had already found in them a source of profound spiritual energy during the retreat he had made under Pierre Favre in Speyer in 1542.[51]

These days of retreat intensified the strong and beautiful friendship between Truchsess and Jay. Truchsess, then forty-five years old, had a wide intellectual formation that started at the aristocratic house of his father, the baron von Waldburg, and extended through the universities at Dole, Parma, Padua, and Bologna. At the latter university he studied law under Ugo Buoncompagni, the future Pope Gregory XIII. With his intelligence and attractive personality, he received several responsible posts in the Church, and in 1543 he was assigned to the see of Augsburg and granted the title of prince.[52] Sensitive to the need for drastic changes in the German Church, he found in Jay a wise counselor. Years deepened the friendship between the bishop and the Jesuit, who together became one of the more effective alliances for reform in southern Germany in the ten years between 1543 and 1553.

Jay hardly had time to direct Truchsess through the first week of the Spiritual Exercises when he was again caught up in the religious turmoil of the empire and the critical tensions between Pope Paul III and Emperor Charles V. A burning issue of the day was how to achieve religious peace in the empire, by a general council of the Church or by a national council of Germany. In June 1544 Charles, taking the latter position, announced that a diet would be convened on 1 October at Worms and that there the religious differences within the empire would be discussed. This announcement placed a heavy burden on the German bishops.[53]

The Synod of Salzburg

To prepare the position he would take at Worms, the archbishop of Salzburg, Ernst von Bayern, decided to convene a synod. Besides his suffragans, he invited Truchsess, von Hutten, and Jay. All agreed to attend.[54] Jay left Dillingen on 15 September.[55] At Salzburg he discovered that the archbishop wanted him to participate actively in the synod. He then realized that he was uncomfortably caught between two fires. It was not easy to refuse the wish of the archbishop; yet, Jay's instinctive loyalty to the Holy See made him halt at even the most remote affiliation with a movement that tended to prescind from the pope's authority on questions of faith. And this synod of Salzburg, free from all bad will as the archbishop himself might be, was nevertheless pointed as a preparatory step toward the emperor's diet at Worms with its unmistakable suggestion of nationalism in questions of religion.

Jay was candid with the archbishop. He explained that, as a priest sent into Germany by the pope, he should not participate in assemblies such as the archbishop's synod without the approbation of the pope himself or his own Jesuit superiors.[56] The archbishop yielded—to a degree. Acknowledging the cogency of Jay's argument, he nevertheless asked him to stay at hand in the capacity of private theologian. This distinction satisfied Jay's conscience, and he remained to accord von Bayern the benefit of his advice.

In order to give precision to his own thought, and for his own private use, Jay wrote out two conclusions on the passionately debated issue of the relation of the national synod to the Holy See. His first conclusion was: bishops, without the approval of the Holy See, should not agree to the discussion of theological questions in secular diets. The second was: even though the Protestants should agree with the Catholics on all points of faith, they should, if they refuse obedience to the pope, still be regarded as heretics and schismatics.[57] Truchsess circulated copies of Jay's paper. By word and deed Jay imported into Germany that particular loyalty to the papacy that distinguished the new Society of Jesus. The synod closed with the prelates deciding not to discuss religious issues at Worms or at any other secular assembly. Truchsess formally endorsed this position.[58]

At the close of the synod at Salzburg, Truchsess and Jay separated for a short time. Truchsess went on to Worms for the diet scheduled there. Jay, who refused some money offered him by Truchsess, headed back to Dillingen, where he arrived on 14 November.[59] Meanwhile at Worms the program of the diet, which was scheduled to open on 1 October, broke down because the imperial officials had trouble getting the sessions under way. Truchsess had been there since mid-November. Shortly after his arrival, during the continuing dreary delays and procrastinations, he summoned Jay to join him at Worms. Once on the scene, Jay moved among the personnel of the diet, repeating his now familiar theme of the need for strength and fortitude among the bishops in their defense of the faith.[60] In December exciting news from Rome broke the monotony at Worms. On the nineteenth Pope Paul named Truchsess a cardinal, the only German among the thirteen nominees.[61]

Jay's Gift to Cardinal Truchsess

On 1 January, 1545, Jay presented the new cardinal with an especially attractive New Year's gift, a catena of quotations on the qualities that should distinguish a bishop. He drew on the Gospels, the Epistles, the Acts of the Apostles, the fathers of the church, as well as a number of the church councils such as Nicaea, Sardica, Carthage, Orleans, Toledo. He called his work *A Bishop's Image* (*Speculum Praesulis*), an accurate title, for in clear, sharp lines the quotations mirrored the ideal bishop, zealous, chaste, learned, prudent, devout.

In 1556 Cardinal Truchsess sent a copy of Jay's work to the bishop of Eichstätt, Eberhard von Hürtheim. For seventy years this copy lay in the library of the episcopal residence in Eichstätt until it was discovered by one of the most industrious German Jesuit scholars of that age, Jakob Gretser. Gretser published the work in 1615, dedicating it to Truchsess's successor in the see of Augsburg, Heinrich V von Knöringen. He addressed this caution to his readers: "Do not look for diffuse and subtle arguments about

SPECVLVM
PRÆSVLIS
EX VERBIS SACRÆ SCRI-
PTVRÆ, CANONVM ET
Doctorum,
JAM OLIM
A R. P. CLAVDIO IAIO,
VNO EX DECEM PRIMIS
SOCIETATIS IESV PATRIBVS, SA-
CRÆ THEOLOGIÆ IN ACADEMIA
Ingolſtadienſi Profeſſore con-
ſcriptum,
ET REVERENDISSIMO AC ILLV-
STRISSIMO PRINCIPI AC DOMINO, DO-
mino OTHONI, S. R. E. Cardinali ampliſſimo, Epiſcopo
Auguſtano, Domino & Præpoſito Elvvacenſi,
ſtrenæ Ianuariæ loco oblatum, Anno Sa-
lutis M. D. XLV.
Nunc primò in lucem editum,
ET REVERENDISSIMO AC ILLV-
STRISSIMO PRINCIPI AC DOMINO, DO-
mino HENRICO, OTHONI in Cathedra Auguſtana
Succeſſori meritiſſimo, dedicatum.
INGOLSTADII,
Ex typographeo Ederiano apud Eliſabetham Angermariam.
Anno partus virginei M. DC. XV.
Impenſis Ioannis Hertſroi Bibliopolæ Monacen.

Title page of Jay's *Speculum Praesulis*

the episcopal office in this *Speculum*. If you want to find arguments of that kind, it is elsewhere that you will have to satisfy that
desire. Our author's purpose was to put together a New Year's gift
from only, and if I might say so, the unadorned words of Scripture,
the canons, the councils, and the doctors. . . . Yet Claude Jay
was a man of that kind of learning that he could have discussed

this theme in a learned and wide-ranging manner, if he so chose''
(*valuisset, si voluisset*).[62]

For Cardinal Truchsess the *Speculum* was an eminently
agreeable gift. Fed by his personal, pastoral interest in the character of the episcopal office, he had a penchant for this genre of
literature. He discussed this subject with Archbishop Robert
Vauchop of Armagh. Gretser printed the eighteen chapter headings of that conversation. Truchsess also spoke with Bishop Luigi
Lippomano of Verona. At his request, Lippomano made a draft of
that colloquy. On it Lippomano penned his personal dedication of
the work to Truchsess.[63]

With his gift Jay contributed to the swelling tide of awareness
of the importance of the episcopal office in the reform of the
Catholic Church. Prominent men of the fifteenth century, Jean
Gerson, Lorenzo Giustiniani, Antonio de Firenze, and Domenico
dei Domenichi, wrote on the duties and the personal piety that are
called for by the bishop's charge. Biographies of men who had
filled this office with honor began to appear. This literary tide
poured into the Council of Trent, where episcopal renewal became
the main key to ecclesiastical reform. Jay's *Speculum* flowed from
his own sensitivity to this dominant exigency of the Catholic
Reform.[64]

The Diet of Worms

On 24 March 1545, after a delay of about six months, Ferdinand, King of the Romans, finally opened the Diet of Worms.
There Jay gained a deeper insight into the tangled religious situation. What he saw was almost the identical spectacle Pierre Favre
had witnessed in the same city in 1540. The theme was the same:
the creation of a religious peace in Germany; the protagonists were
the same: Protestant and Catholic princes standing armed behind
their respective theologians; the denouement was the same: a
chaos of the wrangling and mutual incrimination.[65]

During the preparations, Pope Paul III on 14 November 1544,
revoked the suspension of the Council of Trent, and set the reopening for 15 March 1545. According to the emperor's commitments,
made when he was planning this particular Diet of Worms, religious issues were to be raised only in the event that a general
council of the Church had not yet been convoked. This meant,

with the announcement of Trent's reopening now formally published, that the Protestants were to be deprived of the opportunity of using the imperial diet as a sounding board for their teachings. But they were resourceful and had their tactics prepared for this situation. They simply charged that the council being assembled at Trent was neither free nor truly Christian; therefore it was not a genuine general council; therefore no restrictions should be placed on the discussion of religious questions at Worms. Hardly had the diet opened than a solid impasse developed between the Catholics and Protestants.[66]

Jay's role at Worms kept him for the most part behind the scenes; in private conferences, he clarified the issues for the bishops and prevented conflicting religious and secular claims from confusing their thoughts. This was a major contribution.[67] Jay also did considerable work in the confessional. The rise of Protestantism had created some complex moral problems for Catholics, and many came to Jay with their doubts. Many also made the Spiritual Exercises under his direction.[68] In regard to his preaching at Worms, Jay wrote to Ignatius on 21 September 1545:

> I do not know exactly what to say about what I have achieved by my teaching and preaching here. If what many people tell me is true, others have found more satisfaction in my sermons and lectures than I myself have felt. Cardinal Farnese told me at the time I went to greet him that the king of the Romans had spoken most laudably of my preaching, that I should keep up the good work, that I had gained quite a following, and many other such compliments.[69]

As at Venice, Ferrara, and Rome, the sick of Worms received Jay's special attention. This exasperated a Calvinist minister named Wilhelm Seibert, who vividly expressed his annoyance with Claude Jay. After remarking that Jay used to watch through the night with the sick, he continued:

> At Worms and elsewhere the first members of the recent sect of Jesuits seduced many people from the holy gospel. . . . One in particular, who led a hypocritical life, was night and day in either the churches or the hospital. He ate, drank, and slept little, did not boast of his achievements, as is usual among those knaves. In the eyes of several he made a fine impression, and thereby induced them, to the eternal loss of their souls, to come back to popish idolatry. This was the achievement of this contemptuous, hypocritical blackguard and others of that tonsured rabble.[70]

Seibert's words gushed forth from a milieu heavy with suspicion and acrimony that crippled any constructive efforts at the diet.

The highlight of Jay's preaching experience at Worms was the occasion on which he spoke in the presence of the emperor and his entourage. More than anything else it was a signal triumph over his own natural timidity. Jay knew himself well, and he confessed to Ignatius that this timorousness could grow to mountainous proportions. At no time had he felt so scared. Yet once he had opened his mouth, he was carried away by the multitude of thoughts that rushed in on him. "Never before," he said, "have I felt greater ardor in the pulpit."[71]

While at Worms Jay met for the first time the young Jesuit who, for more than half a century of toil in Germany until his death in 1597, was to become known as the second St. Boniface and the Apostle of Germany, Peter Canisius. At this particular time, Canisius was in Cologne holding in check the unabating efforts of Archbishop Hermann von Wied to hand over his diocese to the Protestants.[72] In May 1545 Jay asked Canisius to join him at Worms. Nicolás Bobadilla was already there as aide to the papal nuncio, Girolamo Verallo.[73] No record remains of the conversations between these three Jesuits, the twenty-four year old Dutchman, the thirty-six year old Castilian, and the forty-one year old Savoyard, all with experience of the religious problems in Germany, but Canisius wrote to Pierre Favre on 12 August 1545 to tell of his impressions of Jay. As far as Canisius was concerned, Favre had already been enrolled in the catalogue of the saints, and one of the qualities he most admired in his hero was the quiet charm of his conversation.[74] It was this same quality that he noted in Claude Jay. Canisius wrote Favre:

> The conversation and preaching of Master Claude, unfailingly filled with piety and sweetness, gave me certainly the greatest pleasure. But not I alone was delighted with his sermons. Those which he delivered in Italian on feast days so pleased King Ferdinand, the emperor, and certain other prominent men that they would not let up in their request that he put them into writing and then give copies of them to read. While I was at Worms, he employed me as an amanuensis, so I am in a position to state this as something of which I am absolutely sure.[75]

Among those who heard Jay preach was Cardinal Alessandro Farnese, the papal nuncio at Worms. Here was forged one of the many links of affection which this influential grandson of Pope Paul III had for the Society of Jesus. Farnese, inspired also by Truchsess's reports on Jay's achievements in Germany, conceived a profound respect for the Jesuit. He saw in Jay a focal point from which emanated a wide and beneficent influence in Germany.[76] Twenty-three years later, in 1568, Farnese laid the foundation of the Church of the Gesù at Rome, an enduring monument to his affection for the Society of Jesus. The diet foundered, as so many before had done, in a wild sea of theological differences and politics. Cardinal Farnese, afraid of being murdered by the Protestants, fled Worms in disguise. On 4 August 1545, the diet was recessed.[77] Jay had witnessed the failure of the imperial power with all the prestige of the Hapsburgs to achieve a settlement of the religious issues of the age. Soon he was caught up in the gigantic effort of the papacy to do the same.

By the bull of 19 November 1544 Pope Paul III convoked the general council for 15 March 1545, but many complications caused postponement. In the consistory of 6 November 1545 Paul announced that the long delayed council would meet at Trent on the third Sunday of Advent, 13 December.[78] Truchsess, who felt that he could not leave Germany, asked Ignatius that Jay might be his representative.[79]

Demands for Jay's Services

During the four months before Jay reached Trent, demands on his time were many. At Dillingen he heard confessions, including those of Italians, French, and Spaniards who were in the town, and gave the first week of the Spiritual Exercises. Some Lutherans came to him and tearfully asked to be received back into the Church.[80]

Then there came another call for help from Bishop Moritz von Hutten of Eichstätt. The emperor, unrelenting in his drive for religious settlement and chagrined by the collapse of his recent efforts at Worms, had summoned still another diet for 6 January 1546 at Regensburg. As a preparation for the diet itself, Charles arranged for a religious colloquy to start on 30 November 1545, also at Regensburg, between eight Catholic and eight Protestant theologians. As presidents of the debates Charles designated von Hutten and Friedrich von Furstenberg.[81] Von Hutten, to prepare himself for his coming responsibility, wanted to confer with Jay. Truchsess therefore dispatched Jay to Eichstätt. For a few days the Jesuit and the bishop together went over the problems of the forthcoming colloquy. Von Hutten then wanted to detain Jay and to keep him at his side during the debates at Regensburg. This Truchsess, with his own plans of using Jay at Trent, refused.[82]

Then a request came from Milan. Sometime toward the end of the year 1545, the governor of the duchy of Milan, Alfonso Avalos y Aquino, the Marchese del Vasto, tried to secure Jay's services as tutor for his son and as a spiritual director in the city. Jay had to decline. From Dillingen, in a letter which he evidently did not send immediately, dated as it was under 27 October and 25 November, Jay informed Vasto both that he could not leave Germany without the leave of his superiors and also that Cardinal Truchsess planned to dispatch him to the Council of Trent.[83]

An Attempt to Reconcile Bernard Ochino

And then Ignatius too had a special assignment. At Augsburg at this time, acting as pastor for the Italian Lutherans there, was the former vicar general of the Capuchins, Bernard Ochino, whose flight to Geneva in 1542 had shaken the Catholic world. A person who knew Ochino and wanted to try to bring about his return to the Catholic Church asked Ignatius to help. Ignatius was willing to do all he could do, even to see the pope personally, but he felt that he should first have a letter from Ochino expressing his desire for reconciliation. Ochino's advocate — Hugo Rahner thinks that it was Vittoria Colonna — told Ignatius that she would write the former friar and solicit such a letter.[84] Since Jay was in Bavaria at this time and not far distant from Ochino, Ignatius wrote Claude, suggesting that he visit Ochino, if he thought it prudent, and offer the services of the Society of Jesus to ease his way back to the Church. Ignatius also enjoined Jay to keep this particular correspondence confidential and not to let Ochino know that Ignatius had taken the initiative. He dated his letter 12 December 1545.

Speak to him and tell him that we are prepared to help him in every way possible in a spirit of complete charity, if he would but grasp this opportunity to use our services in the Lord. Besides, with the purpose of motivating him, you might prod him with questions about what he is accomplishing and what he hopes to achieve; you might tell him that everything can be set in order; and you might offer your help to bring about a favorable resolution of the affair here in Rome. If he is afraid, assure him of the Society's aid, since, besides myself, Master Laynez and Master Salmerón are here. In his natural concern for his person and his problems, he can be sure that we and he are of one mind. Whatever you can do in this affair, be it to get a letter from him or anything else, make sure that he does not find out that I have written you from Rome. With all possible brevity keep us posted on what happens. In no way should he learn about this letter of ours.[85]

Ignatius's plan failed. By the time his letter reached Dillingen, Jay was already at the Council of Trent as the representative of the bishop of Augsburg.[86] And Ochino, despite the efforts of Catholic friends and admirers, continued in his commitment to the Protestant cause until his death at Schlakow with the Anabaptists in Moravia in 1564.

The Advocate of Jesuit Schools

Before Jay went to Trent, he had carried off the most significant apostolic feat of his life: he persuaded Ignatius of the imperative need that Jesuits become educators. His nearly four years in Germany convinced him that the key to reform in that country was education, and that his Society of Jesus was the most effective instrument at hand to carry this out. By his earnest advocacy of it, he became one of the most cogent influences—if not the most cogent—that pointed Ignatius toward the apostolate of formal education. The years 1545–48 were the critical ones for Ignatius on the question of Jesuits assuming the role of teachers. Unforeseen events happened in different areas of Europe that together formed an alliance to turn Jesuits into schoolmen. These developments occurred in Padua, Gandía, Messina, and Germany. At Padua: by April 1545 Ignatius realized that the program at the University of Padua was seriously flawed and was inadequate for the intellectual formation of the Jesuit scholastics who were studying there. Four years earlier, in 1541, Ignatius and five other Jesuits who were in Rome for the election of their first general drew up a list of points reached in the evolving Society that demanded further reflection. In one of these points, they directed that the academic program of the scholastics be carried out completely at the university. There were to be neither classes nor lectures in the Jesuit collegiate residence (*no estudios ni lectiones en la Compañía*). Faced, however, by the sporadic and uncertain program of lectures and literary exercises at the University of Padua, Ignatius, on the advice of Laynez, changed the ordinance of 1541. He directed that Jesuit professors teach the defective courses within the Jesuit residence.[87] At Gandía: in March 1545 Ignatius accepted the offer of Francis Borgia to found a college at which Jesuit professors would teach not only Jesuit scholastics but also some recently converted Agarenes, those descendants of Christians who had apostasized to the Mohammedan religion in the seventh century. By 1547 the superior, Andrés Oviedo, importuned by the people of Gandía, admitted some of their sons to the classes of the scholastics and the Agarenes.[88] At Messina: in 1548 Ignatius acceded to the recommendations of Father Jerónimo Doménech and Juan de Vega, the viceroy of Sicily, and opened a school designed largely, though not exclusively, for lay students.[89] But earlier than these three influences were the letters Ignatius received from Claude Jay from Germany in late 1544 and early 1545.

For Jay the decisive experience had been the year of lecturing in theology at Ingolstadt, 1543–44. It turned him in the direction of education. At Ingolstadt he found theology "close to complete interment" (*quale per tutto e sepolto*). Scriptural studies he found "utterly lifeless" (*e tutalmente extincto*). Students in the theology faculty were practically nonexistent. The decadence at Ingolstadt, he found, reflected the wider problem of the general decay of Catholic life in Germany.[90] So degraded had the German clergy become that the vocation to the priesthood had lost all appeal. No German youths of wealth or standing had any desire to be priests.[91] By the end of the year of lecturing, Jay had sifted his thoughts and reached a practical conclusion: the hope for the German church lay in the establishment at the universities of colleges for poor boys, which, he hoped, would produce theologians of distinction. This information and suggestion Jay sent to Ignatius on 14 November 1544.[92]

Important Correspondence on Education

This particular letter initiated a rapid and fruitful dialogue by mail with Ignatius. Ignatius answered on 11 December 1544; Jay replied to this on 21 January 1545. These three letters are among the most important in the early history of Jesuit involvement in education, delineating as they do the inception and growth of a policy by the encounter of ideas in the minds of Jay and Loyola.

The steps swiftly followed each other. On 14 November 1544, Jay reported to Ignatius that he (Jay) had recommended to three German bishops that they create colleges or residences at universities for poor boys who showed promise of becoming worthy priests.[93] On 11 December 1544 Ignatius went beyond Jay's plan and suggested that Jay persuade the bishops to found at the universities colleges (residences) for Jesuit scholastics, which colleges would be centers for spiritual renewal among the Germans.[94] On 21 January 1545 Jay in his response alerted Ignatius to the reluctance of the German bishops to found colleges for other than students for the diocesan priesthood, and then, pushing beyond Ignatius's idea, proposed that Jesuits become lecturers at the German universities.[95] Ignatius agreed. Within a period of about three months, Jay had moved Ignatius toward the project of Jesuits becoming formal educators. Then in quick succession followed the events at Padua, Gandía, and Messina, mentioned above, that made the role of education in the Catholic Reform so persuasive to Ignatius.

Jay's letter of 21 January 1545 was therefore of seminal significance in Jesuit history. He made several points. These are worth recording, since they fill out the context within which he made his basic educational proposal to Ignatius. First, at the moment there was no hope of creating Jesuit colleges (residences) in Germany. Jay, on Ignatius's advice, had spoken to three bishops, Moritz von Hutten of Eichstätt, Ernst von Bayern of Salzburg, and Otto von Truchsess von Waldburg of Augsburg, and suggested that they establish university residences for Jesuit scholastics who would be sent into Germany from other countries. The bishops balked at the idea of supplying financial backing for foreigners. They preferred a program of recruitment of German youth who would remain within their own dioceses and eventually fill the pastoral vacancies in Germany.[96]

His second point: in view of the negative stance of the bishops in regard to Jesuit scholastics, the next hope for Catholic Germany was in the creation of residences at the universities, where poor youths with the intention of becoming priests could study Sacred Scripture and scholastic theology. In this reiteration of his advice of the previous year, Jay added his fear that, unless each bishop set up this kind of establishment for ten or twelve poor young men, Germany would end up with no priests.[97]

His third point: in order to get this kind of project going, the Society should supply men to run the bishops' colleges and to lecture publicly in the universities, particularly "men in whom was realized the harmony of holiness and learning" (*persone docte et spirituale*).[98] This combination was essential in Germany, because "a person, no matter how good he might be, if he is not considerably learned, is of little account here."[99] Jay suggested the appointment of Diego Laynez, Alfonso Salmerón, and Guillaume Postel as men stamped with "holiness and learning" (*spirito et doctrina*).[100]

His fourth point: quite possibly room could be found in these residences for some Jesuit scholastics, whose way of life would be a good example for the diocesan students and would attract some German youths to the Society.[101]

His fifth point: the acceptance by a Jesuit of a lectureship in a university created a problem for the Society. A stipend was attached to the university chairs. By their vow of poverty, Jesuits were committed to work gratis and without remuneration. These conflicting ideas crossed swords in Jay's mind. At odds were his heartfelt desire to help Germany and a basic principle of Jesuit life. "For my part, I am of the opinion that, even though our vocation does not take within its natural scope such posts as those of university professor and lecturer, yet in the extreme need prevalent in this poor country, it would clearly be the very best decision to have some of our Company take over this responsibility."[102] Jay's solution lay in a simple refusal of the stipend. This refusal in itself, Jay felt, would give edification, which in turn could very well attract German youths to the priesthood and so save the faith in Germany.[103]

His sixth point: although the three bishops whom Jay had befriended were centrally concerned about filling the ranks of priests in their own dioceses, Jay asked nevertheless for literature on the foundation of Jesuit university residences, the process of founding them, the studies and customs followed in them, their rules and their constitutions.[104]

A Long-range Resolve

Jay's analysis of the Catholic condition in southern Germany forged for him an imperative in his life. "In every way possible," he wrote Ignatius, "I shall not give up my determination that by one means or another the study of theology, now totally entombed, will be restored to the university."[105] Ignatius supported Jay's determination. He submitted a list of possible Jesuit appointees to the post of university lecturer in theology, and asked Jay who in his opinion would be the best choices. Ignatius's list included, besides Jay himself, Laynez and Salmerón. Jay replied that his own talents did not measure up to the task but that he would in a spirit of obedience take it on if Ignatius directed him to do so. He preferred Laynez and Salmerón, with a slight reservation about the latter. Salmerón's relative youth—he was then thirty—might work against him, since, as Jay explained, youthfulness in a professor did not sit well with German students.[106]

Despite the seriousness of this exchange between Ignatius and Jay, four years were to pass before a team of Jesuit teachers arrived at Ingolstadt, and eleven years were to go by before a Jesuit college was founded there. Intricate negotiations, as shall be seen, slowed the process, but Jay by gentle and sweet compulsion opened the discussions with the German bishops in 1544–45 and kept the talks going. Jesuit presence in the German universities as lecturer and student became Jay's major preoccupation, and he closed this period of his life just before the Council of Trent by speaking frequently with the bishops at the Diet of Worms (1545) about the foundation of Jesuit university residences.[107]

Summary

Jay's first German experience lasted a little less than four years. In this brief period he learned much about the Catholic Reform in its hopes and its needs. The hopes: he became the personal friend of three bishops of important sees, Salzburg, Eichstätt, and Augsburg. The intense desire of these bishops to have the services of Jay revealed a determination to achieve a renewal of Catholic life. The needs: from hard daily experience, Jay formulated Germany's religious needs under two headings. The first was pastoral: a key bulwark against the advance of the Protestants was in the example of devout and holy lives of Catholics. Jay, therefore, continued what Favre had started and which became a hallmark of the Jesuit enterprise in Germany: a vigorous sacramental life. The second need was intellectual: essential to the Catholic Reform was the education of a holy clergy. Jay initiated what became one of the most striking characteristics of the Catholic Reform in Germany: the Jesuit university residence.

To these two needs, pastoral and intellectual, Jay responded as a scholar trained at the University of Paris and as a priest formed in the Spiritual Exercises of Ignatius of Loyola. He brought to bear on the German situation that harmony of *pietas* and *eruditio* that distinguished the first Jesuits. His own formula for Catholic success was the presence of "men noted for their learning and holiness" in the universities. With this conviction he gave a fresh vision to the Catholic Reform in Germany, and set the needle that would for centuries point the course of the Jesuit effort in the lands beyond the Rhine and the Danube.

CHAPTER III

TRENT

1545–1547

Introduction

This chapter covers the short period from December 1545 to August 1547. They were Jay's conciliar years. During this period, first at Trent, then at Bologna, he engaged in the debates through the first nine sessions of the council.

While Jay was immersed in this conciliar business, princes and bishops in other areas, Austria, Germany, and Italy, tried to disengage him from the council in order to have his services within their own jurisdictions. One of these, Duke Ercole d'Este of Ferrara, who eventually prevailed, had Jay dispatched to Ferrara, and so closed Jay's immediate contacts with the council.

At the Council of Trent

On 13 December 1545 Cardinal Giammaria del Monte, the senior legate to the council, celebrated the solemn mass of the Holy Spirit in the cathedral of the Tyrolese town of Trent. After the mass Cornelio Musso, bishop of Bitonto, one of the most stirring sacred orators of the day, preached a sermon of high hope. "Gathered as it is at the gate of the empire," he said, "may it [the council] effect the reunion of Germany with the Roman Church. To the realization of so high a purpose all must contribute—Latins and Greeks, Spaniards and Frenchmen, Germans and Italians— everyone must give of his best.'' So with great solemnity opened the general council which Pope Paul III had been trying to assemble for years.[1] Jay arrived at Trent three days later, the first Jesuit to do so. Cardinal Cristoforo Madruzzo, the bishop of Trent, could not have been more gracious in his welcome. He gave Jay extensive faculties for hearing confessions and preaching as well as the power to delegate these faculties to others. The three cardinal presidents, Giammaria del Monte, Marcello Cervini, and Reginald Pole, gave him a pleasant reception (*hilari vultu*).[2]

Jay had hardly arrived at Trent before he found himself the center of a delicate diplomatic controversy. When Paul III issued his original bull for the convocation of the general council, he ordered all prelates who by law or by privilege had a deliberative vote to attend the council unless prevented by a legitimate obstacle. Otto Truchsess von Waldburg, faced with the serious problem created by the emperor's determination to open still another imperial diet at Regensburg despite the general council, had a cogent reason to excuse himself from attendance at Trent. That was why he sent Jay in his place with the title of procurator, or deputy.[3] But ever since the pope's original bull, there appeared ominous signs that bishops in several countries, not at all anxious to travel to Trent, were going to resort to the excusing clause and send representatives. Paul III realized that a general council without as many bishops present would lose its suasive power, and therefore on 17 April 1545 he issued the bull *Decet nos*, a blanket order that deputies of absent bishops would be refused the right to vote.[4]

Despite the comprehensive nature of the pope's order, it remained morally impossible for some of the German bishops to leave their dioceses because of the imminent danger that their sees might fall captive to the Protestants during their absence. Paul could not but yield to the hard facts and issued the brief *Dudum* on 5 December 1545, making an exception for the German bishops.[5] Then it was that Jay arrived at Trent. He found the papal legates in a frustrating situation. They felt that an exception made for the Germans would cause an outcry among the other nations. Yet, they were anxious to avoid offense to a man of Truchsess's ecclesiastical stature by a denial of recognition of his representative. They then resorted to some adroit diplomacy. They held in abeyance the papal exception in favor of the Germans; then allowed deputies to attend the council, but with consultative rather than deliberative vote.[6] On the list of the second session of the council, right behind the legates, cardinals, ambassadors, archbishops, bishops, appeared the title ''Procuratores,'' with the solitary entry: D. Claudius Jaius.[7]

The first period of the council, embracing the first ten sessions, extended from December 1545 to September 1549. From March 1547 to February 1548 the meetings, including the ninth and tenth sessions, were held at Bologna. That February the council was practically suspended; in September 1549 formally and definitively so.[8] The major achievements of the council during these years were the decrees, issued at Trent, on the sacred books and traditions, original sin, justification, the sacraments in general, baptism, and confirmation; and then the discussions, at Bologna, on the sacraments of penance, extreme unction, orders, and matrimony. For most of this first period, until August 1547, Jay took an active part in hammering out the decrees.

Jay on Scripture and Tradition

The first subject on which Jay spoke concerned Scripture and tradition. It involved him in one of the more intricate theological inquiries of the sixteenth century, heightened by the issues raised by Martin Luther and John Calvin. Two legacies from the Middle Ages clouded the problem. The first was a strong religious movement that in its quest for the ideal Christian life criticized, in the name of Scripture, the structure and system of the Church. The second was a pervasive obscurity in terminology. The word *tradition* lacked preciseness. The fuzziness of concept became apparent when the speakers at Trent sometimes used the word in the singular, sometimes in the plural. A double heritage, therefore, of an intense religious disposition to cast Scripture in the role of adversary against the visible Church, and of ambiguity about the term tradition, filled the halls of Trent with a thick theological haze.[9]

On 23 February 1546 Jay intervened. What he said affected

the entire course of the debate. He made a vital distinction: "There are traditions that belong to the faith and must be accepted by us as endowed with the same binding force as the Gospels; there are others, such as those of a ceremonial nature, that do not carry the same weight." (. . . *nam quaedam traditiones ad fidem pertinent, et eae pari auctoritate cum evangeliis a nobis suscipiendae sunt. De aliis autem, quae ceremoniales existunt, non ita*).[10] Jay, therefore, drew a sharp line between dogmatic traditions and nondogmatic traditions.

The initial haze that surrounded the debates on tradition belied the valuable work done at the University of Paris at least a quarter century earlier. At Paris articulate and energetic Josse Clichtove gave most of his attention in his controversial writings to the refining of the concept of tradition. Jay, who arrived in Paris in late 1534, seven years after Clichtove left the university for Chartres and when memory of him was still fresh, probably knew the Belgian's theology of tradition. The brace of distinctions he put before the council's bishops stumbling in their perception of tradition he probably learned at Clichtove's school of theology. It was a Parisian gift to Trent through the courtesy of Claude Jay. To this phase of Jay's thought might justly be applied a phrase that has been attached to Clichtove's concept of the Church: "Tridentine before Trent" (*déjà tridentine avant la lettre*).[11]

The distinctions that Jay proposed won influential support. Girolamo Seripando, the erudite general of the Augustinians, intervened on the same day and welcomed Jay's distinction. One of the council's presidents, Marcello Cervini, recognized its import and gave it his support.[12] Jay had swept away a big part of the web of confusion that had been spun about this subject. In its decree, Sacred Books and Traditions: Those to be Retained, the council embraced Jay's distinctions and used terminology resonant of his. Jay had spoken of "traditions that belong to the faith" (*traditiones quae ad fidem pertinent*); the council spoke of "the traditions themselves that belong both to the faith and to moral conduct" (*traditiones ipsas, tum ad fidem, tum ad mores pertinentes*).[13] Jay had said that certain particular traditions "are to be received by us [as invested] with an authority equal to that of the Gospels" (*pari auctoritate cum evangeliis a nobis sucipiendae sunt*); the council said that these particular traditions and the sacred books should be received "with like reverent dispositions" (*pari pietatis affectu et reverentia*).[14]

Exactly a month later, on 23 March 1546, Jay made a second intervention during the discussions on Scripture and tradition. Again he presented a distinction: the central reality is the gospel (*evangelium*); distinguished from the gospel are the two forms in which the gospel is transmitted, the Scriptures and the traditions.[15] Here Jay did not formulate a fresh approach, but he did articulate with clarity and precision a long line of Christian thought that still had vitality at the opening of the sixteenth century: the gospel is revelation; Scripture and tradition are modes of expressing this revelation; revelation enjoys the primacy in this interrelationship.[16] Close to Jay in its expression, the council in its decree considered the gospel as "the source of all the Christianity which comes from the apostles," and which was eventually passed on through two different forms, the sacred books and the apostolic traditions.[17]

Jay on Clerical Education

Two weeks later, on 6 April, Jay spoke at a congregation over which Cardinal Cervini presided. In the last stages of the debate on scripture and the apostolic traditions as the final decrees were being hammered out, the question on the floor was: Holy Scripture: Misuses and Correctives.[18] A refined aspect of that broad question was the training of diocesan priests and the creation of teaching positions in Holy Scripture at the principal churches. Jay addressed himself to this. Influenced no doubt by his German experience, he emphasized that the problem was more than a scarcity of teachers; it was a dearth of students. Some churches, he pointed out to the congregation, did indeed have teachers but no one to listen.[19] He advised that in these cases it be arranged that all the priests attached to a particular church be present for the lectures. He then came to his favorite theme. Where there were no priests, he recommended the establishment of collegiate residences "where students might be instructed and developed."[20] This was an echo of his voice at Salzburg, Eichstätt, and Ingolstadt. Jay carried to Trent the conviction formed in Bavaria: collegiate residences had to be founded at the universities, where an educated clergy could be formed.

Jay's proposal had wide implications. He was trying to break through several centuries of history. He saw the destitution of the system of clerical formation that had been consolidated at Lateran Council IV in 1215. The Lateran system had envisaged a residence for aspirants to the secular clergy at each cathedral. Through three centuries two developments in European society eroded the position of these cathedral schools: the rise of the universities and the breakdown of feudalism. Jay recognized the need to go beyond the blueprints of the thirteenth century, but his call for a modern educational structure hit a stone wall.

The best minds at Trent felt that the reform of clerical education was in the revitalization of past legislation. Even the leading humanists at the council did not perceive that they were attempting a drastic recasting of ecclesiastical studies with a moribund program.[21] This issue, discussed in the debates before the fourth session (8 April 1546), spilled over into the discussions before the fifth session (17 June 1546). In the latter session the council substantially endorsed what had been enacted at Lateran Council IV in 1215.[22] History, however, was on the side of Jay. At the twenty-fourth session (11 November 1563), when Jay was dead ten years, his proposal found a partial endorsement in canon eighteen, which called for the establishment of a seminary in each diocese.[23]

On 8 April, two days after Jay had his intervention about the establishment of colleges, the council issued two decrees in the fourth session, one entitled The Sacred Books and Traditions: Those to be Retained, the other The Vulgate Edition of the Bible and the Way to Interpret Holy Scripture.[24] Four centuries later the former decree remained a theologically vital document. During Vatican Council II, the conciliar fathers had it very much in mind as they forged the seventh article of the Dogmatic Constitution on Divine Revelation. This article, in its final form, was "consciously based closely on the Tridentine text."[25] Jay's reflections on Scripture and tradition at the Council of Trent entered into the achievement of Vatican Council II.

Biblical and Scholastic Tensions

For the next two months after session four, the council had two other issues under consideration, the one pastoral, the other dogmatic. These issues were the formation of priests and bishops, and original sin. Jay contributed to the debates on both questions. Those debates revealed an inner tension between two mentalities: the biblical and the scholastic. The former, with its strong thrust toward the sources of Christianity (*ad fontes*), was brilliantly represented in some of the finest figures at the council: Marcello Cervini; Reginald Pole; Girolamo Seripando; Pietro Bertano, bishop of Fano; Tommaso Sanfelice, bishop of La Cava; and Cornelio Musso, bishop of Bitonto. Taddeo Cucchi, the abbot of Pontida, near Bergamo, spoke in the name of the rich Benedictine tradition and depicted scholasticism as a potential hotbed of discord.

The opposing school of thought, however, had its competent spokesman in Spanish Dominican Domingo Soto. Soto reined in the rapid forward march of the humanists. He reminded the council that scholasticism had played an important role in the defense of the faith against the Protestants; he argued that scholasticism was essential to theological disputation; he warned that a deemphasis of scholasticism by the council would be an invitation to the Protestants to conclude that the Catholic Church was admitting that it had been wrong in its predilection for scholastic thought. At this stage of the council, the humanists and the scholastics shared about equal influence, but in about ten years the scholastics climbed to the ascendancy.[26]

Jay basically identified himself with the biblical humanists. But he brought to their program and to their discussion something unique, his firsthand knowledge of Germany. When he spoke he did so from the broad perspective that his years at Regensburg, Dillingen, Salzburg, and Ingolstadt had given him, and from his intimate knowledge of the deplorable state of the priesthood in Germany.

This perspective, adding as it did the dimension of Germany to the debates, gave a special orientation to the interventions that Jay made through April and May. On 13 April, at a meeting presided over by Cardinal Cervini, the theologians considered the draft of the decree entitled Holy Scripture: Lecturers and Preachers.[27] Jay said that he favored the general tenor of the decree.[28] But he had reservations. The German crisis impelled him to suggest an alteration. Aware of the Protestant stress on ''Scripture alone''

73

(*scriptura sola*), he urged that the decree call on Catholic preachers to treat not only Holy Scripture but also the apostolic traditions.[29] In the final draft of the decree, the title dropped the phrase "Holy Scripture" and read simply Lecturing and Preaching.[30]

A further consideration at this meeting of April 13 was the question of imposing a *methodus* or short compendium of Catholic dogmas as an aide for the better grasp of the doctrinal contents of Scripture. Jay advised caution. Again the complex situation in Germany troubled him. He voiced his apprehension about the Protestant reaction to a *methodus*. To put aside the older doctrinal outlines formulated in the scholastic tradition in favor of a new work, Jay feared, might be interpreted by the Protestants as an implicit conciliar condemnation of the scholastics. He reminded his fellow theologians that in Germany teachers in the scholastic tradition were despised.[31]

This rather unnuanced opinion showed that Jay had been impressed by the extreme views of those humanists who echoed Ulrich von Hutten. They indeed held scholasticism in contempt. And it was the memory of this contempt that Jay carried to the Council of Trent. But he had evidently missed more moderate voices. Many German humanists perceived a value in scholasticism; they recognized a danger in the rejection of a tradition so profoundly molded by the scholastics. The mutual respect and admiration that prevailed among some scholastics and humanists in Germany Jay did not catch. The views of the extremists dominated his memory. Fearful that the council, by turning to something new, might seem to be concurring in the disparagement of the scholastics, he recommended that the *Sentences* of Peter the Lombard be retained rather than that a new *methodus* be composed. Actually, the issue of the *methodus* did not find a place in the final decree.[32]

On 7 May Cardinal Cervini again presided over a congregation engaged in preparing the final form of a decree on teachers and preachers of scripture. Jay made three points in his intervention. The first: the chair of scripture should receive high priority in the intellectual formation of monks and religious.[33] Jay endorsed the views of the Dominican bishop of Bertinoro, Tommaso Casellus, who insisted that the study of the Bible was not "a preliminary step but the very purpose of education,"[34] and who called on general chapters and provincial superiors to give priority to the chair of scripture and to assign to it only the more learned of the teachers in a monastery or religious convent.[35] Jay went further. He suggested that clerics who were capable of following a class in scripture be obliged to attend.[36]

His second point: the oath to be demanded of preachers should be dropped. To guarantee high quality in preaching, the draft of the decree determined that preachers would be compelled to take an oath to the bishop or the parish priest to avoid heresy, contentious questions, and silly matters in the pulpit.[37] Jay dissented.[38] Others did too. The oath was dropped from the final form of the decree. Jay's third point: a particular phrase in the draft about studies in monasteries and religious convents should be dropped. The decree described monasteries and religious convents as places where "studies are wont to flourish" (*in quibus studia vigere solent*).[39] Jay knew that in Germany this was far from the truth and recommended a change to the more realistic phrase: "where studies can be properly carried out" (*ubi commode haberi possunt*).[40] The council in its final form fixed on the words: "where it can correctly be done" (*ubi commode fieri queat*).[41]

On 20 May a general congregation was assembled. The question was the same: Sacred Scripture: lecturers and preachers. Once again Jay brought his preoccupation with Germany to the floor. He knew that a decree about teachers of scripture that ignored the dearth of men qualified for the teaching positions would be mere fantasy. With his personal realization of the scarcity of educated priests, he cautioned against the haphazard establishment of professorships, "especially in Germany," and recommended that central monasteries that could serve several others be chosen.[42] When Jay spoke, it was Germany speaking (*Vox Jaii vox Germaniae*). Jay's presence at Trent underscored the absence of the German bishops and the privation the council suffered because of that absence. On 17 June 1546, at the fifth session, the council approved the decree Lecturing and Preaching.[43]

Debates on Original Sin

The dogmatic decree, issued on the same day, concerned original sin. At least four times Jay spoke at the general congregations. His statements on those four occasions fitted into the

75

theological pattern taken by the decree, notable for its absence of scholastic terminology and for its biblical tone: original sin is transfused by propagation, not imitation; concupiscence, which remains after baptism, is not sin; baptism really and effectively, and not by imputation, removes original sin.[44]

The aspect of original sin that especially preoccupied Jay was its relationship to the Blessed Virgin Mary. In three of his four interventions, on 31 May, 8 June, and 14 June, he requested a change in the decree's wording so that the freedom of the Virgin Mary from the taint of original sin be not compromised, "lest offense be given to the Blessed Virgin and those who contend that she was conceived without this sin" (*ne offendatur B. virgo et ii, qui eam conceptam sine hoc peccato asserunt*).[45]

Jay placed himself with the majority of the council on an issue which had divided Dominican and Franciscan theologians since the work of Duns Scotus. Through the centuries, the opinion in favor of the Immaculate Conception gained in adherence, and at Trent, under the influence of the doughty fighter, Cardinal Pedro Pacheco, almost attained the status of a conciliar definition.[46] The council, however, desirous of avoiding delay by a protracted debate, compromised by referring to the constitutions of Pope Sixtus IV in 1477 and 1483 and by simply stating that "the Blessed and Immaculate Virgin Mary, Mother of God," was not included in the decree.[47] Jay linked the Society of Jesus in an explicitly theological way to this mounting devotion to Mary just as Ignatius linked the Society to it in a spiritual way by the important role of Our Lady in the *Spiritual Exercises*. Jay the theologian at Trent reflected the spirit of Ignatius the mystic at Manresa. Devotion to Mary became the inspiration of one of the Society's chief instruments of apostolic enterprise, the Sodality of the Blessed Virgin Mary, initiated in 1564 by the Belgian Jesuit John Leunis and reaching within thirteen years a membership of thirty thousand youths.[48] Jesuit fidelity to the doctrine of Mary's Immaculate Conception carried through the centuries and reached its climax in the work of the Italian Jesuit Carlo Passaglia, one of the chief architects of the dogma promulgated in 1854 by Pope Pius IX.

Ambiguities on Justification

The next session of the council, the sixth, did not occur until seven months later, on 13 January 1547. Through those seven months the debates were intricate and intense. The issues were thorny and complex: justification and the residence of bishops in their dioceses. On the question of justification Jay became deeply involved.

This question clamored for clarification. Luther had taken the problem that reached back to the Pelagian controversy and cast it into a new formula: the central condition for justification is the confident certitude of one's forgiveness.[49] As early as 1518 Luther wrote: "See to it that in no way do you trust in your receiving forgiveness because of your contrition but rather because of the word of Christ, who said to Peter: 'Whatever you loose upon earth will be loosed in heaven.' Thus I say that, if you would obtain the priest's forgiveness, trust and believe intensely that you are forgiven, and you will truly be forgiven."[50]

Cardinal Tommasso de Vio (Cajetan), the skilled Dominican theologian, quickly discerned the profound implications of Luther's thought on justification. He detected that Luther, by making certitude of one's forgiveness the central condition of justification, had forged a new and untraditional definition of sacramental grace and made the uncanny remark: "For this amounts to building a new Church" (hoc enim est novam ecclesiam construere).[51]

Few other theologians outside Germany, however, realized the implications of Luther's thought.[52] Ambiguity and uncertainty hung like a cloud over the field of Catholic theology not only in the academic and scientific formulation of the doctrine but also in its practical impact on theories of spirituality.[53] This obscurity persisted to the opening of the council. Only four years before the council assembled, Emperor Charles V convened on 5 April 1541 at Regensburg a high level religious colloquy of noble and ambitious design, at which a key problem was the meaning of justification. Philip Melanchthon, Martin Bucer, and Johann Pistorius were the Protestant collocutors. Johannes Eck, Johann Gropper, and Julius Pflug were the Catholics.[54]

Together the theologians hammered out an article that they felt expressed the essentials of Christian belief on justification, while leaving room for continuing theological reflection on the more abstruse aspects of the question. Gasparo Contarini, the papal legate at Regensburg, endorsed the formula.[55] Calvin at

Geneva found it acceptable. But Rome and Wittenberg rejected it as ambiguous.[56] Obscurity therefore still prevailed when the council opened at Trent. Cardinal Marcello Cervini evaluated this unhealthy situation: "A handful of theologians who had achieved but little" (*pauci admodum et paucissima*).[57] This doctrinal ambiguity spilled over into Christian life.

Justification and Spirituality

Since the onrush of the Biblical Renaissance, two influential and diverse theories of spirituality developed among the Catholics. At the council, Cardinal Pole represented one; Claude Jay the other. Reginald Pole, since his exile from England in 1521, emerged as the guiding star among several men and women in Italy, first at Padua and then at Viterbo, who were seeking a deeper interior life and a more profound personal holiness that they hoped would radiate through the Church in a movement of reform.[58] Some Benedictines inspired like groups at Padua and Venice. The theology of these men intent on the life of the spirit (*spirituali*) was distinctly biblical. They found scholastic thought to be "Darke, intangled, difficult and beastlie."[59] The spirituality also of these persons was decidedly biblical. As they moved closer in their religious aspirations toward "Scripture alone" (*sola scriptura*), the more they felt the attraction of Luther's "faith alone" (*sola fides*) as the key to man's salvation.[60] The central doctrine of the Protestant Reform led them to a feeling of complete confidence in God alone, freedom from a complex set of ecclesiastical precepts and regulations, release from the impulse to strain toward good deeds. Personal experience deepened these attitudes, which, for these holy people, mirrored a more mature and a more interior spirituality.[61] Men of integrity and influence in the Church aligned themselves with Pole: Federigo Fregoso, Gasparo Contarini, Gian Matteo Giberti, Marcantonio Flaminio, Giovanni Morone, Alvise Priuli.

Claude Jay represented a school of spirituality with a different orientation—and the one that would actually become the dominant spirituality of the Catholic Reform. Jay, formed in the *Spiritual Exercises* of Ignatius Loyola, articulated in theological language and in his life Rule 16 of Rules for Thinking with the Church in

78

the *Exercises*: "In the same way, much caution is necessary, lest by much talk about faith, and much insistence on it without any distinctions or explanations, occasion be given to the people, whether before or after they have faith informed by charity, to become slothful and lazy in good works."[62] This school of spirituality gave good works an important role in man's salvation.[63]

Schools of Spirituality in the Council

The *spirituali* entered the council severely crippled. At the religious colloquy at Regensburg in 1541 the papal legate, Cardinal Gasparo Contarini, prominent leader among the *spirituali*, received a caustic dressing down by Rome for his role in forging the theological articles that he hoped would ease the reunion of the Lutheran and Roman churches. Cardinal Alessandro Farnese, the papal secretary of state, authored the barbed reproof of 29 May 1541 that profoundly humiliated Contarini.[64] A little more than a year later, on 24 August 1542, this ecumenist and mentor of the *spirituali* died in Bologna. The day before, Bernard Ochino, vicar general of the Capuchins and the most forceful Catholic preacher in Italy, left Florence on his flight north to cross the Alps and join the Protestants at Geneva. The day after Contarini's death, the twenty-fifth, another vibrant preacher, Pietro Martire Vermigli, also left Florence and hastened towards the Alps and the refuge he sought among the Protestants at Zurich. The Catholics of Italy were stunned.[65] Gian Matteo Giberti recognized the meaning of those three days in August 1542: the end of the era of the *spirituali*.[66]

Jay shared many of the aspirations of the *spirituali*. In the debates on Scripture at the council, he made clear his deep sympathy for the biblical renaissance in the reform of the church. But he brought to his task the skills of the trained theologian, skills that Pole and others of the *spirituali* did not have.[67] He had learned the "distinctions," to which Ignatius had referred. The *spirituali*, however, shared the Erasmian mistrust of the Latin zeal for definition and the Erasmian resentment of the theological specialist.[68] Jay, realizing the need for clarity of concept and sharpness of distinction, called extensively on his professional theological training during the debates on justification. He made his first intervention on 12 July 1546.[69] Cardinal Pole did not hear him, since three weeks earlier, on 28 June, Pole had left the council because of serious physical and mental strain.[70]

Jay on Justification

Jay's first intervention was a lengthy one. He followed with other extended interventions on 21 July, 8 October, and 23 November.[71] He also made a short comment on 17 August.[72] Jay sensed the extremities that had to be avoided, the fiducialism of Luther and the voluntarism of Pelagius. With a lucid grasp of the distinctions and subtleties within the corpus of theological reflection on grace, he inferred the need of human free works: "works, therefore, are necessary, because that faith [as preached by Luther] alone was not adequate" (*ergo opera sunt necessaria, quod illa sola fides non sufficiebat.*)[73] Yet, free human acts did not exclude the need of God's help, and Jay insisted on "free will which is itself assisted by God" (*postea liberum arbitrium, etiam adiutum a Deo.*)[74] Then, in his intervention of 21 July, with rich scriptural and patristic resources, including St. Augustine against Pelagius, he insisted on God's continuing aid to remain and grow in justification.[75] Jay therefore was sensitive to the richness of that profound feeling for man's utter dependence on God for salvation to which the current Augustinian renaissance had attracted Protestants and the Catholics of the school of Pole and Morone, and which found its theological expression in the formula *fides sola*.

Perhaps the most complex aspect of the debate on justification was the question of *duplex justitia*. Johann Gropper, an eirenic Catholic theologian from Cologne, had endeavored to bridge the differences between the Lutherans and the Catholics by both his intellectual attitude and his theological reasoning. He insisted that the subject of justification had to be approached with an unbiased mind and that an a priori rejection of Luther's theology must be avoided. He advanced a theory which, for man's final justification, called for further application of *justitia Christi* to supplement the deficiency of personal justice, *justitia inhaerens*.[76] In the council the most distinguished theologian to advance this theory was Girolamo Seripando. Intellectually formed in Augustinian ideas and a dynamic conception of grace, Seripando registered during the debates his reluctance to accept scholastic definitions as the best way of expressing the vitality and the fullness of God's life in man as put forward in the New Testament.[77]

On 8 October Jay lined up his ideas on *justitia* in orderly manner. The whole thrust of his arguments repudiated Gropper's theory.[78] Jay leaned toward those theologians who tried to make clear that personal sanctifying grace (*gratia inhaerens*), effecting an ontological union with Christ, cannot be separated from the grace of Christ (*gratia Christi*) and can only find its explanation in the mystical body of Christ.[79] Two weeks later, on 26 October, Diego Laynez gave for about two hours the most extensive analysis and criticism of the *duplex justitia* theory heard at the council. But Laynez was doing hardly more than administering the coup de grace to Seripando's position. Carmelites, Dominicans, and Franciscans had already hammered it down. Besides, the novelty of the theory made it suspect to many in the council.[80]

Jay, Laynez (and Salmerón too, as will be seen), formulated their interventions in the technical and professional language of scholastic theology. Even though they spoke of man's ineffable union with God, their arguments were coolly metaphysical, their accent was speculative, their conviction was intellectual. But these three Jesuits came before the council from a context far wider than that of scientific theology. They came from the prayerful and personal experience of the Spiritual Exercises and the truths of God's love for man and the world, of God's activity within man and the world, and of God's presence in man and the world. Theirs was a formation not in mind alone but also in heart and will.

The teachings of these Tridentine Jesuits bore a certain resemblance to a spiritual pattern that had been strong among the humanists in Rome, a pattern that emphasized God's friendship for man and his divine intimacy with him. Preachers at the papal court, at least to 1520, articulated that pattern. A preacher in 1492 proclaimed that ". . .in the Virgin's womb and on the cross, he kissed us and renewed all reality."[81] This accent on God's intimate love for man among the humanist preachers in Rome meshed with the intellectual and spiritual formation of the Jesuit masters from Paris. The Jesuit doctrine on justification jumped into silhouette at Trent from a landscape of ascetical, spiritual, and intellectual principles.

The Decree on Justification

On 13 January 1547, at the sixth session, the conciliar fathers unanimously approved the work of seven arduous and exacting months. While profiting from the controversies among Catholics and the negotiations for reunion with the Protestants, they nevertheless advanced beyond them, because they "were fully conscious that their task was to create a new thing, not merely to copy an existing model."[82] Not content with the catchwords of controversial theology, and going to the core of the problem, they marked out the boundaries that separated Catholic dogma and Protestant theology. This was their purpose. To settle opinions disputed among Catholics was not their intent.[83] The two hinges on which the decree swung were the need of God's grace and the free cooperation of man in his justification. On both Jay had spoken with clarity and precision.

Embedded in the decree was a distinctive pastoral orientation. The beginning of the decree read: "Since at this time, not without the shipwreck of many souls and harm to the Church's unity, a certain doctrine on justification is being spread abroad, the sacred ecumenical and general council of Trent, proposes for the praise and glory of Almighty God, the peace of the Church and the salvation of souls. . . ."[84] This pastoral orientation explicitly recognized the place of man's works in his achievement of salvation and made the decree "one of the foundation stones of counter reformation spirituality. . . ." This spirituality "sprang from a triple alliance": the Tridentine teaching on justification; the thrust of that age toward practical works of charity; certain new developments in ascetical teaching and discipline.[85] Although his contribution was not so awe inspiring as that of his two fellow Jesuits, Laynez and Salmerón, Jay as a member of an order explicitly dedicated to apostolic engagement, had a positive share in the forging of the decree that gave dogmatic underpinning to their spiritual vision.

Had the doctrine of this decree been honed with the finesse of Trent some fifty years earlier, the course of the surge toward reform might have been different. This at least was the view of Adolf von Harnack. He perceived the penetration and balance of the decree and judged that if its teaching had penetrated the life of the church, say, at the time of Lateran Council V (1512), the Protestant movements would not have evolved as they did.[86]

Jay on Episcopal Residence

Whereas the dogmatic decree on justification attained unanimous assent, the reformation decree on the issue of episcopal residence failed to receive acceptance and remained a source of divisiveness even until the council's third period (1562–63).[87] Through the late middle ages a breakdown had occurred in the unity of benefice (*beneficium*) and ecclesiastical office (*officium*). As financial recompense and pastoral duty became separated, bishops received the revenues and delegated their episcopal and priestly duties to a vicar. In 1215 the Fourth Lateran Council discerned these evils, insisted on the obligation of episcopal residence, and condemned the accumulation of several benefices by one person. But exemption and dispensation were convenient ways to circumvent the legislation. At Rome the papal curia, especially the cardinals, profited by these stratagems.[88]

At Trent, the two traditions, zeal for genuine reform and the curial resistance to change, met in confrontation. The debates bristled. The exchanges were barbed. Jay participated, but not extensively. When he spoke on 10 January 1546, he took the hard line. With his vivid experience in Germany behind him, he extolled the role of a pastor living with his flock and urged that bishops be forced under severe punishment to reside in their dioceses.[89] Others, too, had the same conviction. But it was impossible at the moment to break the grip of the bureaucrats, and the issue of episcopal residence did not reach its resolution until the council's third period in 1562–63.

Jay on the Sacraments

The next session of the council, the seventh, took place only a month and a half after the sixth, on 3 March 1547. It issued a dogmatic decree on the sacraments in general, on baptism, and on confirmation. Compared to the long labor on the decree on justification, the rapidity of the sacramental decisions was striking.

This rapidity indicated the "firm sacramental consciousness" that flowed from the living, unbroken faith of the medieval church in the sacraments as the channels of God's grace. The confidence on this subject contrasted with the initial faltering on justification.[90]

Cardinal Cervini, even during the debates on justification, looked forward to the problems of sacramental theology. Jay reported to Ignatius on 30 January 1547 that Cervini had asked Laynez and Salmerón to compose a list of Protestant errors on the sacraments and a corresponding list of Catholic teachings as found in the councils, papal decrees, and patristic literature.[91] Girolamo Seripando, and probably other theologians too, shared this task.[92] The fruit of this tedious labor came to the fore on 17 January 1547, when thirty-five errors about the sacraments in general, baptism, and confirmation, accompanied for the most part by citations from Luther, Melanchthon, Bucer, and Hermann von Wied, were read at a general congregation.[93]

Exactly a month later, on 17 February 1547, Jay made an intervention. He criticized the first of the listed errors in regard to baptism. The error read: "There is no true baptism in the Roman Catholic Church." Jay denied that the Lutherans said this. He held, rather, that they denied sincerity in the administration of baptism in the Roman church (non sincere administratur). This intervention reflected Jay's insistence that in the presentation of Catholic doctrine vis-a-vis Protestant teaching the Reformers' positions be given accurately.[94] His firsthand knowledge of Protestant doctrine impelled him to insist that any position of the Reformers chosen for denunciation should be verifiable. In the final form of the third canon on baptism, the council avoided mention of the Lutherans and simply declared that to hold that the Catholic Church does not have the true doctrine on the sacrament of baptism is anathema.[95]

On 1 March 1547 Jay made a few small suggestions for changes in the wording of some of the canons. One was adopted, three were not.[96] Two days later, on the third, the council at the seventh session issued the decree on the sacraments in general, on baptism, and on confirmation. This decree had the very limited objective of delineating Catholic doctrine sharply and pointedly in an age when that doctrine was contested by the Protestants. Even though the Tridentine "canons on the sacraments cried aloud for integration in the inner life and hierarchical structure of the Church," the council deliberately, and unfortunately, did not venture to give a vision of the breadth and depth of sacramental life in the Church such as the Council of Florence had suggested a century earlier in the *Decretum pro Armeniis* of 22 November 1439.[97]

Preoccupation with Germany

Since December 1545, for fifteen months Jay had given his energies chiefly to conciliar business. Yet other events, in other quarters of the world, engaged him also. These happenings brought him a mixture of joy and anxiety. During June 1546, for example, Jay's thoughts turned toward Cologne and the friend he had made at Worms two years earlier, Peter Canisius. Johann Nopel, coadjutor bishop of Cologne, had recently ordained Canisius a priest. Jay, having heard of Peter's exhausting round of apostolic work, and calling on his own personal experience, wrote him an intimate letter on the basic need of a profound sense of prayer in the life of a hard-working priest.

I have heard that you have offered your first mass. This news, my Peter, has moved me deeply. Would that I had been able to assist at this mass and to have been filled with that awareness of the divine presence which, I am sure, invaded your own being. Who could possibly be devoid of joy during the enactment of these divine mysteries when at the bidding of a man God becomes present and dispenses so many heavenly gifts. Great is the awesomeness of Christ that he should will to come when you call; that you should have the power to summon him.

Mind that you prove yourself worthy of this divine favor. And reflect on how imperative it is that you, raised as you are to a sublime pinnacle, be alert lest you demean yourself in the pursuit of mean ambitions. If you have climbed to the heights only to climb down again, you really have not gone aloft. I am moved the more to give you this advice, since I hear that what you are achieving is visible to all and that you are receiving the praises of men, an experience fraught with deceit. He sails close to danger who steers his ship to the gently blowing wind of human applause. That man is carried far off course; his port he will miss.

Go down, my Peter, deep into your being. When you have penetrated to the very depths, feel there the intimate meaning of humility. I think it unwise to be glued constantly to books and always to be up to your ears in activity. As the soul of the body is robbed of its vitality by the importunate demands of work, so the spirit and fire of God, dampened down by the hustle and bustle of external business, eventually is extinguished. Therefore I press you to take time out not only from your preaching but also from interior debates within your mind and heart so that you may hear God in that silence in which he reveals himself. The man who without respite sweats over books is not always the one who makes the greatest headway. The one who is diligent in prayer often learns even when he is not in the formal activity of learning.

Take the example of the Angelic Doctor of the Church, who had no more effective master than Christ teaching from the cross. Whether he had occasion to speak or make a comment, he sought advice from Christ. And he received it. Imitate him, my Peter. And note: when you do so, then indeed you will have one who is teaching you the very best.[98]

Besides Peter Canisius, other people continued to remind Jay of his ties to Germany. On 31 January 1546 Johann Cochlaeus, one of Pierre Favre's first German friends, wrote Jay about the uncertain beginnings of the new religious colloquy begun at Regensburg on 27 January 1546. He listed for Jay the main issues and the chief participants. "You know," he wrote, "how intently I desire to hear from you. I ask that you let me have a good batch of letters."[99] And on 29 April 1546 Cardinal Truchsess wrote a note of encouragement to Jay, urging him to continue as his conciliar representative with unflagging diligence. "What you are doing brings me as much gratification as anything you could give me. I am most obligated to you."[100]

Preoccupation with Colleges

Not only these people, and others, remained in Jay's memory. Very vividly the intellectual experience at the University of Ingolstadt and the conviction of the need of Jesuit collegiate residences in Germany remained with him. This conviction broadened beyond the borders of Germany, and this Jay transmitted to a French bishop at the council, Guillaume Duprat of Clermont in Auvergne. Duprat became seriously interested in the Jesuits.[101] Jay showed him letters from Jesuit missionaries in India, the bull *Injunctum nobis* of Paul III lifting the restriction on the Society's numbers, and a plan for founding a Jesuit college. [102]

The idea of Jesuit colleges began to grow on the bishop, and at least four times during 1546 between February and October Jay wrote Ignatius about Duprat and his growing interest in setting up a college for Jesuits in France.[103] For example, in February or March—the month is uncertain—he told Ignatius that he was hoping that with the arrival of Favre, Laynez, and Salmerón the pieces in the educational business would all fall into place. Colleges were definitely on Jay's mind. The last sentence of his March letter read: "Again I have written to the bishop of Eichstätt about setting up colleges in Germany."[104] And in July Jay related how the fine performance of Salmerón and Laynez at the council fired Duprat's desire for a college.[105] Jay planted in good soil, for four years later Duprat turned over to the Society for use as a college the Hôtel de Clermont in Paris, destined to be a source of distinction and anxiety for the Society.[106]

Nomination to the See of Trieste

In September 1546, during the debates on justification, Jay was filled with a stabbing horror that filled several months of his life with anguish. The trouble started with two somewhat mysterious and noncommittal letters. From Prague on 21 August 1546 King Ferdinand of the Romans wrote to Jay, informing him that he had ordered Urban Weber, the royal confessor and bishop of Laibach, to set up a rendezvous with Jay in order to "transact with you diligently and in my name some business of no small moment."[107] From Oberburg on 3 September Weber wrote to Jay, suggesting Venice as a meeting point, where "you will be able to see the official credentials of His Royal Majesty and once having read them to hear from me his message."[108] It all sounded mysterious.

Yet Jay had an inkling of what was afoot. He had heard that Ferdinand had wanted to make a Jesuit the bishop of Trieste and that Nicolás Bobadilla had refused the offer made to him [109] Deeply disturbed, Jay spoke to Cardinal Cervini. Cervini advised him to go and speak with Weber. Jay left Trent on 19 September and arrived at Venice on the twenty-third. What Jay feared came to pass. Weber told Jay that Ferdinand wanted him to be consecrated bishop of Trieste.[110] Weber came very close to not delivering this message, because he was almost lost in the Adriatic off Venice. As Jay told Ignatius: "The day the bishop of Laibach reached here, he nearly drowned in the Adriatic Sea. Then the next day he put me in peril of drowning in the sea of episcopal grandeur."[111] And so began what were perhaps the three most unhappy months of Jay's life.

Trieste was on the highway between Germany and Illyria, and with the caravans of merchandise that moved south from the empire travelled the ideas of the Lutherans.[112] Pietro Bonomo, a cultivated and devout priest who had been bishop of Trieste since 1502 until his death in 1546, could give his diocese but divided attention, since he had been chancellor for Emperor Maximilian as well as administrator of the great see of Vienna. Ironically enough, one of the watch dogs who barked the loudest because of the danger to the flock of Trieste was the famous Pier Paolo Vergerio, who as bishop of Capo d'Istria apostatized in 1549.[113]

Ferdinand of course understood the strategic importance of Trieste as the key city that opened into both the north of Italy and the country of the Serbs and Croats. A member of the Company of Jesus, reasoned the king of the Romans, would be just the man for such an important diocese. He approached Nicolás Bobadilla, then in the neighborhood of Ingolstadt as chaplain of the Spanish and Italian soldiers on the ever shifting field of battle within the empire. Bobadilla refused.[114] Ferdinand then decided to turn to Jay. He had observed Jay at Worms the previous year and had apprized his qualities of zeal, intelligence, and devotion to the Holy See.

Of all the first Jesuits Jay was probably the most averse, in a deliberately explicit and conscious way, to the idea of ecclesiastical honor. Repudiation of dignity seems to have been uppermost in his mind when he placed himself in the hands of Pierre Favre in Paris in 1535. In his copy of the Little Office he had written some thoughts taken from St. Augustine and St. Gregory the Great. "Unbecoming is it to have an appetite for high office even if one fills it with credit." "Let the strong in virtue take on the office of ruling only under constraint: let the unworthy go not near it even under compulsion."[115] In his *Bishop's Image* he evidenced the lofty esteem he had for the episcopal order.

Once Bobadilla had refused Ferdinand, Jay was on his guard and began to formulate his own reasons for refusal against the day when the king's finger might possibly point toward him. Thoroughly in love with his Jesuit vocation, he was distressed at the prospect of being removed from a life of obedience under Ignatius. Trepidation was on every word of the letter he sent to his father in Christ. On 13 September he wrote:

> I have always had a fear of benefices and ecclesiastical dignities. I turn my back on them now more than ever. The more important they are the more repugnant they are to me. By God's grace I am happy in my life of poverty according to my vocation, although I do feel discontented with myself, since I each day give offense to our Lord by my sins. I do not know how to rule myself. I would do well, therefore, to be on guard against taking on the obligation of governing others.[116]

On 25 September Jay sent Ignatius a detailed account of what happened when he went to Venice to meet Bishop Weber.

> I left Trent on 19 September and reached Venice on the twenty-third, the same day the bishop of Laibach arrived. He told me that the next day, after mass, he would communicate to me the reason His Majesty had given him this particular mission. The next day, accordingly, at ten o'clock we met. He then handed me the message from His Majesty. When I had finished reading it, he gave a wide ranging speech about the king's good and holy desire to provide worthy ecclesiastics for the episcopal office, about the needs of the church in Trieste, et cetera. He capped his little speech with the statement that His Majesty wanted me to accept the bishopric of Trieste. I listened through his whole line of reasoning, and although I had resolved on what I was going to say, I nevertheless asked him for time to think the matter over.
>
> I, therefore, withdrew, went to a nearby church, and there prayed for about an hour. I then returned and said, in substance, that after prayerful consideration I felt in conscience I should not accept. I gave some of my reasons and told him of my gratitude to His Majesty, et cetera. He entreated me time and again to think more of the matter, using all his powers of persuasion to get me to accept. After I left his residence and returned to the Convent of The Trinity, he sent me a number of messages urging me to accede. He, nevertheless, received no other reply than the one I had already given. I answered, as best I could and in the same vein, the letter of His Majesty.[117]

A Duel over the Episcopal Appointment

Jay's friends noticed that he had lost his usual serenity and pleasantness. He became hesitant and preoccupied.[118] As his realization of the import of Ferdinand's designs grew on him, in consternation he wrote pleas for help in all directions. He directed at least two letters to Ferdinand himself.[119] In December, three months later, when he could almost feel the pastoral staff being placed in his hand, he sent a troubled plea to Pope Paul. His reasons poured right from his heart: a conviction that the episcopal obligations were beyond his capacity and that what he regarded as his personal failure to rule his own soul made him unfit to rule others; the conviction that the acceptance of an ecclesiastical dignity was against the whole purpose and spirit of the Society of Jesus, which had been blessed by papal authority; the conviction that the acceptance of a bishopric by one Jesuit would open the door to others, much to the scandal of the faithful, who would then see men expressly dedicated to the repudiation of honors actually accepting them; the conviction that the individual Jesuit, by vocation ready to move from one point of the world to another, once made a bishop would be cramped within the confines of his own diocese.[120]

Jay's letters to the pope and the king of the Romans were necessarily formal and phrased in the stilted language called for by the custom of the age. But when he turned to Ignatius, it was the frightened son writing freely and without inhibition to his sympathetic father.

> With all my heart I beg Your Reverence to deign to block such a command of obedience being given to me. I can say without fear of contradiction that, if holy obedience did not tie me to Trent, I would be whole heartedly set on fleeing some place where no command to take a bishopric would ever find me. I hope in our Lord that His Holiness, at whose feet our Company has had its beginnings and by whom it has been confirmed, will preserve it in its humility and simple lowliness to God's greater glory and to the greater good and salvation of souls.[121]

Ignatius promptly rushed to the rescue of his distracted son. The proposal to make Jay bishop of Trieste was but one other instance of the many attempts by prelates and princes to place a mitre on the head of one of his Company. First, King John of Portugal in 1543 wanted to make Rodrigues the bishop of Coimbra; in March 1546, the same monarch nominated Pierre Favre as patriarch of Ethiopia; in 1545, Laynez was requested to accept

the see of Laibach; in the summer of 1546 Ferdinand asked
Bobadilla to take Trieste. At the time Jay was storming heaven
and earth that he be excused, Paschase Broët was declining an
episcopal appointment that had been offered him. A real danger
had arisen that the Society of Jesus would disappear from the
face of the earth by being absorbed into the hierarchy of the
Church.[122]

The king of the Romans had a vigilant and industrious representative at Rome, Diego Lasso de Vega. Vega assured his
prince: "I shall give myself no rest until this business is finished."[123] Ignatius was warned by Bernadino Maffei, one of the
pope's secretaries, about the pressure being applied at the Vatican by the Hapsburg diplomats. He went, therefore, to Ferdinand's ambassador, but found that Lasso de Vega was not to be
moved. Back he went to Maffei, who had the further disquieting
information that all the cardinals, save Pole and Badia, were on
the side of the king of the Romans. Ignatius's first thought was
to visit each of the cardinals individually. On further reflection
he decided to go directly to Pope Paul III himself.[124]

Paul received Ignatius most graciously and allowed him to
draw up his arguments against the consecration of Jay. Ignatius's
reasons were fivefold. First, the Society of Jesus was born in the
spirit of humility. It could not, therefore, with the acceptance of
ecclesiastical dignities, carry on its apostolic work without serious hurt to itself. Second, presupposing Jay's acceptance of the
bishopric, it would be morally impossible for other professed
fathers to refuse similar offices, and, in view of the Society's
small numbers, its virtual destruction would follow. Third, Jay's
consecration would checkmate the universal character of his
apostolate. As a bishop he would be restricted to his own diocese,
but as a priest of the Society he had the world before him. Fourth,
the acceptance of an honor by a Jesuit would be a source of
scandal to the faithful. The Society's attitude toward positions
of honor was making a deep impression on Catholics. To open
the door to the acceptance of them would vitiate that impression,
and the scandal given would outweigh the good Jay could achieve
in a single diocese. Fifth, the Society would suffer grave internal
harm. The novices and scholastics had left the world and entered

the Society to live in poverty, chastity, and obedience. If they should see elder Jesuits accept honors, they would either, being scandalized, leave the Society, or begin to entertain secret ambitions to attain similar honors one day themselves.[125]

Paul heard Ignatius through to the end of the arguments. But he was far from convinced. In fact, he praised the choice of Jay as an act brought about by the Holy Spirit through the instrumentality of King Ferdinand, and he backed up this judgment with the first verse from the twenty-first chapter of Proverbs: "As the divisions of waters, so the heart of the king is in the hand of the Lord: whithersoever he will, he shall turn it." Ignatius stood firm. With modest insistence he again tried to persuade the pope. Paul concluded the audience by an exhortation to Ignatius that he recommend the whole business to God, promising at the same time that he himself would reconsider it.[126]

The outlook, however, was not encouraging. Even though the ambassador of Emperor Charles V, Juan de Vega, worked against Ferdinand's ambassador, Diego Lasso de Vega, and went to the pope and pleaded Ignatius's cause, he was told that the Holy See had no intention of disappointing Ferdinand by a refusal. The consistory in which Jay's appointment to Trieste was to be announced was scheduled for 10 December. Three or four days before, Ignatius visited a number of cardinals then at Rome. Two of the sacred colleges he did not bother to call on, judging that it would be pointless to interview the one delegated to introduce the business of Trieste in the consistory, as well as the stormy Neapolitan so unlikely to be sympathetic to a Jesuit appeal, Gianpietro Carafa. Despite all his efforts, Ignatius won over not more than half the cardinals then in Rome. Those he failed to convince thought in terms of the Church's need for holy and learned bishops, which the Society of Jesus was in a position to supply. This was the situation on 9 December, the day before the consistory.

Ignatius had one last recourse. Among his penitents was Margaret of Austria, young wife of Ottavio Farnese, grandson of the pope. Of Margaret, a woman of little promise because of her domineering and difficult character, Ignatius as her spiritual director formed a magnificent figure of genuine stature. "The relationship between Ignatius and Margaret is perhaps one of the best documented examples of the influence that the hidden power of a truly Christian spiritual direction can have even upon politics."[127] Ignatius took the case to Margaret. She sent a quick message to Pope Paul, asking him to defer the business of Trieste until an answer was received to the plea she personally had sent to Ferdinand for the withdrawal of Jay's nomination.[128]

On the tenth the cardinals assembled for the consistory. Pope Paul approached the chamber of this solemn session; just before he entered, he called Diego Lasso de Vega aside and told him that the vacancy of Trieste would not be filled for the time being. Ignatius breathed easily again. Lasso de Vega tried to soften the chagrin of defeat in his report to Ferdinand with an observation on Ignatius's vigorous campaign. "Be sure," he said, "that there had been more noise and more to-do about the filling of this see than if there were an election of a pope."[129]

Ignatius's Victory Against the Episcopal Appointment

All now depended on Ferdinand. Besieged on all sides, he received letters from Ignatius and Cardinal Rodolfo Pio di Carpi in Rome, and from Jay at Trent. Bobadilla in Germany, and Salmerón and Laynez at Trent persuaded some of the German bishops to add their voices to the chorus of protest. Cardinal Pio di Carpi, the Society's protector in Rome, stressed the harm he felt the Church would suffer from Jay's elevation to the hierarchy. Such an event, he argued, could begin a process of removing the foundation stones of the Society of Jesus, few in number, and completely obliterating the new edifice. And further, the great spiritual harvest being gathered by the Society of Jesus could be damaged if the impression got abroad that the Jesuits, even while explicitly repudiating honors, were actually on the hunt for them.[130] Also in Rome, Leonor de Osorio, wife of Juan de Vega, the imperial ambassador, swung her important influence onto the side of Jay.[131] Ignatius had no greater supporter among the Roman ladies than Leonor, of whom he spoke as "my spiritual daughter in the Lord."[132] She sided completely with Ignatius in his stand on the episcopal issue and told him that she was prepared to lose all she had rather then see any

Jesuit accept a bishopric.[133] Word reached Jay that she preferred to see him at work in a hospital than immersed in episcopal splendor.[134]

On 9 January 1547 Ferdinand, worn down by the sheer insistence of the opposition, began to retreat. Wearily he instructed his Roman ambassador to drop the matter until he received further instructions. Later that same month, or early in February, he struck his colors. He sent word to Jay through bishop Weber that he had given up the idea of placing him over the diocese of Trieste.[135] So was finished what Jerónimo Nadal described as "the episcopal ordeal" (*tribulatio episcopatus*).[136]

The Quest for Exemplary Bishops

The "episcopal ordeal" had a significance much wider than its effect on Jay's personal life. It revealed a desire, rich with spiritual implications, among spiritual and lay leaders to reform the hierarchy. To place in each diocese a fervent shepherd had become an essential pivot in church renewal. Cardinal Madruzzo and Cardinal Cervini felt that Jay should accept the bishopric of Trieste because the good of the Church demanded it. The good of the Society had to be secondary. Ignatius, using the same norm, the common good of the Church, reached a different conclusion. He judged that restricting Jay to a single diocese would hurt the common good. Madruzzo and Cervini, despite their personal convictions, did not press their argument. Compassion for their deeply troubled friend—and in Cervini's case, respect for Ignatius—restrained them from actively seconding Ferdinand's choice.[137]

This movement for episcopal renewal not only touched the lives of most of the early Jesuits; it also reached into the ranks of the Theatines, who became a literal nursery of bishops. Before their first century was out, they gave more than two hundred to the hierarchy. By 1768 almost one-third of their forty-five hundred priests had become bishops.[138] These new Theatine bishops had a beacon in their first superior, Gianpietro Carafa, bishop of Chieti and later Pope Paul IV, one of the most aggressive champions of spiritual renewal in the sixteenth century. The newly arrived Theatines and Jesuits parted company on the question of accepting places in the hierarchy.

The Council's Move to Bologna

Jay's joy in his freedom from the episcopal office was soon augmented by another joy. On 3 March 1547, about a month after the close of the Trieste affair, his dear friend Peter Canisius entered Trent. Peter came to the council as a theologian for the bishop Jay himself was representing, Cardinal Truchsess. Peter's experience at Trent had great significance for his own life and for the Catholic Church in Germany. The cosmopolitan atmosphere of the assembly burned into his mind the conviction that here at Trent was the hope of an undivided Christendom. And this conviction he carried back into Germany with such fire that his future achievements are understandable only in the light of the council.[139]

Peter entered the council when it was in the grip of a severe crisis that came to a head only a week after his arrival and caused the assembly's transfer to Bologna. Relations between Pope Paul III and Emperor Charles V had been deteriorating. Two of the council's presidents, Cardinals Cervini and del Monte, disliked Trent and felt inhibited there by the awesome power of the emperor.[140] On 6 March Enrico Loffredo, bishop of Capaccio, died after a brief illness. During the next few days others became sick and died. Typhus, probably carried into Trent by soldiers returning from the German battle front, spread rapidly. Panic gripped the personnel of the council. On 10 March the majority voted to move to Bologna. The next day Cardinal del Monte announced the change of site. With the last note of the *Te Deum*, hysteria seized many as they quickly mounted horses and boarded boats. Fourteen bishops, an imperial minority, claimed that there was no epidemic and protested the transfer.[141]

This conflict within the council caught Jay and Canisius between two fires. As delegates of a German bishop, they felt pressure from the imperial group to remain at Trent. Charles V was known to be against the transfer of the council to the interior of Italy; Cardinal Madruzzo, whose see of Trent was within the Holy Roman Empire, tried to keep Jay and Canisius from leaving.[142] The two Jesuits, as members of a religious order with a special vow of obedience to the pope, felt an obligation to move to Bologna. Jay had also received orders from Ignatius to move with the council.[143] He therefore made strong protests to Madruzzo and Truchsess against their restraint. The two cardinals finally yielded and allowed Jay and Canisius to leave Trent, "so that," as Polanco observed, "they might be obedient to their superiors."[144] Laynez and Salmerón, who had no ties to the empire, had gone three days after the scare of 11 March. Jay and Canisius left a few days later. On or a little before 21 March they arrived at Padua, where they found Laynez nursing Salmerón, who was grievously ill.[145]

Over a month passed before Jay joined the council at Bologna. For about four weeks Salmerón had to be cared for. Despite the gloomy prognosis of the doctors, Salmerón's strong body and the nursing of the Jesuits combined to bring him back from the threshold of death, and with surprising rapidity he recouped his forces.[146] At mid-April he was again able to take to the road, and joined Jay on a brief excursion from Padua to Venice to visit a good friend of the early Jesuits, Andrea Lippomani, prior of the Monastery of the Most Holy Trinity. Lippomani "received us as his own sons," Salmerón wrote Ignatius.[147] After a visit of three or four days, Jay and Salmerón returned to Padua. Then they headed for Bologna, where they arrived on probably 27 April. Laynez and Canisius were already there.[148]

Pastoral Concerns at the Council

When the Jesuits entered Bologna, they had behind them more than some fifteen months or so of theological debate and research. They also had a wide pastoral experience.

On a Sunday in September 1546, a strange procession wound its way through the streets of Trent. Seventy-six of the poor, each with a brand new wardrobe, marched to one of the churches, heard a sermon, and then marched to a house outside the city, where they were treated to a meal. It was the Jesuits who were behind this organized charity. On 30 September 1546 Salmerón gave Ignatius a detailed description of how he, Laynez, and Jay, with the approval of the papal legates and the cardinal of Trent, drew up a list of all the prelates and ambassadors at the council, of how they visited these dignitaries each in turn, and asked alms for the poor, of how the contributions enabled them to clothe the seventy-six who took part in the unusual procession.[149]

Jay, Salmerón, and Laynez therefore learned early in the council that their presence at Trent meant more than just theology. It meant service to the poor, a penchant that Ignatius and his friends had shown so dramatically in Rome. And Trent had its share of the poor. A colony of them settled outside the city, where the legates and bishops sustained them with alms. Two councils, therefore, preoccupied the Jesuits: the one of the theologians, the other of the beggars.

Ignatius's Instructions to the Jesuits at Trent

This extraconciliar activity of the Jesuits at Trent was the implementation of instructions that they had received from Ignatius. Ignatius viewed Trent as more than the theater of theological debate. He saw it as another spot on the earth for pastoral work by the Society of Jesus. Indeed, he made it the prime purpose of the Jesuit presence in Trent (*lo que principalmente en esta jornado de Trento*).[150]

Ignatius's instructions, composed during the early months of 1546, had three main divisions. The first division concerned the relations of the Jesuits to other men at the council, especially in their conversations with them. Ignatius stressed the need to listen to others, and to hold their peace in an effort to appreciate the feelings, the ideas, and the aspirations of those with whom they spoke. He repeated the advice: Be slow to speak. In a situation that does call for speaking up, Ignatius counselled the Jesuits to present both sides of a disputed point, to avoid attachment to their own viewpoint, and to speak with calm, humility, and deference to a more sound judgment.

The second division touched on pastoral concern for others. Ignatius called this the main reason for the Jesuit journey to Trent. He encouraged preaching and lecturing in order to inflame souls with the love of God. He urged them to hear confessions, to give the Spiritual Exercises, to teach catechism, to visit the sick, to comfort the poor, "even bringing them a little gift, if possible." The third division pertained to the personal lives of the Jesuits at the council. Ignatius directed them to meet together each night for an hour to discuss their experiences, to vote on

97

their next program of action, and to correct each other mutually and in turn.[151]

In composing these instructions, Ignatius stressed the pastoral more than the controversial. He did not anticipate the influential roles that Salmerón, Laynez, and Jay were to assume in the conciliar debates and in the briefing of the bishops. He did not envisage them standing shoulder to shoulder with Pedro Pacheco, Girolamo Seripando, Domingo Soto, and Juan Bernal Diaz de Luco. Not a whisper do the instructions carry about the refutation of the Protestants. But they do list a litany of those in need: the poor, the sick, the ignorant. Yet Ignatius did not minimize the council. Nine times he repeated his injunction that the Jesuits at Trent seek the prayers of others for the conciliar enterprise.

Three years later, in 1549, as will be seen, Ignatius issued another set of instructions for still another mission. The set of 1549 marked out a route different from that of 1546. Three years of experience as general of the Society shaped in Ignatius a more modulated cast of mind as he grew in his appreciation of the role of learning in the reform of the Church.

Jay at Bologna

When Jay and Salmerón arrived at Bologna on 27 April by way of Padua and Venice, the council had been under way for a month.[152] The Bologna period of the council's history was brief, since early the next year, on 16 February 1548, Pope Paul suspended deliberations. Jay's participation was even briefer, only from late April to early August 1547.

Jay reentered the council with a different status, a change that reflected the papal-imperial tensions. Since the imperial group remained at Trent, the officials of the council withdrew Jay's title as deputy of Cardinal Truchsess of Augsburg and allowed him admittance only as "a plain theologian" (*simplex theologus*).[153] Jay and the other theologians labored with no immediate prospect of their work being synthesized in the form of a decree, since on 1 September Emperor Charles, deeply angered by the transfer of the council from Trent, opened a diet at Augsburg to remedy the religious chaos in Germany independently of the council, and since Cardinal Cervini realized that the publication of any dogmatic decrees at Bologna would only seriously irritate the already inflamed relations between the emperor and the pope. Cervini sensed that the council away from Trent would soon have to come to a halt.[154] The labors of the theologians seemed, therefore, to be an exercise in futility. But actually the next two periods of the council (1551–52 and 1562–63) would enter into the harvest prepared at Bologna.

During the less than four months that Jay was at Bologna, he made interventions on a wide variety of issues: contrition for sin, matrimony, indulgences, purgatory, prayers for the dead, the sacrifice of the mass. These subjects fell under the rubric of the sacraments. On 6 May 1547, he spoke on matrimony at a congregation of theologians. He addressed himself to two specific problems: clandestine marriages and polygamy. Clandestine marriages: on this pastoral problem that troubled many bishops, Jay took the position which the council in its last period (1562–63) would reject by its decree *Tametsi*. Jay held that a marriage, even though entered into without witnesses and a priest, could not be dissolved as long as the parties had given their consent.[155] *Tametsi* would prescribe the presence of a priest and two witnesses as requisite for the validity of a marriage.[156] Polygamy: this issue had been heightened by the marriage of Philip of Hesse to his "conjugal concubine," Margaret von der Saale, that had taken place on 4 March 1540 with the dispensations granted by Luther and Melanchthon. Jay spoke against polygamy, proposing theological and historical arguments. Theologically marriage has, he said, three ends: children, faith, the sacrament, ends that polygamy cannot attain. And history showed, continued Jay, that Pope Nicholas II excommunicated King Lothair in 863 for polygamy and removed the archbishops of Trier and Cologne for their assent to this marriage.[157]

On 6 July Jay spoke on purgatory and prayers for the dead. At a congregation of theologians attended by more than seventy-six delegates, including sixteen prelates, under the presidency of Cardinal Cervini, Jay affirmed by scriptural citations and historical references, including one as remote as a letter of St. Ambrose and one as recent as a work of John Fisher, the existence of purgatory and the effectiveness of prayers for the dead.[158]

Three days later, on 9 July, a congregation of theologians,

again under the presidency of Cardinal Cervini, discussed the sacrament of penance. Jay made a short but important intervention. Through the centuries before Trent, theologians developed a distinction between contrition and attrition, perfect sorrow and imperfect sorrow, repentance motivated by love of God and repentance prompted by fear of punishment. Luther repudiated attrition as a gallows repentance. Jay spoke for the attritionist tradition and urged that the council describe attrition as *true* sorrow. He asked specifically for the word *veram*.[159] Jay, therefore, shared in the council's strenuous effort to achieve clarity of expression and to dispel the muddled thinking that brewed the "theological fogginess" (*theologische Unklarheit*) that beset the Church's understanding of penance in the early sixteenth century. Four years later in the fourteenth session 25 November 1551, in the fifth canon on the sacrament of penance, the council declared that sorrow prompted by fear of punishment is true sorrow.[160]

Almost a month after his important intervention on "true sorrow," again at a congregation of theologians on 6 August, which included forty masters of theology and sixteen prelates under the presidency of Cardinal Cervini, Jay upheld the sacrificial character of the Mass and opposed the Lutheran position that ruled out private masses.[161] Four days later he was in Ferrara. This abrupt change was the culmination of the efforts of several people in different parts of Europe to acquire the benefit of Jay's talents.

Widespread Requests for Jay's Services

While Jay was at Trent and Bologna, memory of him lived on in Germany. On 29 March 1547, Bishop Moritz von Hutten wrote to Jay from his see in Eichstätt. He addressed his letter to Jay as follows: "To Claude Jay, a theologian worthy of an esteem founded in his learning and devotion, a unique friend of mine, currently at the Council of Trent, now in session" (*Doctrina et pietate venerando theologo d. Claudio Jaio, tridentini, in concilio nunc agenti, amico singulari*). He announced that Leonhard Marstaller, doctor of theology at the University of Ingolstadt, had died, and asked Jay to take the vacant chair.[162] On 18 April 1547 Cardinal Truchsess wrote to Jay from Dillingen and expressed his regret that the council had been transferred.[163]

Then on 8 August he sent a forceful letter to Ignatius requesting that Jay be returned to Germany. He made his judgment lucidly clear to Ignatius. "If there is anyone," he wrote, "who can be of help to Germany it is the all-kind (*Bonissimo*) Master Claude. At this moment he is capable of achieving so much here that you and the entire Society could do nothing more pleasing to God than to dispatch him to Germany immediately.[164]

Already, however, other hands were reaching for Jay, and it would be over two years before he would again see Germany. Most of those two years Jay spent in Ferrara. Ultimately, the reason Jay found himself in Ferrara was a conversation between Duke Ercole and an archdeacon of Modena, Guido de Guidoni, a man whom Ercole especially admired. One of Jay's nineteenth century biographers, Jean-Marie Prat, S.J., rather circumspect in his approach to the question of Ercole's morality, made this cautious judgment: his religion was not always the norm of his conduct.[165] In the spring of 1547 Guido, with the candor of a friend, challenged Ercole about the seriousness of his religious practice. Ought not he who had so many advisers in things temporal have one for the guidance of his spiritual life? This happened to be a moment for this child of the Renaissance to display the pious side of his nature. With tears welling in his eyes, Ercole implored Guido to find him a spiritual guide, a learned and holy man into whose hands he could place his conscience.[166]

Guido thought of Laynez, Broët, and Jay. He decided, however, not to suggest any name until he had first written to Ignatius. He told Ignatius that he felt a French-speaking Jesuit would be preferable. When Guido stressed the ability to speak French, he had in mind the French Princess Renée, Ercole's wife of Protestant sympathies. Loyola replied that he left the choice in Guido's hands.[167] Laynez, in a letter to Ignatius from Bologna, on 27 April 1547, listed the qualities of Jay that appealed to Guido: his learning, his age, his all but French identity in language and background, his prudence, his good reputation arising from his renunciation of the episcopal see [of Trieste] (*por las letras, edad, lingua y nacion quasi francesa, y prudentia, y gracia, y buen odor con la renunciacion del obispado*).[168] The last item, Jay's adamant refusal of the bishopric of Trieste, had made an especially deep impression. Guido therefore suggested Jay to

Ercole. Ercole in turn made his formal request to the Pope through Cardinal Alessandro Farnese.[169] On 23 July Cardinal Farnese ordered Cardinal Cervini to dispatch Jay to Ferrara. On 3 August Cervini replied that he would do so as soon as Jay had expressed his opinions on the subject of the Mass.[170] On the sixth Jay did this, and on the tenth he reached his new assignment. Later that month, on the twenty-sixth, Cervini broke the news to Cardinal Truchsess that he could not expect to receive Jay. He told the German cardinal that he had interceded with Farnese in Rome for Jay's assignment to Germany but without success.[171]

Jay's transfer to Ferrara had Ignatius's hearty approval. In early August 1547 Ignatius wrote to Jay recalling the great kindness of Ercole to the Society during its days of troubles before Pope Paul III gave his approval in 1540. Ignatius's praise of Ercole was lavish.

> I can say in all truth that there is no prince or lord who has shown us as much goodwill as the duke of Ferrara, or has contributed more efficaciously to the strength of our enterprise and the formation of our Society. Therefore there is no one toward whom we have greater obligations. . . . I most insistently recommend that in all situations where the duke will ask your assistance for God's glory you strive to prove by your work the desire which we, you and all of us, have of performing that service to which we are obliged.[172]

Ignatius also forwarded to Jay, as a reminder, copies of Ercole's earlier testimonies in favor of the Society.[173]

Summary

The Tridentine experience was a full one for Jay. For twenty months at Trent and Bologna he stayed close to his task. The study of this relatively obscure theologian throws a special light on the operations of the council, for it intimates that a large measure of the council's achievement was the travail of many forgotten men who brought to their task intelligence, erudition, and dedication. Too often the theological reflection at Trent has been viewed as the unique craftsmanship of the giants: Seripando, Pacheco, Soto, Laynez, and Salmerón. Some of the bishops at Trent lacked intellectual depth and theological expertise, but a quiet paging through the twelve massive volumes of the *Concilium Tridentinum, Diariorum, Actorum,*

Epistularum, Tractatuum Nova Collectio, edited by the Görres-Gesellschaft, with their thousands of interventions and opinions opens up a vista of the council's aula and church, wherein sounded the voices of able and forgotten men: Tommaso Cassellus, Pietro Bertano, Egidio Foscarri, Taddio Cucchi, Cornelio Musso, Pedro Guerrero, Georg Drascovics, Claude Jay. The reform that flowed from the council into the Church's life owed much to those knowledgeable men whose names are buried amid the pages of archival documents and large scholarly tomes. Jay was in that company.

CHAPTER IV

FERRARA AND BAVARIA
(1547–1551)

Introduction

This chapter takes Jay through four years, from August 1547 to April 1551. Once more Jay did pastoral work at Ferrara for Duke Ercole d'Este. Then in Germany, at Ingolstadt, he again took over a lecturer's chair in theology. Later, at Augsburg, he once more participated in an imperial diet, during which he received from the Protestants an invitation to join them in Saxony for theological discussions. Finally, he received the reward of his incessant appeals for the foundation of Jesuit colleges: Ferdinand, King of the Romans, promised to found one at Vienna.

A Chilly Reception at Ferrara

After Ercole's flow of tears and the great flutter of correspondence, Guido de Guidoni had reason to feel that the most expansive and magnanimous of welcomes would be prepared for Jay. This was especially so, since Jay had won the respect and even the warm attachment of Ercole in 1537 and 1538. But the duke's memory was short. And Renaissance princes were known for their extremes. The Ercole of August turned out to be far different than the Ercole of the previous April. Once more, as ten years earlier, Jay stood before the famous ruddy brick castello, only to find the door to the duke's chambers closed to him.[1] Instructions were transmitted that he was to take up quarters at the Hospital of Sant' Anna. Jay met Lanfranco del Gesso, the chief minister, but at least ten days passed before he was admitted into the princely presence.[2] In an unenthusiastic letter to Ignatius, which he wrote in August or September, Jay mentioned that the duke only proposed for solution some problems of conscience. "If for the future my dealings with him are not more frequent than they have been up to now," sighed Jay, "little good can be hoped to be achieved with the prince, either for himself or for the Society."[3]

Someone who knew the strange situation then warned Jay that Ercole, confusing Jesuits with Theatines, let it be known that he was not too anxious to be seen in conversation with the recently arrived priest, lest his people, possibly with a sneer of derision at his piety, begin to refer to their prince as a Theatine.[4] "I wonder," confessed Jay to Ignatius, "whether my coming here is not due more to the insistence of Master Guido than to any great desire of the prince."[5] He then asked Ignatius what should be his proper course: bide his time until summoned by Ercole, or take the initiative and ask for an audience. Access to Duchess Renée was even more impossible. Twice the duke expressed the desire to hear Jay give the weekly theological talks he had undertaken in the city, but always some cardinal or prince happened to be passing through Ferrara, and the reception of these dignitaries absorbed all Ercole's time and attention.[6] Jay's ministry was limited, aside from these discourses, to the celebration of mass for the patients at Sant' Anna, hearing confessions, and giving some talks at the orphanage of Santa Maria della Rosa. Those in charge at Sant' Anna, for a time at least, were none too happy to have Jay with them, since they had a suspicion that he was planning to take the management of the institution into his own hands.[7]

As 1547 drew to a close, Jay, with the unpleasant feeling that he was unwanted, continued to wonder for what purpose he had come to Ferrara. Not much encouragement came from the bishop, Giovanni Salviati, nor the vicar general, Ottaviano del Castello, who said they wondered the very same thing.[8] Then came a change. At Easter of 1548 Duke Ercole went to confession to Jay, a sign of a thaw in the frigid attitude of the court.[9] Unfortunately, not a single letter of Jay's from October 1547 until August 1549, a period of twenty-one months, has come down to us, but there are a few clear indications in other sources to show that the duke had abandoned his aloof and remote attitude and was once more the cordial prince of 1538. Polanco recorded that Ercole went regularly on the major feast days to Jay for confession and holy communion. Other men inside and outside the court also went to Jay to receive the sacraments.[10]

Troubling Moral Questions

Frequently during 1548 and 1549 Jay received difficult moral-political questions for solution from Ercole, his brilliant *fattore* or minister of state, Lanfranco del Gesso, and the minister's pious and generous wife, Donna Maria Frassoni del Gesso, whom the Ferrarese referred to simply as the *Fattora*. These questions troubled Jay. He found them unpleasant and he frequently turned to Ignatius for advice.[11] On 21 January 1549 Ignatius replied: "As I have advised you previously, be patient for a little time more and soon all will work out well."[12] On 11 August 1549, in what may have been his last letter from Ferrara, Jay again referred to Ercole's moral problems.[13] Some of these moral questions most likely dealt with the campaign against vice which Ercole launched in his duchy in 1548 and which Jay possibly influenced.

With the thoroughness and ruthlessness of his forebears, Ercole waged a fight against blasphemy, sodomy, and other offenses. In his decree of 2 July 1549, blasphemers who had not been deterred by the standing penalties of three years' exile and the perforation of the tongue, and who had lapsed four times were threatened with amputation of the tongue. Those guilty of sodomy were to go to the gallows, suffer the burning of their bodies, and the confiscation of their property. Laws were passed against those who impeded the reception of the sacraments at Easter and who equipped persons with arms for their private vendettas.[14] A year after the enactment of this legislation, Jay, then in Germany, wrote Ercole: "I experience the deepest consolation in Christ when I reflect on the laudable provisions Your

Excellency has made against indecency, blasphemy, and cruelty."[15] A strange commendation of Renaissance savagery from the mild and merciful Jay.

Near Disaster in Venice

For a brief spell Jay became free of the Este. In the middle of April 1548, he interrupted his work at Ferrara and went to Venice in order to help in the negotiations with the senate for the procuring of some property for the Society within the Serene Republic. Laynez had come from Florence and joined Jay on the trip. They arrived at Venice on 18 April.[16] Pedro Ribadeneyra joined them from Padua.

May 1 came near being the last day the three Jesuits spent in this world. They boarded a gondola and sailed to Murano, one of the Venice's island suburbs, to see the papal nuncio. On their way back a storm suddenly arose, the gondola began to fill with water, and the wind carried them out to sea. Jay and Laynez gave themselves up for lost. Not so Ribadeneyra. "Not a second did I fear," he recalled, jauntily as ever, "in my confidence that the Lord would not allow us to perish in such circumstances because of the holiness of these blessed fathers."[17] The struggle was hard, but by mighty efforts they finally brought the gondola back to the safety of the lagoons. And soon Jay was again back on terra firma of Ferrara and a safe distance from the Adriatic.

Final Months in Ferrara

Throughout the city Jay's popularity grew. During the winter of 1548–49 the price of grain spiraled upwards and the hospital filled with poor people suffering malnutrition. In the spirit that prompted Ignatius and his companions to succor some three thousand persons during the terrible winter ten years earlier in Rome, Jay worked day after day in the wards of Sant' Anna among the human wrecks brought in from the streets. His talks at the church of Sant' Anna drew more and more listeners. After each discourse his path from the pulpit led directly to the confessional.[18] One day in January 1549 the temperature dropped to a particularly low level. A heavy snow blocked the streets. Jay judged that he would have no hearers on such a day and did not go to the church. Soon people were pounding at his door, demanding their preacher. He learned his lesson, that even in the ice cold church the people of Ferrara would be there to hear him preach about the mysteries of their faith.[19]

Yet, despite these successes, Jay failed in a latent purpose of his mission to Ferrara: the conversion of Princess Renée. When two years earlier Guido de Guidoni chose Jay in preference to other Jesuits largely because French was his native tongue, he had in mind the intelligent, lively princess from France, who through twenty years had been the center of Protestant sympathies in Ferrara. But Jay had made no impression. Renée remained aloof and even ill disposed toward him.[20]

Assignment to Ingolstadt

This failure and a desperate cry for help from Bavaria terminated Jay's two year stay in Ferrara. A key bastion in the uncertain fight for the religious allegiance of Germany was the University of Ingolstadt. Jay knew from personal experience the uncertain fate that hung over Ingolstadt, since he had filled for a year the chair of theology left vacant by the death of Johannes Eck in February 1543.[21] Through that year of lecturing, he learned much about the dying Church in Bavaria. Eck's death underscored the severe drainage among Catholic intellectuals.[22] The number of theological students had been dropping steadily. Between 1493–1517, of the 205 who offered their first masses in the diocese of Eichstätt, seventy did so in Ingolstadt; between 1518–30, of 172, twenty did so in Ingolstadt; and in the seventeen years between 1531–48, of forty-five, only nine did so in Ingolstadt.[23] As faculty and students moved toward the brink of extinction, Jay reported the almost complete eclipse of theological and scriptural studies.[24]

Duke Wilhelm viewed this scene with dismay. Appalled by the prospect that the Lutherans might turn the strongest intellectual center of the Catholic Church in Germany into another Wittenberg, he laid serious plans to halt the decay. In the last days of December 1544, he chalked a design to set up a special college at Ingolstadt for theological students.[25] He made his own the precise objective that Jay had been advocating for the past five years in his conversations with the bishops of Salzburg, Eichstätt, and Augsburg.[26]

The duke's initial efforts met rebuff. He appealed to the University of Cologne for scholars to invigorate Ingolstadt's theological faculty. Cologne's answer was negative. He turned to Louvain. Their answer was the same. Robert Vauchop appealed to the University of Paris. He failed.[27] The duke then sent his plea through Cardinal Madruzzo of Trent to Pope Paul III and Cardinal Alessandro Farnese, the pope's grandson. He asked especially for Balthasar Fannemann, the Dominican suffragan bishop of Hildesheim. Here he succeeded, and Fannemann was assigned to the faculty of Ingolstadt.

In 1548, after three and a half years of qualified success, Wilhelm made another appeal to Rome. In August of that year, he sent his secretary, Heinrich Schweicker, to the papal court. Ostensibly the Schweicker mission was to seek confirmation of the new bishop of Salzburg, George von Pappenheim, and to seek a tax abatement in some areas. The real reason, however, was to procure another theologian for Ingolstadt.[29] Out of the Schweicker negotiations emerged the request for Claude Jay and possibly a second Jesuit.[30] This in turn blossomed into the three-man team of Jay, Salmerón, and Canisius, assigned by Ignatius to Ingolstadt. In mid-September 1549, Jay took leave of the gracious and interested Duke Ercole, now hardly recognizable as the cold, aloof, and indifferent prince of two years earlier. The duke insisted that he was releasing Jay to Germany with the proviso that he would one day return to Ferrara.[31]

Ignatius Loyola's Concern for the Intellectual Apostolate

Ignatius Loyola gave high priority to the assignment he entrusted to Jay, Salmerón, and Canisius. By now he realized the vast influence that scholarship was to have in the conflict of religions in Germany, and he wanted the three Jesuits equipped with a doctorate in theology before they put foot inside the lecture halls of Ingolstadt. He spoke to Cardinal Marcello Cervini about the problem. On 9 August 1549 Cervini wrote to Cardinal Giammaria del Monte, recommending that the three Jesuits be granted the doctorate.[32] Del Monte arranged, therefore, that the three stand for the doctoral degree at the University of Bologna. He recommended to the Dominican bishop of Minori, Ambrozio Catarino, that he obtain the services of two other Dominican doctors of theology and with them compose the examining board. Catarino enlisted the help of Vincenzo Villa Placentinus, the dean of the theology faculty at Bologna, and Vincenzo de Quintano, a master in the university.

On 2 October the three Jesuits faced the three questioning Dominicans.[33] The examination was a stiff one. Salmerón's diploma spoke of his subjection to a "difficult, severe, and awesome examination" (*arduo, rigoroso ac tremendo examini*). Angelo Massarelli noted that Jay, Salmerón, and Canisius lived up to the expectations of a brilliant performance. Catarino and his fellow examiners saluted in a special way the display of learning they had just witnessed. On 4 October the three Jesuits received their doctoral degrees in theology.[34]

Besides their degrees from the University of Bologna, the three Jesuits also received special instructions from Ignatius. Ignatius sent them a lengthy document, eight pages in the *Monumenta Historica Societatis Jesu*. It was specific and precise, divided into four parts. Part one spelled out the double purpose of the mission: the renovation of the Catholic faith and religious practice in the University of Ingolstadt and, as far as possible, in Germany; and the foundation of a Jesuit college at Ingolstadt. Part two outlined the general means designed to achieve that double purpose. Part three detailed the approaches more apt for achieving the spiritual rejuvenation of the university. Part four listed the ways more appropriate for forwarding the establishment of a Jesuit college.

This document heralded changes that had taken place in Ignatius's thinking. As has been seen in chapter three, Ignatius sent Jay, Salmerón, and Laynez, when they were at the Council of Trent in early 1546, an instruction that gave priority to the pastoral ministry of visiting the sick and aiding the poor. Of twenty-one specific directions, nine directly touched the pastoral ministry; seven dealt with social conduct, especially in the public articulation of opinion; and five on mutual examination and correction.[35]

Here, three years later, of his forty-four specific recommendations, Ignatius directed only ten toward pastoral concerns. Of these ten, only one touched the corporal works of mercy. "Off and on, time should be given to those pious works that are more visible, such as aid to those in hospitals and prisons, as well as to other poor people, works that usually make a good impression in the Lord.'' The other nine touched preaching, counseling, hearing confessions, guiding others through the Spiritual Exercises. The other thirty-four points focused on the university scene.

Ignatius made several cardinal points. He stressed the interior attitudes that should guide the three Jesuits at Ingolstadt: genuine affection for all, concern for the things of Christ; interior humility; love of the truth. Essential for the success of the mission were those external expressions of their interior attitudes: being patterns of modesty and charity; showing kindness to others; winning the love of others by modesty and charity; adapting to German customs; accepting no recompense for their labors.

Ignatius realized that public teaching was at the heart of the assignment to Ingolstadt. He recommended composure, interior and exterior, in handling the intellectual issues; reflection, study and avoidance of precipitous judgment. He called this maturity. In their public lectures, Ignatius urged his friends to present solid doctrine unencumbered by excessive scholastic terms, genuine learning marked by lucidity, careful preparation free of verbal conceits. He urged them to collaborate closely, to weigh their experiences with one another, to stay in touch with him and the other Jesuits in Rome for advice.[36]

Ignatius' shift in thinking about the ministry happened in the wake of new experiences between 1546 and 1549. During that period he had opened colleges at Gandia and Messina, both of which received lay students. Formal education as an apostolate took deep root in his mind. In the Ingolstadt mission, he gave as much significance to the foundation of a Jesuit college there as to the spiritual renovation of the university. Jay, Salmerón, and Canisius carried into Germany the fresh convictions of the growing Ignatius.

Mixed Reception at Ingolstadt

The route to Ingolstadt took Jay, Salmerón, and Canisius through Trent, Dillingen, and Munich. At Munich Duke Wilhelm received them most cordially, and on 12 November sent them on their way to Ingolstadt in the company of his secretary,

Heinrich Schweicker.[37] They arrived at Ingolstadt the next day. Their welcome to the university was in the grand manner. They were led to a large chamber, where in the presence of all the doctors and professors Chancellor Leonhard von Eck gave a rousing speech of welcome, in which he told the Jesuits how much their arrival had been anticipated, how everybody hoped for their success, "and other things along that line" (*et alia hujusmodi*), as Polanco remarked.[38] Peter Canisius returned the compliments, and then all retired to the refectory, where a feast in full German style was prepared. The next day the Jesuits were assigned their permanent rooms in the main college of the university and provided with books, all with an eye to enable the new professors to follow their way of life, "at once religious and Italian in its style" (*modo religioso atque italico*), undisturbed by the revelings of the Germans.[39] Von Eck lined up a program of lectures. To the Dominican bishop Balthasar Fannemann, he assigned the Gospels; to Salmerón St. Paul's Epistle to the Romans; to Jay the Psalms; to Canisius the *Sentences* of Peter Lombard.[40]

All this fanfare and programming could easily give the impression that Von Eck had rooms bursting with alert, interested scholars, all breathlessly awaiting the professors' opening lectures. But when the Jesuits looked down from their desks, they beheld a pitiful student body of fourteen, ten of whom presented the blank and uninspiring faces of disgruntled illiterates who were in class against their will. To Polanco Canisius dejectedly wrote: "Would that there were four or five for whom we could hope that our lectures would be of advantage. The students of Ingolstadt, few as they are, can hardly be said to overexert themselves in the study of literature and especially Holy Scripture."[41]

Jesuit Plan of Action at Ingolstadt

Canisius, Salmerón, and Jay discussed the dispiriting situation among themselves. They were united in their conviction that the salvation of Ingolstadt as a center of learning depended on the foundation of a Jesuit college, since, with a group of Jesuit scholastics gathered there from all over Europe, it would not only raise the intellectual tone of the student body but would also assure a reservoir of future professors. Laudable as was this plan, it did not automatically carry with it the solution to the vexing practical problem of just how to present it to Bavarian officialdom. The three Jesuits debated the question at length, said several masses, prayed much. They finally decided that Chancellor von Eck was the man to be approached and that Jay should be their spokesman.[42]

An opportunity presented itself on 17 December 1549. Von Eck heard Salmerón lecture that day, and was delighted. A few hours later he returned to the university to look Salmerón up for consultation. When he arrived, Salmerón, Canisius, and Jay were together in Jay's room. This gave Jay the opening he was looking for. The cornered chancellor had to listen as Jay piled up argument after argument for the foundation of a Jesuit college at Ingolstadt. Jay laid stress on the assurance that such a college would provide an invaluable influx of competent students and professors, then the greatest need of the university. He gently challenged the Catholic spirit of Duke Wilhelm by mentioning what Catholic princes of other lands had done. "I pushed the point," he wrote Ignatius, "that we Jesuits could not but anticipate a college from a duke who was so authentic in his Catholicism, so expansive and keen in his determination to assist the university." Jay finished his little speech to von Eck with a little appeal to the chancellor's vanity. "I told him that no better promoter of the project could be found than his honored self. I soft-soaped him a bit, but not over much lest he take us for a group of flatterers."[43]

Von Eck was not hard to win over. He told the Jesuit trio that he had in fact been thinking of this kind of enterprise for two years, ever since Jay's earlier sojourn in Bavaria. With an air of self assurance, he said two or three times in Italian: "Leave it to me ((*Lassate fare a mi*). I know the mind of my prince."[44] The next day, the eighteenth, von Eck was back at the university to hear Peter Canisius lecture. He was delighted with Peter's performance. Again Jay, Salmerón, and Canisius pressed von Eck about the prospects for a Jesuit college. They showed him letters from an impressive array of cardinals who liked the Society: Farnese, Maffei, Cervini, Pio, Borgos, Verallo. Once again, on the nineteenth, von Eck returned, this time to hear Salmerón lecture. He assured the Jesuits that he had put aside ten thousand gold florins to construct the college. The Jesuits entreated him to be careful that in the application of funds from vacant benefices to the college the Society be not entangled in any legal wranglings. Von Eck replied: "Leave it to me."[45]

Encouraging Signs at Ingolstadt

The chancellor was as good as his word. On 6 January 1550 Canisius wrote Ignatius that von Eck had promised to ask the Holy See for permission to transfer some empty monasteries and some vacant benefices to the foundation of a Jesuit college.[46] These negotiations were at the moment temporarily suspended, since the papal throne was still vacant after the death of Pope Paul III on 10 November 1549. But with the election of Pope Julius III on 8 February 1550, Duke Wilhelm dispatched his secretary, Heinrich Schweicker, to Rome to negotiate with the new pope, the curia, and Ignatius Loyola the endowment of the projected college.[47]

Meanwhile at Ingolstadt, despite the discouraging intellectual quality of the Jesuits' students, Peter Canisius felt optimistic about the Society's impact on the university. For several reasons Christmas of 1549 marked a high point in Canisius's enthusiasm: after a month and a half at Ingolstadt the Jesuit teaching program was going along "in an astonishingly gratifying way" (*con mirabile satisfactione*); a notable number of students confessed and received holy communion in the Jesuit chapel, which he hoped would become a monthly practice; these students turned in their copies of the works of Luther, Bucer, and Melanchthon; the rector of the university, Franziskus Zoanettus, confessed to Salmerón; Canisius himself preached the Latin sermon in the Frauenmünster; Jay spent Christmas with Moritz von Hutten, "who has the deepest affection for Father Claude," and who insists that he have a Jesuit aide always at hand.[48]

Setbacks at Ingolstadt

Then, only three months later, came March 1550, a month of harsh disaster. On the sixth Duke Wilhelm died. On the seventeenth Chancellor von Eck died. Heinrich Schweicker, Wilhelm's secretary, had hardly arrived in Rome to negotiate the Jesuit college when these calamities erased the reason for his being there.[49] All the bright hopes of the Jesuit trio at Ingolstadt went down into the graves of the duke and the chancellor. To add to the gloom, Luigi Lippomano, the bishop of Verona, wrote on 5 March to Cardinal Alessandro Farnese, complaining about what he regarded as the waste of Jesuit talent on thirteen or so students, "of whom about ten are illiterate and go to class because they are under constraint to do so."[50] Clearly Lippomano did not share Canisius's optimism. Around the end of March Ignatius ordered Salmerón to return to Italy.[51] The enterprise of only five months seemed to be breaking apart.

Albrecht V, Duke Wilhelm's successor and lavish creator of Munich's Medicean era of art, libraries, and music, hesitated about the Jesuit college.[52] Georg Stockhammer, successor to von Eck in the post of chancellor of Bavaria and protector of the university, also held back from implementing his predecessor's plans. The wearisome trek over the hard ground of persuading Bavaria's officialdom had to start over again. After six months of inaction at the court, Jay, Salmerón, and Canisius approached Stockhammer and asked him to press their project with Duke Albrecht.

An Important Educational Document

The memorandum they left with Stockhammer under date of 10 June 1550 was one of the more explicit Jesuit documents on religious reform in Germany in the mid-sixteenth century.[53] They made several points: the chief need of the age was the edification that radiates from personal holiness; the union of personal holiness and sacred learning, of piety and wisdom, has an especially convincing force; a Jesuit college at Ingolstadt could provide the answer to this current need by guaranteeing competent professors, keen students, and alumni who would enrich German life as preachers, lecturers, teachers; the Jesuit community as a group of men in whom holiness and learning harmonized would have a forceful impact on the religious tone of Bavaria and would even attract German youth to enter the Society of Jesus. Basically the memorandum recapitulated Jay's earlier convictions.

The three Jesuits capped their argument by an appeal to the international character of the Society of Jesus. Their own presence at Ingolstadt, one a Spaniard, one a Savoyard, and one a

Dutchman, demonstrated the Society's ability to summon men from various nations in response to an exigency in Germany. At the moment Jesuit scholastics were studying at Paris, Louvain, Cologne, and other university towns. From these reservoirs of talent some young men could be channeled into Bavaria, and Ingolstadt would then benefit from what other universities enjoyed: the presence and "attraction of devout learning and instructed devotion" (*eosque provehimus ad piam eruditionem et ad eruditam pietatem*).[54]

This document was one among many on the subject of Catholic reform. Composed by men who sensed the desperate needs of the age, it presented the institution of the Jesuit college as one solution. History bore out the accuracy of their proposal. This document also revealed that the Jesuits from their origins were conscious of their wide international resources and how these could be used in an era of intense nationalism. "In no other age was international activity more necessary for Catholicism than in the sixteenth century; in no other age was it more difficult of achievement."[55] By their institutional fluidity—and by their universal charity, to which Jay, Salmerón, and Canisius explicitly referred—the Jesuits succeeded in bringing off this difficult achievement.

Departure from Ingolstadt

In the midst of this uncertainty about the future, on 24 June 1550 Jay received orders from Truchsess, who had the pope's backing, to withdraw from the grasping university and repair to Augsburg.[56] In that city the emperor was planning another diet during the coming summer, and Truchsess, again wanting Jay's services, requested the pope and Ignatius to detach Claude from Ingolstadt.[57] Bishop Moritz von Hutten of Eichstätt suspected what was afoot and worked hard to keep Jay at the university, convinced as he was that his withdrawal would spell the utter ruin of an enterprise filled with bright promise. Of the three Jesuits, Jay exerted the wider influence, and this von Hutten recognized.[58] Among the scholars who felt the spiritual and intellectual impact of Jay's presence and who became one of his penitents was a master of the Collegium Georgianum, Erasmus Wolf.[59]

Truchsess, however, prevailed and on 26 June 1550 Jay left Ingolstadt for Augsburg. Indignation ran high in the university against Truchsess, the marauding bishop who was snatching their Jay from them. Men unashamedly wept when they spoke about it. On the day of his departure, a number of the leaders in the university came to him for confession and holy communion. It was their way of tempering their profound sorrow.[60] Jay joined Truchsess at Dillingen, and the two went on together to Augsburg.[61]

Jay's departure from Ingolstadt had painful repercussions also at the Bavarian court. Duke Albrecht, deeply annoyed, dispatched a protest to the pope, requesting Julius III that he forbid the removal of the three Jesuits, men who, as he said, could not be praised enough for the good they achieved in eight short months. He assured the pope that he was "girding himself" to found a Jesuit college.[62] But two months later, by order of Luigi Lippomano, bishop of Verona, who was acting with the pope's and Ignatius's approval, Salmerón also left Ingolstadt.[63] Jesuit presence there shrank to the solitary figure of Peter Canisius.

Jesuit Replacements at Ingolstadt

The Society, however, had no intention of deserting the university. A stir of Jesuits at Augsburg proved that. Jay had been at Augsburg with Cardinal Truchsess for two and a half months when on 9 September two Jesuits, the German Peter Schorich and the Dutchman Nickolaas Floris (usually known as Goudanus from his home city, Gouda), arrived there on their way to Ingolstadt to fill the slots vacated by Jay and Salmerón.[64] Two days later, the eleventh, Salmerón arrived there on his way to Verona.

At this Augsburg crossroads one subject preoccupied the four Jesuits, both those who had left Ingolstadt and those who were going there: the foundation of a Jesuit college. On the twelfth, the day after Salmerón's arrival, the four descended in a group on Chancellor Stockhammer, who also happened to be then in Augsburg. Their purpose was clear: to break Stockhammer's vacillation about initiating a Jesuit college. Stockhammer received the Jesuits, told them that Salmerón's departure pained him but that Goudanus's assignment tempered his sorrow

117

somewhat. He then said what they wanted to hear: his hopes for a Jesuit college at Ingolstadt were high. The same day, the twelfth, Schorich and Goudanus set out for Ingolstadt, led by the guide who had brought Salmerón to Augsburg. With this guide Stockhammer sent instructions to his chamberlain that he care for the needs of the newly arriving Jesuits.[65]

Meanwhile at Ingolstadt pressure mounted to get Jay back. Men in the university badgered Jay himself with their letters they wrote to the pope; the duke sent a memorial to Rome through the Scots Archbishop Robert Vauchop.[66] News of these moves evoked Jay's habitual diffidence, and he wrote Ignatius on 18 September 1550 that he lacked the talent to be a lecturer in theology.[67]

Remembrance of Ferrara

Jay had to think not only of the hurt feelings at Ingolstadt. He remembered that Prince Ercole of Ferrara had released him on condition that he would return. On 24 June he wrote to Ercole to explain that Truchsess, with the approval of the Holy See, had ordered him to Augsburg. He added:

> Certainly, my most illustrious lord, when it is clear that it is the will of God and my superiors, gladly shall I return to the service of Your Excellency because of the great obligation which I and the entire Society have to you. I say this also because of the special desire that God has given me for the salvation of your soul, for which by God's grace I always pray to the Divine Majesty. In like manner I pray for your illustrious duchess, your very upright and expansive children, for the prosperity of your felicitous duchy, and especially for the noble city of Ferrara, in which I always experienced great charity.[68]

The tender remembrance of Jay in that "noble city of Ferrara" was the foundation stone of a Jesuit college there. The pious *Fattora* and wife of the minister of state, Donna Maria Frassoni del Gesso, had wanted Jay to start a work dear to Ignatius in Rome, the care of fallen young women. Jay's summons to Germany frustrated that. Then on 1 June 1550, eight months after Jay had left Ferrara, Lanfranco del Gesso, the minister of state, died. From that moment his widow, Donna Maria, pressed for a Jesuit college. This Ignatius opened in June 1552.[69] For Jay the *Fattora* could have erected no better expression of the Jesuit presence in Ferrara.

118

The Diet of Augsburg (1550)

At the new diet in Augsburg, which opened on 26 June 1550, Emperor Charles faced intractable political and religious problems. The central political issue was the succession within the royal family to the farflung Hapsburg lands. To Augsburg therefore went not only Charles, his son Philip, and his sister Mary but also his brother Ferdinand and Ferdinand's son Maximilian. Guarding the utmost secrecy, the principals had their long and quarrelsome debates in the house of the Fugger family.[70]

The central religious problem was the German reaction, Catholic and Protestant, to the Council of Trent. Several events had eased the tension between the emperor and the Holy See, which had become severe in the spring of 1547, when the council had been transferred to Bologna. On 13 September 1549 Pope Paul III formally suspended the council. On 10 November of the same year Paul died. The new Pope, Julius III, immediately assured Charles of his desire to work with him for the peace of the Church and to reopen the council either at Trent or at another place congenial to the emperor.[71] Charles for his part was anxious to cooperate with Julius and the council. Religious peace within the Empire, which like a wraith had been eluding Charles for thirty years, now hung on the assent or denial given by the Protestant princes at Augsburg to the authoritative role of the council.

During his nine months stay in Augsburg between July 1550 and April 1551 two major concerns preoccupied Jay: first, the current imperial diet, and second, the foundation of Jesuit colleges in Germany. Of his many letters to Ignatius at this time, only seven have survived, and these pointedly reflect these two concerns. In the first of these seven letters, dated 4 September 1550, Jay sent an encouraging report to Ignatius about his first concern, the diet.

> Here in the court of the cardinal of Augsburg, as well as in the meetings assembled by him, I have no insignificant opportunity to promote the cause of Christ and the salvation of souls. I have frequently engaged in private conversation with many men of various nations—and, sad to say, of various beliefs—partly with a view to refute error, partly to settle disagreements, partly to encourage lives of virtue. With God's grace I have frequently and happily succeeded. A good number, both here and at

119

Dillingen, have come to me for confession. Several young men, about nineteen years old, have abjured the heretical teachings they had imbibed since their earliest years and have been reconciled to the Catholic church.[72]

Jay's second concern, now habitual with him, was the foundation of Jesuit colleges. He continued his relentless propaganda among the bishops and officials of the Empire. In this same first letter from the diet he voiced optimism. "On the question of the founding of colleges that would be stamped with the spirit of holiness and the Catholic faith, I have conferred with many important men, who impressed me as being inclined toward that type of pious work."[73] For the benefit of inquirers, he and Peter Schorich had composed a descriptive folder in four chapters about the nature of a Jesuit college, the procedure in founding one, its regimen, the purpose of its students, and the kind of housing needed.[74]

Jay's principal targets were King Ferdinand, Bishop Urban Weber, the king's almoner, and Jacob Jonas, the king's chancellor. Ferdinand Jay knew from the earlier diet of Augsburg in 1543. Weber he knew from their meeting in Venice in 1545, when the bishop communicated Ferdinand's desire that Jay become bishop of Trieste. From the protracted "episcopal ordeal" of 1544–45, both the king and the bishop had at least a general idea of Jay's and the Society's principles. By mid-September 1550 Jay had explained at least twice to Weber the nature of the Society's institute, the way Jesuit colleges were established and run. Jay also showed the bishop a copy of Paul III's bull of confirmation of the Society, as well as the bull *Iniunctum Nobis* of 14 March 1544, by which Paul lifted the original restriction of the Society to sixty professed members.[75]

The Promise of a Jesuit College in Vienna

The breakthrough came sometime that summer of 1550. In two conversations which Jay had with Jakob Jonas, the vice-chancellor confirmed that King Ferdinand had committed himself to founding a Jesuit college in Vienna. On 12 September Jay wrote to Ignatius: "As I have told you in my letter of 24 August the chancellor of the king of the Romans has informed me that His Majesty has decided to put up a college in Vienna for the Society. He has also mentioned that His Majesty wants two theologians to go to Vienna right away to start lecturing, to find a convenient spot for a dwelling, and to direct construction according to the requirements of our Institute."[76]

On 11 December 1550 Ferdinand sent his formal request to Ignatius. He lined up his reasons cogently: the religious crisis in Austria highlighted the need for education in sound Catholic doctrine and morality; the colleges of the Society of Jesus in other lands had been efficaciously meeting this need. To get the project underway, Ferdinand requested two Jesuits for Vienna immediately. He wanted them to start their lectures even before the erection of the Jesuit residence, because he felt that by their teaching "they would lay stronger foundations for the college." One of the Jesuits he desired to be Jay, "a recent friend of mine, both charming and dear to me" (nobis jampridem notus ac gratus et charus est).[77]

Early in 1551 Ignatius replied and acknowledged Ferdinand's request. He used this letter as an affirmation of his commitment to education as a source of religious renewal. "Among the several remedies that must be used for the sickness that widely infects Germany, let one be a program to place in the universities men who by the example of a holy life and by the integrity of Catholic teaching will involve themselves in helping others and spurring them to better things. The idea is not just something advisable and useful. It is an out-and-out necessity. Or better, it seems to be an inspiration from God."[78]

Meanwhile Jay continued his propaganda among the bishops at the Diet of Augsburg. Results were promising. On 18 September 1550 he reported to Ignatius that Johann von Isenburg, archbishop of Trier and elector of the Empire, was giving thought to starting a Jesuit college, and that Truchsess seriously was looking for ways to found one.[79] Peter Canisius interpreted these signs correctly. He discerned to the proximate foundation at Vienna the harbinger of greater things to come. On 28 December 1550 he wrote to Ignatius: "This college at Vienna will be our first, so long desired, among the German people. We have no doubt that very soon, with Christ's help, another at Ingolstadt will be added. That this might be accomplished, we should earnestly pray the Father of mercies that King Ferdinand in his exceedingly great piety and that his son- in-law, the duke of Bavaria, will be won over to such a project. Then other princes in Germany, as the need for colleges is borne in on them, will gradually fall into line in imitation of them.''[80]

Episcopal Reserve about Jesuit Colleges

Despite Canisius's optimism, Jay knew that the German bishops still had serious reservations about Jesuit colleges. Late in December 1550—the day is unknown but it was very close in time to Canisius's letter of 28 December—Jay sent a brief and carefully ordered letter to Ignatius. He reviewed the difficulties involved in setting up Jesuit colleges in Germany. For five years he had been trying to convince the bishops, but many of the earlier problems still remained and had to be faced realistically.

Jay listed them for Ignatius: the reluctance of the bishops to move without the consent of their counselors and canons, some of whom favored Lutheranism; the little likelihood of the college's scholars being able to preach in German, a fact borne out by most of the Jesuits who had already taught at Ingolstadt; the negative attitude of the bishops toward foreigners; the likelihood that the scholars, on whom the bishops had founded their hopes, would be transferred by the pope elsewhere; the bishops' desire that the students of the colleges be funneled at their ordination into the empty German parishes; the legislation in several cities against new religious orders; the desire of would-be founders to run the colleges according to their own ideas. The difficulties of 1544 remained.[81]

Two Moves Toward Religious Peace

During these months when Jay concentrated so much of his energy on the foundation of Jesuit colleges, a dawn of modest hope for a religious settlement broke over the diet. In two distinct moves, initiative came from Rome and Saxony. The move from Saxony centered on Jay.

The Roman initiative appeared at the diet in the person of the papal nuncio, Sebastiano Pighini. For seven months Pighini negotitated with the Protestants a program for their participation in the Council of Trent. He promised them a safe-conduct and the status of consultants with the same freedom of discussion enjoyed by the Catholic theological consultants. He asked the

Protestants to recognize that the definitive vote rested with the bishops, that earlier decisions of the council should not be re-opened, that the pope's competence to convoke, suspend, or close the council should not be in dispute. At first the electors of Saxony and Brandenburg balked. After more give-and-take, they relented. The imperial dream of a religious unity built with German participation in the general council seemed to be within grasp.[82]

The Protestants, however, gave their formal acceptance only after they reserved the right to make "observations" on the council's earlier defined articles. The foundations of unity, therefore, were laid on sand. Emperor Charles chose to ignore the reservations; Pope Julius at first did not know about them. The fatal flaw became visible to all in early 1552, when the diplomatic representatives of Würtemberg and Saxony arrived at Trent voicing protests and reservations. They insisted on a more adequate safe-conduct, the annulment of the council's earlier decrees, and the definition by the council of its authority over the pope.[83] This was the material of which parapets were made. Another move toward religious peace was routed.

An Invitation to Saxony

During the flurry of excitement about Pighini's mission to Augsburg to persuade the Protestants to go to Trent, Jay received an invitation to go to Saxony. Impressed by Jay's modesty, spirituality, and clarity of mind, and moved by the hope of religious peace, the representatives of Duke Moritz of Saxony thought of inviting him to Saxony for conferences with Philip Melanchthon, then at Wittenberg. Headed by the chief of the legation, Christoph von Carlowitz, a man with Catholic sympathies who maintained contact with Cardinal Cristoforo Madruzzo, the Saxons went to the leading princes of the diet and asked that Jay be permitted to go to Saxony.[84] Peter Canisius explained this unusual development and its background to Ignatius in his letter of 30 April 1551 from Ingolstadt.

> In that assembly of the German princes, he [Jay] has gained for our Society of Jesus results such as no one else has ever achieved in Germany. He has explained the name, the origin, the accomplishments, the progress of the Society in such a way, and has so impressed the Germans, that he

has gained their approval of and trust in our men as they cultivate this particular vineyard of Christ. . . . He whom the Spirit of God once possesses, him he adorns with many gifts, especially when the common good and Christ's glory so demand. Not only was he most acceptable to Catholics and a distinct encouragement to the strengthening of their faith, but he also gave satisfaction to the key Lutherans of the diet, who most willingly listened to his exposition of our faith. They questioned him about the most controversial of religious matters; they put forward their own arguments, especially on the subject of justification. Several bishops were present on these occasions.

Superb artist that he is in understanding and treating with persons, Jay responded with the utmost modesty, uncovered the roots of perplexities, communicated freedom from doubts, illuminated the truth—and in such a manner that Catholics and Protestants were filled with admiration . . . The agents of the duke of Saxony felt that his modesty, graced by learning, and his learning, graced by modesty, would be more effective with Melanchthon and the other teachers of Saxony—as indeed they had experienced its power within their own ranks—than had the bitter disputations of other apologists (*plus effecturam apud illos eruditam modestiam, et modestam eruditionem illam, qua ipsi iam fuissent adiuti, quam profecissent acres aliorum disputationes*).[85]

Duke Moritz's legates felt sure that their prince's religious sentiments were the same as Jay's. Jay was ready to head for Saxony, although he hoped to have Laynez with him.[86] It seemed that Jay was to have what was denied Favre ten years before, a meeting with Melanchthon, when at the Colloquy of Worms of 1540–41 both men were present but protocol prevented Favre from speaking with the Protestants.[87]

In contrast to the official formality that frustrated Favre's ecumenical aspirations, it was something very dear to Jay that blocked his own hopes to build a bridge to the Protestants: the opening of the Jesuit college at Vienna. King Ferdinand, as has been seen, wanted Jay to share in the new Jesuit-Hapsburg cooperative venture. Pope Julius III supported Ferdinand; still more, Julius disapproved of the Saxon mission.[88] Jay, therefore, had to stand fast outside the door opened by the Protestants. Canisius spoke of the Saxon invitation as an opportunity merely delayed rather than conclusively blocked.[89] But Canisius was wrong. Jay was never able to visit Melanchthon.

The initiative taken by the Saxon legation at Augsburg and Jay's positive response were among the few still sputtering candles of religious eirenicism in Europe. But by the 1550s they were doomed to practical extinction. Men who were of mature years in 1517 and knew by personal experience the meaning of a united Christendom were fast dying. For the generations that followed, the religious division of Germany had by now entered the political, social, and cultural life of the empire. The fracture had lasted too long. The concord of a few theologians could hardly undo the fait accompli.[90] But for Jay, blighted hopes in Saxony yielded to the fair promise of Austria.

Assignment to Vienna

Keen as Jay was for the college at Vienna, he shrank from any part of responsibility in its inception. Keenly aware of the need of men of profound learning to staff the college, Jay, once Ferdinand had made his decision, feared that a lectureship would fall to him. And this he tried to forestall. On 12 September 1550 he wrote to Ignatius:

> I humbly ask that men, learned not only in theology but also in languages, be sent in order that the college's opening will create a good impression with this people, who make a very great deal of the knowledge of languages. And if you could send either Master André des Freux or Master Juan Polanco, or some others who like them have, with an adequate knowledge of positive and scholastic theology, a good grasp of Latin and a passing knowledge of other languages, I think that it would be an excellent move. I say this in view of the attitude of this people, among whom little account is made of a professor's erudition if he is without a sound command of Latin and a moderate mastery of Greek and Hebrew.
>
> Since the chancellor on another occasion asked me in the name of His Majesty if I would be happy to go to Vienna when His Majesty founds the college, I think that he will make a specific request for me. If that should be the case and I am ordered to Vienna, I humbly ask Your Paternity to see to it that I am sent as the servant of my companions rather than as a master. Prescinding from all other factors that make me unfit for a university chair, I have a definite awareness of the great weakness of my memory. So pronounced is this weakness that I do not think that I would be able to measure up to the demands of a daily lecture, nor even of one every other day. Therefore, in regard to this impending assignment to Vienna, I judge that I am more fit to be a porter, a sacristan, or servant, than a lecturer in theology. On this point Your Reverence can obtain more information from Master Alfonso Salmerón. Yet, in every circumstance I surrender myself to whatever holy obedience will see fit.[91]

Ignatius however had a more realistic appreciation of Jay's qualities. On the first Sunday of Lent 1551, Jay received a letter from Ignatius designating him superior of the prospective college at Vienna.[92]

Cardinal Truchsess and the Spiritual Exercises

Any thought, however, of an immediate departure for Vienna Jay had to put aside. Cardinal Otto Truchsess desired to make the Spiritual Exercises through a month's period. Twice under the guidance of Pierre Favre, at Regensburg in 1541 and at Speyer in 1542, the cardinal had made the Exercises in part. Now, nine years later, he approached King Ferdinand, who was still at Augsburg, and asked that Jay's departure for Vienna be postponed until after Easter. Ferdinand graciously consented.[93]

Before Truchsess started the Exercises, Jay first paid a visit to his friends Peter Canisius and Nicholas Goudanus at Ingolstadt. He traveled during February. The journey to and from Ingolstadt was most unpleasant.[94] The weather was inclement. The Danube had overflowed its banks. Roads were indiscernible. Cold weather had turned the inundated fields into sheets of ice. At one spot on his way back from Ingolstadt to Dillingen, Jay had to give up the idea of going farther until the ice had melted and the floods had subsided. Once again en route, his horse was feeling its way along when it plunged into a deep ditch filled with water. The body of the animal pinned Jay down. Only by the most frantic efforts and the help of a companion did Jay escape drowning. Soaked to the skin, covered with mud, his right shin cut, he finally reached Dillingen, and eventually Augsburg.[95]

On 2 March Truchsess and Jay set out for a monastery a two-day journey from Augsburg. At the monastery Jay directed others as well as Truchsess through the Exercises.[96] Almost complete silence covers the details of that month of prayer and intimate conversation between two friends seriously dedicated to the service of Christ. While at the monastery, Truchsess also preached and administered the sacrament of confirmation. Truchsess, absorbed in the Spiritual Exercises, symbolized the hinge on which swung the spiritual renewal of the church as envisaged by the Council of Trent: the leadership of devout bishops. The council felt the impact of the overwhelming demand on all sides for episcopal renewal, recognized it as one of the clearer "signs of the times," and so gave high priority to episcopal reformation. Truchsess at prayer was articulating Trent's aspirations. And in this role he was in large measure a Jesuit creation, inspired and guided through several years by Favre, Canisius, and Jay.

Jay esteemed Truchsess highly. In his letter of 11 July 1550 from Augsburg to Ignatius, he delivered a little eulogy of his friend.

> He is much inclined to the things of God. Without fail he has reading at table. He has put aside clothes of silk, dresses quite simply, and always in his cardinal's garb. He recites the breviary most devoutly. Very often he says mass. He preaches on solemn feast days. Every day he carries out some spiritual practice as is done in our Society. His table is marked by great moderation and by what is ordinary. He does not go in for banquets or noise, and almost always eats with only one or two theologians. He gives alms generously, especially to his college [not a Jesuit college], where he feeds and clothes twenty-four scholars without mentioning the professors of theology, liberal arts, rhetoric, and grammar, an undertaking that reflects the supernatural character of his life.[97]

After the retreat, on the Wednesday after Easter, Truchsess and Jay went to the estate of the cardinal's family, a two-day journey away. There in the presence of his eighty-one-year-old father, the Baron Truchsess von Waldburg, his brother Wilhelm, and several other people, Cardinal Truchsess performed a five hours ceremony of dedicating a very beautiful chapel erected by his brother. His reverence and obvious devotion inspired those present.[98]

After the retreat and his visit to the Truchsess estate, Jay made one last quick trip to Ingolstadt to see Peter Canisius before he set out for Vienna. Duke Albrecht of Bavaria had Jay to dinner and expressed his sincere regret that Vienna was being enriched at a cost to Ingolstadt. But he realized that Jay's directives had come from his superiors. Albrecht added further that he was satisfied in that it was the king of the Romans who was profiting from the transfer. On 21 April, with Fr. Peter Schorich and Petronius Zanelus, one of the cardinal's domestics, Jay finally started eastward toward Vienna.[99]

Summary

Jay's experiences through the four years 1547–51 cast in bold relief some of the more notable lineaments of Catholic life in mid-sixteenth century. They did so in at least three ways: first, they illustrated the pervasive influence of the secular powers on the directions taken by the churches, Catholic and Protestant. At Ferrara, where the policy in the Castello could seriously affect the progress or regression of religious activity, Jay tended to measure his success or failure by the coolness or cordiality of Prince Ercole. At Augsburg he shared in an effort by the emperor to bring religious peace to Germany, when Charles applied his imperial, military, and political might to create a stepping stone for Protestant participation in the council. Religious issues, political maneuvers, military engagements made a tangled net in which Europe was bound at mid-sixteenth century.

Second, Jay's experiences instanced a major difficulty encountered in Germany by the disciples of Catholic reform: a reluctance among the leaders, secular and ecclesiastical, to try new ventures. Jay started his propaganda for Jesuit colleges in either December 1544 or January 1545. Repeatedly he articulated his formula for Germany's spiritual renewal: Jesuit colleges, staffed by men in whom were harmonized holiness and learning, as colonies of spiritual strength amid a people in disarray. The breakthrough came only five and a half years later.

Third, these four years heightened the awareness among the first Jesuits that they possessed a unique strength in their international character. Jay in his dealings with the German bishops emphasized that the Society could be an aqueduct channelling the waters of spiritual renewal from Italy, Spain, France, and Portugal into Germany. Salmerón and Canisius joined Jay in this argument. They represented an international viewpoint strongly at odds with the mounting nationalism of the day.

CHAPTER V

VIENNA
1551–1552

Introduction

This chapter covers the last phase of Jay's life, from April 1551 to August 1552. Jay crowned his labors with the realization of his great ambition to have a Jesuit college founded among the German-speaking peoples. And it was a college whose character, as he had promised would be the case, was distinctly international.

Introduction to Vienna

On the feast of St. Mark, 25 April 1551, Jay reached gracious Vienna, dominated by the towering spire of the Stephansdom. Visitors from Bosnia once looked in awe at this spire and stammered, "More money went into that than could be gotten for the entire realm of Bosnia." This spire looked over an affluent city, splendid in its stone houses of high facades, elegant iron work, large windows, arched doorways, broad courts. In contrast to this material affluence, the religious condition of the Catholic Church in Austria was desperate. Year after year the advancing tide of Lutheranism cut away more and more the shoreline of the

Church's position in Austria. The religious crisis seriously affected the University of Vienna.

The seeding ground for many of the Austrian clergy was in the halls of learning that looked out over Vienna's Universitätsplatz, but only the previous year, 1549, the faculty of theology became temporarily extinct after a decade of gasping for breath with its two lone professors. Bishop Urban Weber lamented that Vienna had seen the ordination of not a single priest in twenty years.[2] Things improved a trifle by 1551, when there were three professors lecturing to ten students. But of these ten, hardly one was equipped to follow lectures in theology. And the three professors had indicated their intention to quit the university soon.[3] Of the Hapsburg provinces, some were scarcely a tenth, some hardly a thirtieth, untouched by Luther's theology. With the Protestant stress on faith and the merits of Christ, works of charity, prayer, fasting, all fell into desuetude. Parishes were without priests. Sacramental life was dying.[4]

The day after his arrival, Jay called on King Ferdinand. He discovered that the king had anticipated his coming by the appointment of Bishop Urban Weber and the rector of the university as a committee of two to find a suitable residence for the Jesuits. The best place that they could discover, at least for the time being, was a section of the Dominican convent near the university. Its walls, shaken and cut by shells, brought up memories of the severe Turkish bombardment of 1529. In 1551 a section was used to house a group of workmen and their families. Jay was afraid that settling the Jesuits there might give offense to the Dominicans. His instinct was right, for the vicar of the monastery openly showed his displeasure when he heard the suggestion.[5] A compromise was worked out whereby the Jesuits moved in as temporary guests, whose rent was cared for by King Ferdinand. Ferdinand was aglow with delight. An alert man, quick thinking, expansive and open, he spoke in terms of a foundation to take care of thirty Jesuits. In his conversation with Jay, he turned to the subject of the Society's founder. He was aware, he said, of Ignatius's noble birth and he recalled how one of Ignatius's brothers just about eight years earlier had fallen on the field of battle against the Turk.[6]

One major need at the temporary residence was furniture.

Bishop Urban Weber assumed responsibility for collecting beds, desks, and chairs, and he gave himself to this project with great energy.[7] There was really no time to lose. Ignatius had written sometime after mid-April that some scholastics would be on their way to Vienna as soon as possible.[8] Further news arrived from Ferdinand's ambassador in Rome that a band of Jesuits had left Rome on 28 April. Under the direction of a Belgian Jesuit, Nicolas Delanoy, eight scholastics were in a group which was augmented by two others at Bologna. After a month's travel that took them through Trent and Innsbruck, they boarded a river boat for the five day ride down the Danube to Vienna. During the time that they were south of the Alps, they frequently preached in Italian and Latin. Once in Germany, however, the edification they gave had to be a silent kind, articulated "in naught but a peaceable kind of patience" (*tranquilitate tantum et patientia*) recorded Polanco, since the language of the people of the Empire was a mystery to them. They reached Vienna in early June.[9]

The great metropolis was a maze to the eleven newcomers and they had no precise information about where to locate Jay. They found their way to the governor of the city who, noticing that they carried letters addressed to the king of the Romans, ordered that every courtesy be shown them. They then went to the episcopal residence of the bishop of Vienna, Frederick Nausea. Jay was not there. Next they went to the home of Bishop Weber. Here they found Jay. The bishop with typical magnanimity opened up his house to them until their own residence was completely equipped. The next day they presented themselves to Ferdinand, who received them with great warmth, "not just with courtesy but with love" (*non humaniter solum sed et amanter*). These men from Rome, expecting to receive the amplexus from their royal host, thought it a bit curious that instead the king extended them his right hand. This, Polanco said, interrupting his narrative to explain, was the German way of greeting one.[10]

Finally the Jesuits were able to move into their section of the Dominican convent. Not all was as quiet as they would have liked. With the families of the workmen in their part of the structure, there were the calls of the children and the bustle of the housewives to intrude on their study and recollection. And despite Bishop Weber's generous efforts to appoint their home, the scholastics had much work to do in making doors, windows, beds, racks, and tables.[11]

The Jesuit Academic Program

Shortly after the Jesuits had set up their community, they inaugurated their academic program in the university. Jay, despite his natural fear of the lecture hall, began his discourses on St. Paul's Epistle to the Romans; Fr. Nicolas Delanoy started his lectures on the Fourth Book of the *Sentences* of Peter Lombard; the ten younger Jesuits became the nucleus of the theology classes. Besides their theology course at the university, the scholastics followed a private program of studies at their residence. Their earlier training had suffered from serious deficiencies, but despite these shortcomings the young Jesuits were told to follow the public courses in theology. Realizing their weakness in philosophy, they did not attend the public lectures on that subject, partly because several of the masters were not Catholic and partly because they felt that they could not afford to let their reputation as learned men suffer damage. So they had their own private lessons in the seclusion of their residence.[12]

The intellectual activity inside the Jesuit quarters was intense as the young men resolutely tried to make up the missing parts of their intellectual formation. Delanoy taught dialectics; Georg Schorich taught Greek; Erard Dawant taught rhetoric; Juan de Vitoria taught the *De Amicitia*. Repetitions were the daily fare. Disputations were held on certain days of the week. There were exercises in verse and prose composition. On feast days one of the scholastics preached in the refectory during meal time. Then there was the house work to be done. Polanco observed: Not even the teachers were spared the work in the kitchen.[13]

This obvious diligence could not adequately compensate for the hodgepodge nature of the scholastic program, and it was this that made Ignatius somewhat displeased with the beginnings of the Viennese community. He knew from bitter personal experience the wasted expenditure of energy in a poorly organized program of studies. He did not want his men to move into philosophy without a solid foundation in humane letters, nor start theology without a thorough training in philosophy. But here was an instance where for the time being the ideal had to yield to the circumstances of the moment.[14]

The Quest for German Vocations

Jay's community was a cosmopolitan group, made up of Belgians, Italians, and Spaniards. At the university they could feel at ease because Latin was the language of the lecture hall, but between them and the people of Vienna rose a solid barrier: the German tongue. It was simply beyond them. On 16 December 1551 Claude lamented to Ignatius: "As far as preaching is concerned, not one of us is capable of doing so in German. Nor do the Italians and Spaniards among us, indeed not even the Flemings, have any hope of learning that language. It is far too difficult. For my part, I have been stationed in Germany about ten years and I have not been wanting in industry in trying to learn it. Nevertheless, I still can neither speak nor understand it. Possibly our Flemish brothers could learn it, if they are freed from their studies to converse in German with other scholars of the university, who ordinarily speak Latin."[15]

The best solution to this problem was to have German-speaking Jesuits. Two or three months before Jay wrote his lament to Ignatius, Peter Canisius had received two novices, Karl Grim and Lambert von Auer, into the Society and sent them on to Jay. They were from the Tyrol and had already received their bachelor degrees.[16] On 9 October 1551 Jay told Ignatius of their coming, and correctly estimated them when he said that they were talented young men "of considerable natural endowment" (de bono ingegno), for they did excellent work in later years.[17] The king of the Romans, delighted at their arrival, explicitly accentuated the importance of German-speaking Jesuits. For the same reason, that of rapport with the people, he hoped that Bohemians and Hungarians would enter the Society.[18] Grim and Auer themselves sensed the significance of their vocation, for before they left Ingolstadt they confided to Peter Canisius that they thought the entry of a single German into the Society was an event comparable to the entrance of twenty Italians or Spaniards.[19]

German vocations clearly preoccupied Jay. To his letter of 9 October 1551 to Ignatius he added a happy postscript, relating that he had two German boys, aged eighteen, working in the kitchen. These boys were talented, conscientious, and seemed to like the Jesuits.[20] Jay clearly had hopes that they would become novices, since the German-speaking scholastics were those on whom rested the Jesuit hope of making close and effective contact with the Austrian people. At the end of 1551, a third Ingolstadtian and two other Germans swelled the novitiate to five and the community to eighteen. In the refectory the German novices preached in their native tongue. To these sermons the Flemings especially were supposed to pay strict attention, with the hope that in the near future Jesuits could step into the pulpits of Vienna's churches.[21]

Theological Renewal at Vienna

Jay's success as a lecturer was striking. Clarity, order, courtesy were his main traits as a teacher. Lutheran doctrines had been abroad practically unchallenged. With his rare gift of contesting an opinion without giving offense, Jay quickly cleared the theological air at the university. Experience in Germany and at Trent had given him a comprehensive grasp of the Protestant positions.[22] Francesco Orlandini recorded that Jay developed his matter "with courtesy and apt expression (*facilitate ac felicitate*).[23] And Peter Canisius, who would soon be on the scene in Vienna, drew this picture of Claude's classroom manner. "Even though he was weighed down with years, he did not let up in his unbroken program of teaching, which he carried out to the greatest satisfaction of his hearers, and which was characterized by a certain wonderful charm and sweetness of manner, making it practically out of the question for anyone to take offense at him. His procedure in the classroom was marked by clarity, ease, moderation, precise method, as he presented lucidly and courteously those difficult proofs on justification, predestination, faith and works, and other like controversial problems. With no small labor he also put those proofs into writing."[24] Probably the finest tribute of all to his teaching was the steady attendance of the students.[25]

Ferdinand became fully absorbed in the renewal of theological studies at Vienna. By mid-July 1551, he did two things: first, he assembled the heads of the Austrian provinces at Vienna, at which meeting they decided that each province should recruit a certain number of students who would take up the study of theology, become priests, and fill the empty pastorates; and second, he requested that the Society assign thirty scholastics to Vienna, who, accompanied by excellent professors, would by their example in public theological disputations and exercises, as traditionally carried out in Paris and Spain, provide an inspiration to others.[26]

King Ferdinand's plans and desires Jay sent to Ignatius on 21 July 1551. He also told Ignatius that the only three lecturers in theology beside himself and Delanoy were two canons and a monk who intended to withdraw soon. Because of these departures, the obligation to lecture daily, the time consumed in preaching to the Italians in Vienna and in hearing confessions, Jay asked Ignatius for another Jesuit doctor in theology.[27]

Nicolas Delanoy's experience in the classroom added another reason for asking Ignatius for help. Delanoy attracted only a few students to his class. His subject matter, the *Sentences* of Peter the Lombard, had little appeal for the Austrians. Further, Delanoy, soft-spoken in his delivery, won commendation more for his erudition than his manner of teaching. Jay felt, therefore, that his associate, gifted with an aptitude for administration, should leave the lecture hall and make way for a Jesuit replacement.[28]

Ignatius answered Jay immediately. Through Juan Polanco he sent on 8 August one of his most revealing letters about the role of education in the renewal of the Church.[29] The exigency for well-trained priests in Germany Ignatius knew from the letters of Favre, Jay, Canisius, and Bobadilla. The instrument to meet this exigency he found in the educational structure and methods he had personally learned at the University of Paris. In his letter to Jay he drew a blueprint of clerical training, by which he gave to the hopelessly drifting University of Vienna the compass of the rich educational tradition of Paris. For the aspirant to the priesthood he outlined a solid grasp of Latin letters, and preferably of Greek and Hebrew also, as the essential cornerstone; then a course in philosophy carried out with repeated exercises; then, and only then, the capstone of theology. The preparatory courses in literature and philosophy taught "in the Parisian fashion" (*al modo di parigi*) should, he wrote, be handled by teachers who in their personal thirst for theological learning would keep before the eyes of their students the ultimate goal of theology. The Society was prepared to supply King Ferdinand with this special brand of teacher, experienced in the methods of the University of Paris and keen for the advancement of theological understanding.

This program, Ignatius insisted, demanded time and patience.[30] He told Jay that he welcomed Ferdinand's avowed dedication to the renewal of theology at Vienna—but with a caution. He could not promise Ferdinand immediate results. Even though Austrian parishes were without pastors, the quality of the carefully trained priest would justify the protracted wait. Ignatius made it clear to Jay that he should not allow Ferdinand to pressure him into a program designed for quick and instantaneous results. He was applying his principle of preferring the more permanent to the less durable in the choice of means to the greater glory of God.[31]

Meanwhile King Ferdinand began to implement his plan to set up a college for the diocesan seminarians from the Austrian provinces. In Vienna, in a building not far from the Jesuit residence, he gathered almost fifty young men. The rules for the administration of the house were submitted to Jay for approval. Teachers and prefects consulted him. The dependence of this seminary on the Jesuit college gave Jay another reason to bombard headquarters at Rome with pleas for more men. In December, 1551, he sent an urgent letter to Ignatius.

> Yesterday the director of the seminary came to confer with me on ways to guide the students in their moral and intellectual growth. In the course of our discussion about spiritual things, confession, Holy Communion, prayer, Mass, he told me that he wanted his students to make their confessions to me and that he would like to have some of our men teach them the principles of Christian doctrine on feastdays. It is my hope that this arrangement will produce great results. I have no doubt that Your Reverence deeply desires to provide this college with more men. And I am sure that the same holds for all our other colleges. Yet, I know for certain that you do not have available as many men as you would like to take care of the needs of all.
>
> Despite this, I cannot restrain myself from the humble plea that Your Reverence devise some way by which you can succor this college in Vienna. Aside from the immense gratification it would give the king and his counselors, in whose estimation we enjoy high standing, I am convinced that the college in this city has the potential to achieve the most gratifying results, not in Germany alone, but in the neighboring kingdoms as well, Bohemia, Poland, Hungary, etc. If there is any place where our Company experiences the need to win the good will of the people by scholarship, it is especially here in this country. And if in any country ecclesiastics, priests, brothers, religious groups, and such things as exterior mortification are held in contempt, it is particularly in this area, here in the north. In fact, they are emphatically despised, scorned, and vilified.[32]

Benevolence of Austrian Officialdom

The Jesuit residence became a favorite port of call for Urban Weber, and he was constantly inquiring whether anything was needed. He had the practice of arriving at mealtime, unannounced and with distinguished company, so that his companions might be edified by the frugality and simplicity of the Jesuit meals. One day Weber brought the rector of the university and a certain distinguished abbot. With them they carried an attractive variety of food and wine to supplement the ordinary community fare. The Jesuits, anxious to greet such honored guests with fitting dignity, rose to the occasion and gave an exhibition of their scholastic acumen by short sermons in German and Greek, a debate in Greek, and some disputations in philosophy and theology. Polanco gravely noted that the meats and wines went untouched, so spellbound were the guests by the performance of their hosts.[33]

Jay's community continued to be the apple of Ferdinand's eye. Generous with funds, the king of the Romans was ever alert to forestall any needs. Late in 1551 he returned to Vienna from a visit to Styria to learn that the Jesuits were short of vestments. Promptly he sent them two complete sets. A few days later, with almost his entire retinue, he arrived at the residence and went through it from top to bottom. When Jay thanked him for his gracious and friendly visit, Ferdinand insisted that if anything was needed, they should not hesitate to make it known.[34]

A New Catechism

With his Jesuit collegiate residence set up and his school for prospective priests started, King Ferdinand took still another step in the direction of restoring Catholic life in Austria. He convened the officials of the University of Vienna and told them that he wanted a compendium of Christian doctrine composed for use in his realm. Not that there was any dearth of catechisms in Germany. The printing press was hardly put together before any number of little books with explanations of the Apostles' Creed, the Our Father, the Decalogue, and with such themes as *The Hope of a Sinner* and *The Art of Good Living* made their appearance. One particular catechism, *The Foundation of Eternal Happiness*, appeared in 1498 in Cologne, and before twelve years had passed it had gone through six editions. A catechism by the Dominican

137

Johann Dietenberger went through eight editions before 1550. In the early sixteenth century, in Cologne alone, seven different catechisms were put into the hands of the people.[35]

These publications, however, were not of equal value. Some were too drawn out, some were even defective in the accurate expression of doctrine. Ferdinand wanted a work with the Hapsburg blessing on it and especially designated for use in the Hapsburg lands of Austria. It was to be the work of the theologians of the king of the Romans; it was to be printed at Vienna; it was to be placed at the disposal of all teachers in Austria. Ferdinand wanted it to be up-to-date in its treatment of current theological problems. Besides, he desired it to be so organized that it would contain between its covers all that a good Christian ought to know. Ferdinand was asking not just for the sun and the moon; he was ordering a theological cosmos from the leaders of the university. They did not keep the responsibility very long. Neatly they eased their own shoulders by proceeding to place the burden at Jay's doorstep.

Jay was convinced that he was unequal to the task and tried to deflect the assignment by pointing to the many catechisms already in print, especially those by Pedro de Soto, Johann Gropper, and the Synod of Mainz.[36] Unsuccessful in this maneuver, he did what all the early Jesuits instinctively did when faced with a knotty problem: he turned to Ignatius.

> Master Nicolas Delanoy and I are of the opinion that we cannot measure up to this assignment. Prescinding from other reasons that come to mind, we have neither the material with which to work, nor the talent to organize it, nor the time to do it. Master Nicolas, in addition to his responsibility of running the college, has to give each day a public lecture at the university and a private one to our own men at home. I too must lecture each day. It is not clear just where we would find the time to spend on our other assignments. . . . We humbly beg Your Reverence to deign to make known to us your will in this matter. If you want to see this compendium written, we ask you for the honor of God to assign someone who has the talent for it. We shall give him all the help we can. Master Peter Canisius and Master Nicolas Goudanus, both at Ingolstadt, are not able to help, since they are too far away.[37]

Jay sent that letter on 9 October 1551. His help arrived the following March, five months to the day later. And it came in the persons of the two men he felt he could least hope for, Peter Canisius and Nicolas Goudanus.

Conflicting Claims of Vienna and Ingolstadt

The assignment of Canisius and Goudanus to Vienna was the result of a most delicate diplomatic maneuver. Duke Albrecht of Bavaria, in whose realm was located the University of Ingolstadt, was married to King Ferdinand's daughter Anne. Ferdinand, looking to the progress of his Jesuit college in Vienna, was anxious to take the two Jesuits away from his son-in-law. At Rome, Ignatius too was anxious to transfer Canisius and Goudanus from Ingolstadt because the duke was procrastinating about committing himself to the foundation of a Jesuit college there.[38] Albrecht continued to think only in terms of Jesuit presence in the faculty of theology, whereas Ignatius insisted on the wider goal of a Jesuit college that also embraced the humanities and philosophy.[39]

Through 1551 Ingolstadt, therefore, preoccupied Jay and Ignatius almost as much as Vienna. The two Jesuits felt that the university of that Bavarian town, after Vienna, should be the site of a Jesuit college. Jay, in February 1551, while still at Augsburg, saw his hopes for a breakthrough dashed. He had had his eyes on two empty monasteries at Ingolstadt, which he was sure the deceased Duke Wilhelm had intended to assign to the Society. But on 18 February 1551 the apostolic nuncio to King Ferdinand, Girolamo Martinengo, showed Jay a letter from Rome revealing that Duke Albrecht was negotiating the transfer of the two monasteries not to the Society but to the university proper.[40] That same day Jay sent a letter to Ignatius with the disappointing news. He added: "The most illustrious Duke of Bavaria has become cool in his feelings for Alphonso [Salmerón] and myself because of our departure from Ingolstadt."[41]

Ignatius's Insistence on an Ordered Curriculum

Five days later, on 23 February 1551, Ignatius, through Polanco, wrote to Jay. Once more he reaffirmed his conviction that the Jesuit college, with its integrated program of humanities, philosophy, and theology, was what Ingolstadt should have.[42] Ignatius told Jay that he had written to Moritz von Hutten, the university's chancellor, about the success of the Jesuit college at Coimbra, which King John III of Portugal had founded. This Jesuit college had become the intellectual center of renewal for the Church in Portugal and in the Indies, a role that Ingolstadt, once it had a Jesuit college, might perform in Germany. Ignatius also reminded von Hutten that the deceased Duke Wilhelm IV had planned to found a Jesuit college at Ingolstadt.[43]

Later that same year, on 22 September, Ignatius wrote directly to Duke Albrecht. Again Ignatius made a strong apologia for a rounded and coordinated curriculum of humanities, philosophy, and theology, an ideal that could be realized at Ingolstadt by founding a Jesuit college there.[44] As the point of departure of his argument, he used Jay's assessment: what this German university needed as much as professors was students; the preparation of theology professors was not enough; students too had to be properly trained to take up theological studies. Ignatius insisted on this with Duke Albrecht.

> The students I have in mind are those inclined by personal desire to take up the study of sacred theology avidly and diligently, mentally trained in the lower branches of knowledge, and capable of making progress in theology. But how many of the students of theology at Ingolstadt have this background? I hear that those—I write this with sorrow—in whom either proper disposition or intellectual formation, or both, are not lacking are most rare. For they either dislike theology, or they do not have the solid foundation given by the lower faculties for making headway in it.[45]

These words of Ignatius had all the resonance of Jay's reports about the Ingolstadt scene.

Diplomatic Maneuvering

Ignatius, however, failed to break the procrastination of Duke Albrecht. Then began one of those adroit maneuvers in which Ignatius sometimes engaged with the great ones of Europe. Ignatius, King Ferdinand, and Pope Julius III formed a diplomatic phalanx against the vacillating Albrecht. Ignatius held back from taking the lead in the application of this pressure. Lest he hurt the duke's feelings, he refrained from ordering Canisius and Goudanus from Ingolstadt to Vienna.[46]

The Jesuits in Vienna, however, did not share this inhibition. They urged Ferdinand to take the initiative.[47] This Ferdinand did. On 4 December 1551 he wrote Ignatius, explaining that Jay and Delanoy were carrying a heavy load of work and that they needed the help of one or two more theologians of equal piety and learning.

We have heard that at the University of Ingolstadt there are two other outstanding theologians of your Society, men of German provenance, whom you would like to transfer elsewhere. Although it is our wish not to do anything to the prejudice of the most honored Albrecht, Count Palatine of the Rhine, son of the duke of Upper and Lower Bavaria, our own most dear relative and prince, by attracting these two men from his university to ours at Vienna, nevertheless, if you have decided to recall them from Ingolstadt and to send them elsewhere, we kindly ask you to send them to our college in Vienna rather than to some other.[48]

Ignatius first thought of suggesting that Ferdinand himself personally ask Albrecht for Canisius and Goudanus. But then he feared that this would create tension between the king and the duke. So he evolved a plan designed to satisfy King Ferdinand, and at the same time not to offend Duke Albrecht. He arranged that a request be filed with Pope Julius III in the name of Ferdinand for two Jesuit theologians for Vienna, without specifically mentioning Canisius and Goudanus. Knowing Julius's desire to satisfy King Ferdinand, Ignatius then advised the pope that the only two available and suitable men were Canisius and Goudanus, and suggested that the pope order that these two be loaned to Vienna until the time when Albrecht would decide to establish a Jesuit college at Ingolstadt. This Julius did.[49] And on 28 January 1552 Ignatius, in the name of the pope, wrote Canisius to leave Ingolstadt for Vienna within ten days after he and Goudanus received the letter. The letter reached Ingolstadt on 23 February.[50]

The next day Canisius broke the news to Duke Albrecht. The duke, distressed by Ignatius's move, begged Peter that he and Goudanus stay until he represented to Ferdinand. But realizing that this would keep them beyond the ten days set by Ignatius, he decided to release them and to send an envoy to Rome to ask for their rapid return to Ingolstadt. Moritz von Hutten too was troubled, and although he gave Canisius and Goudanus his blessing, he expressed deep anger with Claude Jay, whom he regarded as the villain of the piece. On the twenty-eighth Canisius and Goudanus boarded a river-craft and sailed eastward. "In such wise," observed Polanco, "was the Jesuit residence at Ingolstadt closed."[51]

Only in 1556, four years after Jay's death, did Albrecht yield to Ignatius's position. For the Jesuits their college at Ingolstadt became known as Ignatius's Benjamin, the child of his old age.

On 22 July 1556 Ignatius sent the last of his nearly seven thousand letters. It was to Peter Canisius and closed with a fervent request for news of the college then aborning at Ingolstadt.[52]

When Canisius and Goudanus left Ingolstadt for Vienna on 28 February 1552, they brought with them two more German novices, one named Johann Dirsius, to increase Jay's community to the number of twenty-five.[53] In that most cosmopolitan city, the new arrivals broadened the international character of the Jesuit group, which had recently added Dalmatians to the French, Flemings, Spaniards, Italians, Germans, Austrians, Dutch, and Hungarians already there.[54]

Educational Developments at Vienna

Less than two months after Canisius and Goudanus arrived at Vienna, a significant development occurred at the Jesuit residence. Lay students began to attend the classes designed especially for the Jesuit scholastics. King Ferdinand had desired this.[55] It was in keeping with the general norm applicable to all Jesuit residences where scholastics were in study.[56] When more commodious rooms became available at the Vienna residence, the Jesuits announced their policy of opening their lectures to the public.[57] This move paved the way for the erection of a separate Jesuit school designed primarily for lay students.

At the beginning of summer, Canisius began the work that weighed so heavily on Jay's mind, the compendium of Christian doctrine ordered by King Ferdinand. Jay had actually started on it, and with Goudanus's help he had done a great deal to determine the order of the work and the points of doctrine to be explained. Now he was only too happy to turn it over to Canisius. He also put in Peter's hands two manuscripts of his own composition, which Peter was able to use in the actual writing of the catechism and in the preparation of his lectures at the university. One was a bulky work of 342 pages, evidence of the wide range of Jay's theological knowledge, in which he had noted the opinions not only of the great medieval doctors and theologians but also the contemporary thinkers: Johann Cochlaeus, Albert Pighius, Desiderius Erasmus, Juan de Valencia, Johannes Eck, and Johann Faber. In thesis form he lined up refutations of the teachings of Luther and Calvin on such subjects as the nature of the Church, celibacy, vows, the saints, the Holy Sacrifice of the Mass, purgatory, original sin, and Holy Scripture. He devoted a page to the teachings of his fellow Jesuit Diego Laynez on the subject of Church and law. His second and smaller work treated the intricate subject of justification.[58]

Jay's Death

On 30 July Jay, absorbed in his beehive of activity, wrote to Ignatius about the various problems the Jesuits faced in Vienna. A week later he was dead. His health had been failing, but he was not inclined to make much of it. At the beginning of August he was racked by fever and chills. Each day brought an increased weakening of his energies. Eventually he was not able to comprehend what was said to him, and then he lost his power of speech. On the feast of the Transfiguration, 6 August 1552, at two in the afternoon he received the sacrament of extreme unction. At five he gave his soul to God. He did not see Ignatius's last letter to him, written eight days before, to ask him to recruit candidates for the German College in Rome.[59] That he would have to do from heaven.

King Ferdinand and Bishop Weber felt his loss keenly.[60] Otto Truchsess wept bitterly when the news reached him, and he requested Jay's copy of the New Testament as a remembrance of his dear friend.[61] Because it was feared that in time the extension of the city's fortifications for the inevitable battles with the Turks would mean the razing of the Dominikanerkirche, they buried Jay in the Franziskanerkirche.[62] Peter Canisius preached at the funeral. His sermon has not been preserved, but we have the letter he sent to Ignatius the day after Jay's death.

> Our Reverend Father, Master Claude, even though he had an attack of fever and had suffered a fourth recurrence of the tertian ague, was in no way despaired of by the two doctors, the very best in the city, who visited him twice a day on five successive days. Then too, he received our most solicitous care. Despite all this, the Lord, holding all under his rule, willed to show forth his providence and heavenly goodness. And lo, Master Claude gave up his holy soul to the eternal Creator, to whom be praise through ages on end. Fortified with extreme unction, while all the fathers and brothers were standing nearby, he went from us, his sons, to that other world. He departed, as did St. Martin, leaving in them who stood by the most intense desire to keep their Claude among them, if such had been the pleasure of the omnipotent Lord. He went from us showing us the right way to go to Christ both in life and in death, a death for him all the more happy in view of the

143

increasingly severe labors, dangers, calamities that now rise up before our eyes in the shape of the nearby Turk, heresy, war, the fierceness of which has probably never before been seen in Germany. It was on the feast of the Transfiguration of our Lord Jesus Christ that Father Claude, taken out of this vale of tears, ascended the holy mountain to behold Christ with flawless vision and to delight with St. Peter in the beauty of the divine nature, the object of his desire for so many years.

I do not intend to give a detailed picture of how admirably this holy father lived and how, over and over again, he gave us an example of virtue. For you are aware, Reverend Father, that up to the present no member of the Society has done more work among the heretics of Germany and has endured as much as he. Everywhere he stayed he always left the sweetest of memories. To such an extent did he arouse souls to piety that nearly all wanted to keep him in their midst. Even though he was weighed down with years,[63] he did not let up in his unbroken program of teaching, which he carried out to the greatest satisfaction of his hearers and which was characterized by a certain wonderful charm and sweetness of manner, making it practically out of the question for anyone to take offense at him. His procedure in the classroom was marked by clarity, ease, moderation, precise method, as he presented lucidly and courteously those difficult proofs on justification, predestination, faith and works, and other like controversial problems. With no small labor he also put those proofs into writing.

Since the Most Serene King of the Romans esteemed him greatly, since courtiers, prelates, professors so frequently called on him, since he was superior of our residence and was taken up with the care of all the brethren, he ran into many obstacles to his teaching. Nevertheless, with great attentiveness he continued to run his regular daily class, which was attended by a large-sized audience that included several priests and prelates.

But, as I remarked above, I do not intend to sketch the life of this reverend father, who was elected by God to be of the group of our first fathers and who in later years stood before men as a very apostle of Germany. I speak what is in my heart. Most deeply loved by the princes and bishops of Germany, he gave them much help at the imperial diets. It is well known with how much favor his presence was recognized at the general council in its sessions at Bologna and Trent. . . . Conscientious in his practice of poverty, he used to walk about the palaces of the nobility in a common, worn out habit, all the time withstanding the princes as they offered to provide everything he needed, and even more. He followed an admirable order in the regularity of his life. Every day—this he himself often told me—he used to meditate on some phase of Christ's Passion. Many were the beautiful sermons he developed on the round of mysteries in the life of Christ. He was a faithful and pious devotee of that form of prayer known as the rosary, studying the mysteries of the Incarnate Word in that order presented by the Church, at one time the Resurrection, at another the Nativity, etc.

I have not the slightest doubt that many will feel his death very deeply.

It is my hope that we, his sons, deprived of so good a father, whose first interest was the management of this college, may hold on to the inheritance of those singular gifts by which his entire life, by divine grace, was distinguished and made resplendent. Every one feels his passing most intensely and speaks of him as an angel of God and as father and protector of all Catholics.[64]

That was the heartfelt tribute of a great saint to a man in whom he recognized exceptional holiness.

Enduring Quality of Jay's Work

Jay died with the knowledge that he had achieved his deeply personal apostolate among the German-speaking peoples: the foundation of colleges. This he realized in Vienna in a three-fold way: first, in the inauguration of a Jesuit collegiate residence; second, in the establishment of a college for diocesan seminarians; and third, in the admission of lay students among the classes for the Jesuit scholastics, a prelude to a separate school for lay students. This school came into being in early 1553, about eight months after Jay had died.[65]

The import of Jay's Viennese foundations became evident only after his death. This was so in at least two ways. First, the college of Vienna broke the logjam of ecclesiastical and princely procrastination and set free a great stream of enthusiasm for the founding of Jesuit schools. Leopold von Ranke wrote that one of the most remarkable phenomena of history was the Jesuit educational program in sixteenth-century Germany. The growth and influence of Jesuit schools among the German peoples, said Ranke, was "a case for which the history of the world could probably not produce a parallel."[66] By 1580, from Paderborn and Heiligenstadt in the north to Luzern, Innsbruck, and Halle in the south; from Trier in the west to Vienna and Graz in the east, three German-speaking Jesuit provinces were either operating or at the point of opening nineteen schools.[67]

And second, Jay's college at Vienna with its staff of competent professors and Jesuit students avid for learning made the intellectual waves that moved across central Europe and saved university life within the Catholic regions of the Hapsburg domains. By the early seventeenth century, no Catholic university within the empire, save Salzburg, which was in the hands of the Benedictines, was founded or maintained without Jesuit help.[68]

145

Jay lived on in the memory of Vienna. In the middle of the seventeenth century, during a solemn mass at the Stephansdom in memory of the deceased members of the university, a gradual composed of iambic dimeters, was sung. In this gradual Claude Jay, among other distinguished professors, was lovingly recalled.

Rudolphus quartus Archidux fundator Athenaei,
Triumphet cum exercitu coelestis aciei.
O ita post hunc praecipuus immaculatae Matris
Assertor, laetus videat vultum aeterni Patris.
Sic Thomas Haselpachius, et Doctor Argentinas,
Jaius, Petrus Canisius, et anima Becani.[69]

Jay had begun a tradition of Jesuit presence in Vienna that was carried on by Peter Canisius and Martin van der Beeck (Becanus), who too left their imprint on Catholic life in the great Hapsburg metropolis.

PART II

ALFONSO SALMERÓN

CHAPTER VI

ALCALÁ TO TRENT
1515–46

Introduction

This chapter covers the first thirty years of Alfonso Salme-rón's life, from 1515, the year of his birth, to early 1546, when he received orders to go to the Council of Trent. As a young man Salmerón attended the University of Alcalá, where he received a lifelong orientation toward scriptural studies. Then he moved to the University of Paris, where he met Iñigo de Loyola and joined him and some of Loyola's friends in a brotherhood which eventually became the Society of Jesus. Salmerón's earliest experiences as a Jesuit included a papal mission to Ireland; extensive preaching in northern Italy; and designation as a theologian at the Council of Trent.

Early Years

On 1 June 1527, after three separate official investigations that extended over six months, Juan Rodriguez de Figueroa, vicar-general of Alcalá, pronounced sentence on one of the city's university students. Under pain of excommunication and banishment from Spain, the student was forbidden to discuss religion with anyone, publicly or privately, until after he had completed four years of study, and then only with the permission of local ecclesiastical authorities. He had become a sign of contradiction at Alcalá. Some said that he was a saint, others called him a heretic. Late in June he quit Alcalá.[1] Shortly after—perhaps in 1528—while people were still talking about the mendicant scholar who had run afoul of the authorities because of his begging, his catechetical instructions, and his austere life, Alfonso Salmerón enrolled in the university. Twelve- or thirteen-year-old Alfonso heard the gossip, and for the first time the name of Iñigo de Loyola fell upon his ears.[2]

Salmerón was born in Toledo on 6 September 1515. His parents were from two small villages near Toledo, Alfonso from Olias, and Maria Diaz from Magano.[3] Salmerón had at least one brother and two sisters.[4] He did his early schooling at Toledo. Then he moved when he was about twelve years old to the new university at Alcalá, where he underwent what was perhaps the most formative intellectual influence of his life.[5]

The Spanish Biblical and Cultural Renaissance

Spain was then at the high tide of a cultural renaissance. Rising from the cultivated court of Juan II of Castile (1419–54), this intellectual revival flowed steadily and widely until the close of the sixteenth century. Schools evoked a love for cultivating beautiful Latin and for speaking it with ease and grace; people cultivated "romance," the beautiful language of Castile; scholars opened the doors to Italian humanistic influences with translations of Boccacio; savants cultivated archaeology, philosophy, and classical philology. The Spanish universities welcomed these new currents, and printing presses, the first of which was established at Zaragoza in 1475, spread the fresh inquiring spirit throughout the peninsula.[6]

Closely entwined with this vigorous and popular humanism was a movement of spiritual renewal. Exactly thirty years before Salmerón's birth, Micer Gonzalo de Santo Maria published at Zaragoza a Castilian translation of the Gospels and Epistles for Sundays and feasts.[7] In 1502 and 1503 Ambrosio Montesino, a Franciscan, issued in Alcalá a Castilian version of *The Life of Christ (Vita Christi)* of Ludolph the Saxon, a work which by

150

reason of its dependence on the Gospels spread wide knowledge of the New Testament throughout Spain. Montesino, in 1512, widened this movement of popularization with his Castilian translation of the Gospels and Epistles used in the liturgical year.[8] The Spanish soul was familiar with the gospels.[9]

Into this brisk and learned setting stepped influential churchmen who assessed the new intellectual and spiritual movements as valuable instruments for elevating the tone of the clergy. Hernando de Talavera, Hieronymite confessor of Queen Isabella, pressed this viewpoint with the queen. Cardinal Pedro González de Mendoza of Toledo—quite notorious for his scandalous private life—gave munificently to the creation of a cultivated clergy.[10] Isabella responded positively, and one of the marks of the Isabelline Reform Movement was its openness to the fresh cultural and spiritual forces within the realm.[11] The queen made her most valuable contribution to this cause by her appointment in 1492 of an austere Franciscan to replace Talavera as her confessor and by her designation in 1495 of this same friar to succeed Cardinal Mendoza in the see of Toledo. This Franciscan, who became the dominant figure of the Spanish Renaissance, was Francisco Jiménez de Cisneros.[12]

Influence of Francisco Jiménez de Cisneros

Two achievements crowned Cisneros's rule as archbishop of Toledo: the foundation of the University of Alcalá, and the printing of the landmark Alcalá polyglot Bible. With these two achievements Spanish humanism came of age.[13] The University of Alcalá: as early as April 1499 Pope Alexander VI issued a bull authorizing the foundation at Alcalá of "a college for students taught by the faculties of theology, canon law, and arts."[14] Cisneros implemented the bull in stages. On 26 July 1508 some 500 persons gathered in solemn assembly in the Church of Santiago in Alcalá to signal the formal opening of the new university. Cisneros called the institution the Colegio de San Ildefonso. Gradually he added some eighteen other colleges.[15]

To this organism Cisneros gave a distinctive orientation that set it off from the medieval universities at Salamanca and Valladolid: a strong emphasis on the biblical languages, Hebrew, Greek, Latin. Although he set up chairs of theology, Thomist,

Scotist, and nominalist, he insisted that biblical and patristic learning permeate the university. Explicitly he forbade the study of civil law. Canon law he permitted only as a complement to theology. The Cisneros touch stood out in the august solemnity with which the university celebrated the feast days of St. Jerome, St. Augustine, St. Ambrose, and St. Gregory.[16] The primate, however, did not live to see the inception of the college that was to become the finest expression of his educational aspirations at Alcalá. The Colegio Trilingüe, organized around the three chairs of the Latin, Greek, and Hebrew languages, did not open until 1528, nine years after Cisneros's death.[17] Under the rector, Mateo Pascual Catalan, this freshest of colleges provided scholarships for some thirty students, twelve in Latin, twelve in Greek, and seven in Hebrew.[18]

The second notable achievement of Cisneros was the publication of the internationally acclaimed *Alcalá Polyglot Bible (Biblia Polyglota Complutenese)*. Cisneros brought to his position as Primate of Spain a love of biblical studies that went back in years at least as far as the 1480s in Sigüenza, where he had been vicar general of that diocese. Once installed as primate at Toledo, he organized about himself a small Bible academy. After the arrival of the printer Brocario in Alcalá, Cisneros began, in 1510, the work of collecting manuscripts for a new edition of the Bible. He assembled a band of distinguished scholars, the Hellenists Demetrius Ducas and Diego Lopez de Zuñiga, the Hebraists Alfonso de Zamora and Pablo Coronel, and the finest of Spanish humanists, Antonio de Nebrija, who, in the words of a contemporary, "amongst us restored the Latin language and humane learning which for many years had almost been extinguished in Spain."[19]

This "monument of eternal glory to the Colegio de San Ildefonso" guaranteed biblical scholarship the ascendancy at Alcalá. It gave the university a unique position in the rebirth of learning in Spain and set it apart from the older universities born in scholasticism. Cisneros had at hand his most effective weapon in his campaign to break the grip of ignorance on Spain.[20]

Impact of Desiderius Erasmus

In 1516, two years after the completion of the Alcalá New Testament, a Spanish pen for the first time traced at some length the significance of the name of Erasmus. Spain in the midst of her own biblical renaissance could not ignore the *Novum Intrumentum* of the Dutch humanist, and Abad de Husillos wrote about "the good theologian, gifted in Greek, Hebrew, and elegant Latin."[21] So were opened the gates to the importation from the north of Erasmus's spirit of learning, piety, and scholarship to intensify the native renaissance.

Ten years later, in 1526, the fame of Erasmus the biblical scholar was enhanced by the renown of Erasmus the spiritual writer. That year a Spanish translation of *A Manual of the Christian Soldier (Enchiridion Militis Christiani)* appeared in Alcalá. The translator wrote exultantly to Erasmus: "At the court of the emperor, in the towns, in the churches, in the monasteries, even in the inns and on the roads, everyone has the *Enchiridion* of Erasmus."[22] Through the decade 1516–26, Erasmus was the subject of sharp debates that enlivened the academic community at Alcalá. The Dutchman's popularity reached its peak between 1527 and 1530.[23]

The debates that Erasmus occasioned were part of a very fluid situation in Spain as various styles of spiritual practice succeeded one another in rapid order.[24] Around 1500 one prevalent devotion centered on the Passion of Christ and on the imaginative representations of scenes from the Passion. About 1520 a distinctly different form of spirituality emerged to push aside devotion to Christ's humanity and the imaginative recollection of his Passion. This form had two expressions, one, that of the *dejados*, who in their spirit of self-abandonment to God concentrated on the divine gifts to men; and the second, the *recogidos,* who in their thirst for recollection turned to the contemplation of the divinity. The teachings of the *dejados* and the *recogidos* came to be dubbed Illuminism. In the mid-1520s these teachings impinged more and more sharply on the Spanish intellectuals. Then appeared Erasmus's *Manual of the Christian Soldier.* Erasmus brought his ethical and rational approach to bear on Christian teaching. His doctrine became grafted on the Illuminist tradition and communicated its own spiritual flavor.[25]

Student at the University of Alcalá

At an early age Alfonso Salmerón met the full rush of these

strong biblical, cultural, and spiritual streams. Around 1528, when only about thirteen years old, he enrolled at the University of Alcalá, at the moment of Erasmus's highest popularity.[26] Among the first students at the newly established Colegio Trilingüe, endowed with three chairs of Latin, Greek, and Hebrew, and placed upon the patronage of St. Jerome, the patron of scriptural scholars, Salmerón found himself completely at home in the study of the Latin and Greek classics.[27] He had an exceptional memory. To the wonder of his fellow students, he could recite entire orations of the classical authors. Recognized as one of the outstanding students in the university, he took the top prizes with ease.[28]

Years later Bernadine Realino, who knew Salmerón in Italy, remarked that Salmerón's memory was the best he had ever encountered.[29] And Bartolomé Perez de Nueros, who worked closely with Salmerón in his writing projects, wrote:

> When I reflect on his sermons, replete with theological doctrine, permeated with scriptural concepts and breathing a spirit of holiness, I am at a loss to discover when he found the time to study, except to say that the Lord, having given him the most tenacious memory of any man I have known, communicated a great deal to him in a short time. With the greatest of ease he retained the Latin and Greek poets he read many years ago. So much so, that at the least suggestion he used to recite for us whole passages in Latin and Greek as if he had just learned them.[30]

Although Salmerón had not begun his theological studies at Alcalá—he had done at least some philosophy—he thoroughly imbibed the university's enthusiasm for biblical and theological studies. At this early stage in his life, he set his eyes on the star of scriptural learning and never deviated from that course. As an old man he wrote: "I avow that from my youth I was strongly inflamed with the love for these divine and sacred studies, and that compared to these the other intellectual disciplines seemed mean."[32] Within the entire corpus of Scripture, the Gospels absorbed him most. For him the Gospels were the kernel and compendium of all the sacred writings; the key that opens an inexhaustible thesaurus of spiritual strength; a splendid sun, bathing with its radiance the Old Testament; our daily bread and an inexhaustible fountain for the relief of our hunger and thirst; a sea of God's immense wisdom.[33] In his last years, when he endeavored to write an extended commentary on the Holy Scriptures, he justified his enterprise, despite the existence of many old and recent treatises: "So lofty and rich are the Sacred Scriptures that there ever remains for those who come after matter for reflection and writing.[34]

Whether Salmerón formed a firm judgment on Erasmus during his years at Alcalá is not clear. Within a few years, however, he would do so. And in a most strenuous way, as shall be seen.

The Move to Paris

Alcalá gave Salmerón not only a distinctive intellectual orientation. It gave him a lifelong friend, Diego Laynez, from the little Castilian town of Almazán. Laynez, three years older than Salmerón, made a brilliant record at Alcalá.[35] When he stood for his master's examination on 26 October 1532, of the twenty-three candidates, he, in the estimation of all, merited the first place. Official chicanery, however, denied him this honor and placed him third on the list. The university authorities gave the first place to the son of the royal treasurer, and the second place to some other favorite.[36] Laynez, with a quiet smile ever playing about his mouth, large aquiline nose and lively eyes, became Salmerón's fastest friend.[37]

Some time during his stay at Alcalá, Laynez began to think about continuing his studies at Paris. For some reason or other, he also wanted to meet Iñigo de Loyola, about whom he heard so much dispute, and who by this time had left Spain and had enrolled at the University of Paris. Salmerón decided to join Laynez, and so in 1533 the two traveled together northward into the land of the fleur-de-lys. Great was their astonishment when, awed and uncertain, they dismounted in the Latin Quarter of the great French capital to discover that the first person whom they met was no other than Iñigo de Loyola. Iñigo found lodging for them at Collège Ste.-Barbe, where they met Iñigo's close friends, Favre, Bobadilla, and Rodrigues.[38]

Francis Xavier was yet to join the intimate circle of Iñigo's friends even though they had known each other at least four years. Since their first meeting at Collège Ste.-Barbe in 1529, Xavier tended to make sport of Iñigo's aspirations. In his high-spirited way he had decided to become a priest, but a priest for whom the way would be open to honor and affluence.[39] In 1530 he left the

Collège Ste.-Barbe and took up residence at Collège de Beauvais as a regent. In 1531 he sought official confirmation of his nobility and a canonical benefice at the cathedral of Pamplona. Iñigo's rejections of riches and public esteem he found ludicrous and made it a target of jests.[40] In the Latin Quarter he met Salmerón and Laynez, and when he learned that they had come to Paris to find Iñigo, he twitted them for their folly.[40]

Despite Xavier's banter, relations between him and Iñigo remained amiable enough. Iñigo, for example, ventured to advise Xavier to follow the theological lectures of the Dominicans rather than those of the royal theologians. Xavier took this advice. In the spring of 1533, certainly by June, a change occurred in Xavier's attitudes. Disenchanted with his quest for prestige and wealth, he embraced Iñigo's ideals and entered the intimate circle of his friends.[41] Salmerón was close at hand to witness the spiritual conversion of one of the greater apostles in the history of the Catholic Church.

Religious and Intellectual Growth

Soon Salmerón and Laynez discovered that Iñigo had certain aspirations about the following of Christ in poverty, in chastity, and in labor for his cause in the Holy Land. Under Iñigo's direction they made the Spiritual Exercises, a most formative period in their young lives, as they persevered through the thirty days of prayer and discernment under one of the greatest mystics in the history of the Catholic Church. They finished with the determination that Iñigo's ideals would be their own.[42] And on 15 August 1534 they sealed their aspirations in a simple ceremony in the chapel of St. Denis on the side of Montmartre. In the morning of that mild summer day, Salmerón and Laynez joined Iñigo de Loyola, Francis Xavier, Nicholás Bobadilla, Simão Rodrigues, and Pierre Favre in a small crypt of the chapel and there, as described in the essay on Jay, they made a commitment to follow Christ in poverty and chastity, and to make a pilgrimage to the Holy Land.

Paris was therefore a turning point in Salmerón's religious life. It also opened the door to a rich intellectual experience. On 3 October 1536, under the tutelage of Master Francis Xavier, Salmerón received his Master of Arts degree.[43] By that time he had also finished a year and a half of study in the theology faculty of the University of Paris.[44] In three special ways Paris deepened the well of Salmerón's intellectual experience: it gave him an esteem for scholastic philosophy and theology; it enriched his predilection for scriptural studies; and it alerted him to the wide diversity among the scholars of the Northern Humanism.

Scholastic Philosophy and Theology

First, an esteem for scholastic philosophy and theology: the order, clarity, and intellectual discipline of these studies made a lasting impression.[45] Salmerón's esteem for them fitted neatly within the broader framework of his basic attitude of respect for intellectual skills, which, if wisely used, could, he felt, add to the beauty of the Church.[46] He recognized God's initiative in the life of faith. "To receive faith and to gain eternal life," Salmerón wrote, "Christ alone, without human learning, be it Aristotle's or Plato's, is sufficient. This is so because faith is infused by God alone revealing himself. And by him alone is this faith increased and brought to perfection."[47] Yet Salmerón readily recognized the contribution that human learning can make. "Even though the branches of human knowledge cannot beget faith," he continued, "they do create dispositions for the reception of faith, as is evidenced in the examples of Justin Martyr and Augustine. The former by reading the thought of Plato, and the latter by reading a dialogue of Cicero were moved to set heresy aside and embrace the faith."[48] Intellectual skills can be splendid ornaments in the Church.

Among these skills Salmerón gave a high place to scholastic theology, which he regarded as partly divine and partly human: divine because it feeds upon the heavenly given Holy Scriptures and finds in them its principles; human because by the light of natural reason it reaches many conclusions deduced from the Sacred Writings.[49] Focusing on the basically disputatious nature of scholastic theology, "dialectical theology" (*theologia disputatrix*), Salmerón advanced the unusual viewpoint that it had its origins in Christ. As a boy Christ engaged the Jewish teachers in the Temple in questioning and answering them; as a man he frequently encountered the Scribes and Pharisees in debate. And in the early Church Stephen and Paul were "distinguished disputants" (*egregii disputatores*).[50] To continue what was started by

157

Christ, was carried on in the early Church, and in later centuries was continued by Augustine, John Damascene, Bonaventure, Peter the Lombard, Albert the Great, and Alexander of Hales had for Salmerón a positive value.[51]

Growth in Scriptural Learning

Second, Salmerón's years at Paris deepened his predilection for biblical studies. When Iñigo introduced Salmerón and Laynez to the College Ste.-Barbe on their arrival in Paris, he brought them into immediate contact with that particular mold of Christian Humanism that was stamped with the biblical, patristic, and mystical fervor associated with Jacques Lefèvre d'Etaples.[52] And as was seen in the life of Claude Jay, Iñigo himself encouraged the study of what was beginning to be called positive theology, a theology permeated with the spiritual and affective genius of the church fathers. In this setting, Salmerón's predilection for the Scriptures reached new depths. His study of the Bible through the eyes of the Christian writers of earlier centuries gave him resources on which he drew to fill his scriptural commentaries with wide-ranging references to their works. His Spanish commitment to scriptural studies broadened, therefore, in France to embrace a love of patristic and mystical learning.

This comprehensive grasp of Christian learning distinguished Salmerón from the other Spanish scholars of the day who were as avid as he for scriptural scholarship.[53] Melchior Cano, Domingo Soto, Diogo de Paiva de Andrade, Alfonso de Castro marched in the same rank as Salmerón in their dedication to the Scriptures. But they fell behind him in the cultivation of patristic learning. And this patristic orientation was a Parisian thing.[54] In Salmerón's intellectual growth Paris gave the increase to what Alcalá had watered.

A Union of Scholasticism and Scriptural Learning

In a still further way Paris and Alcalá met in concord within the mind of Salmerón: in the entente between his keen skill in scholastic dialectics and his wide erudition in scriptural studies. Neither contended with the other. This entente meant that Salmerón declined to make a total commitment to the Christian Humanism as delineated by Lefèvre. As seen in the life of Claude Jay,

Lefèvre contemned scholastic theology. Salmerón embraced it.
Lefèvre defined theology as "wisdom" (*sapientia*); Salmerón, as
"a science" (*scientia*).[55] Noël Beda, ardent champion of scholasticism, thundered loudly against the weak theological structure of
Lefèvre. Derisively he called him "a humanist trying to be a
theologian" (*humanista theologizans*).[56] Salmerón, in contrast, to
his credit might aptly be called "a theologian at ease in the role of
the humanist" (*theologus humanitizans*) He embraced the finest
of humanistic values; he made his own the strong scholastic structure of clear and precise theological thinking. A decade later, at
the Council of Trent, he gave an impressive demonstration in
several addresses of logically ordered argument and close famil-
iarity with the Bible. Scholastic methodology and scriptural scholarship were intertwined in the weaving of a tough intellectual
texture. And all expressed in lucid and limpid Latin.

Salmerón and Erasmus

Third, Salmerón's studies at Paris widened his awareness of
the various nuances within the Northern Renaissance: the religious
fervor of Lefèvre, with which he partially identified himself; the
scorn of François Rabelais; the philological stress of Guillaume
Budé; the doctrinal ambiguity of Erasmus.[57] The last bothered
Salmerón through the years. Bluntly he accused Erasmus of "the
offense of fence-straddling" (*crimen neutralitatis*).[58] He elaborated this indictment: the slippery faith of the Dutch scholar made
it impossible to place him on the Catholic side or on the heretics'
side; his annotations on the New Testament, in which he scarcely
acknowledged the divinity of Christ, "did severe damage to God's
Church "(*magnum ecclesiae Dei negotium facesserunt*).[59] With
this indictment Salmerón was identifying a pervasive mood that
was abroad in that age, a mood for the relativization of dogma, for
the preferment of peace to doctrinal truth, and for that *via media*
that can affirm without deciding. Erasmus was the most eloquent
spokesman of that mood.[60] This Salmerón could not abide. He
explicitly endorsed an opinion current at that time, that Luther had
hatched the eggs that Erasmus had laid.[61]

To the *crimen neutralitatis* Salmerón added another indictment against Erasmus: The Dutchman's erosion of the moral climate at Paris. In a number of Erasmus's works he found much that

could readily incite youth to vice. At the university he heard catchy tags that responded to the corrosive message of Erasmus. One focused on the Dutchman's *Colloquia*. Students took from St. Paul's First Epistle to the Corinthians (1:15) the phrase: "Evil conversations corrupt good manners" (*corrumpunt mores bonos colloquia mala*), substituted the word *Erasmi* for *mala*, and produced the rendition "The *Colloquies* of Erasmus corrupt good manners" (*corrumpunt mores bonos Colloquia Erasmi*).[62] A second tag was directed at Erasmus's *Praise of Folly* (*Encomium Moriae*). It ran "*Folly* is the death of youth; *Folly* deserves to die" (*Moria mors juvenum*; *moria digna mori*). Salmeron recalled that people sang this "not inelegantly."[63] Books of this kind, to his way of thinking, deserved but one fate: the flames. Salmeron, therefore, cast one of the most articulate spokesmen for reform in the role of a destroyer of reform.

Iñigo de Loyola and Erasmus

Salmeron's acerbic judgment indurated Iñigo's personal reservations about Erasmus.[64] Iñigo had come to Paris with an antipathy for Erasmus, an antipathy based on devotional rather than doctrinal grounds.[65] It went back a decade, to Spain. As early as 1524–26, when he studied at Barcelona, Iñigo on the advice of friends took up the *Manual of the Christian Soldier* in order to improve his Latin and to derive spiritual benefit. He did not finish the work. He found that it chilled God's spirit within him and that gradually, it extinguished the fervor of his devotion. Later, at Alcalá during 1526–27, when his confessor, Manual Miona, urged him to read the book, he refused because Erasmus had come under the fire of authorities in the Church.[66] Internal experience and external authority molded within Iñigo's mind a suspicion of Erasmus.

Iñigo by this time had wide experience in the spiritual attractions and revulsions within his soul, and he had developed an acute sensitivity to what drew him to God and to what repelled him. In the *Enchiridion* he encountered, even in the pages in which Erasmus drew a glowing picture of Christ, a spiritual ambience that was heavily ethical, rational, and dotted with ambiguous expressions.[67] He detected the absence of that ringing call to heroic magnanimity which many modern historians, save a few like David

Knowles and Hugo Rahner, have not fully appreciated. Knowles, with his delicate sensitivity to the spiritual dimensions in history, wrote of Erasmus:

> Erasmus, in this respect resembling an Abélard or a Newman, is one of those men of genius whose complex minds present so many facets that any summary judgment stands self-condemned, and any precise label can at once be criticized. With Erasmus, also, as with Newman again or with Cicero, the marvelous style acts as a charm; while he is speaking to us, all criticism is stilled; he has won us, and we cannot believe that the mind of the master is less sincere than his voice, or that his arguments are less adequate than his language. He is so sane, so persuasive, so humane, that it is only with an effort that we can bring ourselves to examine his words for their implications, their ambiguities, and their failure in direct assertion. . . The 'philosophy of Christ,' which he preached in the *Enchiridion* and in the *Commentaries* and in many another work, is one in which a wide culture and a humanistic moral outlook form the basis of a life modelled on the gospel teaching presented in a purely human fashion. It is a persuasive, seductive ideal, and Erasmus never denies the need of divine illumination and help for the man who is to live a Christian life, nor does he omit to tell of the price that has been paid by the Son of God on behalf of mankind. Nevertheless, it is impossible to feel satisfied that the theology and ascetical teaching of Erasmus adequately recognize the wholly supernatural plane on which the life of Christ moved, and to which the life of the Christian is potentially elevated by baptism, and joined in fullness by the Holy Eucharist—a life which implies depths of love and wisdom and of redemptive suffering of which the unaided human mind could not dream and to which the unaided human will could not attempt to attain. . . .
>
> His religious ideal, though presented with all the seductive charm of reasonable argument and salted wit and grace of language, is a kind of 'low-tension' Christianity, a de-spiritualized religion, that has been well called by a sensitive modern critic the 'modernism' of Erasmus, and it was this that spread far and wide in all the cultivated circles of north-western Europe in the two decades that immediately preceded the papal condemnation of Luther.[68]

Hugo Rahner attributed to this kind of spiritual criticism a basic role in Iñigo's judgment of Erasmus. He felt that Iñigo, with his sensitive spiritual taste and instinct, detected in Erasmus the absence of something that was essential to his own mentality: the role of the visible Church in man's sanctification.[69] Mark Rotsaert chose to press the divergence between Iñigo and Erasmus to the deeper level of personal experience. Their differences did not emerge so much on the level of spiritual and theological ideas.

Indeed, between Iñigo and the Spanish translation of the *Enchiridion*, which Iñigo had picked up, there was in many points, a parallelism of ideas. The basic diversity penetrated to the deeper level of the spiritual experience felt by Ignatius at the time of his conversion. It was a diversity of intense quality.[70]

The conclusion that Iñigo reached in Spain by interior discernment Salmerón came to by theological study. In the intimacy of their friendship Salmerón, who had a wider scholarly knowledge of Erasmus than Iñigo, fortified Iñigo in his view. So did Jay, who with an asperity foreign to him called Erasmus a pagan.[71] In the University of Paris influential men censured Erasmus. On 7 July 1531, three years after Iñigo had arrived there, the theological faculty of the Sorbonne published its censure of a hundred opinions taken by Noel Beda from Erasmus's *Paraphrases* and *Elenchus*.[72] Theology and spiritual discernment combined to diffuse an anti-Erasmian ambience in the Ignatian group.

Early Experiences in Italy

The Paris experience of three years was therefore of supreme moment in the spiritual and intellectual formation of the young Salmerón, for the *Spiritual Exercises* and the university fixed his mind and heart on the lodestar that guided him through the remaining fifty years of his life. From 1536, when Iñigo's friends left Paris at the outbreak of hostilities between France and the Hapsburgs, until 1541, when he was assigned to a papal mission to Ireland, Salmerón shared in the experiences of the little group as described in the essay on Claude Jay. With his friends he cared for the sick in the hospitals of Venice; made the exhausting pilgrimage to Rome over rain soaked roads; debated in the presence of Pope Paul III in the Castel Sant' Angelo; received Paul's approbation for ordination to the priesthood.

The day of ordination brought the one striking exception to Salmerón's participation in the common experience of his friends. On 24 June 1537, when Bishop Vincenzo Nigusanti raised to the priesthood Iñigo, Xavier, Rodrigues, Laynez, Bobadilla and Codure, Salmerón could not join them. Paul III's authorization of ordination included the following clause: ''And you, Alfonso, may be raised to the priesthood as soon as you have begun your twenty-third year.''[73] Salmerón was then two and a half months short of that age. Nevertheless he worked out with his friends the plans for three months of special preparation for their first masses, the first forty days to be spent in absolute solitude, and the rest to include some preaching. Iñigo chose Xavier as Salmerón's companion. Their destination: Monselice.[74]

At Monselice Xavier and Salmerón found shelter in the small and deserted Church of San Giorgio, which stood on a slope that overlooked the parapets of Monselice's city wall. There they slept on straw; there through the night they suffered the torments of mosquitoes. Each day they begged their food from door to door. After the forty days of strict solitude, they added preaching to their program of prayer and penance.[75] Almost two months earlier, on 5 July, the priests of the Ignatian group received authorization to preach from Girolamo Verallo, the cardinal legate *a latere* to Venice. Salmerón alone lacked hat authorization.[76] But at the end of August, when he and Xavier had finished their period of strict contemplative living, he received a document from Gasparo de Dotti, Veralli's vicar-general, which read in part:

> Since it has been requested in your name, Alfonso Salmerón, my dearest son in Christ, that you, who have only been ordained a deacon, and since I know your zeal for the honor of God, your own soul, and that of your neighbor, and realize that you are a good son, learned and Catholic, I can only rejoice at this. We therefore grant you with the present letter the permission to preach the word of the Lord publicly and privately to the people in the territory of Venice. . . . Therefore I have desired to write this with my own hand so that the matter may be more quickly accomplished, and also to indicate that I know you personally and am fully informed about you.[77]

This document was the first official approval of Salmerón for work that was to be the most distinctive of his long life. Salmerón more than anything else was a man of the pulpit. He began his preaching experience at Monselice in the oddest kind of style, the same style adopted by his friends at Vicenza, Verona, Bassano, and Treviso. They took to the public squares; they stood on benches borrowed from an inn or a house; they waved their hats; they shouted their invitation to the people to listen; they gave their sermons in a mixture of Spanish, French, Latin, and Italian. Iñigo wanted to say: Today Holy Mother Church. The French *aujourd' hui* blended with the Italian *offi* and fell from his lips as *hojuordi.*[78] Bobadilla desired to say: I am telling you good and pious things; I shall bring you good wares. If you do not wish to hear, depart.'' His mixture of Latin and Italian created the following: *ego dico vobis bona et pia; io portero robba buona, si non vultis audire, abite.*[79] Many people could not comprehend this babel of tongues; some thought that they were jugglers who had come to town. But somehow their sincerity and spiritual dedication came through the garbled words. After about three weeks of this singular program, Iñigo summoned his friends to Vicenza, which was a day's walk from Monselice. Iñigo realized that the pilgrimage to the Holy Land was impossible because of Venice's entrance on 13 September into the imperial-papal alliance against the Turks. He and his friends had to make fresh decisions about their future.[80]

Salmerón shared in these decisions at Vicenza: first, to identify their brotherhood (*compañía*) as the *Society of Jesus (Compañía de Jesús)*, since Christ Jesus was their only head; and second, to scatter to university towns in north and central Italy and there preach, give the Spiritual Exercises, try to recruit new members for the Society, until Iñigo, who planned to go to Rome with Laynez and Favre, would summon them in the following spring of 1538. By mid-October they were ready to separate. Iñigo assigned Salmerón to Siena. His companion was Broët.[81]

Before Salmerón left Vicenza, he planned for his ordination to the priesthood in Venice. On 6 September he had had his twenty-second birthday. He first returned to Monselice for a short period, perhaps two weeks, of quiet prayer. Broët joined him.[82] Sometime late in October or early in November he was ordained.[83] Then he and Broët headed for Siena.

At Siena they received a most cordial welcome.[84] Giovanni di Lorenzo degli Alessandrini, a man deeply cultivated in art and literature, welcomed them to his home. They began to preach at the Loggia della Mercanzia. Increasing crowds forced them to move to the more ample Piazzo del Campo. There, in their strange mixture of Latin, Spanish, French, and Italian, they spoke daily to the people whose Italian was the purest in the entire peninsula. They taught catechism; they heard confessions. Patrons in the city saw to it that the itinerant preachers lacked nothing in the way of food and lodging.[85]

Experiences in Rome

In mid-April word from Iñigo reached the members of the Society scattered in the north to join him at Rome. Jay and Bobadilla left Ferrara, stopped at Bologna to pick up Xavier, then made for Siena. Here they met Salmerón and Broët, whom they had not seen in six months.[86] The party, now five in number, continued southward, and around Easter, which was 21 April, Salmerón and his friends entered Rome and found Iñigo, Laynez, and Favre at the villa of "the exceedingly magnanimous gentleman" (*molto magnifico Signore*) Quirino Garzonio, the first home of the Society of Jesus in Rome.[87]

In Rome Salmerón did as his friends through 1528–41. He preached; he heard confessions; he counselled; he cared for the poor; he participated in the debates that led to the decision to transform their *Society of Jesus* into a religious order. During the fifteen months of suspense before Pope Paul III issued the bull of approbation of the Society on 27 September 1540, he lectured at the Sapienza, the University of Rome.[88] He also began a work in which he excelled: guiding persons through the Spiritual Exercises. Ignatius judged that of the first Jesuits Salmerón was second only to Favre as a retreat master.[89] During this early Roman period of Jesuit history, Salmerón and Jeronimo Domenech were the two principal directors of the Spiritual Exercises.[90] One of Salmerón's more influential retreatants during 1541 was Luis de Avila, a Spaniard who soon entered the Jeronimites, became a propagandist for the Exercises in his own convent at Talavera and in other Jeronimite communities throughout Spain. To these he sent copies of Ignatius's manual.[91]

In April 1541 Salmerón participated in the election in which Ignatius was chosen as the Society's first superior general. Even in this juridical act, Salmerón's love of the scriptures broke forth in language filled with biblical imagery. His ballot also demonstrated a personal frailty: his verbosity. What Broët said in a single declarative sentence, Salmerón said in a long, tortured statement that has to be broken up for translation.

> In the name of Jesus Christ. Amen. I, Alfonso Salmerón, a most unworthy member of the Society, after prayer to God and mature reflection

on whom I should make my choice, vote for as my superior and superior of the whole Society Ignatius of Loyola, who, just as with his God-given wisdom he generated us all in Christ and fed us when we were children with milk, so now will lead us, grown-ups as we now are in Christ, by the solid food of obedience, and will guide us into the sweeter and richer pastures of paradise and to the fountain of life. I cast this vote with a view to that time when as he [Ignatius] renders this little flock to Jesus Christ, the great Shepherd, we shall be able truthfully to say: *we are the people of his pasture and the sheep of his hand*, and he shall be able joyfully to exclaim: *Lord, of those you have given me I have lost not a one*. May Jesus Christ, the Good Shepherd, deign to grant this to us. This is my judgment. Alfonso Salmerón.[92]

Salmerón's Personality

To the creation of the Society of Jesus, Salmerón brought not only a keen intelligence and a prodigious memory; he had powerful physical energy and a vast capacity for work. Of medium height, he had a strong, well-built body.[93] He was a likable youth, open, candid, without trace of pretense. Iñigo enjoyed his unaffected simplicity and joked about it.[94] Through Salmerón's lively, penetrating eyes there radiated the freshness and innocence of a delightful person.[95] He was the Benjamin of the first Jesuits. When Iñigo and his six companions went to the chapel of St. Denis on Montmartre on 15 August 1534 to pronounce their vows to live lives of poverty and chastity and to go to the Holy Land, Salmerón was nineteen years old. In June 1537, when Iñigo, Xavier, Laynez, Rodrigues, Bobadilla, and Codure were ordained priests in Venice, Salmerón had to wait because he had not yet begun his twenty-third year. Even when Salmerón was thirty years old, Claude Jay, it seems, could not break the habit of instinctively thinking of him as a mere youngster. At Ingolstadt, Jay, as has been seen, in reply to a request of Ignatius for the recommendation of some fellow Jesuits for the work of teaching in Germany, expressed his preference for Laynez and Salmerón, but with a note of caution in regard to the latter: "providing his youthfulness (*juvenilis aetas*) would not compromise his authority with the German scholars.[96] And two years later, when on 26 October 1547 Ignatius wrote to Rodrigues about possible appointees to the post of patriarch of Ethiopia, he ruled out Salmerón, since "he was, to all appearances, such a young and beardless fellow" (*y esta quasi tan moco y sin barbas*).[97]

Assignment to Ireland

When the cascade of individual assignments to work outside Rome fell upon Ignatius' group in the period 1539–41, Salmerón received a challenging mission. On 1 February Pope Paul instructed him to join Jean Codure on a mission to Ireland as papal legate.[98] Reports from Ireland had made the pope anxious for the faith of the people in that remote island on the other side of schismatical England. The English built up a corpus of legislation that, in its application to Ireland, aimed at the mastery of the Catholic church in that country. The Act of Supremacy (1534), the Ten Articles (1536), Thomas Cromwell's Injunctions to the Clergy (1536), and his New Injunctions (1538) followed in rapid order. The suppression of the religious houses in Ireland began in 1535. The Scots archbishop of Armagh, Robert Wauchop, in exile from his diocese, urged the Holy See to demonstrate its solicitude for the Irish by a special mission of Jesuits.[99]

Pope Paul III turned to Ignatius in early 1540, but two years passed before the mission got under way. Initially Jean Codure and Francesco Marsupino, a secular priest from Arezzo and a doctor of canon and civil law (*utriusque legis*), were assigned in March, 1540.[100] Marsupino withdrew from the mission, and in February of the following year Salmerón was directed to take his place. Then Codure became seriously ill and died on 29 August 1541. Paschase Broët succeeded him.[101]

In the six months, from 1 February 1541 to 15 July, Pope Paul III issued at least ten official documents concerned with the mission of Broët and Salmerón to Ireland. Some were delineations of the legatine powers of the two Jesuits; some were letters of introduction and commendation, one directed to Cardinal David Beaton of St. Andrew's, one to King James V of Scotland, one to King Con Bacach O'Neill of Ultonia, one to the archbishops, bishops, and princes of Ireland, and one to the people of Ireland.[102] Finally, in the fall of 1541, Salmerón and Broët started northward, carrying a papal bull commissioning them to "bring back to the unity of the Catholic Church the leaders and the people who have left the sheepfold of Christ and to strengthen those who have remained faithful to the true faith of Christ.[103] They had as a companion one Francesco Zapata, a layman and aspirant to the Society.

At Lyons they met Cardinal David Beaton, archbishop of St. Andrew's and Primate of Scotland. If they had heeded the cardinal's words, they would have gone not a step farther. According to Beaton, Henry VIII had all the cities, towns, forts, and castles of Ireland securely under his thumb; there was hardly any Irish port without an English garrison; the Irish themselves were the wildest people alive, barbarous to an incorrigible degree.[104] Despite the gloomy reflections of Beaton, the legates pushed on to the French coast and sailed from Dieppe to a port in Flanders. Late in December they set out across the wild, cold sea for twenty unforgettable days. The winds were high, ships foundered and sunk, their own ship was twice driven into English ports and the suspicions of the English people were aroused. Salmerón reported to Ignatius, ''Although our dress was a bit in the Roman style, we managed to get through the difficulty by saying that we were Spaniards. And to give the appearance of authenticity we occasionally spoke Spanish, because in England people who come from Rome travel with great peril to their life.''[105] Because of the intense cold, Zapata's feet became swollen and covered with nasty sores. On the last day of 1541 they reached Edinburgh.

King James V and his queen, Mary of Guise, welcomed the legates most graciously. Some Scots at the court who had known Jesuits at Rome diffused an aura of good will by the highly complimentary things they had to say about Ignatius's group.[106] The monarchs asked the priests about their Society and placed at their disposal a guide named Farquhardson for their journey into Ireland. The natural apprehension that Salmerón and Broët felt in Rome as they prepared for their mission was only increased at Edinburgh. Some informants told them one thing, some another. Practically everybody, including Gavinus Dunbar, the archbishop of Glasgow, told them to stay away from Ireland. The French Ambassador, Jean de Morviller, who greatly esteemed the Society, went to the king and queen and urged them to forbid the Jesuits to continue their mission lest they endanger their lives. Three Irish priests on their way to Rome repeated almost verbatim the statements of Cardinal Beaton.[107]

In a quandary, Salmerón and Broët decided that they needed
more accurate information about the conditions in Ireland. While
Salmerón stayed at Edinburgh, Broët went to Glasgow in the hope
of making contact with Irish merchants. Unsuccessful at Glasgow,
he doffed his cassock, donned an Irish kilt, and went to the port of
Irvine, fifteen miles away.[108] There someone gave him a presumably
first hand report that was far less forbidding than anything
they had hitherto heard. Broët returned to Edinburgh, and the two
Jesuits decided, as Broët told Cardinal Cervini, ''to investigate the
island and its problems.[109]

The Irish Experience

Carrying letters of recommendation dated at Sterling 13 February
1542 from James V to the Hibernian chieftains, the two
Jesuits landed in Ulster on 23 February 1542. There they remained
for about thirty-four days. And a grim thirty-four days they were.
The two Jesuits felt immersed in violence, treachery, hatred, spiritual
desolation. ''In a short while,'' wrote Broët, ''we found
things just as was told us, if not worse.''[110]

The bewilderment of these visitors from Spain and France
was inevitable. Tangled issues that would have baffled the expertise
of a seasoned diplomat surrounded them. The Irish chieftains
were falling one after the other like a row of dominoes before the
king's deputy. The first to capitulate was Magillapatrick of Ossory.
With completeness he recognized the king of England as the
supreme head of the Church on earth. O'Connor of Offaly and
O'More of Leix soon followed. Just before Salmerón and Broët
arrived, two of the most powerful of the chiefs rejected the authority
of the pope: Manus O'Donnell, founder of the franciscan house
in Donegal, and Conn O'Neill, hailed by the bishop of Metz as
Ireland's champion of the faith.[111] The legates heard the story first
hand from the abbot of Derry how O'Donnell went down to Dublin
to see the king's deputy, made an alliance with his English Majesty,
recognizing him as the head in Ireland of things spiritual and
temporal and promising to turn over all apostolic legates who
might show up from Rome. O'Neill had even surrendered one of
his sons as hostage. A third influential chieftain, O'Brien from
Thormond, was expected to appear in Dublin after Easter and
follow in the abject train of his fellow leaders.[112]

These capitulations deceived Salmerón and Broët, who did not get beyond Mid-Ulster into the regions of Norman influence, or within even fifty miles of any walled town of the Old English. The highly visible breakdown of Catholic leadership in ecclesiastical and civil society distracted the two Jesuits from the deep feelings of loyalty among the people to the pope. The spectacle of wandering friars, turned out of their homes by the British, grieved the Irish. And it was the friars who kept the channels to Rome open. Even within the Pale, the new religious policies strained the old loyalties to the crown. This strain was to grow into, first, a mild obstructionism, then into violent opposition. Faced with latent hostility within the Pale, the British religious program encountered even deeper rejection in the borderlands, for in those Irish-speaking areas the English launched a simultaneous cultural program of anglicization in language and custom.[113]

These complications eluded the two amateur diplomats. What struck them was their immediate experience with feuds and immorality. Broët's report could hardly have been more disconsolate.

> Our main objective, according to the instructions we received from the very reverend cardinals, was to bend our efforts to the establishment of peace among the chiefs and lords of Ireland, so that in their unity they might the more vigorously resist the king, protect themselves, and even take the offensive, if need be, for the faith and the strengthening of obedience to the Apostolic See. We actually met some of the chiefs, such as MacQuillan and O'Cahen, and others. But our eyes were opened to the fact that the disease of internal strife in this country is a hopeless thing and, in our judgment, irremediable because of age-old hatreds as well as because of a savage and barbarous way of life, worse than bestial and hardly to be believed unless actually seen. Often these people, having become reconciled, establish peace. Then after a month they break their treaties. And then the latter situation becomes worse than the first. So they busy themselves in the plunder of each other's possessions, in the stealing of oxen, cows, and horses, in the burning of farm houses and churches. The man who is the more accomplished in the business of plunder enjoys the greater honor and distinction among them. . . . What does a kingdom amount to whose justice consists merely in piracy? In Ireland no punishment is meted out to culprits, murderers, robbers, the impure. When we asked some prelates why they did not punish the violators of purity in their dioceses, they replied that they were powerless in the absence of the secular arm to carry out the penalties for them. But what is worse, the leaders themselves, spiritual and lay, whose office it is to correct their subordinates, are infected with the same leprosy.[114]

Other somber details filled in the dismal Irish landscape on which Salmerón and Broët had to gaze. Monasteries were destroyed, English immigrants were taking over rich land, bishops faithful to Rome, such as those of Tuam and Kildare, were in hiding in the forests with their hopes pinned on the day when news would come of the death of Henry VIII.[115]

O'Donnell heard that Salmerón and Broët were in Ireland. Through the abbot of Derry he got word to them that he would like to see them, but they were to come to him secretly and on the quiet. He was afraid that the king's lieutenant might discover what he was about and charge him with violation of the treaty with England. The two Jesuits reneged at the idea of meeting in secret. Their stand was: let it be in the open or not at all, since their mission was a matter of public knowledge. So they never met O'Donnell.[116]

The mission was not entirely without consolation. The two priests heard some confessions, gave dispensations from illegitimacy and incest, imparted plenary indulgences. But, all in all, a month was enough to make them decide to retire from Ireland. On 9 April 1542 Salmerón wrote to Ignatius after he returned to Scotland: ''Aware of the small favor we had with the Irish chiefs, of their alliance with and obedience to the king of England, of the fact that no strong city or town was in Irish hands, of the scant hope of establishing peace among the Irish leaders, and at the same time recalling the command we received from the cardinals to return if we were not safe in Ireland, we turned back here to Scotland. . . .''[117]

The report of Salmerón and Broët was misleading. It lacked completeness, balance, and integrality. It omitted several important features in the Irish landscape. The two legates did not sound out the strong but hidden under current of religious fidelity behind the more spectacular show of capitulation to King Henry VIII; they did not sense the inherent weakness of the royal position within the Pale; they did not recognize the significance of the ties of fondness between the Irish people and the displaced friars. Unwittingly they sent the pope a report sadly tilted toward the sombre. But it was the work of tyros, raw and naive in the world of diplomacy. And they were on the spot for only thirty-four distracting days.

Return to Rome

In Rome Pope Paul III followed intently the progress of his two legates, and when he learned that they were spending some time in Scotland, he dispatched a brief, dated 27 March 1542, granting them the same faculties for Scotland that they enjoyed for Ireland.[118] But more than likely they had already left the land of the thistle before the brief arrived from Rome. Back on the continent, they cut across France. During those decades of the early Society, the soldiers of Francis I and Charles V became part of the scenery of western Europe, almost as much as the forests and rivers and hills. And it was a common experience for the first Jesuits, constantly on the road as they were, to encounter these military units of the ever-feuding Hapsburgs and Valois. At Lyons Salmerón and Bröet came to an abrupt halt. Soldiers of Francis I, taking no chances with the two strangers, especially when one was a Spaniard, clapped them into jail.[119]

Salmerón and Bröet surely never dreamed that their names would appear in a secret dispatch to King Henry VIII of England, to be preserved in the calendar of foreign state papers for the perusal of future historians. Yet the incident of their arrest, obscure and small as it was amid the tumult of sixteenth century diplomacy, did not escape the note of one of the most alert eyes of the English intelligence system on the continent. William Paget, member of Stephen Gardiner's household, trained in diplomacy by several embassies in Europe, became in 1543, a year after this incident, King Henry's principal secretary, and during the last four years of the monarch's reign one of his most intimate associates. Paget wrote from Lyons on 31 July 1542 to the King. Paget first wrote his dispatch in Latin and then followed it with an English translation:

> Iuvat totum hic anglice transcribere. There hath lately bin in yor Majesty's land of Ireland two Freres Spainardes sent thither by the Bishop of Rome to practise with O'Donnell against your Majesty. They passed through Scotland with letters of commendation to the King of the Scots. With them was sent for that purpose the Bishop of the Isles' brother, that is, Farquhard Farquhardson, which Bishop lyeth at Icolm Kille, between Scotland and Ireland. The two Spainardes and the Bishop's brother be arrived within these two days in this town on their return from Ireland, where, as they say, they have done no good, because the Scottish King kept not his

promise. And this confession have these two Freres made to the Lieutenant of this town, for here they were arrested for spies.—WILLIAM PAGET.[120]

The imprisonment of Salmerón and Bröet at Lyons was brief. Two cardinals, François Tournon and Nicolo Gaddi, recognized them and cleared their identity with the French authorities. The two Jesuits were released, given horses, and put on the road to Rome.[121] They arrived there in the late fall. For Salmerón, this month in Ireland remained like the memory of a terrifying dream, and in the years that followed, when he searched for a yardstick by which to measure how dreadful a particular experience had been, he had at hand the criterion of the Irish mission.[122]

A Clash with Cardinal Giovanni Morone

Salmerón's next assignment took him to Modena, by way of Ferrara. For four months, until April 1543, he and Bröet rested at Rome after the fatigue of more than a year on the road. Then Ignatius sent Bröet to Foligno at the request of the bishop, Blasio Palladio, for pastoral assistance. At Modena, the bishop, Cardinal Giovanni Morone, discovered that members of a literary circle were popularizing Lutheran doctrine in the city. He asked for Jesuit help.[124] Ignatius assigned Salmerón. Realizing that Modena was then under the jurisdiction of the duke of Ferrara, he ordered Salmerón to go first to Ferrara and there pay his respects to Duke Ercole. But he had more in mind than technical boundaries of jurisdiction. He recalled that Duke Ercole had put the Society in his debt with his influential help during the troubles that hounded him and his friends in Rome during 1538. Salmerón, therefore, made a courtesy call on Duke Ercole in Ferrara before he reached Modena.[125]

Salmerón's stay at Modena was extremely brief, and his departure unhappily abrupt. In August 1543, about four months after his arrival, he received orders from Ignatius to return to Rome. A rift had developed between the cardinal and his Jesuit preacher. Its cause: their disagreement on a point of Catholic doctrine. Salmerón had spoken forthrightly on the supernatural efficacy of good works in the economy of salvation. Morone objected. He took Salmerón aside and remonstrated with him. Salmerón retorted heatedly. Morone lost his patience. He made some unthinking statements. He remarked, for example, that even in offering mass he was committing sin. Salmerón challenged this idea. Morone actually meant to say that his personal distraction of spirit led to negligence and inattention at the altar. This was the sin, not the act of offering in itself. But essential distinctions of this kind were lost in the heat of high tempers. Morone banned Salmerón from the pulpit.[126]

This contretemps between Morone and Salmerón was one of the skirmishes before the grand scale battle at the Council of Trent between a theology that recognized the important place of man's good works in salvation and a theology that stressed "faith alone" (*fides sola*). Morone, like Pole, Flaminio, Giberti, Contarini, Priuli, and others of the "spiritual ones" (*spirituali*), felt the appeal of Luther' *sola fides* and feared any diminution of Christ's role in man's salvation.[127] Salmerón challenged the theology of the *spiritualii* at a moment when they had suffered serious setbacks. During the two previous years, Juan de Valdes and Gasparo Contarini died, and Bernard Ochino and Pietro Martyre Vermigli apostatized. The tide was running against them. Three years before the Council of Trent confirmed Salmerón's view on justification, he had heralded at Modena the direction that Catholic Reform spirituality was to take.

Ignatius, when he heard of the clash with Morone recalled Salmerón to Rome. He then requested Pope Paul III for an examination of Salmerón's orthodoxy. The innocence or fault of Salmerón he wanted clearly established. Paul, however, in deference to Morone's excellent reputation, directed that the matter be dropped.[128] Four years later, when Salmerón was again in northern Italy, Ignatius directed him to visit Morone and ask his pardon for any offense that he had given. The two men met at Bologna. Morone expressed genuine delight at Salmerón's visit, and made it clear that he had no grievance. Further, he encouraged the project of starting a Jesuit school at Modena.[129]

Preacher and Lecturer in Rome

Salmerón remained in Rome from the late summer of 1543 until the winter of 1546. Preaching and scriptural lectures occupied him most. Late in 1543 he gave the Advent course at the court of the imperial ambassador and this wife, Juan and Leonor de Vega.[130] In the fall of 1545 he delivered scriptural lectures three times a week on St. Paul's Epistle to the Ephesians at the Jesuit church of Santa Maria della Strada.[131] He also preached at the Roman church of Sant' Anna de' Folgenami, adjacent to the Benedictine convent of Sant' Anna dei Funari.

The reason Salmerón spoke at this particular church was the marchesa of Pescara, Vittoria Colonna. This cultivated poetess and devout woman, as was related in the portrait of Claude Jay, first met the Jesuits in the persons of Claude Jay and Simão Rodrigues in Ferrara in 1537. She went to Rome and gave her generous support to Ignatius' House of Santa Marta for prostitutes. In late 1544 she took up residence at the convent of Sant' Anna. There she and Michelangelo had long conversations about man's thirst for God. And there she wanted to have a Jesuit preacher. Insistently she asked Ignatius for one. And Ignatius assigned Salmerón.[132]

During most of this stay in Rome, Salmerón had the pleasure of being with his younger brother Didacus. Didacus, curious about his older brother's vocation and friends, left Toledo and went to Rome. There he made the Spiritual Exercises in July 1543 and requested admission into the Society.[133] When Alfonso returned from Modena in the late summer of that year, Didacus most likely had received his formal acceptance into the Society. Through two years he went through his novitiate in Rome. Then on 5 October 1545 he and Pedro Ribadeneyra travelled to Padua to pursue their university studies. Soon after, Alfonso received word that his brother had died on 1 November[134]. The year 1545, therefore, closed for Salmerón on this sorrowful personal note.

Assignment to the Council of Trent

In early 1546 Salmerón's life took a new turn. On 13 December 1545, at Trent, under the guidance of Cardinals Giammaria del Monte, Reginald Pole, and Marcello Cervini, what many Catholics regarded as the great need of that moment in the life of the Church, a general council, finally got under way. Two months later, in February 1546, Ignatius received orders from Pope Paul to send three of the Society to Trent.[135] Ignatius chose Diego Laynez, Pierre Favre, and Salmerón. When he dispatched Salmerón, he directed that, before going to Trent, he preach during Lent at Bologna.[136]

Bologna, a key city of northern Italy and seat of the Bentivo-gli family, was a natural strategic point for an energetic apostolate. Salmerón, in the confessional, in conversation and by his elo-quence in the pulpit, won the good graces of the city and spread the news of the new Society of Jesus. [137] Father Francesco Palmio, who with his brother Benedetto was one the first Italian young men attracted to the Society in Parma in 1539 by Pierre Favre and Diego Laynez, sent a glowing account of Salmerón's achieve-ments to Ignatius on 4 May 1546: large numbers heard with plea-sure Salmerón's sermons; on Sundays twenty- five to thirty people received holy communion; on the first Sunday of the month the number reached two hundred; "and day by day the numbers go up" (*et di giorno in giorno la casa si agomena*). [138] Members of an influential family, Andrea Casali and his sister Violante, im-pressed by Salmerón, became deeply devoted to the Society of Jesus. People in Bologna saw with regret Salmerón's departure on 4 May to join Laynez on his way to Trent. [139]

Summary

Two stamps left their indelible mark on Salmerón during this first period of his life. The University of Alcalá gave him his humanistic and biblical cast of mind, later widened by the theological traditions of Paris. Ignatius Loyola gave him the Jesuit thrust "to the greater glory of God" (*ad maiorem dei gloriam*) as a companion of Jesus. And two early missions revealed the tenor of his future life. Ireland and Modena adumbrated a life that would combine apostolic activity and learning. The man of erudition would be a man of affairs. The man of affairs would be a man of learning. The interplay between practical business and scholarship would be a constant in Salmerón's career.

CHAPTER VII

ITALY, GERMANY, POLAND, THE NETHERLANDS 1546–1556

Introduction

This chapter covers ten years of Salmerón's life, from 1546, when he went to the Council of Trent, to 1556, when he returned from a papal diplomatic mission to the Low Countries. These ten years brought a mixture of conciliar, pastoral, and diplomatic experience. During 1546–47 he was a papal theologian at the Council of Trent. From 1547 to 1549 he preached in northern Italy. From 1549 to 1550 he lectured in theology at the University of Ingolstadt in Bavaria. From 1551 to 1552 he again participated in the general council, this time at Bologna. From 1552 to 1555 he was at Naples, fully involved in fostering the new Jesuit college there, and from 1555 to 1556 he was a member of papal diplomatic missions to Poland and the Low Countries.

Introduction to the Council of Trent

On 18 May Salmerón and Laynez arrived at Trent. There they found their gentle friend Claude Jay, acting as theologian for

Cardinal Otto Truchsess, and Jean Couvillon, a Belgian Jesuit, theologian for Duke Wilhelm of Bavaria. They themselves entered the council as "papal theologians" (*missi papa*).[1] Technically they fell within the group called minor theologians," who were invested with a consultative, or advisory, vote. Their appointment did not give them the ultimately powerful deliberative vote.[2]

Some of the Spaniards at Trent made the men of the new and untraditional religious order feel distinctly ill at ease. Salmerón knew the temper of his countrymen and did not hesitate to speak of them as a more than ordinarily touchy people. "Some," he wrote Ignatius on 4 June, "show us their good will; others look on our work as something laughable; others who are more spiritual minded are on the defensive and voice their scruples and doubts about our Company. Some of these latter even try to pick a fight with us. . . . They are a cautious and difficult people and there is special need of God's grace to get along with them."[3]

The coolness of the Spanish bishops belied their intellectual competence, high moral quality, and sincere dedication to reform in the church. The Spaniards, theologians as well as bishops, excelled most of the others who went to the council Trent. Men of the quality of Juan Bernal Díaz de Luco, Bartolomé de Carranza, and Pedro Pacheco brought to the debates not only intellectual keenness but also "their own tradition of pastors modeled on the lines of the apostolic community and in direct antithesis to the rigid, centralized structures of the medieval Church represented in the Roman curia."[4] Their concept of reform, beginning at the head, threatened the Roman bureaucracy. And it was from the pope, the center of the bureaucracy, that Salmerón and Laynez received their commission to Trent. With such credentials the wariness they met among their countrymen was predictable.

The Jesuits soon wore down the inhibitions of the Spaniards. In the public discussions they showed genuine competence, a wide knowledge of theological sources, a clarity of expression, and a personal integrity in the honest presentation of their theological conclusions. Salmerón wrote Ignatius: "In our appearances before the legates, the bishops, and the theologians, our Lord has given us the grace to present our opinions in a way that gratifies all. Many bishops have asked us for written copies of our viewpoints. We have supplied these to a number of them."[5]

Cardinal Cervini realized that some at the council were theologically limited. To help these men, he devised a plan to have each discussion opened with an explanation of the points at issue, and then to have it closed with a summation, aimed especially at reshaping "what had been badly expressed" (*que estuviera mal dicho*). Cervini assigned Salmerón and Laynez to these key slots on the roster of speakers.[6]

Beyond these public appearances, it was perhaps in the humdrum toil behind the scenes, however, that they did their most effective work. In private conferences with the fathers of the council, in hours of study, in reviewing the written opinions of the bishops, in all those scholarly and time consuming activities which are not recorded in the tomes of Mansi and Ehses, they bore the heat of the day and won the gratitude and respect of the bishops. Salmerón gave some of the details to Ignatius: "There are several learned prelates here, and this includes those whose learning embraces the sacred sciences, who show us their opinions before they speak. They want our criticism. Then there are still others who are not distinguished in theology, although they have made their mark in other disciplines. These ask us, in our conversations with them, to bring them up-to-date on the theological issues. Then they want us to give them, word for word, a statement which they themselves can present in the council."[7]

From Aloofness to Cordiality

On 3 July Claude Jay sent Ignatius at happy report on how the skill of Salmerón and Laynez had converted the aloof Spanish bishops into warm admirers. But Jay's delight went beyond the transformation of the Spaniards. It touched his personal preoccupation. Salmerón and Laynez were proving to be the best advertisement for Jesuit colleges. Jay told Ignatius: "The bishop of Clermont [Guillaume Duprat] was especially delighted with Salmerón and Laynez. When he witnessed them speaking in the congregation on scriptural topics, he was set on fire with the desire to establish a college."[8]

A week after Jay sent his letter, Salmerón confirmed the report on the change of the Spanish bishops. He too wrote Ignatius: "We are in the position to say that practically every prelate of the three nations, Italian, Spanish, and French, likes us and even feels a touch of jealousy if we do not include him on our visiting list. This transformation has gone to the point that the most contentious of the Spaniards now cry our praises from the housetops, invite us to dinner, clue us in on what they have lined up for delivery in the congregations of the council.''[9]

The Debates on Justification

The public appearances of Salmerón and Laynez at Trent that helped change the attitudes of the Spanish bishops focused on the subject of justification. In this, their baptism of fire at Trent, Salmerón and Laynez illumined the issues tied into that knotty subject. A month after their arrival, at the general congregation of 21 June 1546, the conciliar fathers decided to take up the subject of justification, whose importance has been indicated in the essay on Claude Jay. From 22 June to 28 June the congregation of theologians considered six precise questions.[10] At the meeting on the twenty-third, Salmerón gave his opinions in an address that lasted perhaps two hours.[11] Of all the addresses delivered before this congregation, this was one of the two that have been preserved in their entirety. The other was that of Antonio Frexius de Pinarolo, a Conventual Franciscan. Cardinal Cervini, who had a special predilection for Salmerón, took care that these two addresses be preserved.[12] Salmerón's discourse gave a clear exhibition of his qualities as a theologian: breadth of knowledge of scripture and patristics; penetrating power of speculation; precise and lucid control of the Latin tongue; alertness to differing schools of thought, instanced by his ready reference to a work of Philip Melanchthon on the Epistle to the Romans.[13]

A Serious Question from Ignatius

During the glow of these early successes, Salmerón, Laynez, and Jay received a serious question from Ignatius: would it be to God's greater glory for them to withdraw from the council and to work in the cities that were clamoring for Jesuit help? Ignatius needed advice in an awkward situation. Requests for Jesuits from various towns multiplied. Florence, in the persons of Duke Cosimo and Duchess Leonor de Toledo, was especially insistent. Ignatius did not comprehend the impact of his friends on the council, and seriously contemplated their removal.

180

Salmerón wrote the answer for all three. "Yesterday we received Your Reverence's letter of 3 July. Because you requested a prompt answer, we did this morning what you ordered [had a meeting]. The unanimous opinion of all three of us is this: even though it is taken for granted that each and every one of the three of us stands ready to carry out whatever Your Reverence decides upon, we nevertheless feel, in view of the whole picture here, that no change whatsoever should be made for the time being. Otherwise the building that has been just begun in these latter days will come tumbling down."[14] Salmerón appealed to the achievements of the Jesuits in the council. He described them as a special kind of service. He enumerated, as indicated above, the various ways in which the Society was serving the bishops, publicly and privately, in the clarification of theological issues.

The Jesuit team at Trent appealed to the principle of choosing the greater good: The work at the council had wider ramifications than a single college. "By these endeavors here at Trent," continued Salmerón, "no less is the Society's good name heralded abroad, and no less does the Society move forward in its good relations with all the nationalities present here than would be gained by the establishment of a single particular college. Here we are sowing the seed for a future harvest not only in Florence but in other places as well."[15] This appeal of the Tridentine Jesuits looked to the future. A work well done under the eyes of bishops of several countries would open many doors to the Society.

Salmerón, Laynez, and Jay suggested to Ignatius that they remain in the council at least until the arrival of Pierre Favre. By that time a number of factors would have developed: a clearer picture of the situation at Florence; a surer sense of the council's direction; a wider consolidation of the Jesuit presence in the council. At that time a wiser decision could be made about Jesuit withdrawal from Trent.[16] Ignatius was persuaded. For the time being, the three Jesuits remained in the council.

Further Developments on Justification

Salmerón continued to contribute to the lengthy debates of seven months on justification. He made further interventions in the congregation of theologians on 28 September and 16 October.[17] The thrust of his thought was clear. He saw justification as

God's gift which effects deep internal changes within man, changes that free him from sin, raise him to the dignity of a son of God, enable him to observe God's law, and endow him with the right to eternal glory. God as the originator effects justification in its entirety. Man actively cooperates in his use of God's gift. God enjoys supreme dominion; man enjoys freedom. "This is so, because the act of faith is totally ours and totally God's. Our action is totally God's and totally ours. In a like way, handwritten letters are done totally by the pen and totally by the penman" (*Ita quod totum credere nostrum est, totum etiam est Dei; nostrum operari Dei est totum et totum nostri. Sic iidem caracteres toti sunt a calamo, toti a scribente*).[18]

Calling upon Holy Scripture and the church fathers, and following a positive and constructive vision of the dignity to which God has called man, Salmerón advocated insights that became solidly riveted into the structure of the council's decree on justification. He knew the Protestant positions and came to grips with them. But his approach was not defensive. He aimed to build in a positive way, quarrying in the traditions of the church and setting several blocks together to form a solid and cohesive theological structure.

Salmerón's intervention of 16 October focused on the thorny question of "twofold justice" (*duplex justitia*). The question was basically this: is man justified by personal internal grace (*gratia inhaerens*), or is there also required the imputation of the justice of Christ (*justitia Christi*)? Is personal internal grace inadequate for man's justification? Is there need for something additional, namely, the justice of Christ flowing from his Passion and applied to man? One theory answered these questions in the affirmative.[19] It carried the prestige of the eminent Girolamo Seripando, and it reflected his concern for conciliation with the Protestants, set in their theology of imputative justice.

Salmerón found this theory inadmissable. As seen in the portrait of Claude Jay, so did Laynez. The structure of the argument advanced by the two Jesuits was basically the same.[20] Personal internal grace is given to man freely by God through the merits of Christ. This personal internal grace is not, therefore, of man's making but of Christ's. When, therefore, man appears before

God's tribunal, he does so with the justice of Christ. There is, therefore, no need of inputing to man another additional kind of justice. Salmerón made a further point in regard to the term "imputative justice" (*justitia imputativa*), used by the advocates of the twofold justice theory. If man were justified by "imputative justice," he would not be truly justified; he would merely be regarded as such. Seripando's theory fell under the hammering of a formidable phalanx of Carmelites, Franciscans, Dominicans, and the Jesuits Salmerón and Laynez [21]

Justification as a theological problem absorbed Salmerón in an intense way. It had occasioned the unpleasant confrontation between himself and Cardinal Morone at Modena in 1543. During the conciliar debates he assembled his thoughts in the form of a tract. [22] After session six of 13 January 1547, he wrote still another extended tract; then a shorter one, a *tractatulus*; then still further smaller pieces, all on justification. These rest in the Vatican archives, and on some of the manuscripts Cardinal Cervini had made notes and queries. [23]

Salmerón's Sermon at the Council

Three weeks before the close of the debates on justification, Salmerón received a special honor. At the liturgy in honor of St. John the Evangelist on 27 December 1546, he delivered the sermon. [24] Regularly during the council, the bishops and theologians assembled for the solemn celebration of mass, at which a participant in the council, usually one of the more distinguished, delivered the sermon.

These sermons at Trent had common characteristics: they delineated the image the Church then presented to the world; they expressed the understanding that the council had of its own function. Unlike the sermons at the Council of Constance, which faced up to the thorny theological issues of that era, those at Trent evaded the controversial subjects, most likely because the Protestants were not present. The preachers aimed rather at pricking the consciences of the bishops and exhorting them to their pastoral responsibilities. [25] Domingo Soto, for example, exclaimed in one of his sermons: "Lift up your hands! What answer will you make to the judge of the universe if you depart this place with your work

ORATIO

REVERENDI PATRIS MAGISTRI
Alphonsi Salmeronis de Societate IESV *Theologi, nuper in* CONCILIO *Tridentino
habita, in qua ad exemplar Diui Ioannis Euangelistæ vera Prælato-
rum forma describitur.*

*Romæ, per Stephanum Nicolinum Sabiensem Chalcographum
Apostolicum, cum Priuilegio ad Decennium. Anno*
·M D X L V I I· *Mense Martio.*

Title page of Salmerón's Sermon at Trent on St. John the Evangelist

undone?'' Bartolomé de Carranza, preaching on the First Sunday of Lent, 1546, called out: ''Lord, wilt thou at this time restore again the Kingdom of Israel?''[26]

Salmerón in his sermon of 27 December 1546 took this same line.[27] He reminded the bishops that, as Christ had a special love for John the Evangelist, so Christ had a special love for them in their post of pastor; that Christ's love should permeate their lives;

184

that they were the instruments by which Christ's love could return to the sullied church.

> It is granted to them [the bishops] to know many of the mysteries of the kingdom of God, in order that, understanding that they are especially loved by Christ and called in love to the dignity of being pastors, they may pasture the flock of Christ; bear a sincere love toward the sheep; teach love, which is the fulfillment of the law, from their episcopal seat; demand love above all else from their sheep; reprove faults while preserving love toward the people who commit them; raise the standard of love in all their works; finally that they might consider it a glorious thing to be deprived of life rather than of love for their sheep, remembering our Lord's words: "The good shepherd lays down his life for his sheep" (Jn. 10.11). It is your task in love, fathers, who have gathered at this legitimate and ecumenical council to reconcile and mend the most grave religious discords, above all else to put aside your own individual advantage and to make known and propagate the glory of the one Christ, our chief high priest and unconquerable Lord, the glory which has been obscured (I almost said destroyed) by foolish teachings and by our corrupt and profligate ways, ways which have given us a bad name among the infidels. It is also your task to restore the pristine health and the primitive beauty and attractiveness of Christ's languishing and dirtied spouse. Through you, therefore, let the most holy and invincible charity of Christ return to the Church of Christ like a person returning home, the charity in which alone consists the purity of the teachings of the faith, the purging of our ways, and the welfare and renovation of the entire Church.[28]

Salmerón proposed St. John to the bishops as the model for the person who would follow Christ.

> For John followed Christ with discerning mind and with zealous love, in purity of mind and integrity of body, in the continual ministry of preaching and with frequent miracles, in dedicating everything to God at an early age, in tolerating insults with joy, and in so often persevering with constancy of soul when he was threatened with the dangers of death.
>
> Although this following of Christ is necessary for all those professing him, the bishops especially ought to follow very conscientiously, in order that, while the sheep follow their shepherd, the shepherds themselves may follow the chief of all the shepherds, Christ. Christ urges all shepherds today to this following when he says to Peter, the leader of all the sheep, "Follow me," and again, "You follow me." Oh how sorrowful! How greatly it should be deplored as evil, when a shepherd either follows Satan, the prince of darkness, or follows the Lord, with Peter, from afar!
>
> What does it mean, most wise fathers, I ask you, what does it mean to follow Christ from afar? It can only mean to fear the power of princes rather than him alone who is able to send the soul to Gehenna; to withdraw one's presence from Christ's Church and to grow old in the halls of princes; to see

the wolf coming and to flee with vile soul; driven by cowardice, not to place oneself as a wall of defense for the house of Israel; to hide in the earth the money entrusted to one; making a delay in one's payment to the Lord, but striking one's own men servants and maidservants; to eat, to drink, to become drunk and to force, by one's own example, those of lower station to wander far from the kingdom of God; to ignore the divinely inspired scriptures; to be ashamed of the office of evangelizing as if it were something contemptible; finally to look for mercenary gain, to dissipate oneself on luxuries, to swell up with praises, to be disturbed by slight and unimportant injuries, to deny and deny again Christ at the voice of the handmaid.

Make it your job, therefore, fathers, to follow Christ as closely as possible and to stay close to his footsteps, which point out the most certain path of safety and of consequent immortality. We ought not to turn from following the Lord because of certain depraved ways of acting among those now alive, introduced and preserved by Satan.[29]

Salmerón then went through certain failings on John's part that he urged the bishops to avoid: ambition in asking for a special place in the kingdom; envy in seeking the restraint of the man who was casting out devils; vengeance in seeking the punishment of certain Samaritans; sloth in falling asleep in the Garden of Olives. True pastors, said Salmerón, reject ambition, envy, vengeance, sloth. Salmerón called on the bishops to overcome these failings in the name of their love for the Church. He urged them to bring comfort, strength, health to the prostrate, sick, desperate Church.

Wherefore it is certainly impossible that what was brought forth by your forefathers in labors, in watches, in fasting and in tears should now be preserved in pleasures, in sleep, in drunkenness, in luxury and pomp. I grieve to describe the face of the Church like this to you, but zeal and the respect I bear towards you forces me to speak thus, desiring that you might accept the Church herself as your mother, just as John accepted the mother of the Lord for his own mother. He accepted her, I said, as *his own* mother, not as a step-mother, or as a hostile woman as the heretics and schismatics, do, who undertake her destruction in open war and in secret plots. John did not receive her as a servant and a handmaid, as do those who oppress her unmercifully with a heavy yoke, with swords, and with tyrannical terror. He did not receive her for a concubine, as do those who are united with her in an adulterous embrace, those who hunt for ecclesiastical dignities, which they are seeking to take as their own. These people are ignorant of what a pastor really is, and they think that the apostolic office consists of those things with which the wicked abound, with which robbers are made rich, and on account of which tyrants are feared. Therefore she should be received as a venerable mother and a legitimate spouse, to whom sincere love, producing fitting honor and appropriate helps, ought to be promptly and cheerfully shown on account of Christ.

I will now end here my speech, but first I want to beseech and implore you, as fathers who are most respected by me, to fix your eyes on John, whom we have proposed to you as a most perfect model, as an eagle urging on to flight those seeking from him examples of all the virtues with which bishops ought to shine. Just as he stood by the girl when she was brought back to life, and went up the mountain, and was taken into the garden to watch and pray, so you too should be mindful of your vocation to be the sweet odor of Christ in every place, so far as is possible to you, in order that you might be an odor of life and not of death.

You who are evangelists climb lofty Sion, raise your voice in a shout, and take care that those who are not wise become wise, and that those who are wise do not become foolish, and that those who are foolish recover their senses. Attend to yourselves and to your entire flock, and be watchful as if you were watching carefully for him who will return as an incorruptible and inexorable judge, and who will require the blood of the lost sheep from the hand of those who should have been watching over them. Pray that Christ may add strength to those of you who are vigilant that you may be able to conquer every adversity with his help, which is a most glorious and truly apostolic thing to do; and that you may glory in your tribulations endured for the Church.

If Christ's mother was handed over to John in faith, in this same way the Church has been committed to this sacred synod through the Holy Spirit, in order that you, looking again in sorrow and mourning upon Christ crucified, might receive her as your mother, in order that you might raise her up, lying on the ground, with the arms of your authority, in order that you, like very firm pillars might prop her up as she wavers from the sound teaching of faith and doctrine; in order that you might help her who is in great need with the help of your holy canons, through which what has collapsed is repaired, what is crooked is made straight, and what is deformed is reformed. Finally may you do this in order that you, by manifesting continual concern and work, might be able to console and comfort her who until now has been deserted by her pastors. I have spoken.[30]

So closed a sermon that meshed smoothly with the pastoral character of the other sermons at Trent. Salmerón the technical theologian yielded to Salmerón the priest in the cathedral pulpit. Salmerón's sermon was published at Rome and Paris the next year. This gave Salmerón the distinction of being the second Jesuit to appear in print, preceded only by Peter Canisius, who issued editions of Tauler in 1543 and Cyril of Jerusalem and Leo the Great in 1546.[31]

187

The publication of his sermon displeased Salmerón—and for a reason that in view of how the Society's history developed was a strange one. Salmerón felt that publishing was alien to the Jesuit way of life. A young man whom Pierre Favre had attracted to the Society when in Parma, Paolo Achille, informed Salmerón that some of Salmerón's friends were anxious to see the sermon in print. Salmerón told Achille that the sermon had already appeared in Rome, but without his permission. He continued: "I am unable to approve your request to publish my sermon, because I feel that it does not merit reading. . . . My principal reason for this decision, however, is because it seems foreign to our Institute to direct our efforts to the publication of books, a work to be done by men of superior gifts. We are called to a way of life characterized chiefly by simplicity, modesty, and a total charity to our neighbor. While it is true that the publication of books in se is not repugnant to what I have just said, nevertheless it can be an obstacle to and, at times, a distraction from works of the higher kind of charity."[32] Time would change Salmerón's mind.

At least one copy of the sermon reached Spain. The bishop of Badajoz, Francisco de Navarra, sent it to the Spanish court. With it he sent his observations on the worthy contributions made by the Jesuits in the council. Antonio Araoz, who knew his way around the Spanish court, passed the word on to Ignatius. He told Ignatius that Salmerón was achieving more for the Society by his preaching at Trent than he would be working in Spain.[33]

Joy and Pain in the Council

Two weeks after Salmerón preached, Claude Jay's pride in his brother Jesuits broke through nearly every line of a letter which he sent to Ignatius from Trent on 30 January 1547. "By the grace of the Lord, our companions, Don Diego and Don Alfonso, have carried themselves in a most laudable manner in the exposition of their opinions. I certainly think that there is no theologian in whom Cardinal Cervini puts more trust than they. . . . Don Diego has the most acute need, so it seems to me, of a rest of some days from his study and preaching, because he looks quite weak and washed out. Needing the break as he does, he is nevertheless unwilling to give in. . . . What I have said of Don Diego I could also say about Don Alfonso."[34]

More than Salmerón's health suffered because of the intense debates on justification. He lost the friendship of the eminent Girolamo Seripando, member of the Hermits of St. Augustine. Between him and Seripando there developed a distinct chilliness. Seripando, who had propounded the theory of "a twofold justice" (*duplex justitia*) with an eye toward reconciliation with the Protestants, saw his proposals go down in defeat under the blows of Salmerón and Laynez. Seripando was a genuinely great Catholic intellectual leader. The chasm that developed between him and the two Jesuits became common knowledge and perdured even to his death in 1563 during the third period of the council. This bad feeling was one of the personal tragedies that attended the advance of the great conciliar event.[35]

Conciliar Debates on the Sacraments

After the work on justification, the next dogmatic subject on the agenda was the sacraments. As has been seen in the essay on Claude Jay, Salmerón was one of the principal theologians selected by Cardinal Cervini to prepare material for the discussions on the sacraments.[36] On 17 January 1547 Cervini presented to a general congregation a part of this theological research, a list of errors held by the Protestants in regard to the sacraments in general and in regard to baptism and confirmation.[37] Salmerón intervened at the congregation of theologians held on 21 January 1547. The tenor of his address was basically a demonstration, by scriptural, patristic, and conciliar documentation, of the erroneous character of the Protestant positions.[38]

On 3 February 1547 the theologians received for study the list of errors in regard to the Holy Eucharist. Twice Salmerón discussed these articles, on two successive days, 4 February and 5 February 1547. Both discourses must have been lengthy. On the first day Salmerón gave his attention entirely to the first article, which presented the teaching of Zwingli and Oecolampadius that the body and blood of Christ are not really present in the Holy Eucharist but only as in a sign.[39] Salmerón rested his argument on two bases: the constant teaching of the Church, and Christ's fidelity to his Church. After several citations of the Church's teaching, he concluded: "If the Church erred, Christ was not with her; this is false and contradicts his promise."[40] The next day he ranged

189

more widely over the other articles.[41] These discussions on the Holy Eucharist did not enter into the body of the dogmatic decree of the council's seventh session of 3 March 1547, but they served as a valuable preparation for the debates that were to continue into the second and third periods of the council.

Extra-conciliar Activity

In his early letters to Ignatius from Trent, Salmerón described more than theological debates. He gave a detailed account of the time that he, Jay, and Laynez were devoting to the poor and to the work of preaching.[42] Such indeed was what Ignatius wanted, as he made clear in a lengthy set of instructions.[43] Ignatius did not realize, however, that he had placed his friends in a position of stress because of the demands on their energies by pastoral as well as intellectual concerns. Dogmatic discussion and the care of the poor absorbed Salmerón, but he kindles a suspicion that his preference was to be in the streets with the needy rather than in the crowded chambers of the theologians. On 10 July 1546 he intimated this potential conflict of works to Ignatius.

> Although the ministering to the poor of which I speak was in itself sufficient to keep us busy, and, I must admit, congenial as well, the most reverend delegates expressed their wish that we be present at the conciliar meetings, where in the presence of the legates and other prelates the theologians give their judgments on the dogmatic questions under discussion.[44]

Laynez shared this two-pronged experience of Salmerón and Jay. Writing to Ignatius on 18 September 1546 about his fellow Jesuits, and implicitly about himself, Laynez observed: "They carry on in the usual occupations, begging for the poor and working on the question of justification, which has been given to the theologians for review."[45]

Ignatius's lengthy instruction strongly advocated preaching in Trent. This Salmerón, Jay, and Laynez did. But it was not until September 1546 that they were able to do so. Cardinal Giammaria del Monte had placed a ban on public preaching by the theologians during the council. Cardinal Marcello Cervini wanted an exception made in the case of the Jesuits. He gained his point. Salmerón informed Ignatius on 20 October that the men of the Society were preaching in various parishes and that their hearers included an increasing number of conciliar fathers.[46]

So ran the reports to Ignatius from Salmerón. It was a story that took its texture from the floor of the conciliar aula and from the streets of the Tyrolese town.

Prospect of Nicolás Bobadilla at the Council

Not all the reports Ignatius received from Trent reflected honor on his fellow Jesuits in the field. In mid-June 1546 Salmerón passed on to Ignatius, in the name of Jay and Laynez as well as in his own name, some disturbing stories about Nicolás Bobadilla, who had been in Germany since 1542.[47] Salmerón was worried. Although Claude Jay and others recited accounts of Bobadilla's work that did him immense credit, still others drew a picture of a strange and erratic man. To satisfy his conscience, Salmerón decided to brief Ignatius and itemized some of the disturbing stories: Bobadilla was incessantly gossiping about princes and affairs of state; he was quarreling with papal nuncios; he was writing on his own initiative and without advice to cardinals and princes; one letter to the nuncio Robert Vauchop, filled with damaging remarks, fell into Jay's hands and so never reached Vauchop; on one occasion Bobadilla got into a convivial drinking bout and could hardly make it back to his lodgings; Claude Jay, although he asserted that he had never seen Bobadilla inebriated, nevertheless did say that Bobadilla's excited manner of talking and gesticulating could give the impression that he had taken too much wine. Through Cardinal Pole, one of the presidents of the council, Salmerón also heard that Bobadilla was doing some political maneuvering in order to be sent to Trent. This Salmerón dreaded. He told Ignatius: "So if Your Reverence does not do something, it might happen that he will end up here."[48] Bobadilla never did participate in the council. And if Ignatius answered Salmerón, the letter has been lost.

Bobadilla's own correspondence seems to corroborate at least some of Salmerón's apprehensions. Bobadilla basked in the belief that the secular and ecclesiastical leaders of Catholic Germany held him in high esteem. Frequently he developed this theme in his letters to Rome: he enjoyed the favor of King Ferdinand and his queen; he was privy to most of the king's concerns; he transacted much business in the diocese of Passau; he was on intimate terms with the Venetian ambassador; he attracted crowds to the confessional; he is wanted everywhere. One modern historian, James Brodrick, gently judges all of this as the comic naïveté of a genuinely great apostolic worker. One of Bobadilla's Jesuit contemporaries, Jerónimo Nadal, wrote in a more acidulous vein. He interpreted Nicolás's proclamations of his importance in German official circles as a massive display of self-deception. The German princes, judged Nadal, were making sport with one whom they looked on as a clown.[49]

Ignatius wanted to pull in the reins on Bobadilla, who, it seems, never learned of Salmerón's report from Trent. But he hesitated to send an admonition himself. He therefore asked Fr. Miguel de Torres to do so. Torres's letter, which reached Bobadilla on 15 July has been lost, but Bobadilla promptly shot back a reply recounting the perils of war he was enduring in Germany "while you in Rome all sit about the kitchen writing letters . . ."[50]

Salmerón's Grievous Illness

About eight months after Salmerón's fears, real or imaginary, about the presence of Bobadilla at Trent, the council, as described in the essay on Jay, reached a crisis in early March 1547, and on the eleventh was transferred to Bologna. On the fourteenth Salmerón left Trent with Laynez. They stopped at Padua, and there Salmerón's health broke. The doctors judged his condition to be extremely serious and held little hope for his recovery. Laynez, who nursed his friend with tenderness, feared that Salmerón had come down with the same sickness that had spread through Trent, because the symptoms appeared to be similar.[51] At Rome Ignatius and the other Jesuits prayed that God would spare their Father Alfonso.

Despite the gloomy prognosis, Salmerón recovered quickly.[52] A month later he was on the road again, and on 16 April, knowing where thanks were due, wrote an affectionate letter to Ignatius.

> May God, our Lord, be blessed and praised for the many manifestations of his mercy that he deigned to show me during my illness. Besides the blessing of the sacraments of the Church and the membership in such a holy Company, his Divine Majesty has given me remarkable help in the extremity in which I arrived by drawing my will into conformity with his most holy will in a spirit of great contentment and joy, by giving me an intimate knowledge of my sins and failings, and a tremendous hope in the greatness

192

of his pity and mercy. In this mercy, contrary to what the doctors and everyone else expected, he has been pleased, if such a way of speaking be permitted, to bring me back to life. I am conscious of the love and paternal affection with which Your Reverence has us written in your heart. I am convinced that it was prayer, especially that of Your Reverence and the other brethren, that obtained from our Lord what the doctors were unable to achieve with all their care and medicines.[53]

The Council at Bologna

With Claude Jay, Salmerón made a brief excursion to Venice to see their old friend Andrea Lippomano, prior of Holy Trinity Monastery. They were back in Padua by the nineteenth or twentieth. There they stayed four days. Cardinal Cervini became impatient with these stopovers, and pressed the Jesuits with the urgency of the council. He wrote to Laynez, requesting him and Salmerón to lose no time in getting to Bologna.[54] There the two arrived on 27 April.[55]

Immediately Salmerón plunged into the conciliar business. The next day, the twenty-eighth, he spoke on penance at a congregation of minor theologians. One of his main points was the divine institution of confession.[56] Then up to the middle of August he made several interventions. On 4 May 1547, at the congregation of minor theologians, he spoke on holy orders, stressing its sacramental character.[57] On 9 July 1547 he spoke at the morning and evening sessions of the congregation of theologians. In the earlier meeting he aimed to prove the existence of purgatory; in the latter he spoke on the nature of contrition.[58] On 11 July, 18 August, and 19 August, he spoke more at length and elaborated his presentations in greater detail. On 11 July he was the only speaker at the early congregation of theologians, which lasted from 10 in the morning to two in the afternoon. He treated purgatory and indulgences. Realizing the varied way in which indulgences were understood in that period of theological ambiguity, he trimmed away confusion and went directly to the essential idea of the remission of temporal punishment granted to those who, through contrition and confession, are freed of the guilt of sin.[59]

On 18 August, again at a congregation of theologians, he followed the Conventual Franciscan Christopher Bagnacavallus, and, rejecting the thesis that the Mass is a mere memorial, he stressed its nature as a real sacrifice.[60] Since he did not finish his argument, he spoke the next morning, again insisting on the sacrificial character of the Mass, and rejecting the Lutheran position that the canon of the Mass was a "novel device" (*nova inventio*). His presentation, with its emphasis on Christ's Passion and Death, articulated the new emphasis on the immolation of a victim and the shift from St. Thomas's insight of sacrifice as a virtue.[61]

These last two addresses made a deep impression.[62] The wide erudition, especially in Scripture and patristics, as recorded by Massarelli, was massive, a demonstration of Salmerón's especially retentive memory and clarity of presentation. He clearly moved in the current of religious humanism. In the long intervention on the Sacrifice of the Mass on 18 August he quoted Scripture at least twenty-nine times; twelve times he cited theologians and fathers of the Church.[63] In the extended intervention of 11 July on purgatory and indulgences, the balance of citations was different. At least twenty-three times Salmerón referred to papal documents, six times to conciliar documents, nine times to the church fathers and theologians, and ten times to Holy Scripture. Despite the relatively low number of explicit scriptural quotations in this particular intervention, Salmerón traced through it a language permeated with phrases and nuances from the sacred books.[64]

Laudable as was his scriptural predilection, these initial appearances at the council brought to light for the first time a serious flaw in Salmerón's scholarship: his failure in the evaluation of sources. From scriptural and patristic literature he piled up text after text as though each citation carried equal weight. Each reference was a triton. There were no minnows. Salmerón's discrimination fell behind his erudition. This defect remained a constant in Salmerón's intellectual career. It stood out during the next two periods of the council and with glaring starkness in the sixteen volumes of his scholarly reflections that he wrote during the last decades of his life. This defect led Salmerón down the road of verbosity. He coated his arguments with the blubber of words. These blemishes notwithstanding, Salmerón's work remains as a testament to his sensitivity to the current scholarly movement of seeking theological truth in the early sources (*ad fontes*) of Christianity, one of the more fertile facets of the Reformation era.

The preparation and presentation of his interventions took a heavy toll on Salmerón's energies. Cardinal Cervini noted this and ordered him to slacken his pace.[65] The cardinal had been anxious to have doctrinal epitomes of what Salmerón had orally presented, and already had received one, done jointly by Jay and Salmerón, on purgatory and indulgences.[66] He wanted others also, but in view of the strain under which Salmerón had been working, he ordered Alfonso to desist for the time being.[67]

Suspension of the Council

In August the routine of the council ground to a halt. In February 1548 the conciliar leaders provisionally but practically adjourned the council, and on 13 September 1549 formally and definitively declared its suspension.[68]

For the infant Society of Jesus the council had special importance. It was an unveiling ceremony where, in the persons of Jay, Salmerón, and Laynez, the new religious order became known to many of the hierarchy and other religious leaders of Europe. This introduction went beyond the august, distant, impersonal plane of theological debate and public discourse. The Jesuits met many of the bishops on the intimate level of retreatant and retreat master. So many of the bishops wanted to make the Spiritual Exercises that Salmerón, Laynez, and Jay could not satisfy all requests. Some bishops who had been directed by the Jesuits became themselves directors of other bishops.[69] As early as September 1546, both Salmerón and Laynez told Ignatius that many prelates, Italian, Sicilian, French, and Spanish, wanted Jesuits to work in their dioceses.[70]

Even though the council had been suspended, its labors shackled Salmerón for several months to come. The doctrinal summations which Cardinal Cervini wanted still concerned him. On 1 October 1547 he informed Ignatius: "I am now giving my attention to the summaries on the Mass, from which I was interrupted for days by other things. At the moment, because of the cardinal's mandate, it will be necessary to sweat and work. What was very easy for two, Jay and myself, is a real burden for me working alone.[71] Almost two months later, on 26 November he informed Ignatius that he had corrected the five sheets on purgatory, was in the process of translating the abridgement on the Sacrifice of the Mass, and was planning a quick trip to Florence to get Laynez's advice on the summaries he had made.[72]

A Preaching Tour in Northern Italy

This theological work for Cervini Salmerón did in northern Italy. And it was northern Italy that was the theater of Salmerón's other apostolic work for over two years, until he was called to Germany in the fall of 1549. To organize Salmerón's itinerary is like matching parts of a jigsaw puzzle. At Bologna until June of 1548; then during the summer to Venice; then to Padua; then to Verona in the fall of 1548; then to Venice in February 1549; then back to Padua for a short visit; then to Belluno in early March 1549; then to Venice at the end of April; then back to Belluno; then to Saravalle; then to Venice; then Padua; then near the close of August to Ferrara, where he joined Claude Jay; then to Bologna with Jay in early September.[73]

A unifying thread ran through these frequent changes: Salmerón's intense pastoral preoccupation with the spiritual needs of the faithful. This he manifested in several ways. In 1547 at

Centers of Alfonso Salmerón's preaching tour, 1547–1549

Bologna, where he had made a deep impression two years earlier, he made the Church of St. Lucy a center for encouraging a deeper sacramental life. On Christmas Day 1547, about five hundred received holy communion. There he also reconciled many Protestants to the Church.[74] In Verona, on Sundays and feast days, he explained St. Paul's Epistle to the Romans, a project which became more and more popular as time went on.[75] He also preached in some nuns' monasteries and several other churches. He strengthened many who were leaning toward Protestant beliefs, and inspired others who possessed books by Protestant authors to burn them. This zeal, nevertheless, did not deflect him from a charitable and compassionate attitude toward the Protestants.[76] Criticism came from some quarters in Verona, where some people spoke of him as an adorer of the pope and the Holy See.[77]

At Belluno his host was the zealous Bishop Giulio Contarini, a name resonant with the fullness of the Catholic Reform. A nephew of the great Cardinal Gasparo Contarini, Belluno's bishop tried to be worthy of his family heritage.[78] In calling Salmerón to his see, he was renewing an old bond of friendship between the Contarini family and the Society of Jesus, for no one worked more energetically in 1539–40 for the approval of the new order than Cardinal Gasparo. At Belluno, as at Bologna, Salmerón gave the Spiritual Exercises to several young men. Of these, a number wanted to join the Society of Jesus but Salmerón accepted only two, lest he over crowd the Jesuit house in Padua. To the others he held out the hope of eventually being admitted into the Society cither at Venice or Padua.[79]

Salmerón knew his oratorical powers and was not beyond being human enough to preen his feathers a bit. On 27 April 1549 he wrote Ignatius: "By the grace of our Lord I have brought to a close my series of sermons at Belluno. If in the beginning and as I progressed they were a success, they were no less so at their conclusion. The success in fact was far more than I ever anticipated. The striking change that the citizens say our Lord worked in the hearts of those who heard me has been so overwhelming that nothing quite like it has been seen since the days when St. Bernardine of Siena preached there."[80] The man who outlined his schedule when he had not received specific directions from Ignatius—for Salmerón was not acting by personal whim or preference—was the bishop of Verona, Luigi Lippomano, to whom Ignatius had assigned him.[81]

Many different responsibilities lay ahead for Salmerón, but he ever remained the preacher. Sacred oratory ran like a thread through his life. His sermons with their distinctly scriptural cast reflected two major influences, academic and ascetical: the Biblical Renaissance at Alcalá and the *Spiritual Exercises* of Ignatius. At Alcalá, as has been seen, Salmerón became fired with a lifelong enthusiasm for scriptural studies. And in the *Spiritual Exercises* of Ignatius he encountered, of the fifty-two meditations and contemplations of the last three weeks of the *Exercises*, forty-eight episodes that are in the Gospels.[82] This background he cast into apostolic form in his sermons.

The Jesuits and the Renaissance of Sacred Oratory

Salmerón entered upon his preaching career during the flourish of the Catholic response to the Lutheran charge that the preachers of the Roman Church were robbing the faithful of the Scriptures. Early in the sixteenth century, the Protestant indictment had a measure of validity. The thematic, abstract, speculative sermon as sketched out in the medieval *Artes Praedicandi* remained the master in many pulpits of Italy. Pietro Bembo, when asked why he did not preach in Padua during Lent, replied: "Why should I? Preaching is nothing more than some chatter between the Subtle Doctor [Duns Scotus] and the Angelic Doctor [Thomas Aquinas], who are joined by Aristotle as a third party in an attempt to resolve a certain question at issue."[83]

Two fresh intellectual styles, however, gradually whittled away the position of the medieval model. The Classical Renaissance evoked the stirring oratory of the great speakers of Greece and Rome. The Scriptural Renaissance sharpened a lively thirst for the freshness of God's word. In the 1530s impressive speakers like Bernard Ochino and Pietro Vermigli led a renewal in sacred oratory and channeled to the people the intense scriptural devotion they found in the spiritual centers formed by Valdes, Giberti, Morone, and other leading men to the *spirituali*.[84]

Within this milieu Salmerón and his fellow Jesuits, especially Jay and Laynez, created a new genre of preaching.[85] They took the older pattern of the Latin university lecture on Scripture;

they turned it into the vernacular; they adapted it to the comprehension of the people. During a stay in a city, they usually took a single book of the Bible and expounded it from beginning to end on a set day of the week. They stressed the literal sense; they also made moral and doctrinal applications. This form of preaching, distinctly different from the sermon, was called "the scriptural lecture" (la leçon d'écriture sainte).[86] Series of these scriptural lectures, by their format and didactic nature, were a form of adult religious education. They also fitted into that popular awareness of the Scriptures that had been molded during the medieval centuries, when the sacred writings inspired art and literature, religion and culture.[87]

This Jesuit creation of a new form in sacred oratory took place during an era when the preachers in Italy had a strong hold on the people. "Not since Savonarola had the Italian cities turned so enthusiastically to preachers."[88] Pulpits held the religious destiny of the people, and it was this that made the era so religiously critical, since the German experience had shown that governments and preachers could make an explosive combination.[89]

Two schools of theology and spirituality strove for the minds and hearts of the populace. On the one hand, Bernard Ochino and Pietro Martire Vermigli, at the service of Reginald Pole, Gian Matteo Giberti, Gasparo Contarini, and Gregorio Cortese, moved nearer to the Lutheran position of fides sola as they stressed the power of Christ's grace and man's utter weakness.[90] On the other hand, the Jesuits, among others, kept clearly in focus the place of man's virtuous action in salvation. Between these two schools stood the masses (popolo), ready to be won by the eloquence of the sacred orators. Ochino and Vermigli were in demand throughout Italy. The people were eager to hear and learn.[91] Evangelical literature was not limited, as has been thought, to the palaces of cardinals or the salons of distinguished ladies or the chambers of the humanists; it was widely read among artisans and shop-keepers.[92] As many Catholics slipped toward a mystical theology devoid of clearly enunciated dogma, it became impossible to distinguish clearly between the Catholic evangelical movement and the Protestant expansion in Italy. Both were enigmatic.[93]

The theology and spirituality articulated by Ochino and

199

Vermigli seemed to be climbing to the ascendancy. In the summer of 1542 Modena and Lucca moved closer to the brink of the steep descent away from loyalty to Rome.[94] Then, in the August of that unstable summer, Ochino and Vermigli fled Italy and joined the Protestants in Switzerland. These apostasies deeply shook the Catholics. They also gave the coup de grace to the cause of the *spirituali*[95] in Italy.

Even before these dramatic events, indeed even before the papal approbation of the Society, the Jesuits had challenged the doctrines espoused by Ochino and Vermigli. In the Lent of 1538 at Rome, Favre and Laynez challenged the Augustinian Fra Agostino de Piemonte for his Lutheran stance.[96] In 1539 at Parma, Laynez contested a Carmelite friar.[97] And after the critical summer of 1542, the Jesuits continued their challenge to the evangelical pockets in Italy. In 1543—as has been seen—Salmerón and Cardinal Morone had a nasty confrontation on the precise issue of good works in salvation. Salmerón, therefore, in this age of influential preachers, by his many journeys in the late 1540s wove a net of many threads that stretched throughout northern Italy, and so made a notable contribution toward keeping the Italian "popolo" within the Catholic Church.

Practical Business

These travels of Salmerón were not entirely a spiritual odyssey. Ignatius had given him the responsibility of helping to find houses for Jesuits in Bologna and Venice. An assignment of this kind brought out Salmerón's practical side. He had the knack of mastering details. In Bologna, for a long time he searched for a church and house, but even with Cardinal Cervini's help he had no success. On 17 December 1547 he wrote Ignatius: "I have done nothing else these days except walk the streets of Bologna looking over the various churches."[98] More than a month later, on 21 January 1548, he reported to Ignatius that his quest had come to an end. He had hit upon the Church of St. Mary Magdalen on the Via Santi Donati and an adjoining residence.[99] Later, from Venice, on 3 May 1549 he reported to Ignatius about a house that he had helped to acquire for the Society in that city. "Without exaggeration it seems that there is not in Venice a more ample house for a student body of about a hundred. There is besides a very large garden. It is true that to live there conveniently the layout of some money will be necessary, since the windows, being rather high, will have to be lowered in order to obtain proper lighting."[100]

At the University of Ingolstadt

Salmerón's pastoral apostolate of two years in northern Italy was finally interrupted by an order from Ignatius that he place his talents at the disposal of the University of Ingolstadt. As has been seen in the portrait of Claude Jay, Duke Wilhelm of Bavaria appealed to Pope Paul III and Ignatius Loyola for help to save his moribund university at Ingolstadt. On instructions from Ignatius, Jay, Salmerón, and Canisius obtained their doctorates in theology, and the three Jesuits arrived at Ingolstadt in November 1549 amid the plaudits of an exuberant Chancellor Leonhard von Eck.[101]

Three days after the opening of school on 29 November 1549, Salmerón delivered the first lecture of a series designed to cover the Epistles of St. Paul. He opened with the Letter to the Romans. Chancellor von Eck, aglow with enthusiasm for the learning of the recent acquisitions for the theological faculty, attended with some representatives of Duke Wilhelm one of Salmerón's early lectures.[102] So impressed was he that he announced that not even for a magnificent sum of money would he have missed that talk, superior to anything that the old veteran of Ingolstadt, Johannes Eck, would have given.[103]

No copies of this lecture or of the others that Salmerón gave at Ingolstadt survive. But his discourses at the Council of Trent and his volumes of the *Commentarii* intimate that what von Eck heard and enthused about was a rich fabric of scriptural and patristic erudition, dialectical skill, and lucid reasoning, all presented with the finesse of the accomplished orator. This indeed was the precise memory that lived on at Ingolstadt. A legend at the university contrasted the Salmerónian style with that of Laynez. Laynez served his hearers with fine banquets and trays filled with deliciously sweetened and attractively arranged dishes. Salmerón, on the other hand, put before his hearers feasts that were to the utmost exquisitely and splendidly decorated, not aimed at the usual taste of people, and indeed requiring a bit of getting used to.[104] Salmerón's style, therefore, in itself presented a daunting challenge to his listeners.

Disillusionment and Catastrophe at Ingolstadt

In the lecture hall of Ingolstadt, Salmerón's flowing phrases, literary allusions, scriptural nuances met blank stares. As seen in the portrait of Claude Jay, what animated Chancellor von Eck left the theological dullards in the benches unmoved. Salmerón's enthusiasm withered before the uncomprehending gape of the students and he began to lose heart.[105]

To offset this discouragement, Bavaria had very little from her own resources to offer. Salmerón and Canisius stood shoulder to shoulder with Claude Jay in the conviction that Jay had reached five years earlier, that the only thing that could stave off rigor mortis from setting in on the theological life of the university was the foundation of a Jesuit college. They had high hopes that such a collegiate foundation would soon be realized through the generosity and conviction of Duke Wilhelm and Chancellor von Eck. But death rudely shattered these high hopes. In March 1550 duke and chancellor went to their graves.[106] The whole weary process of converting Bavarian officialdom to see the pressing need of a college for the Jesuits had to begin anew, repeating to the new Duke Albrecht and the new Chancellor Georg Stockhammer the reasons that had won over their predecessors.

Life at Ingolstadt, far from congenial, heightened the discouragement. Salmerón, never at a loss for words in Latin, Spanish, or Italian, was tongue-tied as far as German was concerned, and he had to look on helplessly and disconsolately as Canisius enjoyed the apostolic consolation of being able to move among the populace of Ingolstadt, conversing, instructing, preaching.[107] No inspiration came from the local clergy, most of whom did not bother to recite the divine office on the grounds that it was too difficult and too long. Students in other faculties of the university had other occupations far more exhilarating than study, such as rollicking through the streets at night, shooting muskets and blasting away on trumpets, running noisy monster parties, cracking the heads of the unfortunates they might happen to meet, all of which led the professors to opine that Ingolstadt was without peer among the German universities for its spirit of license and lack of discipline.[108]

The German diet too presented problems. During Lent butter was ordinarily forbidden. Oil was permitted. But the three Jesuits found the German brand of oil, so unlike Italian oil, difficult to swallow. The famous professor of medicine at Ingolstadt, Johann Agricola, spoke of the oil of his own country as "our stinking and detestable kind," a possible source of all kinds of ills. Fortunately the pope had granted permission to the Ingolstadtians to use butter during Lent on condition that they make a small offering to Our Lady's Chapel. So the three Jesuits had their butter.[109] But this little amelioration of life in Germany did not blind Agricola to the general dispiritedness of the visiting professors. Suspecting that they were not overhappy at Ingolstadt, he wrote a warning to Heinrich Schweicker, the secretary of Duke Albrecht, with the suggestion that the duke pen a note of encouragement to the fathers. Otherwise he might lose them.[110]

Jesuit Changes at Ingolstadt

Within a few months, as it turned out, Duke Albrecht did lose two of the Jesuits. Bishop Otto Truchsess summoned Claude Jay to Augsburg in June 1550. The bishop of Verona, Luigi Lippomano, intensely irritated that Salmerón had been taken out of Italy in the first place, worked through diplomatic channels to dislodge Salmerón from Ingolstadt.[111] Lippomano, one of the more pastorally oriented Italian bishops, faced a delicate and uneasy situation in his diocese despite the invaluable work of Gian Matteo Giberti, who died there in 1543. To secure the achievements of Giberti, Lippomano needed men like Salmerón.[112] To Cardinal Cervini, Lippomano complained: "God forgive the people responsible for the removal of Don Alphonso from Verona, where he was doing some good, quite in contrast to the situation in Ingolstadt, buried as he is in a hothouse with no one to talk to because he is ignorant of the German tongue."[113] Lippomano made his point with Pope Pius IV and obtained permission for Salmerón's withdrawal from Ingolstadt.[114]

The faculty of the university were sincerely sorry to lose this Spanish confrere, and gave him, "another Eck, and even greater than Eck,'' a testimonial dinner of magnanimous proportions. "The Germans," explained Canisius to Ignatius, "are accustomed to do this as a symbol of enduring friendship."[115] Salmerón quit Ingolstadt on 15 August. That same month two other Jesuits, Nicholas Goudanus and Peter Schorich, filled the posts left open by Jay and Salmerón, and joined Canisius at Ingolstadt to deal with the dullards and the procrastinating Duke Albrecht, who continued to give the tantalizing impression that he was at the point of immediately founding a Jesuit college.[116]

Salmerón's stay at Ingolstadt had a long range historical significance: the inauguration of a strong and perduring Spanish Jesuit presence in the university life of central Europe, which had a paramount place in the renewal of the Church in those areas. A distinguished roll of Spanish Jesuits, formed in the lecture halls of Alcalá and Salamanca, took university posts at the borderline between the Catholic allegiance and the Protestant allegiance, and stabilized the weak Catholic positions. This was a Spanish contribution, widely unrecognized, to the Counter-Reformation.

A Review of the Jesuit Constitutions

On 24 September Salmerón was in Verona, and in about two weeks began a course of lectures on the Gospel of St. Matthew. During Advent he preached in the cathedral.[117] After Christmas he left for Rome, to which Ignatius had summoned him and other Jesuits for a conference of deep import for the young Society.[118]

The purpose of this conference was to review and criticize the order's *Constitutions*, which Ignatius had made his main preoccupation since March 1547, when Juan Polanco became his secretary.[119] In late 1550 Ignatius invited all the living cofounders of the Society, probably including Xavier, as well as other Jesuits to Rome.[120] Salmerón arrived in early January 1551.[121] Others present at the conference included Laynez, Borgia, Diego Miró, Antonio Araoz, André des Freux, Andrés de Oviedo, and Francisco de Rojas.[122] Ignatius presented them with a revised Spanish version of his original text, also in Spanish. For a month, until 1 February, the conference went over this text.[123]

During this month Salmerón was perhaps the most active participant. Some of his criticism was general in nature. He felt, for example, that the *Constitutions* were too long. He asked that the text be shortened and that any amplifications be cast in the form of Declarations. Ignatius agreed, and put much of the text under study in the shape of explanatory Declarations.[124] Salmerón thought that the number of impediments to admission into the Society—there were ten—should be cut to five. Ignatius did this.[125]

Salmerón's other suggestions were more particular. A few of these follow. Text A of the *General Examen* reads: "the end of this Society is to devote itself not only to the salvation and perfection of the members' own souls. . . ." Salmerón proposed that the phrase "with God's grace" be included. Ignatius agreed, and changed the sentence to read: "the end of this Society is to devote itself with God's grace not only to the salvation and per-fection of the members' own souls. . . ."[126] Salmerón had res-ervations about a question asked of one seeking admission into the Society: "Has he come from a family long Christian or one recently converted." This question touched directly on a sensi-tive issue in Spain and Portugal, that of the New Christians and the sincerity of their conversion to Christianity. To ask this ques-tion could spark the accusation of racism on the Society's part. Salmerón, it seems, wanted to remove any grounds for such suspicions. Ignatius deleted the question in the next version he made, text B, but restored it later. It remained in the *General Examen*.[127]

On the important question of penances and austerities in the Society, Salmerón made a prudent suggestion. Text A, the text used at this conference, states that there are no regular penances or austerities in the Society "save those which each judges is more helpful for his spiritual advancement." Salmerón felt that this matter was too serious to be left to an individual's personal inspiration, and therefore recommended the inclusion of the phrase "with the superior's approval." Ignatius accepted the suggestion.[128]

In the *General Examen* Ignatius wrote a wide description of the experiences that an applicant to the Society should expect.

Salmerón thought that the wording could be more precise. Text A reads: "The first experience is in making the Spiritual Exercises for one month . . . in meditating and contemplating his sins and the events and mysteries of the life, death, resurrection and ascension of Christ Our Lord." Salmerón pointed to the distinction between *meditación* and *contemplación*, a distinction Ignatius himself habitually made. Ignatius concurred and changed the text to read: "The first experience consists in making the Spiritual Exercises for a month . . . in meditating upon his sins, contemplating the events and mysteries of the life, death, resurrection and ascension of Christ Our Lord." [129]

Salmerón questioned a statement in part one of the *Constitutions* that touched his past life in an especially personal way. Text A reads that a Jesuit, in order to be admitted to profession, must have passed his twenty-fifth year. Because of his youth, Salmerón had not been permitted to be ordained to the priesthood with his friends in Venice in June 1537. And when he pronounced his solemn vows in April 1541, he was only a bit beyond his twenty-fifth year. He raised these questions, perhaps playfully: is this age requirement of strict obligation; could profession be allowed sometime before the twenty-fifth year? Ignatius left the text unchanged, but inserted a declaration which states that lack of qualifications "such as bodily strength, or the age for the profession, or something similar," if compensated for by other qualities, can be dispensed with by the general." [130]

Salmerón and Laynez jointly sponsored a change in part four, chapter six of the *Constitutions* on the study of biblical languages. Text A reads: "If these languages are learned, the purpose should be to defend in its completeness the version [of the Scriptures] which the Church holds as approved." Salmerón and Laynez proposed two modifications, both of which reflected the scholarly attitudes of the two theologians, who had already served at the Council of Trent. The first modification: do not limit the purpose of studying the biblical languages *solely* to the defense of the approved version of the Scriptures, but rather include in the text the phrase: "*among the ends* which are proposed, one should be. . . ." The second proposed modification: do not propose to defend *in its completeness* the version of the Scriptures which the Church holds as approved, but rather state that one purpose of language study is to defend *"in so far as it is possible"* (*en quanto se pudiere*) the Church's version. Ignatius incorporated both suggestions into Text B, his next text. Seven years later, however, General Congregation I suppressed the second modification and removed the words *en quanto se pudiere*.[131]

On 30 January, two days before the close of the conference, Ignatius made a dramatic move. He directed a letter to the Jesuits at the meeting, rehearsing his infirmities, spiritual and physical, and requesting them to consider choosing another to take his place. He also included a simple statement of renunciation of the office of general. Andrés Oviedo agreed to the resignation. All the others rejected it. Ignatius remained in office. Then on 1 February the conference ended. It was a milestone in the slow, methodical labor of constructing the legal structure of the Jesuit way of life. Nadal sensed its importance and likened it to a general congregation.[132] The minutes of the meeting portray Salmerón as the most active of the participants.

Assignment to Naples

At the close of the conference, Ignatius assigned Salmerón to Naples.[133] This assignment opened a long period that stretched through the remaining thirty-four years of Salmerón's life, in which Naples was his main anchorage. Salmerón's personal history and the early Jesuit presence in Naples merged into one story.

Naples already knew the Society of Jesus through the preaching of Bobadilla, Antonio Araoz, and Laynez.[134] The Neapolitan reception was cordial. Crowds gathered to hear Laynez in late 1548 and early 1549. On 5 January 1549 he reported to Ignatius that many Neapolitans were trying to prevent his departure for his next assignment, Sicily; that he was trying to arrange that Bobadilla replace him; that some of the citizens requested either Bobadilla or Salmerón as a replacement.[135] Neapolitan sentiment was, therefore, friendly to the Society. This sentiment soon crystallized in a request for not only a Jesuit preacher but also for a Jesuit school.

Seven years only had elapsed since Pierre Favre had laid at Gandía the cornerstone for the first Jesuit school that received lay students, but by the end of 1551 there were eight such foundations in Europe.[136] It was almost inevitable that Naples, important metropolis that it was, should in time receive a Jesuit school into the ranks of its cultural institutions. Conditions were excellent. A formidable array of influential men began to formulate plans to open a Jesuit school: Ercole Pignatelli, Duke of Monteleone; Giovanni Alfonso Carafa, Count of Montorio; Lopé de Mardones, master of the viceroy's household and prime minister of the Kingdom of Naples; Dionisio de Caesena, O.S.B.; Girolamo Vignes, and Girolamo de Fonseca.[137] Calculating that the public appearance of a Jesuit in the city would be a sure way to arouse civic interest, these men asked Ignatius for a Jesuit Lenten preacher. Ignatius sent Salmerón. And Salmerón exploited the opportunity to the full.

In the maturity of his energies, eloquent and engaging, Salmerón gave a Lenten course on the Epistle to the Galatians. Four or five times each week he spoke at the Church of Diva Maria. He also spoke at the Hospital of the Incurables, home of more than six hundred poverty-stricken patients.[138] The humanist bishop of Ugento, Antonio Miturno, wrote Ignatius that Salmerón's like was not known in Naples, so attractive was his teaching so intent were his listeners.[139] Friends of the Society began a search for a suitable place for the proposed school.[140] The future glowed with the promise of hundreds of young Neapolitans reciting their catechism and chorusing their Latin and Greek paradigms under skilled Jesuit masters.

The Second Period of the Council of Trent

Then came an interruption, the first of the many that were to break the continuity of Salmerón's work at Naples. After Easter he received a letter from Ignatius, informing him of his reassignment by the pope to the Council of Trent.[141] The new pope, Julius III, whom Salmerón knew as Cardinal Giammaria del Monte and as one of the presidents during the first period of the council, was determined to push through to completion what Pope Paul III had inaugurated at Trent, and assigned 1 May 1551 as the opening date. Julius told Ignatius that he wanted Salmerón and Laynez to carry on where they had left off at the council.[142] There was nothing for Salmerón to do but to put aside the business of his college. But negotiations had at least been started, and others could continue from there.

By now it must be evident that it is the easiest thing in the world to lose track of the sequence of events in Salmerón's life. A baffling list of assignments and missions that took him to Ireland, Scotland, northern Italy, Bavaria, and Naples, as papal diplomat, popular preacher, conciliar theologian, school founder, and religious superior resist all efforts to fit them into a neat, symmetrical design. His future life, if anything, was even more complex.

On his way to the north Salmerón did some apostolic work at Gubbio with his friend Cardinal Cervini until 24 June. Then he joined Diego Laynez at Florence. The two then travelled to Trent, where they arrived on 27 July 1551.[143] The two Jesuits found the council, which had convened on the assigned date, 1 May, almost completely bogged down, since very few delegates had yet come. Their arrival raised the spirits of the leaders of the council, who exclaimed in relief: "Now we believe there really will be a council."[144]

If the cordiality of Cardinal Marcello Crescenzio was any measure of how they were to be cared for, the two Jesuits would have had the most comfortable and agreeable of lodgings. Red tape and a confusion of details, however, landed them the very first night in a stuffy, small, stifling room in the house of the council's secretary, Angelo Massarelli. Laynez and Salmerón referred to it as "the oven." In the room there was neither desk nor chair, only a footstool and a chest, a regular type bed and a truckle bed, which when pulled out made it impossible to take more than two steps within the room. Laynez, Salmerón, and a lay brother named John, Laynez's secretary, made the best of the first night, Laynez and the brother sleeping in the two beds, and Salmerón sleeping on the chest. One such night was enough for Salmerón. Nearby was the home of his friend, Luigi Lippomano, the bishop of Verona, and there he went each evening. Lippomano opened his house also to Laynez and Brother John, but they elected to stay in "the oven" lest they hurt Massarelli's feelings. It took some little time, but finally a suitable room was found in which the Jesuit theologians might conveniently study and receive visitors.[145]

Debates on the Holy Eucharist

Ahead lay nine busy months in the council. Only five of Salmerón's letters for this period have survived. Business began in earnest on September 1, when the twelfth session convened and set the target, 11 October, for the next session. The next day, the second, the theologians received articles on the Holy Eucharist for study.[146] On the eighth, the debates began in the afternoon. Laynez, Salmerón, and Juan Arze, a secular priest, spoke during the first meeting.[147] To Salmerón and Laynez these articles were familiar, since they had been on the committee at Bologna in 1547 that formulated in summary form the teachings of the Protestants on the sacraments.[148]

Laynez concentrated especially on the dogmatic question of Christ's presence in the Holy Eucharist. Salmerón focused primarily on the disciplinary issue of the reception of the Holy Eucharist by the laity under the forms of bread and wine. He stressed that this issue concerned practice, not dogma. He dissected article eight, which asserted that the laity, including children, were obliged by divine law to receive the Holy Eucharist under the forms of bread and wine. He based his opening argument against this article on the long standing tradition in the Church of communion to the laity under the species of bread alone. Tradition was ever one of Salmerón's favorite arguments, including as it did the assurance of Christ that the Church would be free of error.[149]

Salmerón and Laynez deeply impressed the conciliar fathers. Cardinal Marcello Crescenzio had them to dinner once a week, and insisted that Laynez's quartan ague was not sufficient reason to keep him away. Egidio Fuscarario, the Dominican bishop of Modena, was delighted with their addresses and wrote to Ignatius: "Fathers Laynez and Salmerón have discoursed with the ultimate in brilliance on the most Blessed Sacrament of the Eucharist against the Lutherans. I consider myself fortunate to be alive at a time that has produced fathers so learned and so holy."[150] These debates culminated in the decrees and canons of the thirteenth session on 11 October 1551.

Promise of Protestant Presence at the Council

Salmerón's report to Ignatius was moderately encouraging.

He wrote that the conciliar fathers passed the decrees on the Holy Eucharist "with a broad consensus and unanimity of opinion" (*con mucho consenso y concordia de votos*). The groundwork done at Bologna was bearing fruit in the rapid advance of the business. Other doors of encouragement were also opening. Salmerón advised Ignatius that Archbishop Adolph von Schauenburg of Cologne and Archbishop Erasmus von Linburg of Strassburg had arrived at Trent. The German presence at Trent was on the upswing.[151]

This German presence also included a promise of Protestants coming to the council. For seven months, through 1551–52, papal nuncio Sebastiano Pighini negotiated in Germany with the Protestant princes and theologians. Emperor Charles V, in his perennial quest for religious peace in Germany, endorsed Pighini's mission. The nuncio promised the Protestants a safe-conduct and freedom of discussion in the council. He asked of them concurrence on three important points: the definitive vote rested with the bishops; the exclusion of the council's earlier decrees from reconsideration; the competence of the pope to convoke, suspend, or close the council. Some Protestants reneged. Then they relented. But their agreement carried within it a grievous flaw: they reserved the right to make "observations" on the articles already defined by the council.[152]

The news of the Protestants' decision to go to Trent sidetracked Salmerón's most recent interventions in the council. In deference to the awaited Protestant theologians, the thirteenth session postponed its final vote on the issue of Holy Communion to the laity under the forms of bread and wine, which had absorbed so much of Salmerón's time and energy.[153] This move checked the council's momentum. But it was only the first in a series of delays that irritated Salmerón and soured him on the future of the council.

Debates on Penance and Extreme Unction

While the Protestants were taking the road toward the Alps, the grind of routine business went on in the council. Salmerón wrote Ignatius that the next sacraments to be considered were penance and extreme unction, and that the next formal session was set for 25 November.[154] On 12 October the theologians

211

received for their criticism twelve articles on penance and four on extreme unction.[155] Five days later, on the twentieth, Laynez and Salmerón opened the debates. Polanco identified the lead-off speakers as "our two men" (*nostri duo*).[156] They shared the four hours allotted to the congregation that began at three in the afternoon. Laynez spoke on the first eight articles on penance. Salmerón took up with the ninth article.[157] He insisted on two kinds of punishment, eternal and temporal. With the remission of guilt and eternal punishment in the sacrament of penance, there remained temporal punishment, for which satisfaction must be made.[158] Salmerón wanted to continue his discourse and take up extreme unction, but since it was already sunset, the congregation was terminated for that day. Massarelli noted that Salmerón had developed his arguments "with utmost clarity and learning" (*diserte admodum et docte comprobavit*).[159] The fourteenth session convened on schedule, on 25 November, and issued its decrees and canons on penance and extreme unction.[160]

Debates on the Sacrifice of the Mass and Orders

The next matter for study and debate centered on nine articles extracted from Protestant writings on the Sacrifice of the Mass and six on orders. On 3 December 1551 the theologians received these articles.[161] Four days later, on the seventh, the discussions opened at ten o'clock. Laynez was the sole speaker for the four hours until two o'clock. An hour later the theologians again met. For three hours, until six o'clock, Salmerón spoke on orders. His speech was a shoal of distinctions.[162] One of these distinctions he drew between the external and eternal priesthood, which is tied to the sacrament, and the spiritual priesthood, which can be lost by sin and regained through penance. He set up the category of the spiritual priesthood to explain the priesthood of the faithful as it is propounded in the text "You are an elect people and a royal priesthood" (1 Pt. 2:9).[163]

The debates continued through December, until the twenty-ninth. From 5 January to 13 January the conciliar fathers considered the work done by the theologians. By 21 January the decrees and canons were ready for the fifteenth session, which was scheduled for the twenty-fifth.[164] By the narrowest of squeaks, however, they missed formal approval. They were not brought to the floor. Only ten years later did they come up for formal vote, during the third period of the council.

Protestant Presence at the Council

Salmerón got off to Ignatius an explanation of the strange fate of the fifteenth session and the slowdown in the pace of the council's business: the Protestant ambassadors had arrived at Trent and had requested a delay in the voting on the Sacrifice of the Mass and on orders until the advent of their own theologians. This development, Salmerón told Ignatius, upset a number in the council. "Some have interpreted this one way, some another. Some think that it comes down to a tacit suspension of the council because they do not believe that they [the Protestants] will come. Others think that they will indeed come, reinforced by the emperor and the princes who have dispatched them. . . ."[165]

Protestant ambassadors had been arriving in contingents since the late autumn of 1551. The first to arrive were two from the duke of Württemberg on 22 October. On 9 January 1552, two came from the Prince Elector Moritz of Saxony. On 24 January, the eve of the scheduled fifteenth session, the Protestants laid before the council their basic positions: a more secure safe-conduct for their theologians; reconsideration of the council's earlier decrees; repudiation of the episcopal oath of fidelity to the pope; the acceptance of scripture alone as the norm of faith.[166] Salmerón elucidated for Ignatius some of their other actions: a denunciation of the sitting council as neither free, nor universal, nor christian; a demand that it be acknowledged that a council is superior to the pope. Salmerón continued, to say that the Würtembergers presented to the council a book that contained the articles of their faith. This was the *Würtemberg Confession*.[167] These stipulations burst the bubble of optimism about religious unity. The hard reality of basic divisions wiped away the dreams of union in faith among the Christians of Europe. But the improbable hopes lingered on.

These flickering hopes shaped the destiny of the fifteenth session. It convened on 25 January 1552 as scheduled. The Protestant ambassadors did not attend. The council, again in deference to the Protestants, withheld action on the canons and decrees already formulated on the Sacrifice of the Mass and orders. They limited themselves to issuing a more explicit safe-conduct for the expected Protestant theologians, as demanded by their ambassadors. Salmerón told Ignatius that the council issued this safe-conduct with a distinctly clear purpose in mind: "so that the Protestants might come [to Trent] and dispute matters of faith according to the norms of Holy Scripture, the traditions of the Apostles, the consensus of the Church, the authority of the fathers, and the actions of the councils. The council phrased the document this way," continued Salmerón, "because they [the Protestants] demand that Scripture alone be the norm during the debates." Salmerón called the session "a washout" (*session en blanco*). It was prorogued until 19 March.[168]

These developments sapped Salmerón's earlier optimism about the council. Inaction distressed him. He even thought of getting away from Trent. The day after the vacuous fifteenth session, he broached to Ignatius the possibility of a change.

> If the council should slacken off in its intent to get things done, Your Reverence might reflect on the possibility of negotiating with the pope with a view to getting us out of here. I bring this up, since it would be better to head for some city in Italy and get something done there than to stay here and waste time. I make a special point of introducing this suggestion in as much as the legate has named two Italian friars as theologians of the Holy See, one a Carmelite, the other a Conventual Franciscan. What is on deck for debate at the moment is little. And there is no shortage of theologians. To your more prudent and balanced judgment I submit this whole business.[169]

This was a drastic change of mood and attitude from the first period of the council, when Salmerón argued against Ignatius's suggestion that it might be better for him to withdraw from the council and aid in setting up a college in Florence.

Salmerón found no assuagement of his disenchantment in the events of the next three months. On 16 February the archbishop of Trier withdrew from the council. Trent's climate was eroding his health. On 11 March the archbishops of Mainz and Cologne left. Moritz of Saxony was invading their principalities. On 19 March the fifteenth session, prorogued until that date out of courtesy for the Protestant theologians who presumably were on their way, shrivelled up in frustration. Only a handful of Lutherans had come from Wittenberg. The council again prorogued the session, this time until 1 May.[170]

A Proposal from Ignatius

During these debates, Salmerón and Laynez received a surprising suggestion from Ignatius. Ignatius wrote them on 29 November 1551 and proposed a plan whereby the two Jesuits were to try to persuade the council to pass an act of confirmation, or at least of approbation, of the Society. The conciliar movement of the fifteenth century remained a vivid memory, and Ignatius realized that in some countries there were theologians and lay leaders for whom the voice of a general council was a fundamental in the life of the Church. It might be a distinct help toward obtaining official approval of the Society in those particular countries, reasoned Ignatius, if the Council of Trent took the initiative and gave its seal of approbation. Salmerón and Laynez, after consultation with the bishop of Calahorra, Juan Bernal Díaz de Luca, sent Ignatius on 22 December 1551 their firm disapproval of the idea. Their reasons were: no religious order had ever before been approved by a general council, but by the pope only; there was so much important unfinished conciliar business to which the prelates wanted to give their undistracted attention; the Jesuit *Constitutions* were not yet completely translated into Latin, a definite desideratum before anything like the review of them in the council could be undertaken.[171] With his usual wise deference to the judgment of men who were in a position to know a particular situation better than he, Ignatius withdrew his suggestion.[172]

Salmerón and Laynez, nevertheless, did carry through a modification of the plan by visiting various bishops and theologians at Trent and explaining in detail the Jesuit manner of life.[173] During their round of visits, Laynez and Salmerón decided also to brief the intelligent and hard-fighting Dominican Melchior Cano, whose special bugbear was the Society, about the purpose of the Jesuits. The meeting of two hours failed to disabuse Cano of his conviction that the Jesuit order, flawed, as he felt, by basic defects within its juridical structure, was a serious menace to the Catholic Church. Laynez finally asked Cano why he had taken upon himself the responsibility of pope and bishops to condemn what they had approved and continued to approve. Cano, with a smile, retorted: "Sir, would you, as a master of the schools, not have the dogs bark when the shepherds sleep?" Laynez came back: "Yes indeed, let them bark, but at the wolves and not at other dogs." Tempers boiled. Cano shot at Laynez: "Get rid of those [Jesuit] novelties (*Abigite istas novitates*)." Laynez shot back, in Spanish: "[get rid of] istas merdas," and left the room. Before he reached the street, he was struck with repentance, returned, fell at Cano's feet, begged his pardon. Cano made the most of the incident. Polanco recorded this observation: "For Cano this remained a terrible crime, which he used to recall in shocked language and about which he expressed his pain by breaking off his narrative at the unspeakable words" (*Hoc fuit apud Canum atrox crimen, et de quo hyperbolice per aposiopesim referre solet et conqueri*).[174]

Mission to Innsbruck

In March 1552 Salmerón received an order from Ignatius that briefly interrupted his work at Trent. Ignatius directed him to go through the Alps to Innsbruck to see Emperor Charles personally about a prospect he held especially dear: the foundation of a college in the Spanish Netherlands.[175] Ever since 1550 Ignatius had envisioned this college. But he met consistent rebuff. The hardheaded, businesslike sister of Charles, Queen Maria, who was in charge of the Netherlands, held Ignatius at bay. Queen Maria's minister, Viglius van Zwichem, regarded the idea coldly.[176] Ever since van Zwichem had dealt with Nicolás Bobadilla, he had an unfavorable picture of the Society. He recalled the rage of Charles V when he learned that Bobadilla had publicly criticized his efforts to reconcile Protestants and Catholics by the *Interim* at Augsburg in 1548; he noted that Bobadilla wore no distinctive religious garb, as did other religious; he noted that Jesuits did not live in community. "Rather are they fully at liberty," he wrote, "to move and wander about, without companions or witnesses, like Bobadilla, who sat at table with all the world and was always discussing the latest news."[177] Ignatius met therefore a stonewall of rebuff in the high counsels of the Spanish Netherlands.

Salmerón was commissioned to break through that stonewall. He reached Innsbruck on 2 April 1552.[178] He could not have arrived at a worse time to do business with Emperor Charles, for Innsbruck was teeming with rumors of war. The alliance between the French monarchy and the Protestant German princes against Charles, struck at the Lochau heath in early October 1551, was not in motion.[179] On 15 March 1552 King Henry II of France was perched, ready to descend on Toul and the Rhine. On 1 April the Protestant princes were at the gates of Augsburg. Salmerón arrived at Innsbruck on the second. Two days later he left. He had achieved nothing.

Suspension of the Council

The day Salmerón left Innsbruck, the Protestants entered Augsburg. They then turned toward the Tyrol. On the sixth Charles, dismayed and in disarray, fled Innsbruck in the darkness of the night.[180] Salmerón arrived back at Trent amid the swirl of rumors about the ominous events north of the Alps. Fear of invasion by the Protestants swept through the council. The papal legate, Cardinal Marcello Crescenzio, was mortally ill. On 28 April the council decreed the suspension of its work.[181] Less than a month later, on 23 May, the Protestants entered Innsbruck.[182]

Return to Naples

On 2 May 1552, four days after the council was suspended, Salmerón left Trent for Padua. He bore within him sour memories of snags and sawyers. Ten years later, when rumors were circulating that he would be sent to the third period of the council, Salmerón threw up a barrage of reasons why he should be excused. He had it, he said, up to his ears with conciliar business. His immediate assignment after Padua was Florence. Summer was coming on and Ignatius, even though he wanted Salmerón to get along with the business of the Neapolitan college, decided to spare him the summer heat of lower Italy and instructed him to stay in the north, at Florence. There Salmerón remained until mid-September, when he traveled to Rome. There he spent about a month with Ignatius. By mid-October he was back to Naples.[183]

Almost three uninterrupted years in Naples followed. On his return there Salmerón found a school of three hundred young men learning Latin and Greek under five Jesuit teachers. While Salmerón was in the north during the Christmas period of 1551 Ignatius assigned a band of ten young scholastics, French, Flemings, Germans, Italians, and Spaniards, to the college, some as teachers, some as students.[184] He appointed Fr. Andrés de Oviedo the rector, and Nicolás Bobadilla the overall supervisor. On 14 February 1552 classes were inaugurated at a solemn ceremony, at which Fr. Jean Antoine Peltan gave a Latin speech in flowing Ciceronian style.[185] This young school became the focal point of Salmerón's apostolic work life for the next three years.

Neapolitan Problems

From the beginning the school presented Salmerón with awkward problems. The first was jurisdictional. Bobadilla, the superintendent, and Oviedo, the rector, clashed about their authority. Ignatius continually tried to persuade the two men to work together. He sent them long, detailed, and practical instructions. He cautioned them that, although they could make changes in case of necessity, no change could be permanent without his approval. Even though he felt that Bobadilla's high-spirited way of doing things was made to order for the starting of a new institution, he advised Bobadilla to stop using the familiar form of "you." But Ignatius's stream of instructions did not halt the breakdown of harmony between Bobadilla and Oviedo. Bobadilla even accused Oviedo of being somehow involved with Protestant teaching. Stories reached Rome about the collapse of discipline at the school. Some Neapolitans seriously criticized the college because of rumors about "ugly things" (*cose brutte*) that were happening there.[186] Bobadilla made himself persona non grata to some of the Neapolitan civic leaders. Ettore Pignatelli, the duke of Monteleone, told Ignatius that Bobadilla's preaching "rubs his listeners the wrong way." He urged Ignatius to dispatch Bobadilla to preach in the countryside for a couple of months and to replace him with Salmerón in the city.[187]

In late September Ignatius ordered Bobadilla to Salerno. If Bobadilla should find Salerno undesirable, he was to go wherever in the Neapolitan kingdom he found the climate best for his health. Salmerón arrived in mid-October. Bobadilla did not leave until after late January 1553, four months after Ignatius's order to quit Naples. Salmerón set to work to bring order to the college.[188]

Another problem was housing. The accommodations were

inadequate. Renovations had to be made in the school and chapel. Salmerón led the way in the work, carting on his shoulders baskets of excavated earth.[189] Another problem was financial. The Jesuits were living in severe privation. Earlier friends had died or moved from the city. A new viceroy, Francisco Pacheco, had taken office. Destitution threatened the Jesuit community. In 1553 Ignatius gave Salmerón permission to beg. Salmerón then explained to different Neapolitans the needs of his community. Several friends responded generously. One offered a house, which Salmerón, however, refused because it was so tiny that it could not accommodate even three men. The city offered a measure of wheat.[190]

One especially tempting source of revenue opened up, but only briefly. Juan Fonseca, bishop of Castellamare di Stabia, royal chaplain of Naples and member of an influential Spanish family, held the office of prefect of the theology faculty in the University of Naples. Fonseca, "a man of notable learning" (*huom dottissimo*), came to know the Jesuits at the Council of Trent and concluded that they were precisely the men he needed to strengthen his theological staff.[191] In 1554 he asked Ignatius for Salmerón. Ignatius refused.[192] At issue was the practice of religious poverty as understood in the Society of Jesus. The Jesuit *Constitutions* declared that members of the Society of Jesus should not demand or accept alms or stipends "in recompense for masses or confessions or preaching or lecturing or visiting or any other ministry among those which the Society may exercise according to our Institute. . . ."[193]

This was Ignatius's approach to the preservation of the Society in freedom from avarice in the service it gives to God and men. To the chair that Fonseca desired Salmerón to take was attached an annual stipend of eighty ducats. The Jesuit college could have used those eighty ducats, but Ignatius, faithful to his principle, declined. On 3 November 1554 he courteously explained to Fonseca that the acceptance of this particular kind of post was against the Society's *Constitutions*. He tried to ease the refusal by explaining that he had likewise refused the Society's good friend, Cardinal Marcello Cervini, who had sought a Jesuit for a founded chair at the Sapienza University in Rome.[194]

The Lenten Preacher

In this financial crisis Salmerón himself was the best advertisement for the school. The viceroy, Francisco Pacheco, wanted Salmerón to be the Lenten preacher. At the beginning of the year, Salmerón halted his scriptural instructions in the cathedral so that he could prepare these Lenten sermons.[195] Once again he had the special opportunity to use his oratorical gifts, and, if one can judge by his own report, the social elite of Naples hung on his every word during that penitential season. With that naïveté which Ignatius always enjoyed, Salmerón wrote Ignatius on 1 April 1554:

> It has pleased Our Lord that our Lenten sermons have been brought to an end with much glory to him and consolation to the señores who without a single lapse in their attendance heard me. Many expressed the wish that Lent were longer so that they might hear more of my discourses. My audience was very large. But it was more than a matter of numbers; the people attending were distinguished by their high social quality. Not only were there knights, gentlemen of the city, and Spaniards on hand, but some of the titled nobility and the more elite ladies as well. They came not just once or twice, as is their normal practice, but each and every single day. They persevered right to the end with evidence of great taste for the word of God and of advantage to their souls.[196]

Polanco made the note that men were in awe of Salmerón's teaching "to the point of wonder" (*ad stuporem usque*).[197] Jerónimo Doménech wrote Ignatius in March 1553 that Salmerón's fame and effectiveness in the pulpit were spreading beyond the city of Naples to the full extent of the Neapolitan kingdom.[198]

Salmerón's sermons gathered more than spiritual fruit. The material future of the college became bright. "Many of the gentlemen who heard me," Salmerón wrote Ignatius, "felt that it would be a good idea to speak to the cardinal [Alfonso Carafa] with a view to getting permission to make a city wide drive for funds to obtain a house which could be the beginning of the foundation of the college. The cardinal was happy about the suggestion, and on Tuesday of Holy Week he summoned some gentlemen especially equipped for the task of collecting alms."[199] The drive succeeded magnificently. By 1 April a little less than fifteen hundred ducats had been collected. And Salmerón saw the prospect of reaching three thousand ducats.[200] One of the benefactors was a widow, Belotta Spinola, of the widely known Genoese family. She contributed five hundred gold scudi.[201] A month after Salmerón sent the good news about the drive to Ignatius, he left for Rome on 5 May for a brief visit. During his absence the Neapolitan friends purchased a new house, "suitably situated in the center of the city" (*salubris situs in ipso umbilico civitatis*), as Polanco described it. In the middle of August the Jesuits moved in.[202]

Almost immediately the Jesuit community found that they had new and embarrassing neighbors. A pious and poor woman named Feliciana had undertaken the care of six or seven maidens. Each week she led the girls to the Jesuit church for confession and holy communion. When the Jesuits moved into their new residence, Feliciana let it be known that she was going to settle nearby. Salmerón, fearful of scandal, admonished her to stay away. Feliciana, however, persisted, and procured a house next door to the Jesuit residence. The windows of each house looked in on one another. Salmerón forbade Feliciana and her brood to enter the church to receive the sacraments. The sanction worked. Soon Salmerón found places for the group in reputable monasteries.[203]

The Sodalities

Salmerón supplemented his labor in the pulpit and in the school with an apostolic instrument that was a favorite among the early Jesuits: the sodality. He gave a vital impetus to two organizations for lay persons that were initiated by a young Jesuit priest, Giovanni Francesco Araldo. The first, Sodality of Recipients of the Holy Eucharist (*Congregatio Communicantium*), was designed for men. The members received holy communion each fortnight, taught catechism, reconciled enemies, encouraged others to the frequent reception of the sacraments. Ignatius directed that the name be changed to Sodality of the Most Holy Sacrament (*Congregatio Sanctissimi Sacramenti*). By 1557 it numbered about fifty men of diverse social classes, priests, artisans, doctors, whom Araldo called "the gold of this city."[204] The second group, the Sodality of Faithful Followers of Jesus (*Congregatio Devotarum Jesu*), was for women. Its members received holy communion monthly, taught catechism to the domestics of the household, discontinued the use of facial rouge. Years later Salmerón supplemented these two sodalities with a third, designed especially for benefactors and men in the higher echelons of society. These men met weekly for discussion on spiritual topics.[205] College and sodality symbolized the persistence of the union of *eruditio* and *pietas*, of learning and devotion, in the Jesuit apostolate.

Two New Popes

In the spring of 1555, Salmerón was again swept into the flow of international events that took him away from Naples for the next year and a half. The tenth of April was a day of great joy to all champions of Church reform. Cardinal Marcello Cervini, one of those associated with reformers like Gasparo Contarini and Gianpietro Carafa, was elected pope and took the name Marcellus II. Salmerón was a personal friend of the new pontiff and had worked with him at Trent. It was Cervini, in fact, who had kept him and Laynez supplied with bread and wine during the first period of the council.[206] Salmerón wrote to Ignatius and asked his leave to go to Rome to greet Pope Marcellus and to

Cities visited by Alfonso Salmerón on four papal missions

get a little change and relaxation after his strenuous schedule of preaching during the Lenten season. Ignatius agreed and summoned him to Rome. Salmerón also had something else in mind. He was thinking of an abbey, outside Naples, called Cappella, which produced a thousand ducats or more in revenue. The abbey was one of Cardinal Cervini's benefices. And Cervini had indicated his intention to give it to the Jesuit college in Naples. Salmerón hoped to effect the transfer during his visit with Pope Marcellus.[207] At the beginning of May Salmerón arrived in Rome to find the city plunged in deep sorrow. Marcellus had died on 1 May, not a month after his election.

Salmerón stayed in Rome during the tense conclave, which ended on 23 May with the unexpected election of the seventy-nine year old, hotheaded, volcanic Gianpietro Carafa, who chose the name Paul IV. Salmerón paid for his delay in Rome, because the new pope very soon marked him out for a mission to Germany and Poland.[208] For a year and a half he was to be absent from Naples.

Pastoral Problems

During the weeks in Rome before Salmerón set out on this mission to Germany and Poland, Ignatius asked his views on certain pastoral problems. Two years earlier, in 1553, Ignatius had commissioned theologians in Rome, probably Olave, des Freux, and Polanco, to prepare a booklet for confessors. The next year, in 1554, the printing firm of Blado issued, under Polanco's name, *A Brief Directory to Help in the Correct Execution of the Office of Confessor (Breve Directorium ad confesarii munus rite obeundum)*.

Ignatius also wanted a companion volume on holy communion because of the opposition to the practice of frequently approaching the altar. He turned to Salmerón first, on 24 June. Then he turned to Andrés Oviedo. Oviedo did not finish his work, since he was preparing to leave for Ethiopia. He left his unfinished papers with Cristóbal de Madrid. Salmerón worked rapidly—too rapidly perhaps, since his tiny volume needed considerable refining. He gave it to Polanco, who in turn passed it on to Francesco Palmio and Madrid. These tried to give greater felicity to the style. In the fall of 1555, some prints were made.

They did not carry the author's name, and they were meant only for Jesuits. Printing mistakes marred these private copies. Stylistic blemishes remained. Finally, in February 1557, a year and a half after Ignatius first commissioned Salmerón, *A Booklet on the Frequent Reception of the Holy Eucharist (De frequenti usu sanctissimi Eucharistiae sacramenti libellus)* appeared under Madrid's name. The burden of this booklet of many authors was to establish that, for persons with the proper dispositions of heart, it is better to receive holy communion than to abstain. More doctrinal than practical in tone, it helped to create an attitude favorable to frequent, even daily, holy communion.[209]

Another pastoral problem that Ignatius presented to Salmerón, in July 1555, concerned the sacrament of penance. It touched a delicate moral issue. The question Ignatius asked was this: did he [Ignatius] as general superior have the power to dismiss a member of the Society because of a mortal sin of which he learned in confession? Salmerón answered in the affirmative but with the condition that the dismissal itself did not amount to a revelation of the mortal sin. This question seems to have troubled Ignatius for a long time, since as far back as 1547–48 he had put it to the Dominican Master of the Sacred Palace, Egidio Foscarari. And more recently he had presented it to Laynez and Cristóbal Madrid. All replied as had Salmerón. And Ignatius indicated that he had acted on this opinion a number of times.[210]

When Salmerón responded to Ignatius's request for advice, he most likely did so when dining privately with Ignatius. Ignatius took his meals, not in the community's dining hall, but in a room adjacent to his bedroom. He usually invited to join him those whose advice he sought on the Society's business. Salmerón was among these guests.[211]

A Papal Mission to Germany and Poland

Salmerón's sojourn with Ignatius and the other Jesuits at the Society's headquarters came to an end in late July, when the papal mission to Germany and Poland set out from Rome. The mission was headed by Luigi Lippomano, bishop of Verona. Pope Julius III had appointed Lippomano just before his [Julius's] death. Pope Paul IV renewed this appointment. At a time when it was difficult to get the help of "reform priests" for diplomatic posts, Lippomano was unusually successful. He obtained the services of not only Salmerón but also of Bernadino Scotti, Theatine and future cardinal.[212] They left Rome on 27 July.

On the way north, in Bologna, Salmerón met Jerónimo Nadal, who was returning to Rome from a visitation of the Jesuit communities in Germany, Austria, and northern Italy. Salmerón, bringing Nadal up-to-date on the news in Rome, told him that on a single day Ignatius had dismissed ten from the Society. Nadal made this entry in his diary: "I heard from Father Salmerón that on that day Father Ignatius seemed far more cheerful than he usually is."[213]

On 20 August Salmerón's diplomatic party reached Augsburg. This was an especially important stop on their itinerary. At this city, already so prominent in Reformation history, Catholics and Protestants were again assembled in one of those frequent diets that seemed able to emphasize only the chasm between the two religious camps in the Empire. Pierre Favre, in 1541, had stressed the ineffectiveness of religious colloquies as the instrument for the achievement of religious peace. Now in 1555 Peter Canisius voiced the same sentiments to Ignatius. "I have nothing to say about the current meetings except that more harm than good is to be feared for the Catholic cause."[214] Lippomano's task was to persuade the Catholic princes to forestall any decision unfavorable to the Church.[215] Salmerón added what weight he could to Lippomano's arguments. He spoke with King Ferdinand, old friend of Claude Jay and Peter Canisius, and received that ruler's assurance that he was ready to lose his estates, his sons, his own life, rather than favor the Protestants in the least way.[216] But despite Ferdinand's good will, the tide was running in favor of the Protestants, and Lippomano decided to withdraw before he was forced to witness the humiliation of the Church. Salmerón was in his company when he quit Augsburg on 7 September.[217]

Grim Experiences in Poland

Poland was next to be visited. The Holy See felt deep apprehension about Poland because under the last of the Jagellons, the ambivalent Sigismund II Augustus, known as King

Tomorrow, many people were slipping away from their fidelity to the Catholic Church.[218] For thirty-two days, without respite, the two ambassadors pushed through Bohemia and Silesia to Warsaw. For Salmerón the crossing of the Oder River began a reliving of his frightful mission to Ireland, a nightmarish experience that awakened his worst memories of the Hibernian episode. Dolefully he complained to Ignatius:

> Ever since we arrived in Poland, we have run into such conditions for sleeping and eating that I am convinced they are every bit as bad as those experienced in Ireland. The man who passes through this kingdom but once has gone through purgatory, has done penance for all his sins, and in addition has also gained a plenary indulgence. That is how tough it is. Despite all the nuncio's providential concern, very rarely is wine to be found, and only with difficulty any beer. There is no want of water. And even if this tasted like the Tiber, we would prefer it to the beer we get. I shall not bring up the question of sleeping quarters except to say that only with the utmost difficulty can we find a little straw to spread on the ground. I prescind entirely from such things as sheets, mattresses, and blankets. . . . By God's grace we are all well. I feel certain that by the time we get away from here we shall be habituated to endure any sort of work and to suffer any cross sent by Christ our Lord. At least we shall be trained to make a virtue of necessity.[219]

Salmerón sent this woeful letter from Warsaw on 10 October 1555. Another fifteen to twenty days of travel faced the envoys before they reached Vilna, the residence of Sigismund Augustus. The king gave them a cool welcome, a reception which in Salmerón's estimation was a poor reward and not at all commensurate with the severe hardships they had endured. Two means only, announced the king, would he adopt to check heresy in his realm: a universal council, at that time an international improbability, or a national council, always an intrinsic threat of the development of an independent national church.[220] Salmerón made inquiries about the feasibility of establishing a Jesuit school in Poland only to be discouraged by a secretary of the king, who ruled it out as an utter impossibility. Heresy, Salmerón was informed, had a stranglehold on the nobles, and the bishops were helpless to take any effective action.[221]

Sickness and Withdrawal from Poland

Eventually, under the wear and tear of the journey and the

business of the mission, Salmerón's strong physical constitution gave way, and he became ill. According to his own diagnosis, it was due to the change of diet and the severity of the Polish winter. Lippomano decided to relieve his exhausted companion and have him return to Rome to give a verbal report to the pope. So, in early December, after thirty-three or four days at the Polish court, Salmerón said farewell to Vilna and took the road to Austria.[222] In his weakened condition he was not prepared for the rigors of the nasty mid winter weather of Central Europe, and it took over three weeks to reach Vienna, where he arrived on 23 December. He wrote to Ignatius on New Year's Day, 1556.

> We suffered so intensely on the road, especially with frozen feet, that the toes of my right foot were half-dead, and the others were in great pain. My whole body felt like a book falling apart, and I found myself unable to go any farther. By decision of the local bishop, who has passed on word to the pope, as well as on the advice of my brothers here in Vienna, I am staying here to recuperate. I am in the hands of the doctors. I do hope that the condition of my feet is not dangerous.[223]

Salmerón's description of his days in Poland made a deep impression on at least one fellow Jesuit. Three years later, Peter Canisius, himself on a mission to Poland, recalled Salmerón's experience and referred to him as "a man experienced in the rigors and chilling blasts of travel in Poland."[224]

A Papal Mission to The Netherlands

Salmerón, with resilience, quickly responded to the doctors' care. He left for Italy sometime in January. Ignatius directed him to stop at Siena, a city then harassed by the Spanish armies. By his sermons there Salmerón gave new heart to the devastated city, and the governor installed by King Philip II, Cardinal Francisco de Mendoza y Bobadilla, wanted to retain him. Pope Paul IV, however, had other plans for Salmerón and ordered him to Rome. Salmerón reached the Eternal City in April.[225] Immediately he was again caught up in the web of papal diplomacy.

Relations between King Philip II of Spain and Pope Paul IV, who as an ardent Neapolitan patriot deeply resented Spain's presence in Naples, deteriorated to the point of war. Spain not only had the more powerful armies; she had also out maneuvered the Vatican on the diplomatic front.[226] To his dismay, Paul IV had learned in February 1556 that Henry II of France, Philip II, and Emperor Charles V had concluded at Vaucelles an armistice for five years. This truce, greeted by Ignatius with joy, enraged Paul.[227] The pope realized that the Papal States stood alone, helpless and without allies, before the efficient Spanish armies to the north and the south. Cardinal Carlo Carafa, the pope's base and debauched nephew, to whom Paul entrusted the foreign relations of the Holy See, determined to woo France from the armistice. Papal diplomacy now hinged on breaking up the truce of Vaucelles; the pope's isolation had to be ended.

To achieve this objective, Cardinal Carafa arranged a two-pronged diplomatic thrust, one headed by himself to the French monarch, the other headed by Cardinal Scipione Rebiba to the Spanish king, then at Brussels. At the request of Pope Paul, Ignatius assigned Father Martin Olave to Carafa's entourage and Salmerón to Rebiba's. The official guise of Carafa's mission was "to conclude the sacred work of peace." His secret instructions were to drag the French king into war with Spain.[228]

Rome's strategy unfolded quickly and successfully. On 20 June the pope publicly chided Charles V. On 5 July Cardinal Carafa openly berated Philip II. By 13 July he had unhitched France from the truce of Vaucelles, received assurance of French support against Spain, and announced his intention to return to Rome. Cardinal Rebiba's mission to Philip II, actually a camouflage, lost all purpose, and also returned to Rome, where it arrived on 9 September.[229]

Sorrow in Rome

Two great sorrows had come to the Roman Jesuits since Salmerón's departure for Belgium at the end of May. Ignatius had died on 31 July. Martin Olave, prefect of studies at the Roman College, recently returned from the mission with Cardinal Carafa, died 17 August. Salmerón most likely heard of these deaths while he was on the road, but no record remains to affirm this. Back in Rome he broke into tears. Juan Polanco recalled that Salmerón, in deep distress, wondered how the Society's educational program and other works would be able to continue moving forward as they had under Ignatius.[230] And a third death was imminent. About six weeks later, André des Freux died.

Salmerón knew Olave personally, and in at least an indirect way had attracted him to the Society. Olave, a native of Vitoria who had a rich intellectual background that included the doctorate in theology from Paris, was forty-six years old when death came to him. Salmerón and Laynez had known him at the second period of the Council of Trent, where as a secular priest he had the distinction of preaching to the conciliar fathers on Trinity Sunday, 1551. The Jesuits impressed him by their performance at the council. Inspired especially by Laynez, whom he regarded as "a father and a master," Olave entered the Society. By September 1552 he was at the professed house in Rome under the direction of Ignatius, who formed him in Jesuit life by the vigorous means he reserved for the strongest novices. Within a year Ignatius admitted Olave to the profession of four vows. A little later, he named him superintendent, professor of theology, and prefect of studies at the Roman College.[231] This death was a serious blow to the institution that Ignatius envisaged as the model of all Jesuit colleges.

Salmerón was still in Rome when death took his friend André des Freux on 26 October. This native of Chartres was a clever linguist, a musician, an easy conversationalist. He used to play the clavichord for Ignatius when the general was, in the words of da Câmara, "in bed, feeling out of sorts."[232] Laynez described des Freux as being of "more than middling talent."[233] Ignatius made him rector of the German College, and noted that God had endowed him with exceptional gifts in poetry, rhetoric, and construction of musical instruments.[234]

Epigrams Dedicated to Salmerón

Love of Latin brought Salmerón and des Freux together. Salmerón had asked the Frenchman to compose some Latin epigrams. Des Freux at first declined. Then he put together a collection of 251 epigrams, brisk, hard-hitting sallies against the heretics. These he dedicated to Salmerón. The ten-line dedication ran as follows:

> When you asked me to compose some verses,
> I replied that it was beyond me.
> Now that you have stopped asking, I take them up.
> Don't read them, and you will get even with me.

Do I come through as a fickle fellow?
To you it is no secret that this is the wont of poets,
As the Venusine bard tells us.
A sound reason is, however, not wanting:
Anger turns out this verse.
At the sight of the pest of heresy, who can keep his peace?
As in former days Croesus's muted son thrust his voice to heaven
When he saw his father at sword's point,
So now the cords tying my tongue are broken perforce
As I behold my mother [the Church] at the brink of death.[235]

Verses, sharp and biting, follow against Luther, Bucer, Melanchthon, Erasmus, and others. Salmerón most likely enjoyed the onslaughts on Erasmus most because of his personal antipathy for the Dutch humanist. Des Freux evoked various mousey connotations from Erasmus' name, breaking it in two so that it came to mean "you were a mouse" (*Eras-mus*).

Why, Erasmus, did you quit your monastic brethren and cloister?
Your act was not free of a pitiable quest for fame.
For there in the cloister like one living in a ditch,
You were a mean mouse.
You ventured forth into the light to see and to be seen.
But the mountain seems to have brought forth a ridiculous mouse
Even as you, a rhetorician,
Absurdly put on the trappings of a theologian.
Indeed the story is abroad
That even as you rashly wander among the collections of holy books
You have slipped into the mousetrap of heresy.
While you are rattling among and nibbling away
At the teachings of the holy fathers,
Watch out for the savage claw of a hellcat.[236]

These epigrams circulated in manuscript form until 1582, twenty-six years after des Freux's death, when they had their first printing in Cologne. In the edition of 1596, printed in Douai, publisher Jean Bogard wrote: "There is an astonishing battle among typesetters to get these poems to press. No sooner are they printed than they are sold out; no sooner sold than they are worn out from circulation."[237] Salmerón made no reference to these lampoons of his friend, but he must have seen the manuscript dedicated to him. Most likely he was at the deathbed of des Freux during the Frenchman's final illness.

An Interpretation of the Roman Sorrows

Francesco Sacchini, official historian of the Society, recalled what he judged to be the significance of the three deaths in rapid succession, of Ignatius, of Olave, and then of des Freux. All three of the Jesuit houses in Rome, the professed house, the Roman College, the German College, had lost their spiritual leaders and fathers. "The tiny flock (*pusillus grex*) which had its strength in God, did not, however, falter." Ignatius, Sacchini recalled, had so molded the Jesuit houses that death in their ranks did not fill them with the dismay of those who have not hope, but rather brought joy in the realization "that the houses and colleges that were being established in heaven were being peopled with a concourse of those who were taking their leave of the earth."[238]

Until mid-December Salmerón stayed at Rome with Laynez, recently elected vicar general. On the nineteenth, after an absence of twenty months, he was back in the college in Naples.[239]

Summary

This chapter illustrates the complexity of Salmerón's life and the diversity of his experience. It is very easy to lose track of the sequence of events in Salmerón's life. A list of assignments and missions that took him to northern Italy, Bavaria, Naples, Poland, Brussels, as papal legate, popular preacher, conciliar theologian, school founder, and religious superior, resists all efforts to fit them into a neat, symmetrical design. But they illustrate two key features of the new Society of Jesus: its mobility and the availability of its members to the pope. In a multitude of Europe's cities, Salmerón's life showed how the Ignatian intuition was actually realized. Behind all this complex grouping of places, persons, works, there was a firm and clear principle that pulled them all together into a unity: a constant readiness to serve the pope.

Ignatius and his companions had written into their Formula of the Institute: "We are to be obliged by a special vow to carry out whatever the present and future Roman pontiffs may order which pertains to the progress of souls and the propagation of the faith; and to go without subterfuge or excuse, as far as in us lies, to whatsoever provinces they may choose to send us."[240]

This responsibility called for detachment from any personal preference in work and place. From this detachment flowed that Jesuit universality in the apostolate: whatever the pope determines; and that Jesuit mobility and readiness to move at the pope's bidding. Through the ten years, 1546–56, Salmerón made these Ignatian principles incarnate in his personal life. He mirrored the Ignatian ideal in an especially striking way.

CHAPTER VIII

NAPLES, BRUSSELS, ROME, TRENT
1556–1565

Introduction

This chapter begins with the concluding weeks of 1556, when Salmerón returned to Naples after the death of Ignatius, and goes to 1565, when Diego Laynez, the second general of the Society, died. During this near decade the center of Salmerón's activity was Naples, first as supervisor of the college there, then from 1558 as provincial of the Neapolitan province. His correspondence with Laynez is a litany of the perplexities, frustrations, uncertainties that beset the early Jesuit enterprise. Three times Salmerón had to be absent from his province: first, on a diplomatic mission to Brussels; second, as vicar general of the order when Laynez participated in the Colloquy of Poissy; third, as theologian at the final phase of the Council of Trent. This period closes with the death of his close friend Diego Laynez, a death that also closed the first twenty-five years of the Society's life.

Irritants in Jesuit Affairs

Salmerón stayed at Naples from 20 December 1556 through the first nine months of 1557. They were months filled with the alarums of war between Pope Paul IV, backed by some French troops, and Spain. Normal life was impossible; routine business in the Society was disrupted; it was out of the question to hold a general congregation to elect a successor to Ignatius. Among the many points of business was the one about shipping wine from Naples to Rome. To repeated requests from Laynez and Polanco that he send wine, Salmerón tried to explain that the sea lanes were unsafe because of pirates and the state of war. The best he could do was to offer the hope that some day things would be different.[1] "In regard to the problem of shipping wine, have patience. It could be that one of these days we shall have peace."[2]

Regular correspondence suffered too. On 19 March 1557 Laynez wrote to Salmerón: "I just want to make this point. I would be happy if you showed more care than heretofore in your correspondence, getting your letters to us either by ship or by other ways which the merchants know about."[3] A few months later, on 11 June, Polanco took up the same idea, suggesting greater diligence in writing and the use of different routes for posting the mail.[4] One of the items of news which Salmerón was able to get through to Rome was about the repair job being done on the church and the residence. On 19 January 1557 he reported briskly to Laynez: "Here we are carrying through the project of enlarging the church a bit and fixing up a wall of the house which is ready to cave in and shower all of us with bricks."[5] Another item of business was Salmerón's request for more Jesuits to teach at his school. On 19th August 1557 Polanco replied: "As far as supplying more teachers is concerned, Your Reverence should realize that we are having a hard time in finding them."[6]

A Religious Colloquy at Worms

Polanco wrote this letter the day the duke of Alba, the Spanish commander, entered Rome, victor in the Hispano-Papal war. Nine days before, on 10 August, the Spanish forces crushed the French at St. Quentin. Papal diplomatic policy was in shreds. These international events again swept Salmerón into the mainstream of European diplomacy. In September Pope Paul IV summoned him to Rome to join the staff of Cardinal Carlo Carafa's embassy to Philip II, which was quickly assembled to confirm the hastily patched together peace between the pope and the duke of Alba. Salmerón did not know why Paul chose him. Laynez assigned Pedro de Ribadeneyra as Salmerón's companion and as agent at Philip's court for the transaction of the Society's business in the Netherlands.[7]

On 16 October Salmerón and Ribadeneyra left Rome, a week before Carafa.[8] It was a long journey of a month and a half that took Salmerón through Florence, Lucca, Milan, Basle, Salzburg, Spires, Worms, Cologne, Louvain, and finally Brussels, which he entered on 2 December 1557.[9] At Worms he found his dear friend Peter Canisius and another Dutch Jesuit, Nicholas Goudanus. And there he saw at firsthand the frustration of trying to reconcile Protestants and Catholics through an imperially sponsored religious colloquy.[10] This conference, on the eve of its convocation, sent strong waves of expectation through Germany. Convoked five years after the suspension of the Council of Trent, which seemed to have been interred forever, this colloquy led princes and bishops to feel that at last a momentous decision might be reached that would bring religious peace to their distraught country.[11] The delegates came to order on 11 September. When Salmerón arrived two months later, the signs of disintegration were clear. Canisius, one of the most active of the Catholic theologians, urged Salmerón to send his personal observations to Laynez. This Salmerón did on 21 November 1557 in a brief but perceptive note.

Salmerón reported to Laynez two issues, deeply radical, which split the colloquy. Both issues concerned the bases for discussion. The first divided the Catholics and the Protestants. For the Protestants the basis of discussion was scripture alone; for the Catholics it also embraced tradition and the consensus of the church fathers.[12] The second issue divided the Protestants among themselves. For some Protestants the point of departure was the Confession of Augsburg; for others it included matters beyond the confession. Even before the colloquy convened, virulence broke out between the followers of Philip Melanchthon and Matthias Flacius Illyricus. And John Calvin, who sought representation at Worms, was rejected by Heinrich Bullinger.[13] Salmerón told Laynez that the question raised by the Catholics about which Protestants they were to deal with opened wide the schism in the Protestant ranks. He also informed Laynez that he had little sympathy for this kind of meeting.

235

On the Protestant divisions he observed: "Hence the Catholics have hit upon a most lucky opportunity for dissolving the colloquy."[14] Yet he feared that, if the Catholics caused the demise of the colloquy, they would give the impression of "fleeing the light, withdrawing from the battle as though lacking confidence in their doctrine and the old religion which they profess."[15] On the other hand, he did not relish the continuance of the debates. The history of this kind of meeting unfolded a story of futility. At Worms, from what he heard, the Protestant chairmen were dictatorial, forceful, and intent on their own purpose. Catholics did not show this strength. Thus the Protestants stood to gain from a continuation of the talks.[16]

These were some of the impressions Salmerón had of "the last considerable attempt to bring the Catholics and the Protestants together until Leibniz made his great effort in the eighteenth century."[17] In his short stay at Worms, Salmerón's wide experience with current religious controversy was broadened even more as he beheld the assembly of dashed hopes and frustrated idealism. Less than three weeks after he wrote to Laynez and when he was already in Brussels, Peter Canisius sent word to King Ferdinand that the colloquy had come to an end.[18]

Failure and Success in the Netherlands

Salmerón arrived in Brussels on 2 December 1557, two weeks before Cardinal Carafa.[19] There he stayed for most of three months, until March of the following year. This was Salmerón's first protracted visit to this corner of Europe, into which Ignatius had found it so difficult to gain admission for the Society. Until only a year and a half before, the Spanish Netherlands were officially closed to the Jesuits. As has been seen earlier, Emperor Charles and his sister Maria, the competent regent of the Netherlands, rejected any suggestion of Jesuit admission there. Since 1550 Ignatius had been anxious to locate the Society in Louvain. He enlisted the help of Cardinal Reginald Pole, Louis de Blois, Prince Philip, and Pedro de Soto, the emperor's Dominican confessor. All to no avail.[20]

Then on 25 October 1555 took place one of the most moving ceremonies in the history of Europe. On that day Charles, pale and

236

exhausted, surrounded by the Knights of the Golden Fleece, the councillors of the Netherlands, and members of the imperial family, resigned to his son Philip in the great hall of his castle in Brussels his sovereignty in the Netherlands.[21] Ignatius had heard rumors that Charles intended to resign. He moved quickly into the new situation. He ordered Pedro Ribadeneyra to go north to seek from Philip formal admission of the Society into the Netherlands. Ribadeneyra left on 22 October 1555, three days before the momentous abdication.[22] In Brussels he received a sympathetic hearing from two influential advisers of Philip, Gonzálo Pérez and Gómez Suárez de Figueroa, the conde de Feria.[23]

Three months later, on 14 February 1556, he presented to Philip a new formal petition from Ignatius. Philip filed the petition among his papers due to receive top priority. The break came five months later. On 30 July 1556, the eve of Ignatius's death in Rome, Ribadeneyra was invited to a grand dinner party run by Viglius van Zwichem and attended by the conde de Feria and the rector of Louvain University, Ruard Tapper. During the party Ribadeneyra learned that Jesuit welcome to Louvain was assured. In mid-August King Philip signed the document of formal permission for the Jesuits to locate in Louvain.[24]

Papal Diplomacy and Jesuit Business

Now, one and a half years later, Salmerón went to the court of Philip II at Brussels as part of the Carafa papal peace mission. Ribadeneyra returned to carry out the Society's business there. The two Jesuits received a welcome that was almost unanimously cordial. Some members of other religious orders murmured against them, but they were a minority.[25] The conde de Feria, whom Salmerón described as "an uncommon and ardent devotee of the Society" (*singular protector y amador de la Compagnia*), set the two Jesuits up in pleasant rooms near his own residence.[26] Many times he had them to dinner.[27] Cardinal Carafa took care of their living expenses and gave them money for new clothes.[28]

Salmerón's main responsibility in Brussels was as theological adviser to Cardinal Carafa in the consultations about benefices and the provisions and exemptions involved with them. He found the workday extremely short during the winter months in Flanders.

To Laynez he complained that the day was consumed in reciting the divine office, in saying mass and in going to meals, and that the evening shadows fell early, forcing one to return home.[29]

During his stay in Brussels, Salmerón received an invitation to preach a Lenten course in Cambrai. He spoke to Cardinal Carafa, making it clear that he realized that he was at the cardinal's disposition. Carafa freed him, and three times a week he preached in Italian. Those who heard him, Italians and Spaniards, found it a rich experience.[30]

Salmerón's relations with Cardinal Carafa were cordial. Carafa, in his conversations with Salmerón, took the initiative in offering to promote the Society's apostolate with King Philip. Salmerón seized this opportunity to resolve a financial problem at the college in Naples that particularly bothered him. For educators of the sixteenth century, as of the twentieth, finances were high on the list of worries. In 1554 Emperor Charles V had promised Pedro Pacheco, viceroy of Naples, six hundred ducats as an annual income for the Jesuit college at Naples.[31] The glitter of those illusive six hundred ducats stayed in Salmerón's memory, and on this mission to Belgium he thought that he had the chance at last to pocket them. He explained the background to Cardinal Carafa, who promised to take the matter up with King Philip. "Although we have our doubts," wrote Salmerón to Laynez on 5 January 1558, "about the success of this venture of ours, we nevertheless feel that it will serve as an occasion to let the king realize the esteem which the legate has for our Company. So far the cardinal has not brought the matter to the king's attention. But he assures us that he is not forgetting us and knows just when to make the move."[32]

It was well that Salmerón was not too sanguine. About six weeks later, he was forced to write to Laynez as follows: "In regard to the money destined for Naples, it has been so far a case of noise and no action. The cardinal has taken on himself the task of presenting to the king a memorial about the six hundred ducats. So far he has not done so. Nor do I think that he will, although it is true that he has spoken to the conde de Feria and Ruiz Gómez."[33] Eight years later Salmerón would still be wondering about the six hundred ducats.[34]

Beginnings of the Carranza Tragedy

Among the several important men Salmerón met at Brussels was one whose long life was to be overshadowed by a tragedy that would bring embarrassment and distress to Salmerón and Laynez. He was Bartolomé de Carranza, recently nominated by Philip II as archbishop of Toledo and primate of Spain. This Dominican friar from Navarre had taught theology at Valladolid, represented Charles V at the Council of Trent, accompanied Prince Philip to England in 1554, advised Queen Mary in a program of suppression of the Protestants, left England in 1557 for Flanders, where he joined the entourage of the Spanish monarch. Carranza deeply admired the Society of Jesus, inspired most likely by his contacts with Salmerón and Laynez at Trent. "I think," wrote Salmerón to Laynez on 5 January 1558, "that the archbishop will be our good friend and protector in Spain, since I have an inkling that he is happy with what he sees in the Society; also because he knows how much we are loved by the conde de Feria, who was a very dear friend of his before he became archbishop, and is now even more of a friend."[35]

The name of Carranza appeared in several letters that Salmerón received from Polanco at Rome.[36] Polanco raised a sensitive issue. He asked Salmerón to request Carranza to use his influence and authority in behalf of Cardinal Giovanni Morone, who at that time was imprisoned by Pope Paul IV in the Castel Sant' Angelo on grounds of heresy. On 20 February 1558 Salmerón replied that he had spoken at length with Carranza on this subject.[37] Salmerón knew the Morone case intimately. Soon after Pope Paul IV, the brilliant but deeply suspicious Neapolitan, was elected to the papacy, he jailed Morone as well as Egidio Foscarari, the Dominican bishop of Modena, and Giovanni Tommaso Sanfelice, the bishop of La Cave, in the Castel Sant' Angelo because he mistrusted their orthodoxy. Almost immediately shades of the spat in 1543 between Salmerón and Morone about the nature of justification arose out of the past and helped to poison the air against Morone.

Twice Salmerón had been drawn into the formal process against Morone, first, on 25 July 1555, when he gave evidence to Dominican Tommaso Scotti, who was in charge of the investigation, and second, on 9 October 1557, when he answered questions of the defense.[38] Salmerón recalled that Morone had silenced him because they differed on the question of the place of good works in the economy of salvation. Morone's lawyer, Marcantonio Borghese, disputed Salmerón's testimony. He claimed that Morone halted Salmerón's preaching, not on doctrinal grounds but because Salmerón used the objectionable practice of naming individuals from the pulpit and publicly scolding them.[39] Borghese's version of the rift did not win Morone his freedom, and the cardinal remained in prison throughout the rest of Pope Paul's reign. Because of Paul's known volcanic temper, few were ready to step forward in Morone's cause. Among the more courageous few was the Jesuit general, Diego Laynez. Through Juan Polanco he asked Salmerón and Ribadeneyra to do what they could at the Spanish court in Brussels to reduce the injustice in Rome.[40] The Jesuit efforts availed nothing.

A solemn irony hangs over the scene of Salmerón speaking to Carranza on behalf of Morone, because within a year and a half, Carranza, himself arrested on grounds of heresy by the Spanish Inquisition, would implore Salmerón and Laynez to intervene at Rome for him. And Salmerón would step forward; Laynez would hold back.

Return to Rome

The peace mission of Cardinal Carafa to Philip II went off expeditiously. By mid-December 1557, rumors spread that the stay in Brussels would be brief. And so it was.[41] On 25 March 1558 Salmerón left Brussels for Rome. During the first stage of the trip, to Louvain, a horse kicked him on the shin and injured him severely. Salmerón stopped at Louvain but not long enough for the full recovery of the wound. He pressed on to Liège. The wound became inflamed and intensely painful. He was forced to stay in Liège for a month. Ribadeneyra, who had received orders to remain in the Netherlands in order to solidify the Jesuit position there, hastened to Liège to nurse Salmerón.[42]

During the month of forced leisure, Salmerón read a book that soon would pull him to the fringes of one of the more celebrated cases in the history of the Spanish Inquisition. His friend Archbishop Carranza had recently published his *Commentary on the Christian Catechism (Comentario sobre el Catequismo*

240

Cristiano). Salmerón read it, and found it to be theologically acceptable and free of objectionable statements.[43] But in Spain the Inquisition charged Carranza with heresy. These charges eclipsed the bright light of honor that had come to Carranza by his appointment to the see of Toledo. This eclipse never completely passed during the remaining seventeen years of the archbishop's life. And several times, as shall be seen, this tragedy intruded itself into Salmerón's life.

The First Jesuit General Congregation

After his month in Liège, Salmerón left for Cologne, where he arrived on 8 or 9 May. There he stayed until the twelfth, when he started for Rome.[44] On 19 June, accompanied by two other Jesuits, the French Jean Pelletier and the Belgian Everard Mercurian, he reached Rome. Late that day General Congregation I, delayed for nearly two years, convened to elect the successor to Ignatius. Salmerón joined the eighteen others who were able to attend.[45]

Salmerón had several prominent roles to play during the congregation. On the twentieth, the day after his arrival in Rome, he was designated by the delegates to go with Laynez to ask Pope Paul's blessing. Paul received the two Jesuits cordially; he praised the Society; he again insinuated his desire that the Society chant the divine office in choir—he launched into a panegyric of St. Mary Magdalen, visited and levitated by angels at the canonical hours; he insisted that the congregation enjoyed freedom in handling its business; he asked that the delegates always turn to him whenever they felt they needed his help; he placed two cardinals at their disposal to assist them with their problems; he corrected any canonical defects in the convocation of the congregation; he assigned Cardinal Pedro Pacheco, as vice-protector of the Society, to assist at the election of the general; and finally, he gave his blessing.[46]

Back in the congregation Salmerón raised a nasty issue. Between 21 and 27 June the congregation approved some twenty decrees by which it established the technical procedure in the election of the general. On the twenty-eighth it started a four-day period of prayer and inquiry about particular men and their qualifications to be general. Sometime during those days Salmerón

241

accused Nadal of ambition. It was a reckless charge, grounded on no greater authority than mere gossip. Salmerón went to Laynez, the vicar general, and confided that he had heard Fr. Leonhard Kessel say that Fr. Nicholas Wischaven had said that Nadal would be the next general. Laynez took the accusation seriously. He spoke to several priests, including Everard Mercurian, who was superior of Kessel and Wischaven. They had heard nothing. Laynez spoke to Nadal. Nadal replied that he did not know, nor did he care about, what others thought about him. Laynez found no substance in the charge and dropped it.[47]

On 2 July the congregation proceeded to the election. At nine in the morning Laynez offered mass in the chapel of the professed house. The delegates then proceeded to the room in which Ignatius had died. Fr. Cristóbal Madrid locked them in. Other members of the Society took turns praying in the church. Peter Canisius gave an exhortation. An hour of prayer followed. Cardinal Pacheco entered the room and, after the invocation of the Holy Spirit, told the delegates that they enjoyed freedom in their choice and that, although Paul IV still had doubts about whether the general's term should be limited or for life, the pope now actually inclined more toward the latter. This observation relieved the delegates, since it meshed with the Jesuit *Constitutions*.[48] The solemn voting by secret ballot took less than an hour. Laynez received thirteen votes, Nadal four, and Broët, Delanoy, and Borgia one each.[49] Salmerón received none. The delegates may have detected the strain of somberness that would impair Salmerón's future rule as provincial.

Pope Paul IV and the Congregation

Four days later, on 6 July, Pope Paul received all the delegates. He praised the Society; he asserted that even before his election as pope he had looked on it benignly; he pronounced his approval of its institute. Then each delegate knelt in turn before Paul and received his individual blessing.[50] On 24 August this benign attitude changed. On that day Cardinal Bernadino Scotti of Trani communicated to the congregation the pope's request that it consider the advisability of a limited term for the general.[51] The congregation took up the question; decided, unanimously, that the life term be kept; left it to Laynez to determine the way the pope should be informed; wrote a letter to Paul, in which it explained that, ready as it was to obey a papal order, it preferred to remain faithful to the order's *Constitutions*. All signed this letter except Laynez, since he was personally involved, and Canisius and Pelletier, who had left the congregation on other business.[52]

This reply miffed Paul. On 6 September, four days before the end of the congregation, Salmerón again accompanied Laynez to the Holy See. They proposed to explain to Paul the attitude of the delegates.[53] Paul launched into a caustic criticism of the general's life term and the omission of choir He began softly. "Ignatius was a tyrant. The general should be elected every third year." His voice rose. "It is my wish that you recite the divine office in common. Even though it may be a burden to you, you must nevertheless do it. Woe to you if you do not do so." This was the idea Paul came back to time and again: failure to have choir in the Society was a manifestation of softness toward heresy; choir was an essential of divine law in the religious state. "I do not excuse you because you are busy with studies. Cursed be the studies that impede the chanting of the divine office." Laynez and Salmerón knelt helpless before the lava of words that poured from the fiery volcano.

When Paul finished, Laynez raised his eyes and asked permission to speak. He said that not only was he prepared to give up the general's office at the end of three years but was ready to do so at that moment; that the Society could not be fairly arraigned for rebellion against choir, since the Holy See had not given an order against which to rebel; that the Society could not justly be accused of heresy, since it was the particular object of attack by heretics. Paul quieted down. He gave Laynez and Salmerón a supply of rosaries and Agnus Deis for distribution among the members of the congregation. The two Jesuits then beat a hasty retreat back to the congregation.[54] Two days later, the eighth, Cardinal Alfonso Carafa addressed the delegates and in the pope's name ordered them to insert into the *Constitutions* the two items that so obsessed Paul: the triennial term of the general and the chant of the divine office in choir. This was done.[55] The congregation closed two days later, on 10 September.

Appointment as Provincial of Naples

Salmerón returned to Naples with a new responsibility. Laynez designated him provincial of the newly erected Neapolitan province, which embraced the area of the Kingdom of Naples.[56] This appointment—as well as Laynez's election as general—contributed to a crisis in one of the chief apostolates of the Society: the guidance of individuals through the Spiritual Exercises. More and more of the early experts in the Exercises were being absorbed into administration. Luis Gonçalves da Câmara and Polanco were engaged at headquarters in Rome; Jerónimo Doménech became provincial of Sicily in 1553, the first of three separate times that he held that post; Paschase Broët became provincial of Tuscany in 1551, and in 1552 of France; Jerónimo Nadal was named visitor of Spain in 1553, and again in 1561; Pedro Ribadeneyra became provincial of Tuscany in 1560.[57] The delegates of General Congregation I recognized the critical trend in the drain on the number of expert retreat masters, and authorized the general to issue an official directory for all Jesuits on the genuine way of conducting the Exercises.[58]

Despite his administrative duties, Salmerón tried to continue his retreat work. Under his inspiration Naples became a vital center of retreats. As in the pulpits of Naples he became the Jesuit preacher par excellence, so in giving the Spiritual Exercises he became Naples's unexcelled retreat director. Among his retreatants were influential persons in the civic life of the Neapolitan Kingdom, including heads of the noble families.[59]

One of Salmerón's first duties as provincial was the implementation of the Pauline edict on choir. A letter of Polanco's to Salmerón on 23 October 1558 set the tone for the Jesuit reaction throughout Europe. Reporting on the Jesuit choral effort in Rome, Polanco wrote: "On the feast of St. Michael, early in the morning, we began choir with the celebration of mass. I do not think that the people were particularly pleased with our efforts. But the more important thing is to look to the good pleasure of His Holiness."[60] More serious than the hurt musical sensibilities of the people was the detriment to apostolic work. From several Jesuit houses Laynez received complaints of this kind. Teaching especially suffered. Miquel de Torres, provincial of Portugal, suggested that, if Laynez humbly represented to Pope Paul about the gravity of the problem, the pontiff would abrogate his edict. When Torres's letter reached Rome, Paul was dead.[61]

Canonical Problems

Pope Paul's death on 17 August 1559, less than a year since his directive, raised a curious question: did this directive, orally given, die with the pope? Laynez consulted Cardinal Diego Pou, an experienced curialist, and four other canon lawyers. Their judgment was unanimous: the Society was not bound by the Pauline precept and might return to its original practice. Laynez promptly drew up a document in legal form before a notary public, stating his firm determination not to assume a new obligation [choir] for the Society by reason of Pope Paul's edict; that this decision did not mean belittlement of the action taken by Paul, whose authority he recognized; that he was merely declaring that he was opposed to taking on a new obligation [choir] if it did not carry the force of law. He then directed the Jesuit communities to discontinue choir.[62]

The twin problem, the triennial term of the general, arose two years later. On this more important issue Laynez moved with greater caution. He decided to sound out the professed fathers in Europe. He ordered each, in virtue of holy obedience, to state frankly his opinion about the life term of the general, as called for in the *Constitutions*, in the light of Pope Paul's edict. To facilitate thinking on this issue, he submitted lists of reasons pro and con. There were at that time seventy-one professed in Europe. Some ballots were delayed, but by June 1561 fifty-two had been returned to Rome. Forty-eight declared for the life term of the general.[63] Salmerón was with the majority. His vote read in part:

> After consideration of this question and recommending it to our Lord, after weighing the reasons pro and con for the election of a new general, and after looking to the greater service of our Lord and the wider good of the Society, I judge that in no way whatsoever should there be another election. . . . I feel that all that Pope Paul IV ordered by word of mouth to be without binding power subsequent to his death. I also feel that what he said does not conduce to the common good of our Company.[64]

The four in the minority either upheld the Pauline edict or, in their doubt about the intention of General Congregation I, felt a new election should be held, followed by a request to the then reigning pope for the abrogation of Paul's directive. These four were Martino Gutierrez, Bartolomeo Hernández, Francesco Adorno, and Benedetto Palmio.[65]

Francis Borgia made a viable suggestion for the practical implementation of the decision of the majority. To maintain the Society's attitude of respect for the Holy See, he proposed that the issue be submitted to Pope Pius IV for resolution. The General Assistants then petitioned Pius to confirm viva voce, Paul IV's decree notwithstanding, the Society's *Constitutions* on the election of the general for life and freedom from choir. On 22 January 1561 Pius IV, in the presence of Cardinal Ippolito d'Este, abrogated Paul's decree and explicitly enjoined the life term of the general.[66]

Cardinal Morone and the Society

Pope Paul's death not only freed the Jesuits of the Pauline decrees; it also released Cardinal Morone from Castel Sant' Angelo and the Pauline charge of heresy. The sacred college of cardinals released Morone on the passing of the pontiff. On that occasion, Laynez informed Salmerón, then in the Netherlands, that Morone expressed his hurt at Salmerón's testimony during the heresy hearings of 1555 and 1557.[68] Morone's friendly attitude toward the Society became distinctly chilly. But this did not last. A magnanimous and conciliatory man, Morone rose above his personal resentment and gave his support to several Jesuit projects. He helped the Roman College; he aided the college in Modena; he proposed that the Society take over the direction of the new Roman Seminary.[69]

Despite Morone's generous attitude, the spat between him and Salmerón in 1543 became part of the local lore of Modena. As late as 1560 the Spanish rector of the college in Modena, Juan Gurrea, reported to Laynez that he detected a strain of hostility among the Modenese toward the Society, traceable, he said, to the Morone-Salmerón encounter of seventeen years earlier.[70] Laynez's comment was: if the Modenese loved their cardinal, they should imitate him in his devotion to the Society.[71]

Racial Purity

At this early stage in the Society's history, another internal problem tormented it and threatened its unity. It came from without, from a drastic change in Spanish social attitudes. In mid-fifteenth century, civil and ecclesiastical bodies in Spain began to pass a series of legal statutes that placed restrictions on those Catholics who were of Jewish or Moorish lineage, known popularly as New Christians. More and more, as time went on, racial purity (*limpieza de sangre*) became an imperative in Spain's social life. Because of this recent code the New Christians were excluded from positions of authority and honor in the church and in the state.[72]

Some Spanish Jesuits, taken by this latest social attitude, regretted that the Society had not followed the lead of the Hieronymites, the Dominicans, and the Franciscan Observants in excluding New Christians from their ranks. At the court they found strong support in the person of the powerful prince of Eboli. Fr. Antonio Araoz, a personal friend of Eboli, became the most vocal Jesuit spokesman for their viewpoint, and kept Ignatius informed about the court's displeasure at the Society's remissness in not making racial purity part of its internal structure.[73] On 9 June 1553 Ignatius answered Araoz. He told him that he had seen his reports on the batteries that the court and other powers in Spain were rolling into the battle line against the Society's practice of receiving New Christians. On no account, however, would the Society exclude New Christians from its ranks on grounds of race. Till his death Ignatius held to that position.[74]

Agitation for a change in Jesuit policy persisted, but the next three generals, Diego Laynez, Francis Borgia, and Everard Mercurian, held firm. Fr. Pedro Ribadeneyra, who followed these developments closely, thought it significant enough to mention that two of those three generals were themselves Spaniards and very familiar with the leading issues in Spain. Ribadeneyra also took note of the sentiments of Alfonso Salmerón. "Superiors of religious orders," wrote Salmerón, "must be warned that no greater pestilence can spread among religious men than the creation of distinctions between races. By such discrimination those who profess death to the world are through a prodigy of the devil brought back once more to the spirit and pomp of this life. Still more, all the merit of and respect due to the religious life are blotted out."[75]

The Jesuit advocates of *limpieza de sangre* did not relent, and in 1592 they finally broke the line of resistance. Fr. Claudio Acquaviva, the Society's fifth general, faltered and instructed the provincials of Spain that they were no longer to receive New Christians into the Society. He had yielded a few yards. The next year General Congregation V (1593–94) surrendered the entire field, passing legislation applicable to the whole order that excluded from admission all men of Jewish or Moorish ancestry. Even Fr. General could not grant a dispensation. Pedro Ribadeneyra dissented strongly. In especially pungent language he laid out before Acquaviva the reasons for his anger at the Society's departure from the position of Ignatius and other leading Jesuits such as Salmerón.[76] He had opened what turned out to be a protracted contest for the removal from the Society's Institute of what became known as "the impediment of origin." Only in 1946 did General Congregation XXIX bring that contest to a close. It completely erased "the impediment of origin."[77]

The Case of Bartolomé de Carranza

Out of Spain came still another sorrow for Salmerón and Laynez. This time it was obsession with heresy. The touchiness throughout the peninsula about Catholic orthodoxy engulfed their friend and admirer, Bartolomé de Carranza, archbishop of Toledo and primate of Spain. In August 1559, after but a year and a half in his new post, Carranza was arrested by the Spanish Inquisition. His appointment to the see of Toledo was the prey that drew the vultures from all corners of the Spanish skies. Aristocratic churchmen envied this priest of poor parentage invested with Spain's highest ecclesiastical honor; fellow bishops looked coldly on this theologian who had written a book that severely criticized episcopal absenteeism; Dominican Melchior Cano, high in the counsels of Philip II, resented this former professor who had challenged him at the University of Valladolid.[78] Even years earlier, when Carranza had been on his mission to Queen Mary in England and on his travels in the Netherlands, rumors about his alleged heterodoxy began to latch onto his name. Vague charges became more refined: contact with heretics warped his faith; heretical views infiltrated his *Commentary on the Christian Catechism (Comentario sobre el Catequismo Cristiano)*.[79]

The *Comentario* drew Salmerón and Laynez within the currents of this rising storm. Even before his arrest, Carranza spotted clouds on the horizon. When Melchior Cano and the Inquisition took the *Comentario* under review, Carranza in the early fall of 1558 turned to the two Jesuits and requested their testimonial to the orthodoxy of the book.[80] At least three times he appealed to Laynez.[81] On 20 January 1559 he wrote to Salmerón. He reminded Salmerón that he had read the *Comentario* in Liège a year and a half earlier, and requested a statement of approval to offset the mounting criticism.[82] Laynez too asked Salmerón to forward to him a review of the *Comentario*, which he in turn would forward to Spain.[83] On 5 November 1558 Salmerón informed Laynez that in his opinion Carranza's work presented "familiar and generally accepted teaching" (*dottrina commune ordinaria*); was almost entirely taken from St. Thomas; presented no grounds for suspicion.[84] The Jesuit approval sought by Carranza seemed guaranteed.

Then Laynez changed. He began to have misgivings. He explained his doubts to Pedro Ribadeneyra, who was then in England. "The truth is that here [in Rome]," he wrote, "it is known on the basis of sound judgment that the book takes certain positions or expresses them in such a way as to leave a bad taste in one's mouth. Yet the author has all the appearances of being a Catholic."[85] Laynez's hesitation hardened. Three times between 5 February and 5 March 1559, he instructed Salmerón that they were not to throw their influence behind Carranza. On 5 February he bluntly told Salmerón that he did not like the *Comentario*; that he felt that Salmerón had not read the work "judiciously" (*con spirito censorio*). "If you had done so," he wrote, "you would have reached the same judgment as I."[86] Exactly two weeks later, on the nineteenth, Laynez advised Salmerón to say nothing, pro or con, about the work; told him that his favorable report had been received at Rome but was not being forwarded to Spain.[87] On 5 March Laynez, through Polanco, outlined for Salmerón a strategy for working himself out of the embarrassment.

> If you feel it advisable that you write to the archbishop, it would be good to take this line: when you read the book in Liège, you were laid up with an illness; although you recall nothing but worthy and sound teaching in it, it would be necessary, in order to give a formal pronouncement, that you reread it. You might use other like expressions to put across your sympathetic feelings. If, however, you feel that it would be better that you yourself do not write, our father [Laynez] could take on himself the responsibility of explaining your silence by excusing you because of, say, sickness,

etc. Or, you could send a blank sheet with your signature, over which could be written in our father's [Laynez's] sentiments. Wisdom dictates that we be on guard about expressing approval of the archbishop's writings because of the murmurings that one hears here [Rome]. Say what you will about the obligation of friendship and charity, this should be able to be fulfilled, but "with a view to our own safety" (*sicuremente*).[88]

What option Salmerón took is not known.

In this ambivalent way Laynez responded to the pleas of a genuine friend. One of Carranza's first actions in Toledo had been to reverse the policy of his predecessor, Juan Martínez Siliceo, who resolutely opposed the setting up of a Jesuit residence in his see. He negotiated with Francis Borgia, and in October 1558, when he was making his early pleas to Salmerón and Laynez for their support against Melchior Cano and the Inquisition, Father Bartolomé Bustamante, Father Francisco Strada, and two coadjutor brothers entered Toledo.[89] The Jesuits were awkwardly caught between Laynez's genuine misgivings and Carranza's kindness. Three years later, at the Council of Trent, this issue would again surface to trouble Salmerón and Laynez.

Heresy and the Index of Forbidden Books

During this early stage of the Carranza affair, the problem of heresy came from another quarter across the desks of Salmerón and Laynez. It was the new *Index of Forbidden Books*. At the end of December 1558 the first official edition of the *Index* came off the press of Antonio Blado.[90] This stern and rigorous measure of the Carafa pope intimately affected the Jesuit schools. In his contest with heresy, Paul IV decided to do for the universal Church what cities such as Venice, Florence, and Milan had already done, issue a list of publications forbidden to Catholics to read or possess. In February 1558 Cardinal Bernardo Scotti of Trani assembled a commission to work on a list of heretical and suspected books.

Laynez by personal directive of Pope Paul joined this commission. His work was limited to extracting passages from Savonarola and passing them on to the commission for examination. Gonçalves da Câmara, who worked with Laynez, described Laynez's approach as "quite mild and free of severity" (*assai dolcemente et senza rigorosità alcuna*).[91] Perplexity, dismay, anger, alarm greeted the *Index*. Printers and booksellers felt a serious threat to their livelihood. Official reception in civic communities varied. Milan and Naples, for example, wrote to King Philip II for instructions.[92]

Jesuit Schools and the Works of Erasmus

Among the Jesuits, especially the teachers, the reaction generally was dismay. In the classes of humanities Erasmus was a favorite author, but in the *Index* the famous humanist, whose publications in their entirety (*opera omnia*) were forbidden, appeared among the heretics of "the first class" (*primae classis*). A radical reassessment of the text books became imperative.[93] Erasmus had made his entrée into Jesuit education under Ignatius. Ignatius recommended that Erasmus's works—and those of Valdes too—not be used, since Erasmus's orthodoxy was then under fire in many quarters. He preferred authors who were not controversial.[94] Yet he had to face the reality that the early Jesuit schools had no texts of their own and were forced to rely on what was available. Erasmus's *Adages* was especially popular. For the colleges outside Rome, in Padua, Tivoli, Genoa, Bologna, Ignatius made exceptions. The schools in Portugal and Spain also used Erasmus. In 1556, before Ignatius's death, French humanist Jesuit André des Freux published two Latin textbooks. Ignatius felt that they removed the need for Erasmus.[95]

Erasmus, however, held his place in the Jesuit schools as though by eminent domain. Then came the *Index*. The rector of the Jesuit college in Perugia, Giovanni Nicolò Notari, epitomized the quandary of many Jesuit educators: "We have no books other than those of Erasmus."[96] At Naples Salmerón and his community obeyed the Carafan directive with completeness. They removed their many volumes of Erasmus, including two or three copies of the *Adages*, and threw them into the flames.[97]

From several Jesuit communities Laynez received complaints and requests that he petition the Holy See for exceptions in the application of the *Index*.[98] Salmerón was among these. In October or November 1560 he suggested that permission be obtained to purchase copies of the *Adages* for use in the college. "If it were permitted to do so," he wrote Laynez, "it seems that it should be done, since the teachers in this community want to use this particular work."[99] Another Jesuit wondered about the status of Melanchthon's commentary on Demosthenes. Jerónimo Doménech was especially upset by the appearance in the *Index* of Ramón Lull and Ramón de Sabunde.[100] Peter Canisius called the document "insufferable, a disgraceful stumbling block, unable to be enforced among the Germans" (*intolerabilis, petra scandili, inapplicabile tra i tedeschi*).[101]

Laynez in his response as general to the *Index* had first to resolve a doubt. Nineteen years earlier, on 5 November 1540, Pope Paul III verbally (*vivae vocis oraculo*) granted the Jesuits freedom to read books suspect of heresy and other forbidden works. Did this privilege prevail? On 28 December 1558, practically on the eve of the publication of the *Index*, Paul IV stated that permission for possessing and reading prohibited works were reserved solely to the inquisitor. Laynez decided to follow the safer course and recognize that Carafa's action revoked the faculty granted by Farnese.[102]

Relief soon came within a month of the issuance of the *Index*. In January 1559 the printer Antonio Blado published a new edition that contained an important innovation: a *Moderatio Indicis*, by virtue of which permission could be obtained under certain circumstances from the Inquisitor to read forbidden works.[103] Laynez approached Cardinal Michele Ghislieri, who presided over the *Index*, with a list of thirty works for which he asked permission for Jesuits to use. On 30 January 1559 Ghislieri granted the permission. The only Erasmian title was *Absolutissimus de octo orationis partibus constructione libellus*.[104] But within a few years, by 1564, when Pope Pius IV issued his milder *Index*, the list of works by Erasmus was drastically reduced. The *Adages* and many other volumes could once more be freely used.[105]

Problems of Health

Grave decisions of policy such as the proper reaction to the *Index* did not monopolize the correspondence between Salmerón and Laynez. Often the two Jesuits had room in their letters for chitchat. There was, for example, the shipment of preserves and knives for cutting writing quills that Salmerón had sent to Rome. The ship went down at sea and much of the cargo with it. Some of the preserves were saved but only after they had been salted by the waters of the Mediterranean.[106] But the subject of the most personal and mutual interest was the ague.

Whatever satisfaction Salmerón may have found in his new position as superior of the Neapolitan province was dissipated by the paroxysms of fever that laid him low every fourth day after he had reached his headquarters in Naples. Laynez immediately sent off a letter filled with tenderest concern and in which he outlined a program of medication. He could speak with sincere compassion because he personally had been laid prostrate with annoying frequency by the ague of the three-day kind. He wrote:

> It was with some feeling that we learned of the quartan fever Your Reverence is suffering, especially since I have personal acquaintance with the kind of companionship it provides. I hope in our Lord, who has visited you in this sickness, that it will mean greater profit to your soul, and that your body too will be better off than heretofore. I also have confidence that you will not feel the distress that has been mine in my bouts with the ague, since you have a stronger constitution than I. Then too, you have the mild air and the other conveniences of Naples. On the question of remedies: over and above the patience required until the fever has run its course, and the freedom from anxiety about study, sermons, and other exhausting jobs that it affords, I personally have benefited from the following: a warm bed, enemas, broth, especially chicken, exercise, avoidance of food conducive to melancholy. Add to these good wine. Dark wines are, in my judgment, the better, or a moderate portion of white. . . . I also believe it better not to eat much, except on the day the fever leaves you alone; to get out of bed; to exercise a bit; and to engage in some congenial conversation. This is what comes to mind at present.[107]

The debilitating fever hung on despite all Laynez's detailed prescriptions. The following January the general was again expressing his solicitude. "I sympathize with you because I know from personal experience the lassitude and nausea that come with the quartan fever. But I hope in our Lord that the coming of the summer will bring a change."[108] But warmer weather did not bring relief, for at the end of April Salmerón reported to Laynez about fevers that hold him for four and five hours at a time. "Although they are not as long as was usual in the beginning, they have been nevertheless more drawn out the last few days. I am left deflated and drained of energy."[109]

A Report on Jesuit Personnel

Personnel was always a big item in the correspondence between the Neapolitan provincial and the general. Shortly after his arrival back in Naples in the fall of 1558, Salmerón asked for an extra Greek teacher for the school. On 27 November 1558 Polanco sent him good news: "When our Father General saw your letter, he decided to take Alfonso of Ferrara out of his course in arts so that he might lecture in Greek. He is a young man, twenty years old, very intelligent, and most affable, but not very strong physically. He must not be given any work outside his Greek classes."[110] In early 1560 Salmerón complained about the shortage of priests at Naples. On 31 March Polanco reminded him that this kind of shortage was felt throughout the entire Society.[111]

Periodically superiors throughout the Society were expected to send a detailed report on the men in their care to the general. On 1 July 1559 Salmerón drew up an account that draws aside the curtain on the human problems of the Neapolitan community. He started with a curt sentence. "I shall say nothing about Fr. [Cristóbal] Mendoza [the rector] and my relations with him, since I have already briefed you in full on this."[112] Behind that sentence lay a history of tension between Mendoza and Salmerón. In 1555 Ignatius had appointed Mendoza, a native of Jerez in Andalusia, rector of the college. After a year, Polanco described his government as "terrible." Mendoza ruled by fear; he sought the limelight; he let it be known how he differed from other men; he announced, when he arrived in Italy from Spain, that he intended to be a professed father, a status which Ignatius accorded him on 17 September 1554; he was indolent.[113]

Salmerón was appalled by Mendoza's rule, and when Laynez became general he asked that Mendoza be removed. Laynez sought advice in Rome, and on 15 October 1558 wrote Salmerón through Polanco that Mendoza should be left in office, even though he had to admit that Mendoza's "nature and years are not a help." He suggested that some of the rector's duties should be shifted to the shoulders of the minister of the house.[114] A year later, when Salmerón drew up his report, Mendoza was still in office. Thus the curtness of Salmerón's reference to the rector.

Salmerón's report continued in a quiet and objective way. He noted that Fr. Antonio Soldevila was thirty-eight years old, seven years in the Society, teacher of Christian doctrine and a popular confessor, physically weak but strong in spirit. There was Father Giovanni Araldo, eight years in the Society, teacher of the elementary class in the school, a man of great zeal and fervor but at times showing a lack of judgment. For a long time he suffered from a bad leg. Then there was Father Lorenzo Scorzini, twenty-eight years old, eight years in the Society, of mediocre talent. He was sick for a year, first with bad teeth and then for several months with a spell of melancholy, on account of which he frequently omitted his mass. Yet Salmerón saw in him a man of strong spirit and noted: "I think he will be a good confessor."

Then there was Father Giospeh, thirty years old, in the Society three years, a man of great ingenuity in all things. "If he is removed from the college," said Salmerón pointedly, "there will be a great rumpus." Giancola de Otranto was twenty-six years old, in the Society three years, very quiet, depressed, and afflicted with headaches. Father Giancola Petrella was twenty-nine years old, seven in the Society, the minister of the house. Salmerón reported that Petrella sang mass and vespers with grace, that he wanted to go to the Indies, but that his Indies were really in Naples because of the help he gave many souls by his modest and edifying manner. "I am sure that, if Your Reverence realized the good he is doing here, you would not transfer him." And so on through the names of the men who were in his charge.[115] This report seems to indicate that Salmerón in his governing kept a sense of balance and a sympathetic understanding of the limitations of human nature. Yet it was deceptive.

Tension between Laynez and Salmerón

The calm of this factual analysis hid the tensions that had been developing between Salmerón and members of the Neapolitan province. At times he was brusque, quick, sharp; he wrote acidly and with barbed pen; he followed a rigorous line in regard to discipline in the religious life. Complaints went to

Rome, and Laynez counselled him to mollify his regime.[116] The rector of the college at Nola, Juan de Montoya, came under Salmerón's special fire. On 17 December 1559 Salmerón sent to Laynez a charge against Montoya: the rector was a serious detriment to the smooth running of the province.[117] A week later Laynez answered through Juan Polanco. The letter was a quiet exhortation to gentleness and understanding.

> It seems to me in the Lord that he [Montoya] never was nor is now a mean-spirited man. As far as I can judge from his correspondence, in which he writes with all respect for Your Reverence, he is disposed to give up the rector's position. . . . I believe that he is a good man, a servant of God who acts according to his lights and abilities. For this reason, encouraged as I am by his letters, and also because the Society suffers so great a dearth of workers, it does not seem good to change easily the workers we have, still less frighten them, or irritate them. . . . I believe that from now on Montoya will obey with all love, respect, and sincerity. I also trust that Your Reverence will carry the cross of your office with fortitude and equanimity, and that at the same time you will give support to the brothers as we are given support by our Lord.[118]

Despite Laynez's exhortations, peace did not come to the Neapolitan province.

In the autumn of the following year, tensions reached the snapping point. On 1 September 1560 Laynez wrote Salmerón that he was thinking of sending an official visitor to inspect his province. The visitor would be Father Cristóbal Sánchez de Madrid.[119] Salmerón resented Laynez's suggestion. On 7 September he wrote the general that he could see no point in a visitation; there was nothing in the province to be put in order; the colleges were going forward "with vigorous attention to the Society's institute" (*in viridi observantia*); this is what really counted. He asked the general not to give a ready ear to the complaints of the Neapolitan Jesuits. He noted that some of the men Laynez had sent him were "of inferior talent" (*baxa metal de ingenio*). None too graciously he declared his readiness to welcome Madrid if Laynez should insist on carrying out his plan. "Father Madrid will be welcome here more because Your Reverence is sending him rather than for any need that I see in his coming."[120] Salmerón closed his letter of four and a half pages with a cry of discouragement and bitterness. "Your Reverence knows that I am surfeited with Naples and that by God's grace I have struck no roots in the city or its affairs. When Your Reverence finds someone who is better equipped to handle this responsibility and in whom you have more confidence, my quitting this place will be a great relief, a great comfort, and most welcome."[121]

Official Visitation of the Neapolitan Province

Salmerón did not leave his post; and Laynez sent Madrid. The visitor arrived in Naples early in October. Friction soon developed between him and the provincial. Salmerón had a congregation of lay people who used to gather at the Jesuit residence on Sundays and feast days to learn more about the faith and to discuss means of helping others to a more faithful practice of their religion. It was a programme blessed by Ignatius, and it led to a widespread sacramental life among the Neopolitans. Madrid decided that the use of the Jesuit residence for such meetings must be discontinued. "I am convinced," Salmerón forebodingly protested to Laynez, "that dropping the use of the residence will give rise to discontent and complaint as well as an all too real cooling of devotion to confession and holy communion."[122]

Salmerón had adopted a practice common in the other churches of Naples to meet the menace of the flies that swarmed about the priest at the altar during the hot weather. He obtained a fan and had it operated by the sacristan. Madrid looked askance at the practice and concluded that Salmerón was injudiciously adding a new rite to the liturgy. Salmerón's reaction was caustic. "I think that, should he come here in July or August and experience at firsthand the fierceness of these flies, he himself would introduce the fan without the slightest qualm of conscience."[123]

Laynez chided him for his resentment of Madrid's corrections. That was more than Salmerón could take, and he poured out his hurt feelings in a lengthy letter to the general. He argued that no visitations had been conducted in Ignatius's time, nor since. But there he erred, for Ignatius sent Jerónimo Nadal on several missions as visitor. But it was more the person and style of Madrid that irritated Salmerón rather than the fact of the visitation.

On this delicate business of visitation, Your Reverence has sent a man who is just an infant in the life of religious obedience and who has yet to give any evidence or indication that he knows what it is all about. Your Reverence has sent this man to correct others who have been in the Society from its very inception. And what is more, his reprehensions proceed from his own personal quirks in thought and judgment. . . . I must confess, Father, my ignorance, but this whole affair has struck me as an oppressive thing, and I have my doubts whether Father Ignatius, were he alive, would have done the like. According to the rules of charity and forbearance, it strikes me that Your Reverence should want no one, save yourself, to be acquainted with the defects of your subjects. This is all the more true when it touches a pioneer and one of the older fathers. . . .[124]

Salmerón itemized some of the methods Madrid used to gather data. Madrid demanded in virtue of holy obedience that the Jesuits tell him what they knew. He even took his inquiries to laymen. He was most thorough and drew up an interrogation sheet that had thirty to forty items on it. In exasperation Salmerón exclaimed:

I doubt whether a criminal would be pressed with such vigor. O Father, is this the road of simplicity which our company has followed heretofore? Is it not normal for me to feel resentment because I am so treated in the last days of my old age? Thanks be to our Lord that the failures which Father Visitor has discovered are not of such tremendous and scandalous proportions that they should come to such a result as this. . . . In all truth, I can say that some of the faults he has reported are nonexistent. Other things he instances are quite the contrary to the way he presents them. He resembles somewhat the man who makes a notation of an item somebody has told him about without checking it not carefully for himself. . . .

He likewise made it hard for me by the way he conducted the visitation, spending the entire time in conference with one person or another and avoiding me. He has thus given the impression that he came to Naples with no other purpose in mind save to undo my reputation and indict me. I expostulated with him about this, as he himself knows. O Father, who has the resolve to be so perfect that he does not feel a bit, in a human way, treatment such as this? For such a tiny thief such an awesome gallows?

In reference to Your Reverence's statement that I wrote in a fit of anger, I desire to know just how this was so in order that I might confess my fault and ask pardon. But the fact is that I have no remembrance of any such anger, writing as I did as an inferior to his superior, committing myself entirely to Your Reverence and hoping that God will grant that I might make spiritual progress under your direction. True it is that I wrote as a man somewhat distracted in view of the way I was being treated. If in this Your Reverence sees anger, it seems to me that the word anger is a very broad one indeed. By this kind of usage Your Reverence would, therefore, categorize as hotheads all those sons who grumble a bit against their fathers, and those religious subjects who complain a bit about their superiors.

No less do I see why my letter can justly be classified as naught but what you call a bold reprehension of yourself without, in your own words, even the benefit of a little dressing of salt and oil to make it palatable. If to make representation to a superior, to reveal to him our human failings, to bring to his attention our complaints, be they groundless or justified, if all this is to be classified as the giving of a reprehension, then indeed will Your Reverence receive, by virtue of your office, many reprehensions this year. Since it is perfectly correct for bishops, prominent laymen, simple clerics to make representation to the pope, the superior of all, because of some affront or reproach which they feel was unjustly tended them; and since no one says that they are thereby reprehending the pope, then neither can sons who make a complaint to their father be said to reprehend him. Still less should your Reverence think so of me, who place myself in your hands and ask your help. And so my letter had need of neither salt nor oil, since I made no pretense at giving a reprehension. . . .[125]

This outburst revealed what was the most serious flaw in Salmerón's character: his overseriousness. Salmerón felt the onus of his office and found it difficult to carry with a sense of joy and graciousness. Responsibility formed in him a grave and earnest approach to problems. His work at the Council of Trent, involving him as it did intimately with the issues that were at the heart of the religious divisions in Europe, contributed to the shaping of his solemn and sober cast of mind. The joyousness of the youth of Alcalá and Paris fell a victim to age and duty. Laynez took a balanced attitude toward Salmerón's difficulties at Naples. He recognized his friend's talent and dedication, and continued to place confidence in him. He not only kept him in the provincial's post; he soon gave him a position of even greater responsibility.

Appointment as Vicar General

In the early summer of 1561, Laynez, by order of Pope Pius IV, had to put aside his duties as general and accompany Cardinal Ippolito d'Este to the Colloquy of Poissy, that awkward project

of the devious Catherine de Médicis of France. Laynez chose
Salmerón to be vicar general during his absence from Rome.
Salmerón shrank back in dread. On 22 June he wrote Laynez
that he had not been well; that persistent ague and a nasty case
of catarrh conspired to drain his old-time buoyancy, fire, and
initiative; that he appealed to his doctors and consultors for help;
that they judged that the journey to Rome would be a serious
danger to his health.[126] But all to no avail. Laynez left Rome on
2 July.[127] Four days later Cristóbal Sánchez de Madrid of unpleasant memories wrote to Salmerón from Rome. "Because of
the pressure of preparations for his departure, Father Laynez left
no order in writing. But he did say that Your Reverence is to
take his place in governing the Society when you get to Rome,
once the summer heat is over. Meanwhile I am filling the office.
I heartily desire that Your Reverence will come immediately
because I in truth feel the assignment is beyond my powers."[128]

Salmerón remained reluctant to go to Rome. Nearly all that
summer he worried Madrid about an appeal he had sent after
Laynez, then on his way through northern Italy.[129] At the end of
July he cautioned Madrid, "I am on the lookout for Father General's answer, which I feel will bring me freedom from this
appointment."[130] A week later he came back to the same idea.
"I received a letter from Florence from Father Polanco. He tells
me that Father General has not received any letter of mine since
he left Rome. I do not know whether or not my message has met
with some ill fortune. I am not thinking of leaving here until I
get his reply. If you do not judge it out of place to do so, would
Your Reverence try to woo an answer from Father General?"[131]
By mid-August the suspense was over. Laynez's answer arrived,
but it was not what Salmerón had hoped for. Laynez insisted
that Salmerón take over at Rome.

Although his departure from Naples meant dropping the
many irons he had in the fire, it was with a sigh of resignation
he wrote to Madrid. "So, I am planning to start putting things
in order. Obedience is better than sacrifice."[132] By 11 September
he was in Rome. There with the help of Francisco Strada, Juan
Ribera, Cristóbal de Madrid, Pedro Ribadeneyra, and Francesco
Petrarcha—all Spaniards, save the last—he worked for eight

months amid the mass of details that came across the general's desk from all points of the world.[133]

Problems of the Vicar General

These details had a familiar ring. They told Salmerón in a very specific and concrete way that his problems in running the Neapolitan province were not so different from those faced in other areas of the Society. There were the problems of the colleges: At Ingolstadt things were going along reasonably well; many of the boarders, however, were causing trouble in their determination to have a kitchen completely separated from the Jesuit kitchen. Canisius advised the rector, Nicolas Delanoy, to go along with this. He also informed Salmerón that he felt Delanoy was too much of a Martha in his worry about the college and ought to busy himself with spiritual works.[134]

There was the problem of money. Canisius in October 1561 urged the opening of a novitiate in Prague and asked Salmerón that a novice master be sent from Rome. Paul Hoffaeus, rector of the college at Prague, offered a very ample house but asked that the communities of the province give eight hundred florins for the maintenance. If Salmerón would give his approval, Canisius was prepared, despite the poor condition of the schools, somehow or other to scrape together the money and push the important work of a novitiate.[135] Salmerón, however, felt that Canisius ought to hold up for the time being on the establishment of a novitiate in Prague, since many reasons occurred to him why Vienna would be a preferable city.[136]

Then there were the problems of personnel: Juan de Vitoria, the stern, overbearing Spanish rector of Vienna, hard on himself and hard on others, received frequent mention in the Jesuit letters from Germany to Rome. Salmerón had hardly taken over his duties as vicar general when he received a letter from Peter Canisius with the terse observation: "If I am not mistaken, Master Vitoria was getting better but we have heard that he has relapsed into a fever. He is too hard on himself and is reported as taking his sleep in a chair. I therefore wrote to Vienna advising him to take care of his body."[137] One of Vitoria's subjects in the community at Vienna, Father David Eck, alienated from the Society, withdrew from its ranks. Two or three others, possibly taking the cue from Eck, also quit the Society.[138] These defections prompted Vitoria to request assistance in his superior's position, or better still, a successor. Frequently he asked to be relieved of his post. On 18 October 1561 Salmerón wrote to Canisius that Vitoria should be changed.[139]

Zeal for the missions raised questions about the quality of some of the volunteers. A number of the most articulate in their requests to go to the Indies were, in Canisius's judgment, unsuited for mission work because of either deficient learning, or small advance in spiritual strength, or incompetence in languages. Canisius asked whether these, because of their insistence, should be sent.[140] Salmerón replied on 6 December 1561 with a simple and direct negative.[141]

The ineptitude of some scholastics created awkward situations. On 25 May 1562, through Father Francesco Petrarcha, Salmerón admonished Peter Canisius for sending five scholastics to Rome without clearing it through the general's office. Salmerón felt that two of them, the Austrian Christoph Lindaver and the Livonian Nicholas Schricker, should have been dismissed, the former because of his instability and immaturity, the latter for his intellectual slowness. He planned to send them back to Innsbruck, where their dismissal from the Society could be carried out.[142] Canisius recognized the wisdom of Salmerón's businesslike and practical judgment, and wrote to Borgia on 18 June 1562: "May God be blessed. He has freed us from these inept and worthless men."[143] Schricker especially proved Salmerón's wisdom to the hilt, for he balked at the order to return to Innsbruck. Canisius told Borgia: "Nicholas the Livonian— may God protect him—is not planning to come back to us. This weak-minded man is spending his time I know not where in Italy."[144]

The Case of Cristóbal Laynez

The most embarrassing personnel problem Salmerón had to deal with concerned Father Cristóbal Laynez, younger brother of the general. Ignatius had admitted Cristóbal into the Society at Rome on 27 December 1547. For five years Cristóbal moved from one Jesuit house to another, from Rome to Venice, to Padua, to Bologna, to Loreto, to Florence, and back to Rome. Restless and inconstant, he was a poor student.[145] Diego, writing about his younger brother to Ignatius from Florence on 1 October 1552, reported that Cristóbal, as well as three other scholastics, were making themselves difficult to deal with. "He cares nothing for obedience, and studies very little," wrote Laynez. "Now he says that he wishes to perform marvels."[146] In a grave error of judgment, Ignatius allowed Cristóbal to be ordained a priest at Palermo in April 1556.

In August 1559, Diego Laynez, now general, dismissed his incorrigible brother from the Society.[147] Cristóbal went to Spain, wandered about aimlessly, and in the spring of 1561 returned to Italy to ask readmission into the Society. Diego refused to admit him but directed that he undergo a period of probation by serving the sick at the hospital of San Giacomo in Rome.[148] Then Diego, as has been seen above, had to leave Rome on 2 July for the Colloquy of Poissy in France. And Salmerón as vicar general inherited the problem of Cristóbal. Salmerón arrived in Rome by 11 September. By mid-October Cristóbal, again bitten by wanderlust, started back to Spain. Salmerón gave him letters of introduction to the rectors of the Jesuit houses at Siena, Genoa, and Saragossa. Salmerón also directed Jerónimo Nadal to give Cristóbal thirty scudi a year, "not in one sum but in small amounts" as long as he behaved himself. This Cristóbal did not do. He continued to be what Nadal called him, a buffoon.[149]

Scholarly Activity

More congenial for Salmerón than dealing with human frailties was scholarship and study. He received this opportunity during his term as vicar general. Peter Canisius, taking advantage of Salmerón's residence in Rome, asked him to come to the assistance of the Greek scholar, Father Theodor Peltan, of the staff of the Jesuit college in Munich. Duke Albrecht of Bavaria had come upon a hitherto unknown Greek codex of the acts of the Council of Ephesus and requested Peltan to translate the work into Latin. Because of the sorry condition of the manuscript, Peltan found the work extremely difficult. For the sake of scholarly thoroughness, Canisius sent Salmerón a summary of Peltan's work and asked him to check it against the codex in the Vatican library.[150]

Salmerón worked rapidly. On 6 December 1561 he sent word to Canisius that he was engaged in the work at the Vatican library.[151] And on the twentieth he sent further word that some of the emandations were already on their way. Despite the alacrity of his work, Salmerón did not find it completely free sailing. "Perhaps we shall send more corrections today," he wrote. "A number of obstacles, however, are hindering us from making greater speed and progress."[152] On 27 December Salmerón informed Canisius that more notes were on their way. He also revealed that other Jesuits in Rome were busy making copies of the acts of the eighth ecumenical council, Constantinople IV, and suggested that these might be able to be sent to Canisius for publication with Peltan's work or for inclusion with the edition of the ecumenical councils that the Jesuits in Cologne were then preparing.[153] Canisius was most grateful for Salmerón's help. "Nothing," he wrote on 27 December, the same day Salmerón was writing him, "could give us more satisfaction at this time."[154]

Assignment to the Third Period of the Council of Trent

In May 1562 Salmerón received relief from his task as vicar general, but not because Laynez had returned from Poissy. On the eighteenth of the previous January, after two years of exasperating negotiation, the Council of Trent again opened, this time under the guidance of Cardinals Ercole Gonzaga, Luigi Simonetta, Girolamo Seripando, and Stanislaus Hosius. For the third time Salmerón was picked to assist in its deliberations. Two years earlier, when rumors were abroad that the council was to be resumed, Salmerón's Neapolitan friends began to tease him and tell him to put on his harness for the work ahead.[155]

Salmerón himself found no pleasure whatsoever in the prospect of another trip to the Tyrol. Fever and a debilitating catarrh had sapped all enthusiasm for travel. He had tried to forestall any appointment to the council by an earnest plea to Laynez. "I request that I be not sent to Trent because, to tell the truth, I am filled up to my eyes with conciliar business. Besides, there are in Rome any number of the brethren more learned and capable than I on whom Your Reverence can lay your hands."[156] With these two reasons Salmerón included a third: the prospect that Cardinal Giovanni Morone was to be one of the conciliar presidents. Stories to this effect were circulating in Naples. Salmerón shrank from the prospect of working closely with Morone. He knew that his testimony at the heresy hearings on Morone in 1555 and 1557 had irked the cardinal. Although Morone's magnanimity soon thawed his frostiness toward the Society, Salmerón dreaded the embarrassment of being yoked with the cardinal in the same enterprise at Trent.[157]

But to Trent Salmerón had to go. Pope Pius IV had appointed him and Laynez papal theologians at the council. Salmerón's appointment was an instance of rare survival in an ugly sea of rumors. It went back to the long conclave of 1559—which eventually elected Giovanni Angelo de' Medici as Pius IV. During the conclave Medici, in a conversation with Cardinal Otto Truchsess, remarked that he favored reopening the council, that he leaned toward granting the Germans a married clergy and communion under the double forms of bread and wine for the laity. Truchsess, surprised, thought that it would be fruitful to widen a dialogue of this kind, and communicated Medici's views to the other electors. These incidents seeped through the secrecy of the conclave. Rumors spread, even as far as Naples.

The name of Salmerón was caught up in the flood of gossip. One blown-up story had it that Salmerón had issued a statement, which he dispatched to Rome, that Cardinal Medici had said that it would be better to let priests in Germany marry. This story upset Giovanni Battista Ricasoli, the Florentine ambassador at Rome, who was committed to the election of Medici. He complained to Laynez about Salmerón's alleged brashness. Laynez replied that he felt sure that Salmerón would not have taken such an imprudent initiative. He then wrote Salmerón, requesting an explanation.

Salmerón complied. He told Laynez that one day during the conclave he was chatting with a gentleman in Naples. This gentleman brought up the subject of the current papal election and those cardinals most likely to be chosen (*papabiles*), mentioning Giovanni Angelo de' Medici and the gossip about his inclination toward allowing a married clergy in Germany. He then asked Salmerón what he thought of this opinion. Salmerón, as he related it to Laynez, replied, "This position is not Catholic and does not merit consideration." Some persons who overheard the conversation, embroidered it to the point that Salmerón was supposed to have dispatched a statement to Rome, asserting that Cardinal Medici had declared it preferable that priests in Germany be allowed to marry. A simple indication of sympathy toward a married clergy expanded into a hard statement of preference for this policy, and a terse answer to a private question grew into a publicly known dispatch. Yet Salmerón's integrity in Medici's eyes survived this unsettling gossip, for two years later Medici, as Pope Pius IV, designated him a papal theologian at Trent.[158]

Tensions within the Council of Trent

Salmerón found this period of the council, as did all the conciliar veterans, the most edgy of all. Intrigue, mistrust, and strain, all compounded by ugly and careless rumors, poisoned the atmosphere. The precise issue on which the council almost splintered concerned the episcopate: were bishops obliged by divine law to reside in their dioceses? The voices of Salmerón, and especially Laynez, were among the more influential in the settlement of this tormenting issue.

This question arose from a strong desire for reform among the non-Italians, and many Italians as well. In 1560, only two years before the third period opened, more than seventy bishops lived away from their dioceses and in Rome.[159] The champions of reform recognized that this reform had to start with the hierarchy and that it involved two aspects: the insistence that the pastor reside amid his sheep; and second, that the episcopal authority be internally strengthened against the varied intrusions into diocesan life by the Roman curia in the form of dispensations and exemptions.[160]

Many ecclesiastics reacted against this form of renewal. The profiteers from the curial system as inherited from the Middle Ages, perceiving their system being brought to the brink of destruction, argued that the doctrine of episcopal residency by divine law implicitly denied the papal power to give dispensations and was therefore an attack on papal supremacy. A question like the curtailment of the plurality of benefices thus became hopelessly enwrapped in antipapal dress. Others, theologians sensitive to the conciliar ideas of Constance and Basle that were still abroad, felt that the call for a strong statement on the divine obligation of episcopal residence, pastorally and practically motivated and free from theological reasoning as it might have been, actually treaded the sensitive area of episcopalism and conciliarism.[161]

Fear of schism and a repetition of Basle was in the air. Cardinal Seripando wrote that some bishops, in resentment of the curia, "wish to be popes in their own dioceses."[162] News from Trent frightened Pius IV. In May 1562 he ordered his legates to halt further discussion of the residence question. At the same time he ordered the Dominican Pedro Soto, Laynez, and Salmerón to Trent.

Suspicions about Salmerón

Peter Canisius echoed the apprehension that was in the air and related how Salmerón's name was caught up in the winds of mistrust and fear that blew through the council, since the "divine law" party looked with suspicion at the coming of a theologian personally picked by the pope. In Rome the recently arrived Spanish ambassador, Luis de Requesens, noted that Roman gossip listed Salmerón among the papal spies, and added: "Of this I am not sure."[163] Peter Canisius wrote to a friend from Trent in May 1562:

> Father Salmerón's arrival here will not be too happy an event for many, especially the Spaniards, because any number are openly asserting that the pope is sending him to squelch the opinion of those who feel that the council's next decision must be that bishops are obliged by divine law to reside in their dioceses. Some are saying that Salmerón has written a book on the subject. Others assert that he has expressed his opinion in a letter. Since we perceived the prejudice that this perverse rumor can evoke against not one man only but against the entire Society, we went to work to eradicate the mistrust from the minds of at least the leading men here. May the Lord free us from all schism.[164]

Salmerón left Rome in May. With him he brought a letter from the papal secretary of state and nephew of the pope, Carlo

Borromeo, addressed to the presidents of the council, conveying the pope's desire that they graciously receive the learned and widely experienced papal theologian. Salmerón arrived at Trent in early June. There he found with Peter Canisius the Belgian Jesuit Jean de Couvillon representing the duke of Bavaria.[165] By the time he had arrived the presidents of the council had tabled the divine residence issue, promising its reconsideration during future debates on the sacrament of orders.

Debates on the Holy Eucharist

Eighteen months of strenuous theological work lay ahead for Salmerón. As papal theologian and also deputy of Cardinal Otto Truchsess, he made his first public address at this third period of the council at the congregation of the minor theologians on 10 June 1562.[166] The subject matter was the Holy Eucharist, and especially the issue of whether the laity might receive holy communion under the species of both bread and wine. This issue was an insistent one, because Emperor Ferdinand I had been pressing for communion of the two kinds as a way to reconcile the Protestants.

Salmerón opened the debate. On the angle of dogma, he affirmed Christ's presence, wholly and entirely, under each species; further, he held that divine law in no way obliged the laity to receive the Eucharist under the forms of both bread and wine.[167] On the practical issue of church discipline, Salmerón argued against granting the chalice to the laity. He presented six arguments for his position, and challenged seven reasons usually advanced by those who would allow holy communion under both species. Among his main points were the following: the inconveniences and dangers which led the Church of the West to refrain from distributing the Precious Blood to the laity; the possibility that people in areas where the chalice is not given the laity would feel that their reception of the Holy Eucharist was imperfect and deficient; the opening this would give the Protestants to seek other concessions, such as a married clergy; the danger that lack of uniformity in eucharistic practice would break down the sense of unity in the Church and make it seem but a collection of sects.[168]

Salmerón's position on this issue placed him with a large bloc in the council, predominantly Spanish. Their position exasperated Georg Drascovics, bishop of Fünfkirchen, who represented the emperor at Trent. To Ferdinand he wrote: "Since these theologians are almost all Spaniards and little acquainted with the negotiations and troubles outside their own country, they talk as though everything is peaceful and there has been no religious revolution."[169] Drascovics's anger deepened when three months later, on 6 September 1562, Laynez also spoke against the use of the chalice by the laity.[170] Despite these sharp differences of opinion, the bishop of Fünfkirchen remained among the staunchest friends the Society had. When Salmerón and Laynez dined with Drascovics, Polanco, who was also at Trent at this time, had his personal interpretation for Jerónimo Nadal, to whom he wrote on 1 November 1562: "I think that they are making peace."[171]

Salmerón's opening address of 10 June 1562, three hours in length, established him as a leader among the council's theologians. Torellus Phola wrote of the address as "a most beautiful and elegant speech" by "a man well-rounded in sacred theology."[172] Despite the suspicion that surrounded his arrival, Salmerón attained the respect and stature that had been his at the first and second periods of the council. How wrong he was about his own talents and ability to help the council was made clear from a letter that Peter Canisius sent on 18 June 1562 to Francis Borgia, then acting as vicar general in Rome. "It is the general opinion here that Father Alphonso ranks, and deservedly so, as the number one man among the theologians of the council. He has brought great honor to the Society. . . . I have no doubt that the arrival here of Father General [Laynez] will strengthen even more the council's good will toward our men."[173]

Salmerón's Display of Petulance

A month later Salmerón carried on in such a graceless way that he could have soured this good will toward the Society. On 15 July the presidents of the council, at a general congregation, presented the drafts of the chapters and canons on the Holy Eucharist with a view to their formal ratification by the council the next day. Salmerón objected strenuously. Francisco Torres, a secular priest who five years later, in 1567, entered the Society, supported Salmerón. Both told the legates that as theologians sent by the pope they could not give assent to a doctrine on the Eucharist so repugnant to truth and the Catholic faith. Salmerón criticized what he felt was hedging by the council on the correct interpretation of chapter six of St. John's Gospel. In the council were the spiritualists, who held that the eating of the body of Christ and the drinking of his blood in this chapter of John were to be understood in a metaphorical sense. And there were the realists, including Salmerón, who held for an understanding in the real sense. The draft said nothing on this point. To Salmerón this was intolerable. He also felt that it was a scandal that the decree did not address itself to the genuine difficulty embedded in the words "Drink of it, all of you" (*Bibite ex eo omnes*), a difficulty pushed by the Protestant apologists for granting the chalice to the laity. Salmerón expanded still more his censure of the document because the scriptural texts advanced for the Church's authority over the sacraments, he judged, were not ad rem and unworthy of the council. He and Torres left no stone unturned, wrote Gabriele Paleotti, to get the changes they insisted on.[174]

The charges made by Salmerón and Torres that the council's doctrine was repugnant to the Catholic faith disturbed the legates, who promptly consulted several bishops and theologians. These replied that the draft "contains nothing that is not in the highest degree true and holy" (*nihil non maxime verum ac pium continere*). They insisted that the document should remain unchanged because "its teaching is stamped with authenticity" (*la dottrina stava bene*). Yet the protests of Salmerón and Torres disturbed other members of the council. But it was already late in the day, and time for further discussion had run out. And the next day, the sixteenth, the council, brushing aside the continuing objections, ratified the chapters and the canons on receiving the Holy Eucharist under the forms of bread and wine.[175]

Salmerón and Torres took their defeat with little grace. Nasty stories about their reaction floated about. Salmerón was reported to have said that up to that time he had never doubted that a council could not err in faith but now he frankly avowed the opposite. Torres was reported to have said that he used to think that a council did not need in matters of faith the approval of the pope, but now he felt it to be requisite when a council decrees much that is in error. Paleotti heard these stories bandied about, but remarked, "I don't believe two men so learned and so filled with the religious spirit said these things; nor do I know anyone who actually heard them." So ended in ambiguity a distasteful episode in Salmerón's share in the council.[176]

Debates on the Mass

The next subject on the agenda was a delicate one: the Mass. On 19 July the theologians received thirteen articles for their study. In a general congregation on the next day, the twentieth, Cardinal Gonzaga pointed out the heavy pressure of business and the need to keep the interventions brief. He directed that lengthy opinions be presented in writing. He also admonished those who, like schoolboys, made a racket by scraping their feet on the floor when certain speakers were holding forth.[177]

Salmerón protested Gonzaga's curtailment of verbal interventions. He felt that, when one speaks in the name of the Holy Spirit on such grave issues as those before the council, one should be free to follow to its full extent the inspiration of the Holy Spirit. And on the twenty-first he violated the rule imposing a half hour speaking limit. Before the papal legates, imperial ambassadors, 187 prelates, nearly 100 theologians, and more than 2,000 other interested persons, he spoke his half hour, and then continued for another hour and a half. This speaking feat consumed that morning's entire meeting.[178] Salmerón's subject was the sacrificial character of the Mass. In one point he especially stressed that the Last Supper was a sacrifice. Through the texture of his address he intertwined many threads of scripture and patristics—some 70 citations.[179] Massarelli noted that he spoke "with learning and devotion" (*docte et pie*).

Salmerón's brilliant performance, however, exasperated the papal legates by its length. They promptly wrote to Rome about their annoyance. The pope too was displeased.[180] But Salmerón was not the only offender by prolixity. Other theologians, with the honorable exception of Dominican Pedro de Soto, who kept his observations brief and to the point, violated the time limit with their speeches.[181] Finally, after this abundance of oratory the council, in the twenty-second session on 17 September 1562, issued its chapters and canons on the Holy Sacrifice of the Mass.[182]

Confrontation on Episcopal Residence and Jurisdiction

The next subject was the sacrament of orders. On 23 September the theologians began discussion on seven articles. Salmerón again was the first speaker. Before a large assembly that included the papal legates, eighteen archbishops, and 147 theologians, he aimed with an elaborate use of scripture and patristic writings to show the genuine sacramental character of orders.[183]

For ten months the debates went on. For the first week the discussions progressed smoothly enough. Then at the beginning of October the controversial subjects of episcopal jurisdiction and episcopal residence finally returned to the floor after having been tabled the previous May. These questions opened the floodgates of nationalism, acrimony, and vested interests. At issue was the question that even at Vatican Council II was, and still remains, "one of the thorniest legal and constitutional problems in all the history of the Church, one that is at the same time crucial in theology": the relationship between the pope and the bishops.[184]

During the entire council the most important objective of reform was the moral and administrative rehabilitation of the episcopate.[185] The conciliar fathers issued a lengthy list of decrees that affected the lives and duties of bishops: regular preaching; annual visitations; annual synods; foundation of seminaries; and many others. By the sheer amount of this legislation that stressed episcopal duties, the council made the bishop's office a key position in the Catholic Reform.[186] The orientation was distinctly pastoral in the conviction that reform among the faithful was dependent on the uprightness of the bishops.[187] In the sixth session, the council incorporated the words of Pope Leo I in the first reform decree: "On the spiritual soundness of those in authority hangs the eternal salvation of those in the ranks" (*Integritas enim praesidentium salus est subditorum*).[188]

The tempest broke when the council went beyond this practical and pastoral legislation and took up the theory and theological understanding of the nature of the episcopate, especially in relation to the Holy See. The harmony formed at the practical level broke up on the rock of theory. The lightning rod that drew the bolts was the phrase: the divine right of bishops. As a theological question it read: how reconcile the institution of the episcopate by Christ and the pope's supremacy in the Church. This phrase became more refined by two specific questions: does the jurisdictional power of the bishops derive from Christ or from the pope; and does the obligation of the bishops to reside in their dioceses issue from divine or ecclesiastical law.[189] Many bishops, especially those without theological expertise, were in a sea of confusion and uncertainty. Others saw clearly an opportunity to enhance the episcopate. "Let us push," they said, "for the declaration that episcopal residence is of divine law, and we shall be popes in our own dioceses."[190] The same blocs formed as in the spring of 1562. Bishops with a strong pastoral orientation held that the duty of residence incumbent on a bishop issued from divine law and so precluded the dispensations given by the Roman curia. The curialists saw in this attack on their practice of granting dispensations an assault on the papal primacy. The dissension, almost to the point of the dissolution of the council, revealed in grim colors the damage that had been done by the Western Schism of nearly two centuries earlier.

Laynez on Divine Law

Salmerón and Laynez addressed themselves to this dispute with vigor. Laynez carried the greater authority, and in the end his voice was a decisive one in the council. When he took the floor, the council heard the theologian who in that age probably was the most conversant with the notion of divine law (*jus divinum*) and who wrote the most extensively on it.[191] Laynez held a simple thesis: of all who hold office in the church the pope alone can be said, with the certainty of faith, to have jurisdiction by divine right. Unlike in the Old Testament, where the divine law expressed itself in many contingent details of time, place, weight, and measure, the divine law in the New Testament called into existence a unique institution, but one without prescription for minute details, which details would indeed work themselves out in history.[192] This thesis put in Laynez's hand a clear measuring rod. With it he marked out a very limited area that could be attributed to the divine will. Outside that restricted space, he allowed wide scope for human initiative in a changing world.[193] This point of departure gave Laynez his axis on the twin question about episcopal jurisdiction and episcopal residence.

On 20 October 1562 Laynez gave one of his major addresses at Trent. He focused on the origins of episcopal jurisdiction. His opening remarks reflected the suspicions that poisoned the atmosphere. "Some theologians," announced Laynez, "and these are good men, have counseled me not to defend my opinion in this matter lest I give the appearance of fawning on the pope. But God, judge of the living and the dead, is my witness that I have never uttered a word with an eye to the adulation of the pope. . . . Three times I have been present in this council. Always have I spoken the dictates of my conscience. This I do now, and this I always will do, because I look for nothing, I hope for nothing, I fear nothing."[194]

Laynez spoke for three hours. He elaborated a distinction between the power of holy orders and the power of jurisdiction: the bishops' power of orders proceeds immediately from God; their power of jurisdiction, although it resides in the episcopal body by divine right, is conferred on the individual bishop immediately by the pope and not by God. It was an important application of his theory of divine law as revealed in the New Testament.[195] Paolo Sarpi wrote that no discourse at the Council of Trent received more praise or more criticism. Carlo Visconti, bishop of Ventimiglia, was enthusiastic. Muzio Calini Bresciano, archbishop of Zara, was disgusted.[196] A month later, on 24 November 1562, Salmerón wrote Borgia that he felt that the discourse had a generally happy effect, since it illumined the issue, won over some hitherto undecided bishops, radiated tranquility, and checked the acidulous and intemperate language of some at Trent.[197]

Moving toward a Crisis

Salmerón's assessment of the scene was immoderately optimistic. He was writing during the period of elation that followed the arrival at Trent on 13 November of the masterly cardinal of

Lorraine, Charles de Guise, with his impressive party of fourteen French bishops and some theologians. Although de Guise had been defeated in his campaign against the continuation of the Council of Trent and for the calling of a new council, his conciliatory gestures augured harmony and tranquility in the council.[198] By early December, however, the storm winds began to blow. On the fifth Cardinal Luigi Simonetta rejected canons on episcopal residence that Lorraine favored. Simonetta claimed that he discerned in Lorraine's language echoes of the antipapal conciliar movement. The same day François de Beaucaire, bishop of Metz, challenged the fullness of papal primacy.[199]

As these tensions mounted, Laynez gave another major address, on 9 December. He reminded the council that it had been called to refute heresy and eradicate moral decadence in the Church, not to engage in disputes among Catholics, which disputes should be left to the theological schools. He recalled for the council that the question of the source of the sacramental episcopal power caused no trouble; that the question of the source of jurisdictional power, whether directly from Christ or indirectly through the pope (*mediante pontifice*), split the theologians into opposing schools. He recommended that this disputed issue be dropped from dogmatic discussion in the council and be transmitted to the ongoing scholarly work of the theologians. Applying his restrictive principle on divine law as known in the New Testament, he contended that the obligation of residence did not derive from divine law, and that a disciplinary matter should not be elevated to the dignity of dogma. Reaction was mixed. Nicolas Peaume, bishop of Verdun, disapproved. Cardinal Stanislaus Hosius liked it. Suspicions widened. Hostilities sharpened.[200]

In this acrimonious atmosphere Salmerón gave a sermon on St. Thomas on Sunday, 20 December. He touched on several issues of the day, and aggravated some of the bishops. Polanco reported that Salmerón had touched too close to home for some of the prelates.[201] Ludovico Nuccio, secretary of Gabriele Paleotti, said the same thing, and added that several complained that Salmerón should not have spoken in so freewheeling a way in public.[202] Among those offended was the cardinal of Lorraine. Complaints went to Rome. Carlo Borromeo, cardinal secretary of state, admonished Salmerón, and others too, to avoid saying anything in public that would irritate de Guise. Salmerón promptly wrote to Borromeo, apologizing for the incident, and protesting that he had had no intention of distressing the cardinal of Lorraine.[203]

Despite the efforts of Laynez and Borromeo to defuse the explosive issue of divine law, the Franco-Spanish phalanx and the Roman party continued on a collision course. On 20 January Laynez was scheduled once more to address the council on this question. All looked forward to it. But sickness, aggravated by foul weather, forced Laynez to bed, and the meeting was cancelled.[204]

March 1563 was a seriously troubled month. Great uncertainty and uneasiness fell over the council. On the second Cardinal Gonzaga, one of the papal legates, died. He, Laynez, and Salmerón had worked together harmoniously. On the last day of Gonzaga's mortal illness, Salmerón and Laynez twice visited him. Laynez heard his confession and administered extreme unction.[205] On the seventh, Pope Pius IV, without consulting the college of cardinals, appointed two new legates to the council: Cardinal Giovanni Morone and Cardinal Bernardo Navagero. On the seventeenth Cardinal Seripando died. Between this competent general of the Hermits of St. Augustine and the Jesuits at Trent a distinct coolness had developed since 1546, when the intricate question of justification was debated and Seripando's theory of twofold justice (*duplex justitia*) had been rejected in favor of the position taken by Laynez and Salmerón. With the death of Seripando, rumors spread through Trent that Salmerón was gathering material unfavorable to the memory of Seripando. Some delegates complained to Cardinal Simonetta. Simonetta promised to summon Salmerón and have the matter clarified. Nothing further was heard of this.[206]

Salmerón and Gentian Hervet

Salmerón next became involved in a theological skirmish, an event that added to the uneasiness of that worried March. The day after Seripando's death, Gentian Hervet, a French theologian in the entourage of the cardinal of Lorraine who pushed for a conciliar definition that favored the obligation by divine law (*iure divino*) of episcopal residence, sent a letter to Salmerón, contesting his opposition to a definition of this kind. On the twentieth Salmerón visited Hervet and discussed with him the problems of the council. Both lamented the delays, but differed on the cause. Salmerón traced it to the divine law issue; Hervet felt it was Rome's reluctance to face up to the need of curial reform.

The Frenchman in his written message to Salmerón elaborated on his deeply felt personal stand against the Jesuit position.[207] Hervet's approach was basically an attack on the scandal of absenteeism among the bishops, and Rome's inertia in the face of this scandal. The Frenchman disclaimed any attack on the person of Pope Pius IV, "no less pious in reality than he is in name" (*non minus est re quam nomine Pius*). The fault he placed at the door of "several venal bishops and sycophants at the Roman curia who, in their irresponsible desertion of their flocks and their ambitious quest of prominence and empty titles, are no less attached to Rome than are serfs to the soil. So oppressive and blind is this ambition that they prefer to see Germany torn by unending dissensions, all hope of winning England back lost, and France, ever the most powerful and reliable defender of the Supreme Pontiff, snatched from Catholic hands— an eventuality most to be feared at this moment—than to bring themselves to quit Rome and feed their flocks.[208] This was Hervet's theme: the pressing scandal was in flocks unattended by absent and rapacious pastors; the remedy lay in a conciliar decree that bishops must by divine law reside in their sees; the omission of such a decree could not only instigate rumors that the pope did not really want bishops to live among their faithful but could also split the Church by a schism. "Beware, beware" (*Cavendum, cavendum*), he wrote.

In his document Hervet addressed an apostrophe to Pope Pius IV: Do you want to renew the Church? Start with your own house. To Salmerón and Laynez he made an emotional appeal:

> If you are genuine companions of Jesus—and you say that you are— show this in deed. Are you companions of Jesus? Seek the glory of Jesus. Can you be companions of Jesus and not make the glory of Jesus your quest? . . . Stop throwing up to the man in the street that you are defenders of the supreme pontiff's authority. Even the barbers and the half-blind see what those who deny the divinely mandated (*iure divino*) obligation of

episcopal residence are up to with their schemes and projections. You claim that you champion the authority of the vicar of Christ, and at the same time you bring upon Jesus himself, so far as you can, ignominy, shame, disgrace.[209]

Salmerón replied to Hervet's charges on 9 May, the Fourth Sunday after Easter, in a sermon that he delivered before the council. Gabriele Paleotti thought that it was excessively sharp.[210] Polanco reported that it was hard-hitting and practical. Salmerón took to task those bishops who, in his mind, were holding up the council's dogmatic and disciplinary task by beating the air with the theoretical question of divine law and side tracking concrete, practical measures that could be realized in the real order of things.[211] His aggressiveness annoyed the cardinal of Lorraine. De Guise made extended interventions on 12 and 14 May. He did not mention Salmerón by name in his reprehension of "a certain priest" who from the pulpit denounced the council's attention to the great issue of the moment. Lorraine not only launched a strenuous criticism of those who stood by what was known to be Salmerón's position on the divine law issue. He also made a pungent attack on the Roman curia. No one doubted that Salmerón had seriously irritated Lorraine.[212]

Continuing Conciliar Crisis

These feelings deepened that fear of schism which Laynez had felt three months earlier. On 1 January 1563 he had written to Antonio Araoz.

> May God stretch forth his hand, Father, because ever since I heard in France [before I came to Trent] of these interminable questions about divine right, I feared that the French party, zealous and well-intentioned as they are, might under the influence of the devil take these question as an occasion for withdrawing from the council, and this without finishing the business of defining matters of faith and without taking action on reform. From a gesture of this kind would arise primarily scandal or even schism. No good can come from this situation; only harm to sheep and shepherds. To give what little help I can, I wrote to Rome, asking the pope to consider whether it would not be wise to put pressure on the council to get on with the definition of dogma and, in so far as possible, with legislation on reform, and then to close the council.[213]

On 3 March Emperor Ferdinand sent two serious letters to Pope Pius IV after the cardinal of Lorraine had visited the emperor at Innsbruck about the grave developments at Trent. That same month King Philip II sent special ambassadors to Rome about the divine law issue. The secular powers were becoming more deeply involved in the council's business.[214]

The grave issue of episcopal jurisdiction and residence broadened, therefore, beyond the area of theology. The Catholic powers entered the arena at a moment of universal thirst for reform within the Church. Around the standard of reform, French, Spanish, and imperial bishops rallied in a rare display of harmony. The reform they envisaged embraced change "in head and members." Many put their sights on the Roman curia. Despite papal protests of determination to reform the Church at its head, the secular rulers distrusted Pope Pius IV.[215]

Diplomacy and Theology

Cardinal Morone had his work cut out for him. He had to close the chasm of distrust between the secular powers and Pius IV; he had to convince the princes that Rome was not sidetracking the council into trivial affairs; he had to give the rulers a responsible place in serious planning for reform; and at the same time, he had to avoid the pitfalls of conciliarism. Morone, therefore, had the daunting task of balancing the demands of sound theology and delicate diplomacy.

Salmerón and Laynez approached the issue from a more narrow base. Perhaps they did not appreciate the breadth of Morone's task. They saw their role as that of theologians. This shaped their vision of the questions before the council. They handled theological questions with theological tools. And they spoke forthrightly when they thought bishops and princes were theologically aberrant. Talk of this kind easily led to estrangement.

These tension-laden attitudes leaped to the fore in the spring of 1563. The two Jesuits detected an anti-Roman hue in some of the programs for reform. Gentian Hervet's letter to Salmerón, for example, sounded loud the notes of chagrin with the papal curia. In May Salmerón had heard that more prelates were coming to the council, bearing strong feelings against the pope. He wrote Cristóbal Madrid about what he heard. "There is little hope of getting away from Trent soon, for it appears that this game is starting all over again. The talk is that, with the advent of the new legates, some other bishops are coming from Spain, Scotland, and Flanders. 'You have multiplied the people but you have not expanded the joy.' All appear to be coming armed with declarations against the head of the Church with a view to tumbling him to the ground.''[216]

This attitude troubled the Jesuits. They rejected any move that appeared to denigrate the pope. Their determination to safeguard the papal position in the church exploded in a feisty address Laynez gave on 16 June 1563. He spoke for more than two hours. Bluntly he asserted that the reform of the papacy was the business of the pope, not the council. He proclaimed that the choice of bishops was the exclusive prerogative of the pope, not the people; that the vulgar crowd was a beast of many heads whose rule was marked more by rashness than prudence. "I always distrust a crowd, even a crowd of bishops," he exclaimed.[217] Some hailed the discourse. Others were deeply angered. It especially irritated the frayed nerves of the French and the Spanish. Muzio Calini, archbishop of Zara, emphatically criticized the talk, citing in particular Laynez's equating the judgment of an ignorant mob with the bishops legitimately assembled in a council. He deplored Laynez's taunting the French with the intention of ''breaking the unity of the Church and withdrawing from obedience to the head.''[218]

Some took the case to Rome. They formulated their grievance simply: "We are getting nothing done here, thanks to the general of the Society of Jesus."[219] Cardinal Morone too was deeply angered as he beheld Laynez rattling the fragile structure of his diplomacy of conciliation. He disassociated himself from Laynez's position. He declared that he wished the Jesuit had kept his peace.[220]

Toward a Peaceful Resolution

Morone at this critical moment in the council's life was the hero. Ever since 10 April, when he entered Trent as the successor to Cardinal Gonzaga, he plied his diplomatic trade with finesse and patience. Six days after his arrival, he set out for Innsbruck to see Emperor Ferdinand. Through three weeks he labored at restoring trust between the emperor and Pius IV. He gained that improbable goal.[221] Back at Trent, this flexible diplomat worked with the cardinal of Lorraine on the "troubled issue" (*vexata quaestio*) of episcopal jurisdiction and residence. With tact he brought the French to the point where they willingly backed down from their hard line.[222] On 6 July in a conference that lasted five hours, forty prelates tried to work out a new formula. On the ninth, in another conference, Morone urged the prelates to face up to their responsibility and their consciences. More than forty interventions were made. Laynez spoke last. Once again he presented a formula he introduced seven months before: since the issue of the divine origin of episcopal jurisdiction and residence was one debated only among Catholics—and therefore a strictly Catholic question—it would be better to halt discussion, issue no condemnations of either school, and leave it with other questions disputed among Catholic theologians.

Laynez's proposal was decisive. All accepted it. Gabriele Paleotti reported that a great calm followed. In the twenty-third session on 15 July 1563, the council reached a happy detente and a singular triumph for peace in the Church. The decree on episcopal residence, while declaring residence a serious obligation, avoided stating whether it was or was not *jure divino*; and the question of the source of jurisdiction was omitted.[223]

Ignorance of History

If these decrees were a palm of victory for skilled diplomacy, the debates were a display of historical ignorance. The *jure divino* school in its insistence on the immediate divine mandate, and the *mediante pontifice* school in its claim for the mediating power of the pope argued in isolation from the historical evolution of the conferring of episcopal power through the centuries. Both schools therefore failed to set forth a principle that enjoyed continuity with the past. The *jure divino* theologians did not take into account the need that a bishop be in communion with the hierarchy and be dependent on the primatial see in the exercise of episcopal powers, a basic dependence that the current council recognized. The *mediante pontifice* theologians failed to explain the practice in the ancient Church that did not conceive the act of conferring jurisdiction immediately as something separate from the act of consecration.

281

Laynez shared that failure. Embedded in his theology of the Church were the weaknesses of some old positions long since abandoned, such as the thesis that Christ conferred jurisdiction on his apostles through Peter (*mediante Petro*). Laynez's distinction between the two powers, the power of orders and the power of jurisdiction, was pointed, but quite irrelevant to the question at issue, since a bishop at his ordination not only received orders but was also invested with an apostolic office.

This separation of the two acts was a late development in theological thinking, of recent date, the thirteenth century. The evolution of the idea from then to the period of Trent was obscure. Both schools fell into the trap of a mental provincialism that blocked them from reducing to unity, on the one hand, the bishops' divine power of jurisdiction, and, on the other hand, the bishops' dependence on the primatial power of the Holy See for the valid use of that jurisdiction.[224] This unfinished business remained to engage the bishops and their experts (*periti*) at Vatican Council I and Vatican Council II.

Bishops and Jesuits

Years later, when far-removed from the heat of the conciliar debates, Salmerón in his *Commentarii in omnes Epistolas b. Pauli* balanced both sides of this issue quietly and evenhandedly, and then sided with the stance taken by Laynez at Trent. In the seventy-fifth tractatus, he lined up the arguments that the obligation of episcopal residence is of divine law. In the seventy-sixth tractatus, he did the same with the arguments that this obligation derives from ecclesiastical law. He favored the latter. But he felt that a reconciliation could be achieved between the two by describing the obligation of residence as divine "in the broad sense of the word" (*laxe sumpta voce*) because ecclesiastical power, from which the precept derives, has its origin in God, and also because God orders man to hear the Church.[225] Salmerón's presentation of the arguments pro and con was a synthesis of the fissures that ran through the council during 1562–63.

The stand taken at Trent by Salmerón and Laynez became distorted as it filtered down through the succeeding centuries, and left a residue of inaccuracy that depicted the Society of Jesus as habitually harboring a wariness of the episcopate. Laynez's position has been called "a papalist presbyterianism," a description that recalls Cardinal Henry Manning's angular judgment that the only plank between a Jesuit and a Presbyterian was the pope.[226]

Laynez the speculative theologian and Laynez the active apostle, however, cast a different historical shadow. In his theology of orders—and Salmerón joined him in this—he ascribed to the bishops, who received a distinct ordination, a superior hierarchical position over priests.[227] On 23 September 1562 Salmerón elucidated his theory of triple ordination before the council: Christ conferred the sacrament of orders on his apostles on three distinct occasions, first at the Last Supper, when he conferred the power of consecration; then in the evening of Easter Sunday, when he gave them the power of absolution; and then at the Ascension, when he blessed them and gave them the power to preach. On this last occasion he made them bishops, elevating them to a unique and special position in the Church.[228]

Laynez, in his work in the field, labored at the side of bishops Ennio Filonardi in Parma and Giovanni Morone in Germany. This alliance with the bishops was characteristically Jesuit. Salmerón cooperated with Luigi Lippomano of Verona, Alfonso Carafa of Naples, Juan Fonseca of Castellammare di Stabia. Pierre Favre worked closely with Albrecht of Mainz and Philip II of Flehsheim in Speyer; Jay with Pankratius von Sinzenhofer in Regensburg, Moritz von Hutten in Eichstätt, Ernst von Bayern in Salzburg, Urban Weber of Laibach, Otto Truchsess von Walburg in Augsburg; Paschase Broët with Rodolfo Pio di Carpi in Reggio Emilia and Faenza; Jerónimo Doménech with Francesco Orozco de Arce in Palermo; Juan Polanco with Antonio Pou in Bari. And there was a multitude of other examples.[229] Bishop and Jesuit were a familiar pair.

The Carranza Affair at the Council

Six weeks before the momentous twenty-third session, a strange and deviously conceived event occurred. It involved the controversial *Commentary on the Christian Catechism* (*Comentario sobre Catequismo Cristiano*) of Archbishop Bartolomé de Carranza, who had spent four years in the jail of the Spanish

Inquisition. On 3 June 1563 five or six members on the council's commission for the review and revision of the list of books on the *Index* met to take under consideration Carranza's *Comentario*. Laynez and Salmerón, who were members of this commission, received no notice of the meeting. Those present at this rump session heard statements from the archbishop of Granada and the bishops of Orense and Almeria, all of whom affirmed that Carranza's book was truly Catholic. They then, without having personally reviewed the work, voted in view of the testimony of prelates so eminent to approve the *Comentario*. When this devious bit of business came to light a few days later, the patriarch of Venice asked Laynez to explain it. Laynez replied that he and Salmerón knew nothing about the secretive meeting of 3 June.[230]

Polanco passed on to Antonio Araoz his opinion of this backstairs diplomacy. "This action appears to have been ill-advised. Still more, little honor has been done to the archbishop by this kind of conduct."[231] Laynez had the same opinion. He told Francis Borgia: "I wish the author of this book [Carranza] every possible good. But I believe that the way they [members of the *Index* commission] went about approving the work was, for many reasons, illegal. I fear that they have done damage to the archbishop's cause. I also believe that, considering the temper of the times and the position of the author, the book contains statements that would better have been left in the inkwell. I say this even though I am sure that the archbishop's intentions were good."[232] Polanco's reaction to the case was one of relief that the Society had come through unscathed. He wrote Jerónimo Nadal: "Neither the archbishop nor the Inquisition can pick a quarrel with our men."[233] So petered out the clandestine conspiracy to exonerate Carranza during those arduous weeks in which the council moved toward its decisive twenty-third session on orders on 15 July 1563.

Debates on Matrimony

The next business before the council concerned matrimony and the reform of the clergy. Five days after the close of the twenty-third session, the debates opened. Actually, the theologians had started their consideration of matrimony five months earlier, in February, amid the prevailing uncertainty about episcopal residence. On 9 February Salmerón, the first speaker, consumed the entire afternoon session, again with a broad appeal to scripture, patristics, and conciliar decrees in upholding matrimony as a sacrament.[234] He also spoke on the cloudy issue of clandestine marriages. For centuries the Church, identifying the partners in marriage as the ministers of the sacrament, recognized the validity of marriages entered into secretly and without the presence of a priest. A number in the council, in order to remove the many abuses that arose from clandestine marriages, wanted to legislate the need of a priest and witnesses as requisite for a marriage's validity. This raised the question of the Church's power to make this kind of legislation.

In his address of 9 February Salmerón for the first time hedged. He simply presented the arguments pro and con for a change, and then deferred to the wisdom of the council.[235] Salmerón's hesitancy in enunciating a clear personal judgment on this issue arose from an embarrassment that he and Laynez felt. They differed with Pope Pius IV. The pope judged that in the future the presence of a priest and witnesses should be an essential for the validity of a marriage. So he advised the council.[236] Salmerón and Laynez disagreed.

Continuing Divergence between Morone and the Jesuits

The position taken by Salmerón and Laynez widened the divergence between them and Cardinal Morone. Again differing styles jarred each other. Morone tipped his hand on 31 July during the debates on clandestine marriages. In the morning meeting, when it was Laynez's turn to speak, the hour was late. Laynez had prepared his matter carefully, but he said simply: "I do not agree with the decree under discussion on clandestine marriages."[237] Many in the council wanted to hear his reasons. This could have been done in the afternoon meeting. But Morone decided otherwise. He was annoyed with Laynez. He shunned him and Salmerón as much as possible.[238] Polanco briefed Francis Borgia on this unhappy development: the legate habitually avoided the services of Salmerón and Laynez; he entrusted theological questions to less capable men; even when on more vexing issues he did call on the two Jesuits, he did so perforce, either because the pope ordered him to do so, or because the questions were so intractable he had to seek their help, or because he feared that they would speak out against him.[239]

Salmerón had an opportunity to expand on his own reasons against the invalidation of clandestine marriages during an unusual private discussion. Cardinal Stanislaus Hosius, one of the council's presidents was deeply vexed by the question. On 13 and 14 September he arranged debates on it at his residence. He invited several important men, including all the legates, to hear eight theologians hammer out the issue. Salmerón was among the eight. Four argued that the Church had the power to invalidate clandestine marriages, and that the secrecy was in itself sufficient reason for so decreeing. Salmerón joined the three others against this position. The eight theologians divided evenly.[240]

"Small Comfort" for Salmerón and Laynez

Among the theological principles that guided Salmerón and Laynez during these debates was this: a conciliar definition, to be valid, must evoke a moral unanimity among the conciliar fathers. This, they contended, held also for reform decrees, since these, to be vital and strong in the Church's life, must be knit tightly to revealed truth. Durable reformation must be permeated with dogma.[241] In a vote taken in early September on a tentative formula, 134 voted for the invalidation of clandestine marriages, fifty-six against.[242] The size of the negative vote gave Salmerón and Laynez a disquieting uncertainty.

Divisions of this kind carried right into the solemn assembly of session twenty-four on 11 November. By the canon on reform *Tametsi*, the council decreed that, although clandestine marriages freely entered into previously were true marriages, nevertheless for the future the presence of a priest and witnesses would be necessary for validity.[243] Of the council's four presidents, only Cardinal Bernardo Navagero fully approved. Cardinals Hosius, Simonetta, and Morone, in one way or another, deferred the final decision to the pope. Salmerón and Laynez did the same. Two thirds of the council voted approval; one third expressed disapproval. In this the two Jesuits found "small comfort" (*poca consolazione*).[244] Loyalty to the pope had not vitiated their intellectual integrity. Their stand refuted those at the council who

286

had classified them as stereotyped expressions of Rome's policies.

Last Month of the Council

Many questions raised by the Protestants remained for the council: purgatory, invocation of the saints, veneration of images, and relics. The prospect of many more months of labor at Trent troubled Morone. Roman sentiment leaned toward putting these issues in the hands of the pope. But the cardinal of Lorraine insisted that they be handled by the council. Morone worked out a compromise. He endorsed a plan that the council not try to hammer out dogmatic decrees, because of the complicated structure of several and various congregations which that involved. He envisaged instead the more modest objective of formulating less intricate reform decrees, whose function would be the removal of abuses in the Church and a simple enunciation of the Church's teaching.[245]

The pressure to move along with what he thought was a reckless pace in questions so important troubled Laynez. Loosely formulated and emaciated decrees disquieted him. He wrote a lament to Francisco Vargas, Spain's ambassador to Rome, on 9 July 1563. "To be on the level with Your Excellency, it strikes me as being a hard task, in view of such conflicting opinions among so many men here, to reach agreement on the decrees except by paying the price of diluting their language and injecting into them equivocal expressions with diverse significance. The consequence is that one decree is wrapped up in one meaning, and another decree in still another meaning." He surmised, he told Vargas, that he would have to lower his sights to the negative goal of merely preventing damage to the council.[246]

Again Laynez found himself at odds with Cardinal Morone. The scholar and the diplomat continued to draw apart. Laynez, sensitive to the serious implications of conciliar documents, insisted on accuracy and lucidity. Morone, preoccupied with closing the council on a note of harmony between the pope and the secular princes, tended to compromise.[247] Yet, under these trying circumstances, Salmerón and Laynez continued to add to the contributions they had started earlier on indulgences, images, and purgatory.[248]

One of the subjects discussed was the reform of religious orders. The Jesuits, whose *Constitutions* called for a two-year novitiate, became apprehensive when the council hammered out legislation that called for the pronouncement of the vows after a year of noviceship. Cardinal Carlo Borromeo, the papal secretary of state and long a friend of the Jesuits, contacted the legates. Into the decree was inserted a statement that the Society of Jesus was not affected by this particular legislation. Of the 175 archbishops and bishops who voted, one Spaniard cast a negative ballot. He was Bishop Martin Pérez de Ayala of Segovia. His reason: he knew nothing of the Jesuits and therefore could not make a judgment.[249]

Finally the most protracted conciliar enterprise in the history of the church came to an end. Through three periods and twenty-five sessions it had seen the succession of five popes and had felt the guiding reins of thirteen papal legates. On 4 December this question was put to the assembled members: "Most illustrious lords and very reverend fathers, is it agreeable to you that this holy and ecumenical synod be brought to an end?" They replied: "Affirmative" (*placet*). Cardinal Giovanni Morone then pronounced the "Go in Peace" (*andate in pace*); the cathedral resounded with acclaim; tears filled the eyes of many.[250] Only a handful of those present had participated in the three periods of the council. Salmerón and Laynez were two of these.

The three periods of the council unrolled for Salmerón and Laynez experiences that changed keenly through the eighteen years. The first period closed on a note of high achievement and harmony with the legates; the second closed under a cloud of disenchantment and irritation at small progress; the third closed with a sigh of relief, disquiet with hastily done work, and the awkwardness of isolation from the chief legate.

The Impact of Trent on Salmerón

Despite the exacting demands that the council had made on Salmerón, it did not seem to be a significant factor for him during the remaining twenty-two years of his life. Unlike the impact of Vatican Council II on its members, so many of whom hearken back to it as an inspiration and a vision, the influence of Trent as a perduring guide seems to have been minimal for Salmerón.

After he left Trent, only three times in his ample correspondence did he refer to the council. These three references were only passing remarks. In one he made a correction in Pedro Ribadeneyra's life of Laynez; in another, a report on a member of his province, he mentioned that Father Paolo Canozza had accompanied him to Trent; and in a third, a letter to Francis Borgia about the antipathy of Ascanio Geraldini, bishop of Cantanzaro, for the Society, he casually mentioned the faculties that the council gave and did not give to bishops [251] Nowhere in his many letters did Salmerón evidence that the council had become a leaven in his consciousness or that it had cut new routes for him in the renewal of the church.

Salmerón's seeming lack of sensibility to Trent pinpoints one of the deeper problems in Tridentine historiography: to what extent did the council enter into ecclesial consciousness? Strong progress in research makes it increasingly clear that the conciliar event and postconciliar events, despite their complemental nature, had their own special identity, and that frequently after 1563 a creative spirit emerged in the Church that sparked religious attitudes not in the Tridentine mold. [252] In Salmerón's firmament at least, the Council of Trent did not take its place as a guiding star.

A Preaching Stint in North Italy

Six months passed since Morone's *andate in pace* before Salmerón returned to Naples. He, Laynez, Polanco, and Nadal left Trent on 11 December and went to Venice. There the four Jesuits preached and spent Christmas. The Venetian visit became one of the more memorable experiences in Salmerón's preaching career. That Christmas more of the nobility went to hear him than all the other preachers put together. [253] At the urgent request of the doge, Giovanni Battista Lecaro, he prolonged his visit so that he might preach there during Lent. He gave his sermons in St. Mark's Basilica, the Church of The Apostles, and the church attached to the Jesuit college. The Venetians responded enthusiastically. This gratified Salmerón intensely, and he confessed that not even in Naples had he sensed such satisfaction among his listeners. [254]

One topic on which he spoke with singular directness was

immodesty in women's fashions. Pointedly he criticized the in-delicacy of the low breast line of some dresses. Many gentle-women then adopted a dress that became known as a "salmeron" because it fitted up to the neck. Salmerón became a noted figure in the city. As he walked the streets, gentlemen raised their hats, and girls exclaimed: "That's Salmerón" (*Questo è il Salmerón*). At the close of the Lenten course, Salmerón felt exhausted. The doge and other leading men of Venice, in expressing the city-wide affection, tried to keep him there.[255] Salmerón, however, had to move on, but, as he wrote Laynez on 8 April 1564, "I did not dash their hopes that I might visit and preach at another time in Venice."[256]

Laynez suggested that Salmerón on his return to Naples by way of Rome stop at Ferrara, Bologna, and Amelia, and preach in those cities. He recommended Amelia especially because the rector of the Jesuit community felt that Salmerón could achieve a great deal in a few days with Pietro de Petrignano, a gentleman who was a potential founder of a Jesuit college.[257] Salmerón finally arrived in Rome sometime in May. On the feast of Pentecost, 22 May, he preached in St. Peter's Basilica. In late May or early June he left Rome and arrived back in Naples after an absence of three years.[258]

The Gesù Vecchio in Naples

The most visible sign of progress in the province that greeted Salmerón on his return was the new Jesuit church. He had long been identified with this initial introduction of Jesuit architecture in Naples. As early as 1557 he had decided that a more spacious church was needed to replace the small building in the area called *il seggio di Nilo*. In the Society at that time were two members of an artistically talented family of Ferrara, Lorenzo and Giovanni Tristano. Salmerón asked Laynez that one of the Tristanos be the architect and builder. Laynez, however, was unable to free either Lorenzo or Giovanni from other tasks. Salmerón therefore employed a layman, Pilidoro Carafo di Cave dei Tirreni. Cave had hardly started when he died on 7 December 1557. Lorenzo Tristano then took over for a brief period. These erratic beginnings settled into a firm and consistent program with the arrival in Naples of Giovanni Tristano in the fall of 1558.[259]

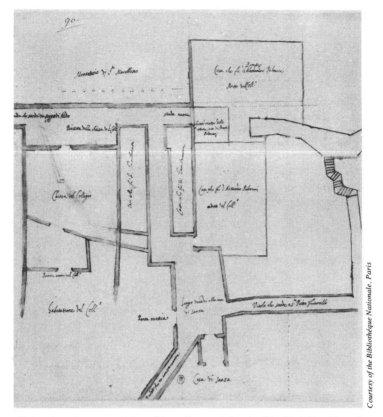

Sixteenth century ground plan of the college and church of the Gesù Vecchio and surroundings, Naples

The artistic and technical development of Jesuit architecture in its Baroque style through the sixteenth and seventeenth centuries falls naturally into three phases: the origins, the early formation, and the triumph. The first two belong peculiarly to Giovanni Tristano. And the first church whose construction he personally directed after his entry into the Society was Salmerón's project, which became known as the Gesù Vecchio, to be distinguished from the later Gesù Nuovo. For four years, until 1562, Tristano worked in Naples.[260]

Tristano developed a master plan on the grand scale that embraced a Jesuit enclave of church, school, and residence as a unit so striking in its sweeping design that it would be one of the most splendid Jesuit foundations in Europe. He envisaged a college building with seventy rooms and with a capacity for ten classes. Father Francesco Araldo was so enthralled by Tristano's design that he wrote in January 1559 that in time the Neapolitan Jesuit complex would be outstanding in its beauty among Jesuit institutions of Europe and would be the source of "the most extensive spiritual achievements" (*grandissimo fruitto*). Six months later, in July, Araldo again expressed his awe, for the church, as yet unfinished, was "large, beautiful, and practically designed for the ministry of word and sacrament" (*grande, bella et attisima a ministerio del verbo et sacramenti*).[261] In 1562 Tristano received another assignment and had to leave Naples. He turned the work over to a layman, Domenico di Verdina. He left a church not yet completed but already superior in the splendor of its lines and in the richness of its decorations to most of the churches of the city.[262] Jesuit architecture had come to Naples. Salmerón's insistence had brought Tristano to Naples, and with him the shape of the Gesù Vecchio, ten years before Giacomo Vignola traced his design of the Gesù in Rome.

The Death of Diego Laynez

Six months after Salmerón returned to Naples in early June 1564, Laynez died in Rome. In January 1565 the general's health took a serious turn. Francis Borgia kept Salmerón informed. "On the feast of the Epiphany," wrote Borgia, "he [Laynez] said to me: 'Tomorrow I want to celebrate mass. It will be my viaticum.' It was his last mass."[263] In the afternoon of the seventeenth, he asked for extreme unction. This he received with deep devotion. Later, an attack of catarrh almost suffocated him. He then went into a coma that lasted forty-three hours. On the nineteenth at two in the morning he expired. He was fifty-three years old. Borgia wrote Salmerón: "After his passing, it was a comfort to look on his body, kiss his hand, gaze in wonder on his countenance."[264]

For some thirty-seven years, ever since their undergraduate days at Alcalá, Laynez and Salmerón had been friends. For thirty-one years they had been faithful to the vows they pronounced at Montmartre in 1534. Salmerón revered Laynez deeply, and this he expressed in the preface of his own magnum opus, *Commentarii in Evangelicam Historiam*. He confessed that in the composing of this work he was dependent on a host of scholars from whom he garnered many bits of information. He likened himself to "Aesop's jackdaw, dolled up in the feathers of many other birds" (*Corniculam aesopi, alienis pluris indutam*). The one scholar, however, whom he singled out was Laynez. To Salmerón Laynez was a man of unique and almost divine genius, learned in an almost miraculous way in many intellectual disciplines, perfected by a preeminently perceptive judgment as well as by an outstandingly broad reading in sacred scripture and the patristic age."[265] Laynez left the Society with some three thousand men, divided into eighteen provinces and spread to the far corners of the world.[266] His death deepened the sunset of the presence of the Society's founders. Only Salmerón, Simão Rodrigues, and Nicolás Bobadilla remained of those who received *Regimini militantis ecclesiae* from Pope Paul III in 1540.

Summary

The ten years of Salmerón's life embraced in this chapter resemble a piece of motley in the disarray of events and jumbled accumulation of facts. But from this confusion three patterns seem to emerge and clarify Salmerón's contribution to the Catholic Reform: his work as a theologian, as a religious superior, and as a popular preacher.

Salmerón the theologian was identified with the Council of Trent. He was one of the few men present in the council's three periods. With rare exceptions—his opinion about the validity of clandestine marriages was one—the theological judgments he expressed in the congregations basically anticipated and meshed with the decrees and canons of the council. Any reliable judgment on Salmerón's significance as a theologian must therefore wait upon a more definitive construction of the Council of Trent.

At the moment the council is enveloped in a crisis of interpretation.[267] Some historians think it an "indisputable fact that a whole epoch of the Church has been fashioned by this council."[268] Other historians judge that the destiny of the post-Tridentine Church lay rather with the spirituality of the Devotio Moderna and the independent sovereignty of Rome than with the council.[269] Still others take a middle course and draw a wide distinction between those in the post-Tridentine Church who took the council as a corpus of definitive and set prescriptions for all religious needs, and those who found in the council a vision of the Church, however vaguely defined, that called for a creative spirit to do what Trent had left undone.[270] Only patient research can resolve these deep divisions in interpretation. Esteem or reproach for Salmerón's role will rise or fall with the mercury in the historical barometer of the Council of Trent.

Salmerón the religious superior was provincial of Naples for eighteen years. By 1565 he had completed half of those years. For eight months in 1561–62 he held the post of vicar general of the Society. In his routine work of dealing with civic communities, the aristocracy, the hierarchy, the people, his fellow Jesuits about schools, finances, and residences, Salmerón was practical, realistic, and intelligent. An overserious cast of mind, however, tarnished the brightness of those positive qualities and deprived his regime of a sense of joy. Under his barbed and hasty admonitions, some of the Jesuits in the Neapolitan province became restive and complained to Rome. But in the balance, Salmerón carried out his administration responsibly and admirably. His concern that his important unit of the Society be preserved in what he called "the diligent adherence to the Society's institute "(*in viridi observantia*) gave added fibre to the cloth of the Catholic Reform in the Kingdom of Naples.

Salmerón the popular preacher continued for many years in the role in which he did his personally most gratifying work. He started in 1537 on the street corners of Monselice, where he and Francis Xavier were preparing for their first masses. He closed thirty-two years later, in 1569 at the Vatican. By 1565 he had only four more years ahead in the pulpit. Pedro Ribadeneyra calculated that Salmerón gave eighteen Lenten series, which involved preaching each day. Almost half of these series were given in Naples.[271]

Salmerón spoke with compelling power. He mobilized a wide array of scriptural texts strategically placed, skillfully maneuvered, and clearly paraphrased. He honed a rick of rhetorical conceits that sustained protracted reflections on scriptural images. He sketched vivid vignettes of daily life in the streets, the shops, the home. Salmerón's oratory had a significance that extended far beyond a show of personal talent. He was but one voice in a large Jesuit chorus that was giving fire to a mighty force of preaching in the Catholic Reform. He belonged to that covey of Jesuits of whom a decade later the English secular priest, Gregory Martin, wrote in his *Roma Sancta* (1581). Martin described the Jesuits going to the poor in the piazzas and preaching

> with ful streame of the plainest scriptures, and piked sentences of ancient fathers, and notable examples of former time, most sweetly exhorting to good life, and most terribly dehorting from al sinne and wickednesse...[272]

Salmerón the theologian, the religious superior, the preacher: these headings best synthesize these ten years of his life.

CHAPTER IX

NAPLES

1565–1576

Introduction

This chapter covers a trifle more than a decade of Salmerón's life, from 1565, when Francis Borgia was elected the third general of the Society, to 1576, when Salmerón resigned from the provincial's post in Naples. Salmerón's correspondence epitomizes some of the serious tensions that rapid growth and expansion brought to the Society. What happened in Naples was happening in other Jesuit centers throughout Europe. Toward the close of these ten years, Salmerón started his most enduring contribution to Catholic life, his vast scriptural commentary in sixteen folio volumes.

Election of Francis Borgia as General Superior

Salmerón remained in Naples until the convocation of a general congregation for the election of a new general. After the death of Diego Laynez, the professed fathers in and around Rome chose Francis Borgia as vicar general. Borgia set 21 June 1565 for the opening of General Congregation II. During the Lent of that year

Salmerón gave a long course of sermons. Because of broken health—Salmerón was then but forty-nine years old—he intended to preach only three times a week. Many people, however, demanded that he speak every day. He yielded. On 4 March 1565 he wrote Borgia: "Although I have had a surfeit of this particular kind of work, I have been foolhardy enough to take up this task on a daily basis lest I disappoint the people who want it so intensely."[1]

Salmerón finished the course utterly exhausted. Because of his depleted energies, he asked Francis Borgia to be excused from attendance at the general congregation.[2] Borgia in turn used all the charm of his warm personality to overcome Salmerón's reluctance. On 4 May 1565 he wrote:

> My Father, never did I think that the occasion would arise when I would face the prospect of denying Your Reverence's wishes. My desire is above all to obey you and nowise to go counter to your inclinations. But in response to your recent letter, I do not feel that I can in conscience go along with my normal desire to yield to your good pleasure, both because of the damage that the Company would suffer by your absence from the congregation and because of the occasion it would provide outsiders for gossip and undesirable speculation. So I appeal in the spirit of charity that Your Reverence do not turn down this task. . . . May Your Reverence look kindly upon our loneliness. May you compassionate your sons, especially this one, who loves you truly. . . . So, committing to your consideration what I have said, I again beg Your Reverence to make haste to come to the congregation.[3]

Salmeron yielded to Borgia's eloquence. Francis, delighted at his success, sent off word to Salmerón that he was arranging for him to live during the period of the congregation in the room used by their loving father Ignatius.[4] On 2 July Borgia was elected general, and it was Salmerón's privilege to announce publicly the decision of the congregation.[5]

Problems in General Congregation II

General Congregation II occurred during a period of crisis in the Society. Among the internal tensions that this body of three thousand men felt were these: the pull between a spirit of activism and the call to contemplation; the pull between the élan of apostolic expansion and overextended resources; the pull between the sound training of the scholastics and the insistent demands for teachers in the schools; the pull between poverty and economic security. On all these problems the congregation legislated.

The Pull between Apostolic Action and Contemplation

This tension developed within an ambience of lament about the alleged decline of the Society's religious spirit from the bright fervor of its primitive period. Those who joined this dirge identified the culprit as an inadequate length of prayer exacted of Jesuits. Francis Borgia was one of the more articulate mourners. So was Nadal. They judged that the remedy lay in precise and juridical legislation that would impose an increased period of daily prayer on each member of the Society.[6]

This position was ably challenged. Paul Hoffaeus, a brusque and incisive German, contested this melancholy chorus. One of his points: fidelity to Ignatius's other spiritual foundations precludes the need for increased prayer. Another point: "The shorter length of time for prayer is not responsible for the spiritual decline." (*die kürzere Gebetzeit nicht shuld am Absinken!*) And still another point: the legislation proposed by Borgia and others is "not an addition to the Constitutions [as the advocates claimed] but a radical departure from them" (keine Ätenderung der Konstitutionen, sondern radikale Beobachtung!).[7]

Ignatius had envisaged the Jesuit as a man imbued with a thirst for a rich interior life who with the guidance of his confessor or superior planned a program of prayer and penance adapted to his work, health, and natural and supernatural gifts. Ignatius explicitly excluded the imposition of a universal law.[8] He deeply respected two fundamentals in the sensitive area of prayer: the diversity of the gifts of the Holy Spirit; and the differences among individuals in their talents and supernatural inspiration. During his lifetime he soundly reprimanded Jerónimo Nadal for advancing the cause of some Spanish Jesuits who desired the legislating of protracted periods for prayer. He failed, however, to scotch this tendency. Proposals to extend prayer by legislation arose in General Congregation I. These the congregation rejected.

In General Congregation II the issue again rose. Who precisely brought it to the floor is not known, but Francis Borgia, the newly elected general, emphatically favored the imposition of a definite period of increased daily prayer. The delegates from France and Germany, including Mercurian and Canisius, opposed this. The Spaniards and the Portuguese favored it. The Italians carried the decisive weight, and they sided with the Spaniards and the Portuguese. Basically, the issue placed three assistancies, the Spanish, the Portuguese, and the Italian, against one assistancy, the German. Salmerón, voting as provincial of Naples, joined the Italian bloc.[9] In the failure of consensus, the congregation compromised. It turned the resolution of the issue over to Francis Borgia, empowering him to increase prescribed prayer to the extent he judged best for the various men and areas in the Society. The congregation closed on 3 September 1565. On 5 November Borgia directed that the provinces of Spain should practice an hour of morning prayer; that other provinces should spend three-quarters of an hour in the morning and a half-hour at night in prayer and examination of conscience over and beyond the examination of conscience previously practiced.[10] Despite Borgia's noble intent, his decree was a grievous departure from Ignatius's inspiration and vision, and evokes resonances of those occasions when Ignatius had to chide Borgia for his waywardness in the practice of prayer. It is a surprise, therefore, to note that during this congregation Salmerón, who had been so close to Ignatius in the composition of the *Constitutions*, took the path of departure from those *Constitutions* in this basic area of Jesuit life.[11]

The Borgian decree suffered at least one failure. It did not silence those who were wont to tint the Society's primitive period in an unblemished golden hue. Voices continued to sound the cry of gloom about decadence. Paul Hoffaeus, as seen, challenged this. A little later, the Belgian Frans de Costere did the same, and in dramatic circumstances. In 1600 Pope Clement VIII, who seems to have been obsessed with Jesuit spiritual decline, lectured the Congregation of Procurators on the defects of the Society. De Costere replied to the pope: "Most Holy Father, I have known the Society since the time of our Father Ignatius and I recall very well what it was then. I also know what it is now. I have seen it. I have felt its pulse in the offices I have held. Now then (and here he lifted up his hands as if he were taking an oath) I swear before God and before His Vicar the truth of what I am saying. The Society now appears to me to be in our days twice as good as it was in the time of our Father Ignatius.''[12]

The Pull between Apostolic Expansion and Overextended Resources

The congregation tried to check the trend toward the multiplication of colleges. Salmerón consistently, even caustically, chided the Jesuits who were, as was Bobadilla, bent on the opening of more colleges. Ignatius had started this unwise trend toward expansion. When he died in 1556, he had started thirty-two colleges designed primarily for lay students. Actually, the total number of colleges Ignatius started was forty-six, since fourteen other colleges, although intended for scholastics, opened their classes to lay students. Ignatius's norm was this: if Jesuits taught Jesuits in Jesuit houses, the lectures should be open to the public.[13] These schools could not be properly manned. Large numbers of priests were necessary, but only at the end of the sixteenth century did priests outnumber scholastics in the Society.[14] The rector of the German College from 1564 to 1569, Guiseppe Cortesono, summed up a common lament: ''the ruin of the Society'' (*la rovina della Compagnia*) is in the acceptance of a multitude of colleges.[15]

General Congregation II could not evade this genuine crisis. In the eighth decree it called for moderation in the acceptance of colleges, and for the improvement of current schools rather than the inauguration of new ones.[16] Salmerón, in his frequent correspondence with two generals, Francis Borgia and Everard Mercurian, gave his strenuous support to this policy. The trend toward increase, however, moved onward. In 1579 the colleges numbered 144; in 1600, 245.[17]

The Pull between Solid Training and the Demand for Teachers

Here the congregation faced an issue of quality. It recognized the prevalence of poorly trained teachers in the colleges. Salmerón had complained to Laynez about the inferior quality of some Jesuits assigned to Naples. Overexpansion bred this shortage of skilled teachers. To man the schools, scholastics were taken from their studies and put into the classrooms. Novices, who received their basic ascetical and spiritual formation in various Jesuit communities, were sucked into the maelstrom of work in the colleges.

Scholastics and novices entered the classroom with little or no preparation. The schools were crippled by ineptitude. Many vocations were shipwrecked. One scholastic in the Neapolitan college, Giovanni Battista Pietrantonio, lamented: "I'm practically a boy. The students do not fear me. They take me for a lark. They are held in check not by whippings or threats, not by talking to or scoldings, but by the grave appearance, the dignity, the authority of the teacher."[18] This dangerous trend toward abbreviated intellectual formation had started under Ignatius. During his generalate, for example, 217 entered the Society in Italy. Seventy-six of these received little or no philosophy, and even less of theology. This trend grew stronger with time. Under Laynez, 342 entered the Society in Italy. Of these, 127 stopped their studies at grammar and humanities, except for the few who also received some little schooling in practical confessional work.[19]

Complaints poured into Rome from several countries about incompetent teachers. Pedro Juan Perpinya, a teacher at the Roman College, wrote in a memorial on Jesuit teachers: "They are wrong who think that any idiot can handle the lower classes of grammar."[20] Paul Hoffaeus wrote from Innsbruck about teachers in the lower classes of grammar: "The heretics are far ahead of us. They have mature and very learned teachers of the humanities.[21] Laynez tried to come to grips with the problem. A year after he was elected general, he directed that thirty scholastics who were teaching in Italy and Sicily should be sent to Rome to study philosophy at the Roman College.[22]

The congregation also took drastic means to resolve this problem. In decree fourteen it called on each province to set up a novitiate, conducted in a special house either attached to a college or separate and by itself, "so that the novices through a two year period could be thoroughly tried in the study not of letters but of mortification and spiritual progress."[23] This decree aimed at removing the novices from the swirl of life in a college. It formulated in a judicial form what Ignatius had basically determined on. In 1547 Ignatius had sent to Simão Rodrigues a detailed argument for the establishment of separate houses for the novices.[24] In the ninth decree the congregation directed that, wherever feasible, each province should have a seminary at which the scholastics would be trained in humanities, philosophy and theology.[25]

The Pull between Apostolic Mobility and Academic Stability

The congregation addressed itself to the conflicting demands of the *Constitutions*, which insisted on a Jesuit's mobility, and the schools, whose academic excellence demanded stability of the staff. Salmerón tended to side with the schools. The congregation tried to formulate a via media. This crisis was Ignatius's making. For him the Jesuit was a member of a Society whose members "ought to be ready at any hour to go to some or other parts of the world where they may be sent by the supreme pontiff or their own superiors."[26] But when he decided to open schools, he introduced an internal threat to this ideal mobility. Schools had to have a measure of stability that ruled out the constant shifting of teachers. Tensions inevitably appeared. Complaints went to Rome about the frequent transfer of personnel.[27]

The congregation tried to honor the imperatives of both mobility and stability. It explicitly recognized the power of the general and the provincials to change men from place to place, "changes often beneficial and even necessary not only to the individual men changed but also for the common good."[28] The decree promptly added a modification: these changes should not be made lightly nor with harm to those deprived of an individual Jesuit's service. It concluded with recognition of the political world of the sixteenth century: due regard should also be had for the laws of kings and princes that might touch on the positioning of Jesuits.[29]

The Pull between Poverty and Economic Surety

Ignatius envisaged professed Jesuits as men who, without any source of stable income, should trust that God "will cause everything to be provided which can be expedient for His greater praise and glory,"[30] and should be "content with whatever is given them out of charity for the necessities of life."[31] Their residences, usually called professed houses, had their support in alms to the exclusion of fixed income. But colleges, established primarily either for Jesuits or lay students, had to have economic security. This Ignatius realized, and decided that these institutions should have fixed revenues, by which students and teachers could be supported.[32] Ignatius conceived the professed houses as the more important and as the normal abode of most Jesuits. Colleges he regarded as secondary, indeed as seminaries to feed the ranks of the professed Society and its coadjutors.[33]

History, however, threw Ignatius's plans into disarray even in his lifetime. In the actual development of the Society, the colleges took over the primary role. And Ignatius condoned this. At his death, he had inaugurated forty-six colleges and only two professed houses, one in Rome and one in Lisbon, with a roster of only eighty-two men from a total of over a thousand.[34] Tensions developed between these two structures of Jesuit community, one oriented to the insecurity of living on alms, the other based on the security of fixed income. When Francis Borgia intimated his desire for an increase in professed houses, Ignatius told him that, especially in those early days of the Society, preference should be given to the colleges with a view to apostolic concern for large numbers of students.[35] Ignatius the executive deviated from the dictates of Ignatius the legislator. This trend, set in motion by Ignatius, continued under Laynez, Borgia, Mercurian, and Acquaviva. In 1579 the Society had 144 colleges and ten professed houses; in 1600, 245 colleges and sixteen professed houses.[36]

With this trend continued the tensions about the implementation of Jesuit poverty. Miguel de Torres, superior of the professed house in Lisbon, energetically expressed this tautness within the Society. On 12 October 1564 he wrote Laynez that the Society was on the wrong track by running colleges, and indeed so serious did he consider this aberration that a general congregation should be called to handle this crisis in Jesuit life.[37] Torres spoke for a sense of dependence on divine providence as opposed to a preoccupation with economic security.

This preoccupation with economic security was heightened even more by the wobbly existence of certain colleges that were poorly endowed. The yen for more colleges shelved prudence and led to the easy acceptance of inadequately funded institutions. Complaints went to Rome about wretched housing and bad food. At Pamiers in France, for example, the Jesuits who under Laynez answered the invitation of the bishop to open a college ended up in an abandoned hovel open to the biting Pyrenean winds and a single bed, which they used in turn. The Jesuits in other French colleges subsisted on a fare of plums, dry bread, and water. Students and teachers almost suffocated from the smoke that arose

303

from the smoldering rotten wood, their only fuel.[38] The health of the scholastics broke down. Ignatius himself saw many scholastics wasting away and dying a short time after their entry into the Society. He invited a group of physicians to a conference. The physicians, appalled at the austere life of many young Jesuits, told Ignatius that they marveled that more scholastics had not died, and recommended a sane program of sleep, rest, diet, recreation. Ignatius incorporated many of these suggestions into the *Constitutions*.[39]

Yet the trend toward the acceptance of inadequately funded colleges continued under Laynez. Some of Salmerón's letters to Borgia and Mercurian read like a somber medical report—one college he likened to an infirmary. He hammered at the basic need for a sound financial basis for the Jesuit educational enterprise. General Congregation II faced up to this problem. In the eighth decree it called for assurance of sound funding of the colleges.[40]

Rapid Growth and Its Impact

This and several others of the congregation's decrees reflected what some Jesuits felt was an acute need: reformation. Mercurian disagreed. He felt that what the young Society needed more than anything was an equilibrium and a regularity in its life, a rhythm and an order in its growth. He used to say: the Society has an exigency "more for form than for reform" (*mas que de reforma, de forma*).[41] Rapid growth made the attainment of the "form "desired by Mercurian an impossibility. By the hundreds young men, many about fifteen years of age, entered the novitiates. In a little more than eight years about four hundred Italians were received into the novitiate at the professed house in Rome. Throughout the Society, in the 1560s, the median age of the novices was nineteen. One in ten was older than thirty. In Spain 9.8% were sixteen or younger; in Portugal 25.6%; in Germany 31.8%.[42] Many came from Jesuit schools. Through the 1590s, 89.5% of those who entered the novitiate at Tournai had been students at the Society's schools. Large numbers were immature, having been closely supervised and, in the case of the boarders, compelled to follow a routine so monastic that some French parents complained that they did not want their sons reared as monks.[43]

Older men also entered the universities. And others interrupted their careers as lawyers, doctors, priests to become Jesuits.
From individual families groups of brothers entered the novitiate.
Under Ignatius there were the four brothers of the Petroni family,
three of the Androzzi family, three of the Coudret, two of the
Maggiori, two of the Reggio. During Laynez's generalate, there
were the four brothers of the Cortesono family, three of the Amo-
dei, three of the Gnecchi-Soldi, two of the Comitoli.[44] By 1565 the
Society numbered three thousand; by 1600, eight thousand five
hundred. Enthusiasm for the Jesuit vocation was contagious. Rays
of romanticism set the Jesuit image aglow.[45]

This enthusiasm had little endurance. Against the tide of
entrants into the Society pulled a mighty undercurrent. Novices
and scholastics left in droves. Precise figures cannot be determined
because of the fragmentation of official correspondence and cata-
logs. But enough is known to be able to describe the exodus as a
grievous rupture in the life stream of the Society.[46] The college at
Loreto was but one example. Between 17 October 1557, and 10
June 1559, some twenty scholastics left the Society either by their
own decision or, as the saying of the day had it, were sent on their
way with God. In July 1559 the number of defections from the
college at Messina was large enough to worry officials at headquarters in Rome.[47]

What was especially disconcerting was the large number of
scholastics who simply walked away from the Society and so
became what in canon law were called fugitives (*fugitivi*). Around
1557 it reached the proportions of an epidemic. From the college
at Argenta, for example, three scholastics disappeared within a
few weeks.[48] Sometimes the *fugitivi* prepared for the road. In
January 1560 Antonio Riva, a scholastic at the college in
Venice, went into action while the community was in the church
for a sermon. He broke open the cash box and made off with 117
gold scudi. Only a week earlier Riva's rector called him an angel.
In Rome a young Jesuit named Prospero broke open several con-
tainers, scooped up money and anything else he could carry,
and disappeared.[49] Turmoil of this nature undermined the quest
for balance and regularity in the development of the
Society.

Opinions about Departures from the Order

The reaction of Jesuit superiors to this unsettled state differed. Salmerón was scornful. He remarked, "The sea throws up the dead body." Among so many who became Jesuits, it was to be expected that some would be "Jews and false brethren."[50] Bobadilla was compassionate. He felt that God in his providence led some men to the Society for just a short period and not for life.[51] Polanco was coolly detached. In language that seemed to have anticipated Charles Darwin, he spoke of a natural process of selection in the Society's life: bad health, temptations, impatience with restraint, dismay at the difficulties of so demanding a vocation, all conspired to eliminate many from the ranks.[52] Laynez pointed to the immaturity of many novices. The open kind of novitiate of the Society, he felt, could succeed with only mature men who had rubbed shoulders with life. "Give me men who have a practical knowledge of the world, because they are the ones for us."[53] Laynez also indicted the inferior talent of some of the novices and scholastics. A good number of those who broke off from careers in law and medicine reflected the low level of professional standards in their university training. Once in the Society, they proved able to study only a morsel of the humanities and a minimum of moral theology.[54]

Pedro Ribadeneyra analyzed the problem more thoroughly and perceptively. He cited, first of all, the ignorance of the order's *Constitutions* among the Jesuits. The first printed copies of the *Constitutions* were distributed only at the end of 1558. The Ignatian spirit had not penetrated the Society even as it moved toward the two thousand mark.[55] Ribadeneyra then cited the dearth of competent novice directors, whom he called "the sentinels of the Society."[56] The direction given the novices often lacked theological expertise. Geared to the practical solution of daily problems and to the arousing of fervor, it found theological nourishment only in a thin body of knowledge. Until 1569, when Diego de Ledesma published his conferences, no Jesuit had put into print anything specifically on the theology of the religious life and its relation to the Society. Jerónimo Nadal had addressed his fellow Jesuits extensively on that subject, but it was not until the early years of the twentieth century that snippets of his conferences began to come off the press. A year after Ledesma's work, Adriaan Adriaenssens published a volume on the nature of the religious life and the excellence of the vows. Everard Mercurian, who recognized the serious need to present the peculiar spirit of the Society within the context of the spirituality of the religious life, relied extensively on Adriaenssens.[57] A twofold ignorance, of the Society's spirit and of a theology of the spiritual life, was, therefore, in Ribadeneyra's mind a key reason for the instability among so many Jesuits of that early and formative period in the Society's history.

Despite the dilated instability, the Society received into its ranks many who reached genuine distinction. These were as "constant as the northern star." Beneath the visibly shifting sands lay a sound foundation. In the sixteen years from the death of Ignatius to the death of Borgia, many of these men of "true-fixed and resting quality "entered the novitiate. Some were over thirty years in age when they entered. Edmund Campion, Francisco de Ribera, Piotr Skarga, Bernadine Realino, Alfonso Rodríguez. Others were between twenty and thirty years old: Francisco Toledo, Julio Mancinelli, Antonio Possevino, Louis Richeome, Juan Maldonado, Juan Villapando, Alfonso Rodríquez (ascetical writer), Alessandro Valignano. And several were teen-agers: Robert Bellarmine, Stanislaus Kostka, Matteo Ricci, Gregorio de Valencia, Gabriele Vázquez, Francisco Suárez, Leonard Lessius, Tomas Sánchez, Gaspar Sánchez, Rodolfo Acquaviva, Jacques Salès. These men rose to genuine eminence in one area or another.

Implementation of the Congregation in Naples

The presence of these men in the Society did not minimize the gravity of the problems that then lay siege in the Society. General Congregation II identified some of these problems and initiated positive steps toward their resolution. This resolution, slow and painful, gradually emerged under Mercurian and Acquaviva. Salmerón, in his post as a major superior, worked closely with Borgia and Mercurian to win a balance and a poise in Jesuit life. When the congregation closed in September 1565, Salmerón returned to Naples. Through the seven years of Borgia's generalate

(1565–72), he continued in the office of provincial of the Neapolitan province. He did the same through the first three years of the generalate of Everard Mercurian.

Although the provincial's duties were exacting, Salmerón reacted strongly against any suggestion that he leave Naples. Two months after Borgia's election, Salmerón heard that Paolo Tripoli, a Venetian diplomat, was on his way to Rome to have Salmerón changed to Venice. Forthrightly he wrote to Borgia on 23 September 1564: "I am sure that you will honor him and at the same time with some kind words knock the idea out of his head."[58] Tripoli failed, and Salmerón remained at Naples. His correspondence with both generals was extensive and revealed in minute detail their common joys and frustrations in meeting the everyday business of the Society of Jesus. Schools, personnel, diplomatic affairs, preaching, all demanded their attention.

Bobadillan Colleges

The implementation of the recently closed General Council II's decrees on the schools preoccupied Salmerón. He had a keen realization of the serious pitfall created by overexpansion. At the same time he found himself swamped with requests for Jesuit schools within the area of his province. Gian Girolamo Acquaviva wanted one at Atri; Cardinal Giacomo Savelli wanted one at Benevento; the city of Salermo wanted one; so did Capua, Pozzuoli, and Cosenza. All these requests Salmeron rejected, and thereby implemented one of Ignatius's later administrative policies: the refusal of "tiny colleges "(*collegiola, collegetti*).[59]

Despite Salmerón's diligence against the *collegiola*, some slipped through his defenses and saddled the province with serious problems. Nicolás Bobadilla was the villain of the piece. He had made several sorties through southern Italy, charming with his zest and panache bishops, noblemen, civic officials. His message was the good news of Jesuit colleges. In April 1562 he wrote to Salmerón from Mileto, reciting the devotion, the tears, the joy that his coming had aroused. "Normally I do the sowing. Others reap the harvest. This was the case in Naples, Loreto, the Valtelline. I hope that the same will prove the case in Calabria."[60] It did. The harvest Salmerón reaped was a series of headaches in the form of what he called "Bobadillan colleges."

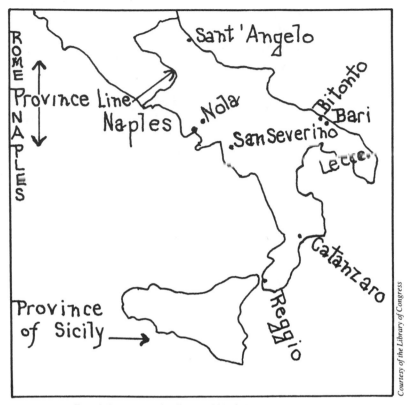

Founded or proposed colleges within Salmerón's jurisdiction

Catanzaro and Reggio Calabria were the sites of two of those "Bobadillan colleges." On one of his early Calabrian tours, in 1553, Bobadilla met a secular priest named Gianpietro Pittarella, who later became a Jesuit. Charmed by Bobadilla's zest for schools, Pittarella communicated this educational ardor to several gentlemen of Catanzaro. In early 1562 the city offered the Society, through Salmerón, a house, a church and 180 ducats. Salmerón transmitted the business to Laynez. Laynez authorized the initial negotiations.[61] The distance between Naples and Catanzaro made so serious a problem that Salmerón was effectively blocked from this Calabrian operation. Laynez depended on the provincial of Sicily to make the on-the-spot inspection of the site.[62] He then sent Pantaleo Rodinò as rector, Francesco Mercado as prefect of studies, a brother for the temporal affairs, and three teachers: Giuseppe

309

Rubies, Giambattista Ninguarda, and Giovanni Tommaso Vitali. The school solemnly opened on 24 October 1564.[63]

Within a year the Catanzaro enterprise was swamped with calamity. Bickering broke out among some of the early enthusiasts. Petty gossip poisoned the atmosphere. Some benefactors did not meet their commitments; they failed to provide even a stable place for the Jesuits to sleep and eat. Normal equipment, even albs, were lacking. The rector Pantaleo Rodinò, wrote Francis Borgia, then vicar general, on 20 February 1565, asking whether he was expected "to keep alive on wind," since the small revenue went into construction. In this intolerable situation, the small Jesuit community broke open in dissension. The three teachers united in a common front against the rector and the perfect of studies. Rodinò wrote Borgia on 3 June 1565 about his teachers' program of harassment. "For two months now I have been living in a veritable hell among these devils." Borgia tried to alleviate the situation by some changes in the personnel, including the designation of a new rector, Giovanni Battista Filippi.[64]

Reggio Calabria was a twin of Catanzaro. From Messina in May 1564 Bobadilla wrote to Polanco of his whirlwind success in Reggio. "I have seen more marvelous things since I began my life in the Society. But I don't think that I have seen the equal in good will and joy, expressed in spirit and in body, [as here in Reggio Calabria]."[65] And of course a college had to follow. Laynez approved. Early enthusiasm yielded to wrangling among a new set of city officials. In early November 1566 Salmerón advised Borgia to quit Reggio if the officials did not adopt a more friendly attitude. He had other reasons too for closing the school. "The viceroy," he wrote, "obtained the inauguration of this college practically by coercion. It is a place exposed to raids by the Turkish fleet every time it shows up."[66] Despite these ominous beginnings, the school survived.

Salmerón worried much about the schools at Catanzaro and Reggio Calabria, since they were located within the jurisdiction of the Neapolitan province. The bishop of the former town, Ascanio Geraldini, "dealt with our men in a nasty fashion" (*tratta mal á nuestra gente*) reported Salmerón to Borgia on 3 February 1566. He also forbade the Jesuits to preach "either before noon or after noon" (*ni á la manana ni á la tarde*).[67] Distance forestalled frequent visits by Salmerón to the troubled college. The distance to Reggio Calabria was even greater. As early as 1567 Salmerón argued for the transfer of both schools to the Sicilian province. Borgia made the transfer.[68] Soon, however, he reversed his decision. In February 1570 he sought Salmerón's reaction to the suggestion that Catanzaro and Reggio Calabria be restored to the Neapolitan province. Salmerón protested against the move. He did not want either place under his care. Borgia, however, overruled his protests on 4 March 1570, "Although this will involve some inconvenience for you," Borgia wrote, "I believe that the burden will be less than trying to govern these colleges from Sicily."[69]

Salmerón kept this issue alive and advanced a fresh suggestion: create a new province, that of Calabria. With a new province, neither the Sicilian provincial nor the Neapolitan provincial would have to worry about Catanzaro and Reggio Calabria. On 5 August 1570 Borgia acknowledged that Salmerón's proposal "would be worth thinking about in time. For the moment, however, since these colleges are so few [only two] and since they are poor, a plan of this kind is immature."[70] Once more Salmerón had the "Bobadillan colleges" of Catanzaro and Reggio Calabria on his hands.

Bobadilla and the College at Sant' Angelo

Sant' Angelo, a tiny town of five or six hundred people in the Abruzzi, was another spot over which Nicolás Bobadilla waved his magic wand and which then produced a college. In January 1565 Bobadilla stopped at Nocera. There the Duchess of Nocera, Giovanna Castriota, received him with, as he reported it, "a thousand demonstrations of kindness" (*mille carenze*). Talk about founding a college followed.[71] Sant' Angelo was a classic example of one of those mere dots on the map that General Congregation II had warned against because they lacked the necessary resources to support a school. As early as 7 October 1565 Salmerón reported to Borgia that Giovanna Castriota was anxious to set up a Jesuit college there. Salmerón looked at the offer from every angle.

> I investigated what would be given as a foundation fund and found it to be a glaring example of niggardliness. The duchess promised a hundred ducats a year. The city would give sixty more, a hundred bushels

of wheat, a field that belonged to the Monastery of Santa Chiara, and I do not know what other trifling things, which all together would, I do not think, come to 250 ducats. Besides the items I have enumerated, there are other things that we are very uncertain we would ever actually get our hands on. I say this because we know from experience, such as we had in Naples, that the promises of a city government are honored the first year, contested in law the second, and completely disregarded the third.[72]

Despite Salmerón's realistic report, Borgia did not want to brush the idea completely aside and decided to send Bobadilla to investigate a little more fully. Salmerón, however, remained set in his opinion and added to his list of formidable reasons against the school the paucity of men. "Really," he wrote Borgia on 3 February 1566, "we have not a single man on hand to give to Sant' Angelo except by interrupting the course of study of our scholastics. Here at Naples we have no one with any preaching ability, as I have already advised you, save Father Pietra Blanca. At the moment he is the only cock who can crow. We have absolutely no one else."[73]

To strengthen his general attitude toward new institutions, Salmerón had the advice of a knowledgeable layman, Lope de Mardones. Salmerón had earlier shared this advice with Borgia when he wrote on 7 October 1565. "Señor Mardones, a man of considerable wisdom and prudence, advises us not to go running off and taking over houses, unless we first set a good price. By this policy we shall acquire good, comfortable, and well endowed houses, although this would not happen immediately."[74]

Salmerón, however, found his hardheaded, practical approach offset by the grandiose, hasty and unrealistic thinking of Bobadilla. Bobadilla seemed to feel that buildings of stone and brick would rise in town after town just by the mere taking thought of them. On 22 September 1565 he suddenly appeared in Naples. Salmerón, though exasperated by his old friend's antics, was nevertheless glad to see him. He wrote to Borgia: "Father Bobadilla arrived yesterday, galloping into town on his white horse. We were tickled to see him, and we enjoyed his line of chatter. At table he did all the talking and we did all the listening. He told us that he was on his way to Apulia to found new colleges. . . . But I think that these colleges will end up as mere mathematical entities such as the others he has been involved in and which he is planning ever and anon.''[75]

Bobadilla's flamboyant demeanor undermined Salmerón's negative decision about Sant' Angelo. In February of the next year, 1566, Bobadilla, still dreaming dreams of new schools, was back in Naples from Sant' Angelo. Salmerón tried to pin him down on just what he accomplished at Sant' Angelo but without success. He reported to Borgia on 9 February 1566: ''Father Bobadilla arrived here this evening on his way from a visit with the duchess of Nocera. He spoke with her about the procedure to be followed in the foundation of a college at Sant' Angelo, but we have been unable to extract a single statement from him about how much money she promised for the foundation. . . . He is the sort of fellow who has the habit of blowing up a mouse into an elephant.''[76]

Two weeks before Bobadilla arrived in Naples, Salmerón had felt pressure from another quarter. This time it came from Hypolita Castriota, sister of the would-be foundress. Hypolita made on her sister's behalf a fervent plea for the desired college at Sant' Angelo. Salmerón again took a hard look at the proposal and again felt unconvinced. On 20 January 1566 he reported his sentiments to Borgia and briefed the general about his answer to Hypolita: that the Society had such a shortage of personnel that it could not meet even its current obligations; that the duchess's offer of a mere hundred ducats a year for support did not reflect great enthusiasm for the school; that Sant' Angelo was a ''tiny town'' (*cibad pequeña*), no place for the Jesuits.[77]

The duchess of Nocera and Nicolás Bobadilla, however, prevailed, and Borgia gave his approval for the opening of the college at Sant' Angelo. But Salmerón's analysis was borne out by hard experience. The house gradually began to fall apart; the annual stipend was collected only after much wrangling; the community hardly received the necessities of life. This was the kind of situation that the General Congregation II had in mind when it warned against the easy acceptance of colleges. In October 1573 Everard Mercurian informed Salmerón that he had commissioned Father Dionysio Vásquez to close the school at Sant' Angelo as well as the one at Teramo.[78]

More College Problems

Shortly after Salmerón suffered defeat on the Sant' Angelo front, he had another "Bobadillan college" left at his doorstep. In January 1565, Bobadilla, on his way to Calabria, wrote to Juan Planco from Naples. He recited the story of his visit to the archbishop of Salerno, Gaspar Cervantes, and their conversation about setting up a college.[79] Two years later, Cervantes insistently asked Borgia to open a college or a novitiate at San Severino, a tiny dot within the jurisdiction of Salerno. Borgia turned to Salmerón for advice. This Salmerón delivered without equivocation on 10 August 1567.

> Through the kindness of some people who are well informed, especially Señor Mardones, I have brought myself-up-to-date on the situation at San Severino and on the question of putting a college or a novitiate there. My informants are universally against the proposition because San Severino is in the wide open country, and in this kingdom of Naples even the populace of a city live with hardly any security. Close by to Nola are two monasteries, one Santa Maria de Pariete, the other belonging to the Canons Regular. It is their daily fare to have to fight off the bandits of the area. There is no doubt that San Severino is the nest and breeding ground of these vagabonds and the spot more disturbed than any other in the world. . . . I have maintained in the past, and I still do, that we should not put our hands on this project lest in time we be forced to drop it, as has been the case with certain undertakings in Spain and other parts of Italy. . . . Besides, I am convinced that the bishop of Salerno wants the novitiate just to have people under his jurisdiction whom he can command, send throughout his diocese to preach and teach christian doctrine, and serve him on his visitations. I believe that this is his motive more than any consideration of our novices.[80]

Despite Salmerón's energetic protest, Borgia allowed the opening of a college at San Severino, and appointed Gaspar Hernández to the rector's post.[81]

Two "Bobadillan colleges" that Salmerón successfully squashed were at Bitonto and Bari. Bobadilla was the *éminence grise* formulating the requests that came in from Cornelio Musso, the bishop of Bitonto, and Antonio de Pozzo, the archbishop of Bari. Both men, in their letters to Salmerón, wrote as though the schools were on the threshold of realization. Behind this correspondence Salmerón recognized the impetuous hand of Bobadilla making commitments for financial support which he felt were inadequate. He told Borgia on 3 February 1566: "It strikes me that these two colleges are brothers, offspring of the same Father Bobadilla."[82] Borgia answered immediately. On the tenth he instructed Salmerón to ask the two bishops that they excuse the Society from opening the proposed schools in Bitonto and Bari because of the shortage of teachers. Borgia backed up his argument by citing the wish of the Holy See that the Society work in areas of greater need, specifically Germany and France.[83]

With his decisiveness and realism, Salmerón never left any doubt about his position on the controversial question of Jesuit expansion. His letters were straightforward, businesslike, often barbed. He advised Borgia against opening a college at Mileto because of the pestilential air and the meagre population.[84] Two years later, in 1567, he strongly urged Borgia to suppress the college at Nola. Even though this college was one of the beneficiaries of King Philip's donations made in gratitude for victory over the Turks in Africa, the province was hard put to man it any longer. On 22 June 1567, Salmerón wrote Borgia.

> My Father, this college is a very disspirited institution. The boys are a sly lot, take correction poorly and run off wailing to their fathers. The fathers then descend on us, voicing their grievances and even breathing threats. Fifteen ducats a year is paid for each one of the students. . . . Our men have to delouse the youngsters, scrub them, and accompany them whenever they go home. It is my opinion, from the little I have observed and from what we have figured out with Father Minister, that in this part of the country thirty ducats a year would be needed for each one.[85]

On the other hand, the school had an ardent champion in its rector, Juan de Montoya. Vigorously he argued at Roman headquarters for the college's preservation. But he realized that he was fighting a losing battle. In 1567 Benedetto Palmio, the Italian Assistant, opened a visitation of the Neapolitan province in Borgia's name. He shared Salmerón's dim view of Nola. In May Montoya, dismayed by these two formidable adversaries, remarked to Polanco: "I am forced to take on in combat two giants [Salmeron and Palmio]."[86] The giants won a partial victory the next year. Borgia closed the boarding facilities of the college and allowed it to continue only as a day school.[87] A year later Borgia turned to Salmerón for advice about the college at Frascati, where progress was unpromising. Salmerón's answer of

October 1569 was clear: "Close it."[88] On the issue of expansion, Salmerón consistently pressed for restraint.

Development in Naples

Nearer home, in his own Naples, the work on the church and the school continued according to the grand design of Giovanni Tristano. In 1567 the spacious structure of the Gesù Vecchio was completed. Under the guidance of another Jesuit architect, Giovanni de Rosis, a decade of work on the mosaics, the marble altar, and the tabernacle of carved wood got under way. The completion of the school was less rapid. De Rosis changed Tristano's plans somewhat, and this involved the demolition of the adjacent Palazzo di Andrea d'Evoli.[89]

To sustain this ambitious enterprise, Salmerón did not forget the promise made by Emperor Charles V in 1554 of an annual income of six hundred ducats for the support of the college. The money had not been forthcoming. As seen earlier, Salmerón, in 1588, during his sojourn in Belgium with a papal mission, tried to get word to King Phillip II about his father's promise. And now, seven years after that promise, he was trying again, cutting at Spanish bureaucracy from several different angles. On 4 March 1565 he wrote Borgia that the viceroy of Naples, Pedro Afán de Ribera, and the city government had written to Philip II about the money; that he [Salmerón] had twice asked Antonio Araoz, a Jesuit favorite at the Spanish court, to push the matter; that Araoz promised that he would do so. "It would be good," continued Salmerón, "if a word of recommendation were sent from Rome." On the margin of Salmerón's letter Polanco wrote: "It will be done."[90] If the money ever was given is not known.

Personnel Problems in Naples

Then there was the question of personnel. Closely connected with the business of running schools was the never-ending demand for teachers. Shortage of men was a perennial problem, and there were occasions when Jesuit superiors seemed to have become engaged among themselves in a tug-of-war for workers. Salmerón and Borgia went through such minor crises together. There was, for example, the case of Father Luigi Massella, a man depressed in spirit and anxious to leave Naples and go to

Rome for a year or two. Borgia was inclined to give a sympathetic hearing to Massella. Salmerón, desperately in need of workers, became very aroused at the prospect of his province being reduced by the removal of one of its members. He sent an excited appeal to the general. "In regard to Father Luigi, please realize that he is no worse that he ordinarily is, except that he is a bit more melancholy, which for him is a natural state."[91] Salmerón pleaded that Massella be left at Naples because he could, despite his depression, at least hear confessions and do some other works of the ministery. Then came a poignant and even bitter cry.

> My Father, it is simply not right that any one can take off from the province merely by saying, 'I am depressed,' or 'I am not happy in this particular work.' . . . If one priest quits the province, then another, and then still another, and if we not empowered to go ahead and ordain others,[92] what is going to become of the province?. . . If the wide spread practice among the men of the colleges of writing secretly to one person or another in Rome to manipulate what they themselves desire, and if the tendency to beg Your Paternity to give them this or that position without paying any heed to the provincials were forbidden and checked, as it should be, then the provincials would not become so disgusted and sour when they see the bread taken out of their mouths, that is, their useful and necessary subjects removed from their jurisdiction. I trust in the Lord that Your Reverence will fully recognize the need to leave Massella here and not deprive the province of so necessary a man.[93]

Again Salmerón's excitability and over seriousness came to the fore as they had done during the generalate of Diego Laynez.

It must have been hard for Borgia to turn aside Salmerón's terribly earnest representation. Placing the province's needs and Massella's sickness in the balance, the general, after consultation with other priests, decided in favor of the latter. When he broke the news to the disconsolate Salmerón, he tried to ease the blow by holding out the hope of Massella's eventual return to Naples. "We decided," he wrote, "to give Father Luigi the consolation of a year or two in Rome after which, I have no doubt, he will go back to Naples."[94]

Massella's ailments revealed one of the great problems of the province, and indeed of the Society: the bad health of many of the men. Sickness was appalling in its extent. In an age when medicine was still notably primitive, many Jesuits fell before the ravages of disease. From the Society's documents a staggering list of victims can be drawn up. There was Father Giovanni Battista Boncuore. On 18 November 1565 Borgia informed Salmerón that Cardinal Alfonso Gesualdo wanted the services on Boncuore for one or two months. Salmerón on 25 November replied that Boncuore should be excused. "He is very flabby and weak. There is blood in his urine. Every day his knees and other parts of his body must be massaged. He feels the cold intensely. . . . Take note, so that you do not make a mistake and lose a good man." Borgia rescinded his order.[95]

Then there were the three teachers at Nola in 1568. On 12 September Salmerón pointedly and with a barb or two filled in the picture for Borgia:

> The other scholastic who was assigned to teach humanities at the college at Nola is in my judgment not suited for the post, because the last time he was there the air of the locality did him no good. At the moment he is complaining of intense headaches and pains in the stomach and kidneys. How he is able to teach and carry on I leave to Your Reverence to figure out, especially since he is living with Master Agostino, who has three or four ordinary pains and aches, and Master Titio Fido, who has as many or even more complaints. And these are Nola's three teachers, or better still, Nola's three candidates for an infirmary where they might be cured, if indeed a cure is possible.[96]

Then there was Father Juan Pareja. In 1575 Mercurian had recommended Pareja as the Spanish preacher at the court of the new viceroy of Naples. On 13 August 1575 Salmerón sent Mercurian his negative opinion. "Six years have passed since he has preached, and during this time all his teeth have fallen out.[97]

In the province of nearly ninety men, some were a source of embarrassment, others of pride. There was Father Giovanni Francesco Araldo. Araldo was a tireless worker, whose efficacy, at least in Salmerón's view, was vitiated by imprudence. On 19 October 1567 Salmerón requested Borgia to transfer Araldo to Loreto.

> He is a great worker, busy in hearing confessions, assisting the dying and other charitable undertakings. He does the work of three men. Yet for all this, he is a foolish man and shows little prudence. As a consequence, therefore, he frequently compromises us in many of our enterprises. While on the one hand he helps us with his public and private acts

318

of mortification, on the other hand, by his prolonged and imprudent conversations with certain kinds of women, he has put the reputation and credit of the Society in the balance. And now he is secretly making a peculiar brand of *agnus dei* with a die that he has in his room. These he distributes to his devotees.[98]

Then there were two lay brothers, Francisco Briones and Alfonso Bravo. They were two of the eight Spanish Jesuits who were with the fleet of Don Juan of Austria at Lepanto on 7 October 1571. Don Juan, who liked Briones, chose the brother for his own royal gallery.[99] In November 1574 he asked Salmerón to allow Briones to sail with the fleet to Spain.[100] Briones then expressed the desire to become a priest. Salmerón on 2 July 1575 sent a strongly negative report to Mercurian. He indicated that the brother had conducted himself indecorously with some noble ladies on the galley when in port, and that he revealed little interior religious spirit.[101]

Brother Alfonso Bravo proved to be an even greater disappointment. After Lepanto he had become restless and like Briones wanted to study for the priesthood. Salmerón felt that Bravo was ambitioning a state for which he was not qualified. To Mercurian he wrote on 1 October 1574, almost the third anniversary of Lepanto. "Alfonso Bravo is a very rude person, a chronic complainer, filled with illusions."[102] Mercurian in his reply advised Salmerón that Bravo could be dismissed from the Society, if he though it should be done.[103] Three months later, on 8 February 1575, Salmerón wrote a brief note, pointed yet paternal, to Bravo, who was then at Catanzaro, informing him that Mercurian had decided that he should not change from the grade of brother to that of scholastic, and urging him to put aside the illusion of studying for the priesthood, which was causing so much restlessness.[104] A month after this note, Salmerón notified Bravo that Mercurian had released him from his vows.[105]

Bravo did not leave the Society quietly. The veteran of Lepanto ended his Jesuit career in a cannonade. He betook himself to Marco Antonio Pescara, archbishop of Consa, and presented himself as a Jesuit authority in moral theology or, as Salmerón expressed it, "a master in handling cases of conscience." Salmerón then briefed Pescara about Bravo's real status.[106] But Bravo had already hoodwinked the archbishop, who had the highest praise for his "Jesuit." "I laughed," Salmerón wrote Mercurian on April 16, 1575, "when I read the archbishop's letter, in which he praised the teaching, the humility, and the holiness of this man. I stand on the adage: 'It's a case of a donkey and thistles getting together'" (*similes habent labra lactucas*). It was Salmerón's way of saying, by way of a classical proverb, that it takes a bonehead to like another bonehead.[107]

The Problem of Cristóbal Laynez

Then there was Cristóbal Laynez, inconstant younger brother of the deceased general, who kept bobbing up in early Jesuit history. The last time Salmerón had seen him was in October 1561, when Cristóbal failed in his efforts to be readmitted into the Society by his brother and returned to Spain. For four years Cristóbal went about Spain and Portugal, embarrassing the Society by his loudmouthed immaturity. Nadal remarked that at Coimbra Cristóbal was acting like a buffoon, demanding help from every Jesuit he met.[108] A short while after Borgia became general on 2 July 1565, Cristóbal returned to Rome, coming, as Borgia informed Salmerón, "with a strong determination to enter the Society."[109] Borgia, however, turned down Cristóbal's request. Cristóbal then set his heart on working in the hospital for incurables in Naples. Borgia sent with him a letter of commendation to Salmerón, suggesting that he, out of respect for Diego's memory, help Cristóbal along in his good desires.[110]

Ten days later, 25 November, Salmerón wrote to Borgia to say that he was unhappy about the arrival of Cristóbal, who already was making a pest of himself by his importunate begging. "I have the impression," Salmerón wrote, "that he is hurting the names of those who recommended him and put in a good word for him. I also fear that he is staining the good and holy memory of our Father Laynez, and so it works out that he is giving offense to both the living and the dead. May it please Our Lord that I am a false prophet and that he will become as holy as his brother."[111] Despite Salmerón's disenchantment, Borgia readmitted Cristóbal into the Society on 14 October 1567, only to dismiss him four years later, in July 1571.[112]

Holiness in the Neapolitan Province

Then there were the members of the province who were a source of pride and inspiration. Father Giovanni Batista Carminata was an eloquent preacher, who made a deep impression on the Neapolitans in 1564. Salmerón knew this and earnestly asked Borgia on 7 October 1565 that Carminata be returned to Naples. "Please note that since last Lent he has not preached at our house and that the people want him very much." Later that month Borgia told Salmerón that Carminata was on his way back to Naples.[113]

With Carminata's name is associated the Jesuit vocation of a saint. Bernadine Realino, born in Carpi on 1 December 1530, recipient at Bologna of the doctorate in civil and canon law (*utroque jure*) on 3 June 1556, lived in Naples in 1564. The Jesuit scholastics he occasionally met impressed him. He heard Carminata preach and was deeply moved. He spoke to Carminata, made some meditations under his guidance, and then made a general confession. On 13 October 1564, Salmerón admitted Realino into the Society.[114]

Ten years later, Lecce became the center for most of Bernadine's life as a Jesuit. In 1564 he joined another priest and a brother to set up a Jesuit house in Lecce in Apulia, midway between Brindisi and Otranto. There for forty-two years he worked as spiritual counselor and became the spiritual father of the town. When Bernadine was dying, the mayor and the chief civil officials visited the old priest, and gathered around his death bed, told him that he was hereby designated Lecce's protector in heaven.[115]

Salmerón and Realino deeply esteemed each other. Of Salmerón, Realino wrote to his father in 1565: "Our provincial, Father Alfonso Salmerón, preached during the season of Lent. He was supposed to do the preaching at Ferrara, but the viceroy of Naples and the entire city petitioned the pope to keep him at Naples. And so it worked out that I heard his every sermon. He is the most literate and talented man I have ever seen."[116] A year later Realino wrote his brother after hearing Salmerón give a discourse on the book of Genesis. "I regard it a singular grace to have begun my Jesuit life at the time of this exceptional man, a most illustrious pillar of Christian truth.[117]

Salmerón for his part recognized the sanctity of Realino. And it was a misunderstanding between the two about the acquisition of property at Lecce that evoked Salmerón's explicit tribute. Backed by some generous friends in Lecce, Realino pushed the business of getting a house for the Jesuits. Salmerón, with his wide experience of the knotty questions of real estate, felt that Realino was disregarding standard procedure by failing to have a regular contract drawn up.[118] Pessimistically he envisaged some Leccean entrepreneurs hoodwinking a naive Realino in a large swindle. Yet, in a letter to Mercurian on 12 February 1575, he exonerated Realino of any malice, testified "to the great goodness and virture of this father, "and wrote of him as being "thoroughly good"(*tutto buono*) despite his trusting business methods.[119] Mercurian cut through the intricacies and formalities by an act of confidence in the gentlemen of Lecce, and did not demand a formal contract. This information he sent to Salmerón on 9 April 1575.[120] The warmth of the response of Lecce's citizens to this decision wiped away any doubts of their sincerity, vindicated Realino's trust, and belied Salmerón's forebodings.[121]

Diplomatic Problems

Then there were the various and disparate bits of diplomatic business assigned him by the pope and the general. One item was the issue of the *Exequatur* in Naples. The government of Naples claimed the right, called *Exequatur* or *Regium placet*, to forestall in its territory the automatic enactment, without civil approva!, of the decrees of the Roman See. This disturbed Pope Pius V, who became supreme pontiff on 7 January 1566. Soon after his election he asked Salmerón through a personal friend, Spanish Jesuit Cristóbal Rodriguez, to speak to Pedro Enríquez y Afán de Ribera, the viceroy of Naples, about the possible easement of the *Exequatur*.[122] Salmerón's early impression of Perafán—so the Viceroy preferred to sign his name—was negative. He found Perafán to be a man "of little congeniality and religious devotion."[123]

Perafán yielded nothing on the *Exequatur*. The debate between him and Salmerón was lively. Perafán argued from his-

322

torical precedent: the hundreds of years during which the government of Naples enjoyed this particular right. Salmerón, admitting his ignorance of precisely how long the practice had perdured, argued from a theological principle: constraint of the church as a violation of the divine law.

This diversity of approach, historical versus theological, stamped the character of the debates. The viceroy pointed to the many popes who made no complaint about the *Exequatur*. Salmerón replied: "Perhaps these were deficient pastors, each concerned more with his own person, his family and relatives. But this present pope is concerned not with flesh and blood but only with the service of the Lord's Church, with the affirmation and strengthening the Church's power, evilly usurped by so many, and with preserving that power complete and intact."[124] Salmerón's efforts, however, did not change the viceroy's mind or the course of history, for through the seventeenth and eighteenth centuries the *Exequatur* remained an abrasive element in the relations between Naples and the Holy See.

In 1566 the archbishop of Naples, Mario Carafa, raised another delicate problem. Through his vicar he repeated an earlier request that the Society take over the responsibility of examining the Neapolitan candidates for ordination, benefices, and the office of preaching. Salmerón advised Borgia against accepting this responsibility. He recalled the seventy-second decree of General Congregation II against accepting this kind of office, although the decree granted the general the power to dispense, if he should feel it wise and expedient to do so. Salmerón also argued that this kind of business could make the Society odious in the eyes of the secular clergy and other religious. "Because we are a new religious order and have made our mark in the city," he wrote, "we are disliked and murmured about. To assume this post will aggravate the situation even more."[125] Borgia concurred in Salmerón's judgment and declined the responsibility.[126]

Current Events

Highlights in current history also found a place in Salmerón's correspondence. Naples, by its location, was especially sensitive to the crucial international events in the Mediterranean, and its citizens followed with lively interest the grievous conflict between the Turks and the naval forces of the Christian states for control of the sea-lanes. In several of his letters, Salmerón passed on bits of information about this contest. In 1565 the Christians freed Malta. On 23 September Salmerón told Borgia that "the entire city [*of Naples*] is lit up and filled with joy" because of the Christian victory and the humiliating flight of the Turks."[127]

Don Juan of Austria won his great victory at Lepanto on 7 October 1571. Before and after this momentous event, Salmerón wrote of the repercussions in Naples. On 8 August Don Juan arrived there from Barcelona. To Cardinal Antonio Carafa Salmerón wrote about the city, "full of splendor, uniforms, and galleons."[128] Again, on 24 August he wrote to Carafa, describing the departure of Don Juan's fleet on the twentieth for Messina, followed by thirty Neapolitan triremes and considerable military equipment. "Where this vast preparation for battle is leading, and what it all adds up to is not sufficiently clear to everyone. This question will shortly be resolved, and we shall be freed of the anxiety of trying to divine what is afoot. Perhaps you are laughing because I, who scarcely ever, as you know, leave the confines of my room, am writing about events about which you are informed by leading men."[129] After the crucial victory, Don Juan returned to Naples in November. Salmerón passed on the good news to Cardinal Carafa: "We have here Don Juan of Austria "the delight of the world and the city." (*delicias urbis et orbis*). By his presence the most noble city of Naples is made illustrious and extraordinarily exhilarated."[130]

The Close of Salmerón's Preaching Career

Then there was the work of preaching. The year 1569 brought a special honor to Salmerón. Pope Pius V chose him as the Lenten preacher at the Vatican. Three years earlier, on 3 February 1566, Salmerón recited a litany of ailments for Borgia: impaired sight and hearing; loss of his principal teeth; the loosening of his other teeth; low physical energies.[131] Now in 1569, asked to preach at the Vatican, he explained to Borgia on 23 January 1569 his reluctance to accept the assignment because of sickness. Severe attacks of catarrh had been assailing him for three months, and the doctors could not give him relief. He felt that if the pope were aware of his condition, Pius would excuse him. Yet he stood ready, he said, to obey the pope's will. And Pius's will remained unchanged.[132]

Salmerón's appearance at the Vatican as a preacher identified him more than anything else with the distinguished school of sacred oratory that made Rome the showcase of Tridentine reform in preaching. This school gradually took form a century earlier, during the Renaissance, when preachers at the Vatican brought to their task a classical vocabulary, a vivid imagery, a focus on God's mysterious grandeur, a style modelled on the fine oratorical works of Greece and Rome. Erasmus criticized those Renaissance preachers as purveyors of resounding Ciceronian periods and mythological allusions. He shot wide of the mark. Those preachers to the papal curia of the fifteenth and early sixteenth centuries knew the complexity of Catholic dogma, and this they declaimed with nuance and unction. A distinctive excellence stamped their work. Kith and kin to those Vatican preachers of the Renaissance were the preachers of the Catholic Reform who followed. They were of the same stock. They took up the classical heritage; they mustered the energies of the scriptural awakening; they kept alive the tradition of oratorical excellence.

Quite early in their history Jesuits became members of that elite clan. Invitations to preach at the Vatican multiplied. Under Pope Paul IV the Jesuits received the prerogative of preaching on Good Friday at the papal court. Between 1555 and 1589, a Jesuit held the post of *praedictor apostolicus*, the official preacher for sermons and exhortations on certain days outside liturgical functions. From the final years of the Council of Trent until the death of Pope Gregory XIII in 1585, the Society's preachers had a special preserve at the Vatican. Salmerón, therefore, was not alone among the Jesuits in wearing the nimbus of a Vatican preacher. He was but one in a long file who had received that distinction and therefore shared in making Rome a model for the Catholic world of excellence in expounding the Word of God. With that distinction Salmerón closed his career as a preacher. At Rome, as recalled by Father Bartolomeo Pérez de Nueros, at the very head of the Church for which he labored so unselfishly, in the presence of the colorful assembly of the pope's household, Salmerón brought to a grand finale his work as a sacred orator.[133]

Generally debilitated, even though he was but fifty-four years of age, Salmerón was unable to go on. Besides a body often wracked by fever, he suffered the discomfort of a nasty case of catarrh—a Neapolitan specialty, one Jesuit observed. Then he lost all his teeth.[134] It was time to yield the pulpit to such younger men as Benedetto Palmio.

Recognition by Later Generations

The drop of the curtain on Salmerón's speaking career did not stop his continuing renown. Among the learned, his name perdured into at least the eighteenth century. In 1600 a volume of his works entitled *A Year's Sermons on the Gospel Parables* (*Sermones in parabolas evangelicas totius anni*) came off the press in Antwerp. A second edition appeared in Cologne in 1612.[135] Cardinal Federigo Borromeo (1564–1631), the erudite librarian of Milan, included Salmerón in his survey *The Sacred Orators of Our Times* (*De Sacris nostrorum temporum oratoribus*).[136] Antonio Vieira (1608–97), the most celebrated preacher among the Portuguese Jesuits of the seventeenth century and one of the more decisive moulders of the modern Portuguese tongue, knew his publications.[137]

In the eighteenth century, the learned preacher and librarian, Francesco Antonio Zaccaria, discovered some of the works of Salmerón in the archives of the Jesuit college in Modena. Zaccaria had especially close ties to Modena, since in 1750 he succeeded the celebrated Ludovico Muratori as archivist and librarian for the duke of Modena. Of his 161 published works, some are descriptions of the archival materials in the libraries of Italy. In one of these, *Literary Excursions through Italy from 1742 to 1752. Volume I (Excursus litterarrii per Italiam ab anno MDCCXLII ad annum MDCCLII. Volumen I)*, he tells that in 1748 he travelled from Milan to Modena to preach a Lenten course in the Jesuit church. While in Modena, he found in the college archives two batches of sermons given by Salmerón in the Jesuit church in Venice, and six scriptural lectures delivered by him in Rome in 1561 on Psalm 118.[138] In the same *Literary*

S. Mattheus

S. Ioannes

R.P.
ALPHONSI
SALMERONIS
TOLETANI, SOC.
IESV THEOLOGI;
Sermones
In Parabolas Euan:
gelicas totius anni.
*Hac Secunda Editione quam di=
ligentissime reuisi, et à mendis
expurgati.*
*VNA CVM AVCTORIS VITA ET IN=
DICIBVS COPIOSISSIMIS %*

Permissu   Superiorum

COLONIÆ AGRIPPINÆ.
Apud
Antonium Boetzerum
M DC.XII

S. Marcus

S. Lucas

Title page of Salmerón's volume of *Sermons on the Parables*

Excursions, Zaccaria quotes a copy he found of the long letter
to Salmerón from Gentian Hervet during the third period of the
Council of Trent.[139] In 1756 Zaccaria again preached in Modena,
this time in the cathedral. His search through the archives of the
Jesuit college this time turned up some scriptural lectures that

Salmerón had given on the Passion of Christ. This he recorded in his *Literary Trip through Italy from 1753 to 1757 (Iter Litterarium per Italiam ab anno MCCCLIII ad MDCCLVII).*[140]

Salmerón's renown also penetrated Protestant lands. In 1580 an Italian Jesuit, Luca Pinelli, made a trip through Switzerland. He met several Protestants, including Theodore Beza and Galeazzo Caracciolo (1517–86), the only son of Marchese di Vico, elegantly trained courtier at the court of Emperor Charles V, devotee of the Neapolitan intellectual circle of Juan Valdes, convert to Calvinist belief, and exile from his homeland. Pinelli's conversation with Caracciolo in Geneva went along pleasantly, even playfully at times. Caracciolo asked about several Jesuits he had known in earlier years, especially Salmerón. Pinelli recounted, in rather corrupt Italian, their conversation and their mutual play on the word "illumine." He recalled that Caracciolo spoke of Salmerón as a great man, "one who would become more of a wonder to the world if he would be illumined [with the Protestant faith]. I, laughing, told him that Father Salmerón had illumination enough for both himself and others too." (*che sarebbe stato di più stupore al mondo se fusse stato illuminato. Io ridendo li disse che il P. e Salmerone havea lume per se et per altri*). So began a debate between the two men on the issue of the true road to salvation.[141]

The Beginnings of a Writing Career

Salmerón's preaching career moved easily into his next preoccupation: writing. Of the first companions of Ignatius Loyola, Salmerón was the author par excellence. Sixteen volumes in folio went to press with his name on the title pages, learned works called *Commentaries on the Gospels and the Acts of the Apostles (Commentarii in Evangelicam Historiam et in Acta Apostolorum)* and *Commentaries on all the Letters of Blessed Paul (Commentarii in omnes Epistolas b. Pauli)*. Francis Borgia was the main influence in setting Salmerón on the path of authorship. Salmerón had kept rough copies of his lectures and sermons, and these, thought Borgia, would make excellent matter for publication if they were but organized and expanded. Salmerón was at first appalled by the idea. On 3 June 1569 he wrote Borgia:

In regard to Your Reverence's instruction that I make a neat copy of
my writings, I find it a difficulty of the greatest magnitude. There is a
vast ocean of such writings; they are undigested; they are in such shape
that I do not know where to begin or what approach to take. Besides, it
is an entreprise that demands both bodily vigor and the assistance of others.
I am without either.[142]

Added to the normal difficulties of organizing material and
outlining his text, Salmerón at first was not able to do the essential reading that would make his work up to date and relevant
to the world of the late sixteenth century. Pope Pius V refused
to give him permission to read the works of contemporary heretics. Two and a half years later, however, Pius died and was
succeeded by Gregory XIII, who, one month after his election,
gave Salmerón the permission that his predecessor denied.[143]

Salmerón, pen in hand, worked away year after year, fighting all the time against discouragement and a sense of futility.
About a year after he launched his enterprise, he dejectedly reported to Borgia: "In regard to this business of being an author,
I am completely at sea. At first I had some little fervor and I
envisaged accomplishing and saying something worthwhile.
With the passage of time, however, I have become convinced
that my knowledge does not measure up to the demands of such
an undertaking. . . . Without exaggeration, what I am doing
comes to this: composing, scratching out, erasing. Nevertheless
I am not quitting the work because of this."[144]

Encouragement then came from another quarter. In the
spring of 1572, Peter Canisius lavishly praised Salmerón on his
potential as an author, and urged him to put his sermon material
into print. Salmerón's answer again reflected the burden of organizing and composing. "To speak frankly, I am at this point
still a novice in this task of writing, which clearly is an elevated
and difficult one and thus meant for few men. I enter upon it
only as an old servant who is passing through as a pilgrim. This
one warning I want to make. My writings are so numerous and
in such disarray that I judge it will take long, serious, earnest,
and exacting work to get them into shape, the way bears lick
their cubs."[145]

Diffidence, too, was an enemy to achievement. Salmerón
had that peculiar low estimation of his talents which sometimes

cripples the energies of gifted persons. He knew the intellectual spirit of his times with its cult for wide learning, erudition, humane letters, and a grasp of scriptures, and he hesitated before it. "In this age, if anyone aims at bringing out a work that is not clever, diligently polished to perfection, strengthened by the force of eloquence and adorned with flowery language, then he can be checked off as having lost time and energy." (*Oleum sane et operam perdidisse videri posset*).[146] But the importunate requests of his fellow Jesuits and the explicit desire of the general, Francis Borgia, overcame this diffidence.

General Congregation III

Borgia's death on 1 October 1572 interrupted Salmerón's writing, since he attended General Congregation III, called to open on 12 April 1573 for the election of a new general. Serious troubles, external and internal, buffeted this congregation. The first difficulty, an external one, was raised by Pope Gregory XIII. Gregory heard widespread complaints about the hispanization of the Society, brought about by the large number of Spaniards in high office. When Polanco, the vicar general, accompanied by Salmerón and a few others, went to petition the papal blessing on the congregation, the pope directly referred to these complaints. He asked Polanco, Salmerón, and the others of the small party how many Spaniards were in the congregation. Half of the forty-six delegates were Spanish. He asked the nationality of the previous generals. All three were Spanish. He then strongly suggested that a non-Spaniard, and specifically Everard Mercurian, a Belgian, be chosen as general.[147] On the first ballot, on 23 April, Mercurian received the election with twenty-seven votes. Of the other nineteen, thirteen went to Spaniards.

Trouble within the congregation followed. The election of the general's assistants was the eye of the storm. During the normal exchange of information about the qualifications of various men, some delegates began to push in an active (and prohibited) way for the election of certain individuals. The congregation reprimanded the campaigners. On 9 May in an atmosphere of peace, the congregation elected the four assistants: Olivier Mannaerts for Germany, Pedro de Fonseca for Portugal, Gil González Dávila for Spain, and Benedetto Palmio for Italy.

Soon murmuring broke out about an election tainted by pressure from secular princes. These stories reached Gregory XIII. Gregory summoned Salmerón to the Vatican on 20 May. He directed Salmerón to communicate to the congregation his papal admonition that the delegates should spurn princely pressure, should close the door to ambition, should blackball no one, should punish the guilty.[149] The next day Salmerón delivered the pope's message to the congregation. The delegates were appalled A majority promptly asserted that the election had been carried out with all integrity. Mercurian, determined to give complete satisfaction to the pope, appointed a commission to investigate the entire affair. The members of the commission were Spanish Alfonso Salmerón, Italian Francesco Adorno, German Paul Hoffaeus, French Claude Matthieu, Spanish Miguel de Torres. For eight days they studied the entire event. Their unanimous decision: there existed no grounds for suspicion about the integrity of the election of the assistants.[150]

General Congregation III brought at least one satisfaction to Salmerón in his role as writer. Applause came from Germany. In its preparation for the general congregation, the provincial congregation of Upper Germany included the following among its recommendations to the general: "That the fathers in Rome, Portugal, and elsewhere, who are engaged in the task of preparing theological works for publication, men such as Alfonso Salmerón, Manuel [de Sá], [Francisco] Toledo, be encouraged and strengthened in their lofty purpose. This holds true for men writing in philosophy and grammar.[151]

Retirement from the Provincial's Office

For three years after the congregation, Salmerón continued as provincial of the Neapolitan province. What gave him his best opportunity to push on with his writing was retirement from this post. Frequently through 1575 he had asked that he be relieved of that responsibility.[152] On 23 February 1576 he recommended that Father Claudio Acquaviva be his successor.[153] Salmerón was then sixty years old, and his catarrh had become more and more an impediment to his efficiency. As much as ten years earlier, in 1566, he reported to Borgia that his sight and hearing were failing and that his teeth were falling out.[154] Mercurian consulted a number of the Jesuits in Rome, including Nicolás Bobadilla, and they all agreed that Salmerón's wish should be granted.[155]

Mercurian then decided to appoint as provincial the promising young rector of the Roman College, Claudio Acquaviva. All went smoothly until the indiscreet Bobadilla again made one of his unpredictable moves. He went to Naples and in a strange volte-face tried to persuade Salmerón not to give up the provincial's post. Mercurian was amazed, and in delicate but clear terms told Bobadilla so. Salmerón eased the embarassing situation by his rejection of Bobadilla's advice and his cordial welcome of Acquaviva to Naples. Acquaviva took the post on 1 April 1576.[156]

Summary

This decade notably altered the pace of Salmerón's personal life. A modulated activity contrasted sharply with the rush of his earlier Jesuit years. The incessant moving about of years before ground to a halt. The conciliar experience at Trent was over. The diplomatic missions that took him to Ireland, the Netherlands, Poland, and Germany came to a close. The preaching in Bologna, Venice, Padua, Ferrara, and other Italian cities of the north was finished. His travels diminished to three short trips to Rome, twice to attend a general congregation, once to preach at the Vatican. By his own description, Salmerón had become a recluse.

This decade also notably altered the Society of Jesus. The death of Laynez left but three living members of the original brotherhood that had gathered about Ignatius. The ten of 1540, all priests, became five thousand by 1576, mostly scholastics. The Society had become lop-sided. Not till 1600 did priests again outnumber the scholastics. Bale and woe entered the Society with the rapid increase. The intimate knowledge of the Jesuit spirit, communicated by the person of Ignatius, yielded to a widespread ignorance of the Society's *Constitutions*. The air of maturity created by older and well educated priests gave way to a burst of romanticism that attracted a host of immature teen-agers.

During this decade too began that slow and painful movement toward a richer theological expertise, a more sound religious formation, a more mature appreciation of the

Constitutions, a realistic understanding of Jesuit life, goals that were gradually realized under Mercurian and Acquaviva. The ''recluse ''of Naples, as a member of General Congregations II and III and as superior of the Neapolitan province, addressed himself to the painful shifts and turns in the Society's history. He did so unambiguously, sometimes caustically, and generally on the side of realism.

CHAPTER X

NAPLES

1576–1585

Introduction

This chapter covers the last nine years of Salmerón's life, from his sixty-first year to his seventieth. Salmerón's activity was in the main scholarship. He continued his commentaries on Holy Scripture; he corresponded with other scholars. The only serious interruption to his routine was his attendance at General Congregation IV in Rome in 1581. Salmerón climaxed his life with a plea for freedom in the theological quest for a deeper understanding of God's revelation. From his large fund of wisdom he urged Acquaviva to refrain from issuing a list of theological opinions obligatory for Jesuit professors. It was an appropriate peroration to his long life of speaking about God's word.

Continuation of the *Commentarii*

Relieved of the burden of superior, Salmerón had the freedom to push on with his writing. This was precisely what Mercurian had in mind. Only two weeks after his retirement, Salmerón wrote to the general: "My infinite thanks for your affectionate letter, in which you exhorted me to two things: first, that I be of good cheer.

I can say that since I was relieved of the care of the province, I find myself cheerful and happy. And second, that I finish my scholarly project. I can affirm that a major motive for surrendering the government of the province was to attend to this task and to bring it, with the Lord's help, to completion."[1]

In the same letter, Salmerón asked Mercurian for help. He requested some fellow Jesuit, knowledgeable in the Holy Scriptures, patristics, and languages, whose function would be to review Salmerón's work and to help in making any necessary emendations. Mercurian and his successor, Claudio Acquaviva, responded somewhat sporadically. At broken intervals they sent three scholars: Robert Bellarmine, Diego Paez, and Bartolomé Pérez de Nueros. Another appointed by Acquaviva but stopped by untimely death was one of the more distinguished scriptural scholars of the age, Juan Maldonado.[2]

As Salmerón scratched away with his quill, something he said years before may have come back to haunt him. As seen earlier in this essay, Salmerón preached an impressive sermon during the first phase of the Council of Trent. A young Italian Jesuit, Paolo Achille, told Salmerón that a number of people wanted to see the sermon published. Salmerón rejected the idea. Among his reasons were the following: publishing is foreign to the Jesuit way of life; publishing can be an obstacle to higher charity.[3] But twenty years had wrought their change. By his own admission, prominent leaders in the Church had urged him, since he could no longer preach because of his physical debility, to turn to writing and put at the service of the church the fruit to his meditation on Holy Scripture and his readings in the church fathers. "I fully realize," he wrote in the preface of his *Commentarii*, "the very glorious and noble kind of work this is, and if I can in some measure carry it out, I would judge that it will be of use to the Christian Republic and the study of sacred letters."[4] Somewhat like St. Jerome, who turned his back on his famous dream and again picked up his Cicero, Salmerón discarded his suspicions about the place of writing in the Society of Jesus and once more turned to his desk.

A Series of Assistants

Salmeron's scriptural commentaries, published in sixteen folio volumes, were an impressive achievement. He had the assistance of an amanuensis, Father Francesco Foliani, and a librarian, Brother Cristóbal López. In its scholarship the work was basically all his, although he received the help of other scholars provided by two generals, Mercurian and Acquaviva. But this assistance was scattered and limited. Robert Bellarmine was the first, but he did not arrive at Naples until more than three years after Salmerón's request. The delay was in part due to the Holy See. Some time in 1578, Mercurian directed the popular and esteemed professor of controversial theology at the Roman College to go to Naples. The grand inquisitor, Cardinal Julio Antonio Sanctorio, who relied on Bellarmine for advice, asked Pope Gregory XIII to cancel Mercurian's directive. This Gregory did. Mercurian made energetic representation to the pope. He did it "with intense warmth of feeling" (*con ogni caldezza*).[5] Only in the spring of 1579 did Bellarmine gain his release from Rome. On 6 June Salmerón wrote Mercurian to announce Bellarmine's arrival and his delight with the learning and talents of the Roman professor.[6] But he enjoyed Bellarmine's assistance for only a brief period. A little more than three months after his arrival at Naples, Bellarmine was back in Rome to make ready for the fall term at the Roman College.[7] During those three months, he had gone over the first four of what, in written form, Salmerón then projected as twelve volumes.[8]

Salmerón's next assistant was Diego Paez, but he reached Naples only in January 1581, a year and a half after Bellarmine's departure.[9] Paez went over the remaining eight volumes, a task that occupied him some eighteen months until his death in mid-June 1582.[10] Acquaviva planned to replace Paez with one of the Society's most eminent scriptural scholars, Juan Maldonado, who for fourteen years had illuminated the intellectual life of Paris by his lectures, characteristically rich with scriptural, patristic, and historical learning. But Maldonado was then doing some work for Pope Gregory XIII. Salmerón's friend, Cardinal Antonio Carafa, intervened and obtained Madonado's release from the Holy See.[11] But on 5 January 1583 Maldonado died at Rome. Three days later Acquaviva, lamenting what he called the grievous loss to the Church and the Society, sent the sad news to Salmerón.[12] Acquaviva fortified his encouragement to Salmerón by sending him scholarly books. In March 1582 he dispatched some writings of

Dionysius the Areopagite, and the following May an edition of the New Testament in Greek and Syriac.[13]

Salmerón's final helper was a Spaniard who gave great promise as a scholar but spent most of his life in administrative posts. Bartolomé Pérez de Nueros y Maynar arrived in Naples in 1584.[14] Salmerón was pleased with his new aide and noted for Acquaviva's information that Pérez was on good terms with the viceroy and his wife.[15]

Pérez was the man who supervised the publication of Salmerón's work. But the first volume appeared only in 1597, twelve years after Salmerón's death. Pérez was among those present at Salmerón's death bed and promised the dying man that he would see his work through the press.[16] This promise he kept between 1597 and 1602. In 1597 volume seven, on Christ's parables and the volume most immediately ready for the press, was printed in Madrid.[17] Between 1598 and 1601 the entire *Commentarii in Evangelicam historiam et in Acta Sanctorum* appeared in twelve volumes in Madrid. In 1602 these were complemented by four volumes of the *Commentarii in omnes Epistolas b. Pauli et Canonicas*. With the name of the editor, Bartolomé Pérez de Nueros, appeared the name of Brother Cristóbal López, Salmerón's companion and librarian.[18]

Salmerón's Method in the *Commentarii*

Throughout these volumes Salmerón used a basically simple methodology. He usually took an event as related by one or more of the evangelists. This he studied within the framework of what he called a *tractatus*—in his analysis of St. Paul's epistles he called it a *disputatio*. He then unfolded the narrative phrase by phrase. These phrases he analyzed from the diverse angles of linguistics, history, and patristics. Basically, he sought the literal meaning of the text. To this analysis he sometimes added a spiritual reflection or theological speculation. Occasionally he used the passage for apologetic purposes. By his critique of language and his appreciation of the cultural and historical background of the Scriptures, Salmerón gave his work a "modern" impress.

Perhaps the best way to appreciate Salmerón's approach would be to compare two of his tracts, the one on the parable of

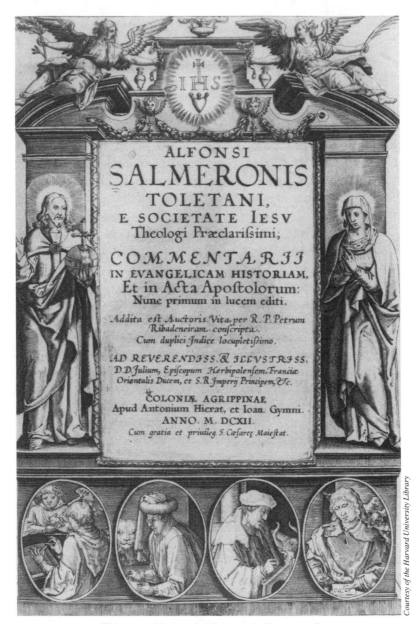

Title page of Volume I of Salmerón's *Commentarii*

the mustard seed (Mk 4:30–32; Mt 13:31–32; Lk 13:18–19) and
the other on the cure of Simon's mother-in-law (Mk 1:29-31;

338

Mt 8:14–15; Lk 4:38–39) with the corresponding sections in *The Jerome Biblical Commentary*.[19]

A comparison of this kind immediately highlights Salmerón's highly comprehensive purpose. His seventeen columns on the cure of Simon's mother-in-law dwarfs the thirty-two lines, less than half of a single column contributed by three authors in *The Jerome Biblical Commentary*, and his nine columns on the mustard seed overshadow the forty lines in *The Jerome Biblical Commentary*.[20]

An example of Salmerón's thoroughness: On the parable of the mustard seed, *The Jerome Biblical Commentary* observes that this seed is not really the smallest of seeds and that the essential note of the parable is that of growth from insignificant beginnings into a full-grown tree.[21] Salmerón makes the same judgment. But he expands this theme more thoroughly. "Great rivers," he writes, "originate from tiny springs. Empires, flourishing republics, art, industry, all have insignificant origins." Salmerón then unfolds a wide background of natural history. Calling on Albert the Great as an authority, he enters into a discussion that touches the relative sizes of a bush and a tree, and the distinctions between the plant, the shrub, and the tree. He then points out that the seeds of the poppy, the rue, and the cypress are all smaller than the mustard seed. But he then shows that the poppy seed, while smaller, does not develop, as does the mustard seed, into a wooded kind of growth with trunk and branches. And the seed of the rue, though it does develop into a kind of wooded species, yet does not attain such height as to resemble the tree-like structure of the mustard plant, and so should be classified as a shrub. The height of the cypress, though greater than the mustard, does not present a problem, because Christ made his comparison among shrubs— the tree-like mustard shrub and others—and not among trees in the strict sense of that word.[22]

Another example of Salmerón's thoroughness: The *Jerome Biblical Commentary* applies the parable of the mustard seed symbolically in but a small number of ways: to the organic unity between the mystery of Christ, which was a disappointment to the Jews, and the kingdom of God, which takes Gentiles and Jews within its bounds; to the kingdom of Nebuchednezzar, which embraced the world and gave shelter to all peoples; to the scandal Judaism felt at the kingdom's modest origins.[23] Salmerón is more complete. Here he presents the variety of ways in which the church fathers interpreted the parable. Hilary, Ambrose, Gregory the Great, and Peter of Ravenna understood the kingdom of God to be Christ; Chrysostom and Euthymius, as the Church; Augustine, as faith; Jerome, as the preaching of the gospel. Salmerón then observes that all of these interpretations are really not so far apart, "because faith and the preaching of the word are not very removed from the Church in which they exist; nor are they that distant from the King in whose name they live."[24]

Both *The Jerome Biblical Commentary* and Salmerón occasionally offer a spiritual reflection. The former, for example, sees the phrase: *She served them*, after Christ had cured Simon's mother-in-law, a suggestion of the "service expected of those who have been served by Christ."[25] Salmerón reflected on the phrase: *And he took her hands*. He discerns in this human act an aspect of the incarnation. "Not as did God in the creation of the world, when he used only a word, Christ in the renewal of the world also used the touch of his hand. He did so because it was incumbent on the Word that he become Flesh, and that this Flesh be immolated on the Cross for us and be eaten by us in the sacrament that we might live."[26]

In one major way *The Jerome Biblical Commentary* and Salmerón differ in their approach. Occasionally—and only occasionally—Salmeron, reflecting the age in which he wrote, wove into his writings an apologetic and polemical attitude. In the tract on the cure of Simon's mother-in-law, *The Jerome Biblical Commentary* simply remarks that this episode indicates that Peter was married.[27] Salmerón uses it as a point of departure for arguing, in view of the marriage among Protestant clergy, for the celibacy of priests. In an intemperate phrase—which was unusual—Salmeron writes: "The Jovinian heretics of our day, in talking about this passage, grunt like pigs and make much of Peter's marriage and having a mother-in-law."[28] Salmerón does not deny—he cannot—Peter's marriage. But, falling back on the passage in Matthew 19: "Behold we have left all things," Salmerón claims that Peter's marriage did not take place after his call to the apostleship and that he had no relations with his wife after that call.[29] Then he gives eight reasons for priestly celibacy.[30]

A Critique of the *Commentarii*

An enterprise so comprehensive raises a serious question about its identity. As a venture in scriptural theology, it is an uneven amalgam of exegesis and theologizing. The scriptural exposition is overextended; the theological development is fragmentary. Irresolution about the work's precise purpose is the rift within the lute. The vastness of the project provokes another question: How steady is Salmerón's scholarly judgment? Salmerón piles up proof upon proof, many of which are of unequal value. The sixteen volumes are a jungle rather than a forest. What Salmerón needed was a sharp machete to cut through the entangled thicket of his overloaded arguments. In the seventeenth century, Cardinal Federigo Borromeo (1564–1631), nephew of St. Charles and founder of the Ambrosian Library in Milan, criticized Salmerón for his uncoordinated learning. In his *The Sacred Orators of Our Times* (*De sacris nostrorum temporum oratoribus*), Borromeo pays tribute to Salmerón for his wide erudition but faults him for his doctrinal and scriptural exposition loaded with arguments that go sailing off in scattered directions.[31]

Salmerón's scholarly prodigality makes him vulnerable to the charge of verbosity. So great an admirer of the early Jesuits as James Brodrick, S.J., tags Salmerón's discussions as long-winded.[32] Salmerón realized that clouds of words can block the light of understanding. He himself criticized the spinning out of patristic citations, for example, as a defect of scholarship. But he also felt that excessive brevity could be a defect. In his "hunting down and digging out" (*cum in venando, ac eruendo*) the correct literal meaning, he aimed to take a via media. "That kind of brevity that darkens our expression with clouds of obscurity must be avoided. Yet it is my hope that a copious flow of words will be balanced by the service they render."[33] Besides, he had a vivid realization of the various problems linguistic, historical, cultural, that intelligent hermeneutics involved. He devoted, for example, 544 folio pages, double columns, to forty-three separate prolegomena on the background, knowledge, and tools one should bring to a study of Scripture, and on the challenges and difficulties that one must encounter in such a study. The entire first volume is a collective prolegomenon. Prolegomena nine, ten, and eleven, for example, he called Three Sets of Fifty Canons (*Tres Quinqua-genas*), in each of which he listed, with explanation, fifty canons for a more accurate understanding of Scripture.[34]

This was the heavy burden he carried as he trekked through the gospels and the Pauline epistles. Father Brodrick's twentieth century charge of long-windedness against Salmerón recalls the same complaint of sixteenth century men, when Salmerón at Trent, to the annoyance of the conciliar delegates, spoke for an hour and a half beyond the limit set for each speaker.[35] Despite these internal flaws of overstocking the proofs and overmassing of words, the *Commentarii* stands as an impressive tribute to Salmerón's desire to deepen the appreciation of the Scriptures within the Church and as an expressive indictment of those theologians whose writings were overabstract, overdidactic, and unconnected with the sacred books.[36]

Salmerón on Erasmus

The great scholar on the sixteenth century whom Salmerón could not ignore was Desiderius Erasmus. As was seen in the section that treated Salmerón's student years at Paris, Salmerón deplored the "doctrinal ambiguity (*crimen neutralitatis*) of Erasmus. On two other scores he also indicted Erasmus: Erasmus's restrictive approach to the study of Sacred Scripture; Erasmus's irreverence.

Erasmus's restrictive approach to the study of Sacred Scripture: Salmerón, while himself appreciating the essential need to grasp; the literal sense (*sensus literalis*) of the Scriptures, felt that Erasmus by his exaggerated preoccupation with this *sensus literalis* had created a rupture with the wider and more comprehensive approach to the sacred books. As a young man, Erasmus had felt the influence of the traditional ways of interpreting Scripture that reached back to the patristic age: the search for the allegorical, the anagogical, and the tropological meanings as well as the literal.[37] In his later years, Erasmus, whose eyes Lorenzo Valla had opened to the need of critical editions of Scripture, concentrated his energies on the use of learning (*eruditio*), especially philology, in searching for the literal sense.[38] This quest for the literal sense Salmerón genuinely appreciated. This he himself seriously sought. But as the singular preoccupation of the scriptural scholar, this he deplored. Erasmus, he felt, had tipped the scales by an emphasis that narrowed the scope of scriptural studies.[39]

This Erasmian imbalance Salmerón attacked. He latched onto a few phrases that Erasmus had used in his Letter to the Emperor (13 January 1522) at the beginning of his *Paraphrase on St. Matthew*. He quoted these phrases and added his own comment. "The ancient doctors of the Church present a spectacle by their allegorical interpretations. Part of the picture is the variety of opinions that they espouse. Another part of the picture is the way in which they carry on, frequently giving me the impression that they are playing games. That is what he [Erasmus] has to say. My reaction is this: with even greater truth we can say that it is these modern exegetes who have been playing games, and destructively so, in their absorption with the literal sense of Scripture."[40] Salmerón met acid with acid.

Erasmus's irreverence: Salmerón described what he called "the spirit of Erasmus" as an attitude of scorn for certain beliefs and practices of the Catholic people. This Erasmian spirit, for example, pervaded those who out of a feeling of hostility spoke of the Immaculate Conception of Mary as nothing more than a fable.[41] Salmerón chided Erasmus himself for his impudent laughing at the custom of saluting the Blessed Virgin in sermons.[42] Erasmus therefore received low scores from Salmerón as he looked back on the scholar who died two years after Ignatius and his friends pronounced their vows at Montmartre in Paris in 1534.

The *Commentarii* in Jesuit Literary History

As a literary monument of his age, Salmerón's *Commentarii* was at once an epilogue and a prologue. It was an epilogue because it closed the contributions of the first band of Jesuits to the biblical ferment of their age.[43] It was a prologue because it led that long and impressive line of Spanish Jesuits, Nadal, Toledo, and Serrario, who carried scriptural studies to new heights of perfection.[44] Salmerón shared in one of the golden ages of the history of scriptural exegesis, an age which, while not achieving new principles and methods of analysis, nevertheless advanced with vigor the traditional methods that had been hammered out by the scholastics in their systematic use of dialectics. The *Commentarii*, come to blossom in Naples, grew from the planting in Alcalá some seventy years earlier.[45] Salmerón the Jesuit had carried the vision of Francisco Jiménez de Cisneros, the Franciscan beyond the Pyrenees, in a way the old primate of Spain could never have dreamed of.

Salmerón and Peter Canisius

Even though immersed in his own massive project of scholarship, Salmerón tried to keep in touch with the literary activities of his fellow Jesuits. One of his dearest friends through the years had been Peter Canisius. In 1571 Canisius brought out his first volume in answer to *The Centuries of Magdeburg*. Since he saw the *Centuries* as basically a collection of deceptive statements about the word of God, he entitled his work *The First Book of Commentaries on Falsifications of God's Word* (*Commentariorum de Verbi Dei corruptelis liber primus*). Salmerón was delighted with it, and in its pages he said he saw reflected the learning, the gentleness, the charity of Peter's great mind and heart. When he heard that Peter's next efforts were to be a defense of the Blessed Virgin Mary, he sent a stirring letter of encouragement.

> Now you have undertaken an even greater project and you are in the fight with your pen for the glory of the Blessed Mother of God. You are pushing the contest bravely and gloriously. Carry on, and may all good fortune attend you. I meanwhile take delight in the high hope I entertain that you, having excelled others by your first book, will easily outstrip even yourself by this second one. . . . If the church fathers of past centuries, whose works had the simple aim of preserving among the faithful the belief in Our Lady's virginity, have attained such a place of honor with posterity, what fruits do you suppose will come forth, what titles to fame and what trophies do you suppose they will merit who fight for not only the virginity of the Mother of God but for her other tremendous gifts as well. . . . Blessed Ildefonso, bishop of Toledo, when he published a book to uphold the honor of Blessed Mary's virginity against certain heretics of his day, received as a fitting reward for his labors a vision of the Blessed Mother attended by a great concourse of angels. . . . From this example you can see the extent of glory you can promise your writings. Immortality is the crown for a book penned for the glory of the Virgin Mother; destruction by fire is the lot of the work of the heretics. . . With far more right you will be able to say of your literary accomplishments what the bragging Ovid sang of his own: 'And now I have put the finish to my work, which neither Jove's wrath, nor fire, nor sword, nor the gluttonous mouth of time shall ever be able to destroy.'

Iamque opus exegi, quod nec Iovis ira, nec ignis,
Nec poterit ferrum, nec edax abolere Vetustas.

Metamosphoses 15:871-72.

Goodbye, dearest Father. If it is not too much bother, please let me know whether you have reached the half-way mark in composing your defense of the Virgin and when you judge that it will be off the press. Take care that from now on you do not allow me to be deprived for so long a time of the fruit to be gained from reading your books. As soon as they are published, be sure to send me one or two copies to Rome at my expense.[46]

Canisius obliged. In 1577 he published his book on the Blessed Virgin and the next year he sent a copy to Salmerón.[47]

A Wider Use of the Spiritual Exercises

During these years of research and writing Salmerón retained his concern for the Spiritual Exercises as a source of Jesuit inspiration. In the Neapolitan provincial congregation of 1576, called for the triennial election of a delegate to the congregation of procurators of that year, Salmerón joined Bobadilla in giving support to a movement that was then gaining momentum in the Society: the frequent repetition of the Exercises by members of the Society.[48] The provincial congregation appealed to the moral authority of these two survivors of the original Ignatian group: "This congregation strenuously and unanimously petitions Father General to direct all priests frequently to make the Spiritual Exercises. This same congregation also feels that the provincial should see to it that this custom, so holy, so proper to the Society, and from which our ancient fathers obtained such profit be extended to lay people as well."[49]

This petition of the Neapolitan province articulated the grass roots movement that urged Jesuits frequently, even annually, to go through the Spiritual Exercises. Jerónimo Nadal was one of the chief advocates of this novel practice, as he travelled through Europe.[50] The widespread movement finally took legal form in the twenty-ninth decree of General Congregation VI in 1608, which required each Jesuit to make the Spiritual Exercises each year for a period of eight or ten days.[51]

General Congregation IV

One final trip to Rome Salmerón had to make in the winter of 1580–81. It was to participate in the general congregation called for 7 February to elect a successor to Everard Mercurian, who had died the previous August. Delegates assembled from Italy, Spain, France, Portugal, Germany, for the most part a new generation of men, unknown personally to Salmerón. Representatives with unfamiliar names like Martin Lebenstein, Pedro de Silva, Emerich Forsleus, Arnold Staventius were taking over the government of the Company which he had helped to found. He and Bobadilla were the only two pioneers yet alive. Favre was dead thirty-five years, Xavier twenty-nine, Ignatius twenty-five. Laynez and Rodrigues had both passed on. Salmerón and Bobadilla alone could tell from personal experience of the day of vows at Montmartre in 1534, of the nights in Rome when they debated the question whether their "Company of Jesus" should be made a religious order.

The fathers assembled in the congregation made a gracious gesture. Before they proceeded to the election of the general, they sent Olivier Mannaerts, the vicar general, flanked by the two old veterans, to Pope Gregory XIII to ask his blessing on the Society. There in the papal court the pope spoke words that could not but have stirred the hearts of Salmerón and Bobadilla, words that were a benediction on all that the first Jesuits had stood for. Gregory said:

> Your holy order, and indeed it is a holy order, is spread throughout the entire world. Anywhere you look you have colleges and houses. You direct kingdoms, provinces, indeed the entire world. In brief, there is in this day no single instruments raised up by God against the heretics greater than your holy order. It came into the world at the very moment when new errors began to be spread abroad. It is all important, therefore, for the good of princes and of peoples (and we desire to add, of Ourselves too) that this order prosper and increase from day to day, and above all that it be governed by good superiors.[52]

With this magnanimous blessing from the supreme pontiff, the delegates of the congregation proceeded to the election of their general. They chose the man who had succeeded Salmerón as provincial of Naples and who then became provincial of Rome, the thirty-seven year old Claudio Acquaviva.[53]

346

A Plea for Freedom in Philosophy and Theology

Four years remained to Salmerón. These he devoted mainly to his writing, encouraged and assisted by the new general. In his turn Salmerón helped Acquaviva. On 18 August 1582, Acquaviva made a request that evoked one of Salmerón's most illuminating letters, revealing as it did the breadth of his view on the need for freedom in the advancement of human knowledge. Acquaviva was concerned about the diversity of opinions in philosphy and theology within the Society. He seemed to feel that this pluralism was unhealthy and that somehow it should be checked. He sought counsel in Rome from a number of theologians and received a diversity of opinions. "Restricting oneself to one particular teaching," he wrote Salmerón, "is not without its problems."[54] He asked Salmerón's opinion. "It will mean very much to me if you get your answer to me as soon as possible."[55]

Salmerón had his answer on its way in less than two weeks. Lucidity, wisdom, common sense marked his letter of five and a half pages in the *Monumenta Historica Societatis Jesu*.[56] Salmerón wrote with an awareness of the guidelines given by Ignatius for theological and philosophical studies in the Society of Jesus. Ignatius, in part four of the *Constitutions*, recommended as theological authors to be studied St. Thomas, Peter the Lombard, or "another author" who would be more suited for the current times. In philosphy Ignatius designated only Aristotle as an author.[57]

With this background of part four of the Jesuit *Constitutions*, Salmerón made several points: first, the practical impossibility of unity in teaching. Unity in teaching would have many advantages, but such unity would be extremely difficult to maintain. "Very rarely will you find harmony of teaching and unanimity of mind and will, and this even among men of outstanding holiness. Our own experience and the examples of history teach us this."[58] Among his examples Salmerón cited Paul and Barnabas, Peter and Paul, Cyprian and Cornelius, Jerome and Augustine, Chrysostom and Theophilus of Alexandria.

Second, the inadvisability of a one school or a one-man authority. No author has yet appeared, nor can one such be hoped for who, in the entirety of his writings, is free of fault and whose judgment, here and there, is not rejected by others. The infallibility of God should not be attributed to man. In the Society there should not be such adamant conformity to a single author that all of us would swear to stand by his words and opinions to the point that we would fight for them as though "for our hearths and homes" (*pro aris et foris*).[59]

Third, the ongoing growth of knowledge. All intellectual disciplines are developed and perfected with the passage of time. Advances have been made over some of the opinions of St. Thomas. Ignatius, Salmerón recalled, was open to advance. Ignatius even hoped that a Jesuit would one day present the body of theology in a fresh and more excellent way. Concurring in Ignatius's dream, Salmerón asked: "Why do we want to begrudge ourselves this glory, if God should deign to give it to us?"[60] Salmerón ruled out therefore any a priori exclusive and complete commitment to one particular theologian of the past.

Fourth, the drawbacks of a list of prohibited propositions. A catalog of prohibited propositions is not a good operative norm. It has not worked. "But if a catalog of this kind is actually drawn up," Salmerón wrote, "let it contain as few propositions as possible, lest the word go out that we wish to restrain the human mind within overtight limits and condemn by anticipation opinions and theses which the Church in no way has proscribed."[61] Holy Scripture, the definitions of the Church, and pontifical and conciliar decrees are adequate norms. "In what touches dogma, let us maintain unanimity and harmony. In other questions, let us enjoy our freedom."[62]

When Salmerón told Acquaviva that the publication of a catalog of prohibited propositions did not work, he was no doubt referring to the decree issued by Francis Borgia in November 1565, in which Borgia published five norms, all negatively phrased, and sixteen opinions that Jesuit masters were obliged to adhere to and teach.[63] This document of constraint was the first of its kind in the history of the Society. Borgia introduced a mode of authority that departed strikingly from Laynez's breadth of vision. Laynez, for example, when he received complaints that Francisco Toledo was propounding a novel explanation of predestination, decided that, since Toledo's exposition was not at odds with defined Catholic doctrine, he was free to explore this mystery down still unexamined roads.[64]

Salmerón shared Laynez's view. The wisdom gained over

some forty years of teaching in Rome and Germany, of advising at the Council of Trent, of counseling papal legations to Ireland, the Low Countries, and Poland, of preaching in a host of Italian cities, all poured into his direct, forceful unambiguous letter to Acquaviva. Twenty-eight years after Salmerón's death, Acquaviva put aside his earlier agreement with Salmerón. During the strained debates with the Dominicans on the nature of efficacious grace, he decreed that Jesuits had to adhere to that school of thought called congruism, a distinctive mold of Luis de Molina's teaching on "middle knowledge" (*scientia media*).[65]

The tendency toward intellectual constraint grew within the Society. In 1650 Francesco Piccolomini, the Society's eighth general, issued a list of sixty-five propositions in philosophy and thirty in theology that Jesuits should refrain from teaching.[66] A series of general congregations then passed decrees that called for the composition of an elenchus of opinions that Jesuits had to adopt or reject. In 1661 General Congregation XI called for a list of dangerous, scandalous, offensive opinions on moral issues; in 1696 General Congregation XIV directed the general to assemble a collection of philosophical and theological opinions forbidden to Jesuits. In 1706 General Congregation XV, anxious about the threat of Cartesianism to Aristotelian philosophy and the faith, did not issue a decree lest the Society incur the public anger of Descartes's disciples, but gave the general a catalog of thirty Cartesian propositions he was to circulate among Jesuit superiors as interdicted in Jesuit books and classrooms. In 1730 General Congregation XVI recommended that the general draw up a list of opinions in philosophy that Jesuits may not hold.[67] The wisdom of Salmerón was shunted aside by future generations of Jesuits.

Death of Salmerón

When the end came to Salmerón, it came quickly.[68] In January 1585 he seemed to have a premonition of his death. He used expressions such as "I have but a short time left," and —here the scripture scholar came to the fore—"The putting off of my body will be soon." One Jesuit in the community observed: "He seems to have a strong desire to die." A sharp decline set in in early February. He said his last mass on 5 February the feast of St. Agatha, to whom he had a special devotion. In the morning of the seventh he began to run a fever. He also suffered a pain in his side, an affliction he had not had before. He told the members of the community: "This time I am going to die." The next day he received holy communion. Asked to bless the 120 Jesuits of the Neapolitan college, he replied: "Rather, they, the servants of God, should bless me."

The doctors relieved the pain in his side but could not bring down the fever. Despite this, they did not feel that this condition was serious. He reacted to their judgment with a quotation from St. Mark: "The son of man is indeed going." When the doctors, urging him to eat, promised their help to make him better, he replied: "It would be better if you helped me to get to heaven." Some Jesuits pestered him with maladroit questions. One asked: "Are you dying willingly?" He quoted St. Augustine: "If it is going to happen sometime, why not now?" Another Jesuit asked: "How does the good fight?" He said in Latin: "My offering has been made, my past, my present, my future" (*Oblatum de prae-terito, presente et futuro*).

On the eleventh Salmerón made a general confession and again received holy communion. After communion the community requested his blessing. He gave it in Latin: "My excellent fathers and dearest brothers in Christ, always have I loved you. And now, at this time, I love you with the deepest of feeling. And if I have not had the opportunity to treat with all of you on intimate terms, I nevertheless have ever loved you and have ever desired to see you attain to that perfection to which you are called in this holy Society of Jesus. Now about to render an account of my life and my sojourn in this world, I have resolved to exhort you to this ideal anew. Since God in his infinite goodness has willed to summon me, as is indeed my hope, I have set my heart on giving you a fresh blessing. I therefore implore our Lord Jesus Christ to deign to protect you, uphold you, bless you so that you will be enabled to respond to the graces of your vocation and attain the Kingdom of Heaven in the name of the Father, and of the Son, and of the Holy Spirit. Amen." When he finished, the Jesuits, one by one, approached his bed and with tear filled eyes kissed his hand.

Salmerón lingered for two more days. Frequently he uttered passages from Scripture, especially the psalms. One phrase he recited was: "I shall be satisfied when your glory shall appear."

When a priest asked him: "You are not going to forget to pray for all of us?" he answered: "You seem to have some doubt, as though I would be ungrateful to all of you." The archbishop, the papal nuncio, the viceroy's son, and other distinguished men of the city visited him. To each he gave his blessing. On the twelfth the doctors still had hopes for his recovery. His devoted assistant in the work on the *Commentarii*, Bartolomé Pérez de Nueros, asked him whether he wished to receive extreme unction. "Yes," said Salmerón, "it will fortify us in our meeting with death." He then asked: "On what day did we celebrate the feast of St. Agatha?" He was told that it was on Tuesday past. "And when will be the octave?" he asked. "Tomorrow" was the reply. Salmerón said: "Then tomorrow will be the end." With profound devotion he then received extreme unction, answering the prayers and litanies in a low voice. Through the night he was heard whispering: "Off to life eternal. Off to life eternal." (*A la vida eterna, a la vida eterna*).

Around noon on the thirteenth Salmerón sent Nueros to the viceroy, Pedro Geron, to say that he was grateful for the viceroy's goodness to the Society, to commend once more the Society to his generosity, and to impart on Geron and his family his blessing. As evening came on he asked that litanies be recited. These he answered. Then he requested that the passion of Christ be read. He listened intently and asked that certain passages be repeated. Toward midnight he noticeably weakened. His voice became inaudible; he could move only his lips; his hands faltered in his efforts to make the sign of the cross; he fixed his eyes on the crucifix. Quietly he gave his spirit to his Lord. It was late on 13 February 1585.

Salmerón's body was placed in a room of the Jesuit residence. The next morning crowds of Neapolitans poured into the house to kiss Salmerón's hands. At two in the afternoon, the Jesuits tried to inter the body with the archbishop presiding over the obsequies. But the crowds, the known and the unknown, made it impossible. The Jesuits placed the body in the middle of their church so that the hosts of people might have the opportunity of expressing their grief and respect. Some clipped strands from his hair and beard; others snipped pieces from his clothing; still others tried to cut off a foot. At nightfall the Jesuits moved the body to the sacristy and closed out the crowds. In the sacristy they coated the body with wax. When darkness enveloped the city and the people had dispersed, behind locked doors and with only their community in attendance, they placed the body in a lined box, and laid it with the remains of other Jesuits beneath the college church.

To the north, in Genoa, the seventy-six year old Nicolás Bobadilla went about his work. With Salmerón gone, he alone of the seven who ascended Montmartre in August of 1534 was alive to tell of the earliest days of that blessed companionship formed around Ignatius Loyola.

PART III

A RECAPITULATION

CONCLUSION

The conclusion of this volume is an attempt to formulate a synthesis after the analysis in the first two parts. It is the gathering of the stalks and bundling them together into sheaves. The trails that wound through part one and part two meant the constant rubbing of shoulders with Jay and Salmerón. The lineaments of the personalities of these two Jesuits became sharper as, through the years, they revealed more and more of their characters. The differences between them unfolded with increasing clarity. How diverse were the vessels that carried the Ignatian ideals became more palpable.

Claude Jay, from the Alpine passes of remote, agricultural Savoy, was an open, friendly, affectionate, attractive person. His most obvious weakness was a diffidence about his talents that made him shrink from taking Johannes Eck's chair of theology at Ingolstadt and the rector's post at the Jesuit college in Vienna. Superiors forced both responsibilities on him, and in each instance he carried out his duties with intelligence and charm. His correspondence radiates his deep emotional attachment to the Society of Jesus, his fears, his anxieties, his piety, and his prayerfulness.[1] Salmerón, from the royal city of Toledo, was a competitive, aggressive, serious-minded man of high intellectual powers. Open and friendly in his youth—Ignatius used to tease him about his naïveté—he became grave and solemn, even gloomy, under the burdens as religious superior and conciliar theologian. His chief weakness was excessive sensitivity, petulance, even a tinge of hysteria, when criticized or challenged. In some ways this brilliant man never grew up. He had a streak of vanity, preening his feathers as he described how men and women hung on to his every word from the pulpit, another Peter Damian. His correspondence crackles with businesslike efficiency and irritation with the incompetence of others. His judgments were often caustic, sharp, biting, which provoked fellow Jesuits to complain about him to superiors in Rome. He was committed to the life of the mind. He revered the scholar's vocation. His *Commentarii* impressed Louis-Ellies Dupon, a scholar of the eighteenth century, as being overbalanced toward intellectualism.[2]

These two men, so different in talent and personality, became immersed in the religious reform of the sixteenth century. Ignatius remained in Rome. They took to the road. Through the thirteen years of his life since the approbation of the Society, Jay was constantly pitching and striking his tent in either Italy or Germany or Austria. In Italy he had short stints in Bagnorea, Brescia, Faenza, Ferrara, Bologna, Trent. In the German speaking lands, he literally shuttled between Regensburg, Ingolstadt, Eichstätt, Salzburg, Augsburg. He closed his days in Vienna. Salmerón ranged even more widely. He worked in Edinburg, Ireland, Brussels, Cambrai, Augsburg, Ingolstadt, Cracow, and a host of towns in northern and southern Italy. He breathed his last in Naples. If, on a sketch of western and central Europe, a pin were placed at each town where Jay and Salmerón labored, the surface would take on the appearance of a military map marking out the disposal of army units in a wide ranging campaign. To a wide span of Europe they more than Ignatius introduced the Society of Jesus. They did so in a number of ways.

Jay and Salmerón stepped into European history as professional theologians, members of a body of men who, in their hierarchy of learning, gave primacy to theology (une véritable primat de la théologie).[3] In Paris they imbibed the renewal of scholasticism set in motion by Pieter Crockaert and Francisco de Vitoria.

356

They knew not only the Scriptures and the church fathers but also the great medieval scholastics. They learned to distinguish, to think in a precise and orderly way. They became skilled woodsmen in the thicket of theology, recognizing the exigency of theological refinement, an exigency that insisted on defining compunction as well as feeling it. "Someone, somewhere, must be interested in compunction's definition, or it will soon cease to be understood that there can be, and is, a certainty about what compunction is and what it is not, and if that certainty goes, very strange things indeed will begin to wander about, claiming the name of compunction in the lost land that once was Christendom."[4]

Often did Claude Jay play the professional theologian. At the University of Ingolstadt, for nearly a year (1543–44), he replaced the recently deceased Johann Eck as lecturer in theology. In 1545 he coached Bishop Moritz von Hutten of Eichstätt on theological issues in preparation for a religious colloquy at Regensburg. In 1546 he represented Cardinal Otto von Truchsess at the Council of Trent. During an imperial diet at Augsburg, 1550–51, he advised Truchsess on the theological issues. Twice he and Salmerón worked together as theologians. At the University of Ingolstadt in 1549 Jay lectured on the Psalms, Salmerón on the Epistles of St. Paul. At the first period of the Council of Trent, in the presence of some bishops they made solid and constructive interventions toward the clarification of the conciliar documents on tradition, justification, original sin, the sacraments, and the role of bishops. Salmerón carried on his theological work, with Diego Laynez, into the second and third period of the council. Twice he served on papal diplomatic missions, to Poland and the Netherlands, as theological adviser to the nuncios.

Their professional training set them apart from those Catholic leaders who deplored renewal through theology and who surrendered to Erasmus's viewpoint that "there was no longer any place for the intellectual construction of Christian doctrine under a scientific form corresponding to the exigencies of speculative reason."[5] Reginald Pole and those of his circle shared a common suspicion of the professional theologian. Without the latter's expertise, they debated the religious issues of the day poorly equipped to handle the subtleties inherent in such questions such as, say, the formulas *fides sola* and *scriptura sola*. Jay and Salmerón came to the same questions with their professional training and were able to help hone with precise language some of the star documents of the council. Through them Europe's bishops became aware of the new Society of Jesus as a resource of theological learning.

Jay and Salmerón also fused Jesuit history into European history in the manner of Christian Humanists. In the sixteenth century men were trying in varying ways to mold a synthesis of the humanism that emerged from the literary Renaissance and the religious devotion that grew out of the scriptural Renaissance the spread of methodical prayer, and the fresh outburst of Eucharistic piety. The Christian Humanist of that age might have said, "I am a man, and I consider nothing divine as foreign to me" (*Homo sum et nil divinum a me alienum puto*). He envisioned "a devotion expressed with literary grace" (*pietas litterata*); he hoped for a Christianity that crowned the achievement of Greece and Rome.[6]

At Paris a student named Guillaume Postel noted that Ignatius and his friends stood out as a group in the Latin Quarter because in their lives they reflected a striking harmony of learning and devotion. In their youth Jay and Salmerón had seriously studied classical literature. At Paris they earned the master of arts degree and moved on to theology. From the Spiritual Exercises of Ignatius they imbibed a deep commitment to the service of Christ in apostolic action. The harmony in their lives of these influences was what Postel noted. So did many others. At Augsburg in 1551 the Protestants were so impressed by Jay's "learned modesty and modest learning" that they invited him to Wittemburg to meet Philip Melanchthon. Dominican Egidio Foscarari considered himself fortunate to have known Salmerón, a priest "so learned and so holy." Angelo Massarelli recalled that Salmerón spoke at the Council of Trent "with devotion and learning." Jay and Salmerón were conscious of this humanist ideal. At Ingolstadt they together argued with Chancellor Georg Stockhammer for the opening of a Jesuit college, since it would have the power to attract German youth "to a learning charged with devotion and a devotion graced by learning." They were telling the German leaders what Ignatius was telling King Philip II of Spain. The Society of Jesus, because it personalized in its members a union of learning and devotion, was able to relieve the dearth of teachers who attained that ideal. "There are too few teachers who combine the virtue and the learning essential to this task [of teaching]. For this reason, Christ Our Lord has inspired the Society with zeal to undertake this very humble, but nonetheless valuable, task of educating youth."[7] Many Europeans, especially in Germany, Austria, and Italy, through Jay and Salmerón, first met the Jesuits as Christian Humanists.

Perhaps the most obvious point of confluence of Jesuit and European history was the school. Jay and Salmerón stood before thousands of Europeans as schoolmen, intent on setting up within the ferment of Europe's intellectual and religious life a new institution, the Jesuit college. Jay, perhaps more than any other early Jesuit, moved Ignatius toward the enterprise of formal education. From the depths of his painful German experience, he cried out that only the Jesuit college could be the life raft of the Catholic church in Germany. Eloquently he pleaded with Ignatius, princes, and bishops. His college at Vienna crowned his efforts of nearly a decade. Salmerón, early in his Jesuit life, became identified with the college in Naples. Between other assignments, he worked to purchase buildings, find financial footing, staff the faculty. During his years as provincial of Naples, he gave his greatest attention to the founding of other Jesuit colleges in southern Italy. Jay's Vienna and Salmerón's Naples won the admiration of the Austrians and Italians, and became important pegs in a web of colleges that numbered forty-three at the death of Ignatius in 1556.

The Jesuit colleges gave a practical embodiment to the ideal of imparting "a learning charged with devotion and a devotion graced by learning." Erasmus and Lefèvre, dreaming of "an intellectual and moral elite," pressed for the union of learning and piety, but it was "an artifical construction, with no deep roots in the mentality of the Christian people, too refined and subtle to act on the masses."[8] Their aspiration was utopian. The Jesuit aspiration was practical. It gripped the masses. Bollandist Alfred Poncelet, with the Jesuit colleges in Belgium in mind, judged that the secret of their enthusiastic welcome by the people lay in their style of education, "more civilized, more thorough, more methodical,'' which in turn had a notable impact on the quality of Catholic life, bringing about "the preservation of the Catholic religion and the securing of it for successive generations, and this through the instrument of belles-lettres . . ."[9] Mutatis mutandis, Poncelet's judgment applied to the Jesuit colleges of other lands in that early age of beginnings. The Society of Jesus entered the lives of many Europeans for the first time when they met Jay and Salmerón wearing the birettas of schoolmen.

If many heard Jay and Salmerón speaking from the lectern in the classroom, far more heard them speaking from the pulpit in the church. As sacred orators did Jay and Salmerón first swing into the ken of thousands. And with them the new Society of Jesus. They appeared at a bewildering time. Preachers, Catholic and Protestant, were vying for the populace. "Not since Savonarola had the Italian cities turned so enthusiastically to preachers."[10] Jay was the first Jesuit to preach in Bagnorea and Faenza. In Regensburg he witnessed large segments of the population give their loyalties to a popular Protestant preacher. From his own pulpit in the same town he tried to reverse the exodus from the Catholic church. Salmerón excelled Jay in oratorical skills. A favorite at Naples, he received acclaim in several cities of northern Italy. Venice tried to wrench him away from Naples. He joined a distinguished line of sacred orators at the Vatican.

Jesuit oratory had a peculiar pertinence to the spiritual aspirations of the age. The breezes of the Scriptural Renaissance were blowing strongly through Europe, Protestant and Catholic. At Trent, Jay banded with the humanists in the council in placing scriptural studies at the core of sacerdotal training. At Ingolstadt, he lectured in the university on the Gospel of St. John; a few years later, on the Psalms. Salmerón, at Alcalá, drew deeply of the scriptural well dug by Francisco Jiménez de Cisneros. Here he found some of his richest spiritual nourishment through his long life, which he crowned with his *Commentarii*. He and Jay as well as the other early Jesuits, poured this scriptural ardor into a special spiritual mold: the scriptural lectures, "a new kind of preaching," whereby through highly refined popularization (*haute vulgarisation*) they taught the populace about the Scriptures.[11] In their scriptural lectures, Jay and Salmerón united the scientific explanation of the classroom with a devotional reflection on the force of God's word in one's life. Behind them lay centuries of the scholastic tradition of seeking clear, objective knowledge in the "holy page" (*pagina sacra*). The key words were: "the question under examination" (*quaeritur*) and "the point to be intellectually grasped" (*sciendum*). And then there was the even older monastic tradition of tasting the spiritual sweetness of the "holy page." The key words were: "the meaning for which the heart thirsts" (*desideratur*), and "the meaning that is to be spiritually felt" (*experiendum*).[12] In their scriptural lectures Jay and Salmerón united the *quaeritur* and the *desideratur*, and the *sciendum* and the *experiendum* into an exposition that was at once informative and inspiring.

Jay and Salmerón were good craftsmen in the making of this new form of preaching. In presenting it to the people, they presented the Society of Jesus. Jesuit history and European history found a rendezvous at the pulpit.

Beyond their scriptural lectures, the Jesuits had at hand another tool, one even more expressive of their spirit and highly personal to their vocation. It was a small book, a manual really, entitled *Spiritual Exercises*, composed by their friend Ignatius of Loyola. With this text as their guide, Jay and Salmerón led hundreds of people through a series of meditations, contemplations, examinations of conscience, and confession of sin, helping them to achieve "the conquest of self and the regulation of one's life in such a way that no decision is made under the influence of any inordinate attachment." Ignatius, formed by centuries-old spiritual insights and methodical prayer, took those older riches, structured them in a dynamic and strikingly personal way, and brought forth a powerful instrument for the renewal of the church in that age. At least some thirteen hundred persons during the lifetime of Ignatius entered into the experience of following the *Spiritual Exercises*.[13] For many of them this was their introduction to the Society of Jesus.

With the *Spiritual Exercises* in hand, Jay and Salmerón became skilled retreat masters and spiritual directors. Jay guided retreatants in Regensburg, Ingolstadt, Eichstätt, Worms, Ferrara, Augsburg, Ottobeuren. At Regensburg he went from house to house seeking people to make the Exercises. He met acceptance;

he met rejection. He found it difficult work. His most famous retreatant was Cardinal Otto von Truchsess. Salmerón did the same work in Rome, Trent, Bologna, Belluno, Verona, Venice, and Naples. He made Naples a vital retreat center.

Jay and Salmerón, therefore, met hundreds of people within the special relationship of retreatant and retreat master, and in so doing gave many of them their first inkling of the Society of Jesus. With the *Spiritual Exercises* they extended far and wide the spiritual experience of Ignatius himself, prolonged into the modern world, "perhaps without realizing it, the trends of northern piety,"[14] and "gave legitimacy once and for all to the idea of the 'method of prayer.' "[15] As retreat masters they piloted the Society of Jesus into the stream of European history.

Retreat masters, preachers, schoolmen, professional theologians. Jay and Salmerón changed their hats often. They were men ever on the move. They mirrored Ignatius's design: a Jesuit's mission should be, unless the pope or the general good dictated otherwise, of about three months duration.[16] Fr. Jerónimo Nadal, a respected exegete of Ignatius's thought, saw his fellow Jesuits as men of the road. "In the last analysis the Society's most effective bivouac is not to be found in the professed houses but on the highways" (*in domibus professis non est ultima vel potissima habitatio Societatis, sed in peregrinationibus.*"[17] As no other group in the church of that era, Jay and Salmerón and their fellow Jesuits gave "consistent testimony to the Tridentine doctrine of the value of good works . . ."[18] They brought Trent to the marketplaces and the highways.

On 13 January 1547, the Council of Trent, at its sixth session, issued the decree on justification. At that session Dominican Tommaso Stella, Bishop of Salpi, gave the sermon. He said: "To this one purpose did the law and the prophets look forward: that man might be made perfect and endowed to achieve in justice every good work, since the fullness of the law is charity, by which a living faith does the things in which God takes delight."[19] Stella hailed the council's achievement in laying a solid doctrinal foundation of the intrinsic goodness of the works done by man raised to the dignity of a son of God. He praised the optimistic conciliar judgment, which one scholar has called an "antidote to the pessimism of the theology of the reformers."[20]

Jay and Salmerón were active in the debates before the decree on justification. They sounded a clear note: man's good works have a significant role in his advance toward eternal salvation. They helped formulate the decree that gave theological underpinning to the spiritual doctrine of man's interior integrity, worth, and dignity. They shared in the making of one of the finest pieces minted at Trent. In this Tridentine theological optimism did they root their labors as preachers, schoolmen, retreat masters, episcopal advisers. They helped formulate the doctrine; they implemented the doctrine. At each point where they guided the Society of Jesus into the flow of European history, thousands met an early fulfillment of the hopes and aspirations of the current council.

These pages identify the several points of rendezvous at which Jay and Salmerón met their age in history. Mutatis mutandis, the experiences of these two of the first Jesuits were the general experience of the young Society of Jesus. These pages highlight how Jay and Salmerón, standing at a tragic parting of the ways in Western Europe, felt the forces of the old and the new. Both men, washed by the deep spiritual currents rising out of past centuries, imbibed them and were enriched by them. Both men, alert to the unfamiliar and turbulent eddies of their own age, changed course and sketched out new channels.

Where they touched thought and piety, they turned out a fresh mint. This handseled work did not issue from any originality of their own minds. Neither was an original thinker. The freshness flowed rather from a power wider than themselves: their membership in the Society of Jesus, their common experience of the Spiritual Exercises of Ignatius of Loyola, their intimate friendship with Ignatius, and their critical review of the Jesuit Constitutions composed by Ignatius. They themselves first had been fashioned into something new. Italians, Belgians, Germans, and Austrians did not meet just Jay and Salmerón. They met the Society of Jesus.

The introductions of the Society of Jesus to Europe were not violent or majestic. They were gentle, like the scattered drops that precede the downpour. A few drops at Bagnorea, or Faenza, or Augsburg, or Eichstätt. Gentle but evident. Ignatius's guiding

363

influence was of course dominant. His companions turned to him in abundant correspondence. He was the center of their union. So he intended the office of Jesuit general to be. But at the center in Rome, he could not be in Salzburg and Trent and Ingolstadt and Naples. Jay, Salmerón, and the others did what he could not do. They went to these cities, and others too, and there sowed the Jesuit message. To tell that story has been the purpose of this volume.

ABBREVIATIONS

AHSJ	*Archivum Historicum Societatis Jesu*
CollD	*Collectio Decretorum Congregationum Generalium Societatis Jesus [XXVII–XXX]* (1923–1957)
CO	*Conciliorum Oecumenicorum Decreta*
ConstSJ	*Constitutiones Societatis Jesu*
ConsSJComm	*The Constitutions of the Society of Jesus*
CT	*Concilium Tridentinum. Diariorum, Actorum, Epistolarum, Tractatuum nova collectio*
DeGuiJes	De Guibert. *The Jesuits: Their Spiritual Doctrine and Practice*
DSpir	*Dictionnaire de Spiritualité*
DTC	*Dictionnaire de Théologie Catholique*
EnSym	*Enchiridion Symbolorum*
EppCan	*Beati Petri Canisii Societatis Jesu epistulae et acta*
EppIgn	*Sancti Ignatii de Loyola . . . Epistolae et Instructiones*
EppMixt	*Epistolae Mixtae ex variis Europae locis*
EppXav	*Epistolae S. Francisci Xaverii*
FN	*Fontes Narrativi de S. Ignatio de Loyola*
InstSJ	*Institutum Societis Jesu.*
LittQuad	*Litterae Quadrimestres*
MonBobad	*Bobadillae Monumenta*
MonBorg	*Sanctus Franciscus Borgia*
MonBroet	*Epistolae PP. Paschasii Broeti, Claudii Jaji, Joannis Codurii et Simonis Rodericii S.J.*
MonFabri	*Fabri Monumenta*
MonLain	*Lainii Monumenta*
MonNad	*Epistolae et Monumenta P. Hieronymi Nadal*
MonPaed	*Monumenta Paedagogica Societatis Jesu (1540–1572)*
MonRib	*Patris Petri de Ribadeneira Confessiones*
MonSalm	*Epistolae P. Alphonsi Salmeronis*
PolChron	*Chronicon Societatis Jesu*
PolCompl	*Polanci Complementa*
SMV	Sommervogel, *Bibliothèque de la Compagnie de Jésus*
TheolSt	*Theological Studies*

NOTES

CHAPTER I

1. W.V. Bangert, S.J., *To the Other Towns, A Life of Blessed Peter Favre* (Westminster, Md., 1959), 7–10.

2. H. Tavernier, "Le P. Claude Jay, sa patrie et sa famille," *Revue Savoisienne*, 35 (1894): 81, 91–93.

3. The name Jay was one of the most ancient in Mieussy. Farther up the valley of the Giffre is the town of Samoens, where there is evidence of the name Jay in the fourteenth century. The spelling of the name gradually became *Gex*. Other variant spellings are *Gets, Gyez, Jayz, Jay*. Ibid., 89–92.

4. Ibid., 90–91.

5. *Pierre Favre, Mémorial*, ed. M. de Certeau, S.J. Collection Christus No. 4, *Textus* (Paris, 1939), 11–12.

6. H. Tavernier, "Le P. Claude Jay," 90. Bangert, *To the Other Towns*, 10–12.

7. Two copies of this work are known to exist, one at the Bibliothèque Publique de Genève, the other at Séminaire d'Aoste. See *Pierre Favre, Mémorial*, ed. M. de Certeau, S.J., 108, n. 1. A scholar, Théophile Dufour, made notes on this work of Veillard. These notes, unedited, are in the Bibliothèque Publique et Universitaire de Genève. See Bangert, *To the Other Towns*, 296, n. 13.

8. *MonFabri*, 843–46. At the end of his abstract, Claude made the notation: "Done at La Roche, May, A.D. 1519, on the feast of St. Urban." Claude also made an abstract of the Fourth Book of the *Sentences*, at the end of which he wrote: "Done at La Roche under the direction of the Reverend Teacher Peter Veillard, most celebrated instructor in the school of this town."

9. Ibid., 491. Bangert, *To the Other Towns*, 9.

10. Bangert, *To the Other Towns*, 93.

11. *MonBroet*, 323.

12. *FN*, 1. 30.

13. Bangert, *To the Other Towns*, 12.

14. G. Schurhammer, S.J., *Francis Xavier. His Life, His Times* (Rome, 1973) 1:260.

15. *MonFabri*, 846. Tavernier, "Le P. Claude Jay," 81–85, 90.

16. Bangert, *To the Other Towns*, 22–23.

17. Ibid., 20–22. Schurhammer, *Francis Xavier*, 1:35, 49, 67–68. Schurhammer lists nineteen variant spellings of Xavier, including these: Chavier, Jabier, Xabierre, Savierr. Ibid., 1:798.

18. Bangert, *To the Other Towns*, 26–28.

19. Ibid., 28.

20. Ibid., 28–31.

21. Ibid., 31–32.

22. Schurhammer, *Francis Xavier*, 1:370.

23. Ibid., 1:211. A. de Aldama, S.J., *Repartiéndose en la viña de Cristo. Comentario a la séptima parte de las Constituciones de la Compañía de Jesús* (Rome, 1973), 24–31.

24. Bangert, *To the Other Towns*, 34–35.

25. Ibid., 36–37. Schurhammer, *Francis Xavier*, 1:213–14.

26. Schurhammer, *Francis Xavier*, 1:260. When writing his *De origine et progressu Societatis Jesu* forty-three years later, Simão Rodrigues said that he could not remember whether Jay had met Iñigo. Most likely he met not only Iñigo but the other friends also. See *MonBroet*, 486.

27. *FN*, 1:658. Bangert, *To the Other Towns*, 40.

28. *FN*, 1:704.

29. Bangert, *To the Other Towns*, 40.

30. Schurhammer, *Francis Xavier*, 1:260–61. J.M. Prat, S.J., *Le Père Claude Le Jay Un des Premiers Compagnons de S. Ignace de Loyola* (Lyon, 1874), 442 (hereafter abbreviated as *Le Jay*).

31. H. Bernard-Maitre, S.J., "Les Fondateurs de la Compagnie de Jésus et l'Humanisme Parisien de la Renaissance (1525–1536)," *Nouvelle Revue Théologique*, 72 (1950): 812.

32. Ibid., 817.

33. Favre, *Mémorial*, 30.

34. R. Rouquette, S.J., "Ignace de Loyola dans le Paris intellectuel du XVIe siècle," *Études*, 290 (1956): 27. Bernard-Maitre, "Les Fondateurs de la Compagnie de Jésus," 817.

35. H. Bernard-Maitre, S.J., "Calvin et Loyola," *Bulletin de L'Association Guillaume Budé*, Troisième Série, numero 2, (June, 1953), 81–84.

36. Schurhammer, *Francis Xavier*, 1:162–63 and n. 119.

37. Ibid., 1:163. Bernard Maitre, "Calvin et Loyola," 78–79.

38. E. F. Rice, Jr., ed., *The Prefatory Epistles of Jacques Lefèvre d'Etaples and Related Texts* (New York, 1972), xix. Lefèvre's endorsement of a chaste and holy Aristotle, freed from the inaccurate editions of the medieval scholars, challenges the simplistic view that the Renaissance was, philosophically, Platonic. E. F. Rice, Jr., "Humanist Aristotelianism in France.

Jacques Lefèvre and His Circle,'' *Humanism in France at the End of the Middle Ages and in the Early Renaissance*, ed. A.H.T. Levi (New York, 1970), 132–49.

39. Rice, *The Prefatory Epistles*, xvi.

40. Ibid., xxiii.

41. Rouquette, "Ignace de Loyola," 27–29. P. Dudon, S.J., "Sur un texte inédit de Salmeron (1562)," *Gregorianum*, 11 (1930): 417.

42. Y.M.-J. Congar, O.P., *A History of Theology* (Garden City, 1968), 171–72. Ignatius Loyola, *The Spiritual Exercises of St. Ignatius* (Westminster, Md , 1951), 159. Some scholars trace Iñigo's ties to the Lefevrian brand of Christian Humanism through one of Lefèvre's active and articulate disciples, the Belgian humanist Josse Clichtove (1472–1543). They think that Iñigo, in the composition of his Rules for Thinking with the Church, borrowed from the 1528 anti-Lutheran decrees of Paris, of which Clichtove was a sponsor and advocate. Rouquette, "Ignace de Loyola," 28. Bernard-Maitre, "Calvin et Loyola," 84. Joseph de Guibert gives this reasoning some probability. *The Jesuits. Their Spiritual Doctrine and Practice. A Historical Study* (Chicago, 1964), 121 with n. 29. Pedro Leturia, who recognizes that the campaign for religious orthodoxy in Paris led by Josse Clichtove, Diogo de Gouvea, and Noël Beda had its impact on Iñigo, nevertheless traces the roots of the Rules back to Iñigo's year in Alcalá, 1526–27. "Genesis de los ejercicios de San Ignacio y su influjo en la fundación de la Compañía de Jesús (1521–1540)," *Estudios Ignacianos* (Rome, 1957), 2:26. Also by Leturia is "Problemas Historicos en torno a las Reglas para Sentir con Iglesia," *Estudios Ignacianos*, 2:181–86.

43. Rouquette claims that Iñigo was the first to use the term "positive theology." "Ignace de Loyola," 28. Yves Congar disagrees. He shows that John Mair used the term in 1509 in his commentary on the *Sentences. A History of Theology*, 171. Joseph de Guibert places the incorporation of the Rules for Thinking with the Church into the text of the *Spiritual Exercises* during Iñigo's Paris period, 1528–35. De Guin, 121. The editors of *MHSJ* put this incorporation of the Rules in the early Roman period during 1539 and 1541. *SpEx* MHSJ 1:33. In either case, John Mair preceded Iñigo by at least a decade.

44. Ignatius Loyola, *The Spiritual Exercises*, 159.

45. P. Leturia, S.J., "Sentido Verdadero en la Iglesia Militante," *Estudios Ignacianos*, 2:152. Historians differ sharply on the issue of Lefèvre's sympathy for certain Protestant theological positions. John Olin, after a review of the divergent opinions, holds that "the thought and spirituality of Lefèvre . . . are fully Catholic." *The Catholic Reformation: Savonarola to Ignatius Loyola*, ed. J. Olin, (New York, 1969), 110.

46. Rice, *The Prefatory Epistles*, xx.

47. Ignatius Loyola, *The Spiritual Exercises*. 159. Ignatius also differed from Lefèvre in other ways. Lefèvre held that "the pursuit of divine things by sense and imagination leads to idolatry and error." E.F. Rice, "Jacques Lefèvre

d'Etaples and the Medieval Christian Mystics,'' *Florilegium Historiale. Essays presented to Wallace K. Ferguson*, ed. J. G. Rowe and W. H. Stockdale (Toronto, 1971), 101. Ignatius taught the use of the senses and imagination in prayer. Eugene Rice states, cautiously indeed, that Lefèvre valued the mystics primarily for their help to him in shaping and clarifying his own theory of knowledge. "Jacques Lefèvre d'Etaples," 100. Ignatius never had an academic purpose of this kind in his looking back to the Christian spiritual writers of the past.

48. Schurhammer, *Francis Xavier*, 1:170.

49. S. Ozment, ed., *The Reformation in Medieval Perspective* (Chicago: Quadrangle Paperbacks, 1971), 7.

50. Ibid., 7.

51. Congar, *A History of Theology*, 171. Rouquette, "Ignace de Loyola," 28.

52. Congar, *A History of Theology*, 173.

53. Schurhammer, *Francis Xavier*, 1:261, n. 108.

54. *EppCan*, 1:416.

55. Ibid., 1:416. Peter Canisius made an index of Jay's work, kept it for a long time, and used it in his lectures at Vienna and in the composition of his catechisms.

56. Favre, *Mémorial*, 26. Postel, who had an exceptional facility in languages, entered the Society in Rome in 1544 but was dismissed the following year because of his mental illness. Schurhammer, *Francis Xavier*, 1:163–64 and n. 131. Postel was inaccurate in identifying the Iniguistas as the creators of a theology that unites *pietas* and *eruditio*. The ideal of this unity of devotion and learning inspired Catholics and Protestants, and permeated the cultural milieu among the Italian and Northern humanists. The many nuances of these words go through all the colors of the academic rainbow of that age. Eugene Rice, Jr., delineates the pronounced differences in emphasis, focus and judgment in *The Renaissance Idea of Wisdom* (Cambridge, Mass., 1958). Although scholars used *pietas* in a wide variety of meanings such as dutifulness to God, holiness, piety, and moral earnestness, the central thrust was always religious. Calvin, Beza, and Viret loved the learning of the past and tried to unite this with *pietas*, a word that "occurs over and over again in their writings." R. D. Linder, "Calvinism and Humanism: The First Generation," *Church History*, 44 (1975): 176. Giles of Viterbo postulated a direct relationship between theology and piety, a relationship that "must be kept in mind if we are to understand his insistence that learning and reform march hand in hand." J. W. O'Malley, S.J., *Giles of Viterbo on Church and Reform. A Study in Renaissance Thought* (Leiden, 1968), 54. Charles Trinkaus writes: " 'Anthropology' and 'theology' belong together in Renaissance thought, and if we find that the humanists' ideas about man were a 'theological anthropology', their significance also is in the fact that they developed an 'anthropological theology.' Their concern for God and religion was

inseparable from their concern with man in his otherworldly destiny and his this-worldly condition." *In Our Image and Likeness. Humanity and Divinity in Italian Humanist Thought* (Chicago, 1970) 1:3–4. Postel's knowledge of cabala was probably more extensive and sympathetic than that of any other cabalist of his time." W. J. Bouwsma, "Postel and the Significance of Renaissance Cabalism," *Renaissance Essays*, ed. P. O. Kristeller and P. P. Wiener (New York, 1968), 254.

57. Bangert, *To the Other Towns*, 147–48.

58. *EppCan*, 1:359. Years later, when Jay, Canisius and Salmerón lectured at Ingolstadt, the men at the University discerned in the three Jesuits the union of *pietas* and *eruditio*. They paid tribute to this union with an inscription that read:

Nuper quantam laetitiam ceperimus
Omnes ex adventu trium theologorum
Claudii Jaii Alphonsi Salmeronis et
Petri Canisii vix dici potest quorum
Praesentia non solum famam de ipsis
Excitatam non minuit sed etiam auget
Quorum singularis in sacrosanctis
Studiis scientia tum in omnibus disciplinis
Exercitatio postrema sanctimonia vitae
Expectationem omnium eamque maximam
Non solum aequat verum etiam superat.
Prat, *Le Jay*, 486–87.

59. Schurhammer, *Francis Xavier*, 1:261.

60. Bangert, *To the Other Towns*, 40–41.

61. Ibid., 41–43.

62. *MonBroet*, 462–64. *FN*, 1:40.

63. *Mon Broet*, 474–75.

64. P. Dudon, S.J., *St. Ignatius of Loyola*, trans. William J. Young, S.J. (Milwaukee, 1949), 233–35. Schurhammer, *Francis Xavier*, 1:139, 302, 310.

65. *MonBroet*, 479–80. There were twelve in this pilgrimage to Rome. Besides the nine who joined the Ignatian group in Paris, there were three others, all Spaniards, who joined Iñigo in Venice: Diego Hozes, Antonio Arias, Miguel Landívar, the last two of whom were former acquaintances from the Paris days. Schurhammer, *Francis Xavier*, 1:301–2, 309–10.

66. *PolChron*, 1: 58–60.

67. Schurhammer, *Francis Xavier*, 1: 334 36.

68. Ibid., 1:336. Sometime during the stay in Rome, Arias and Landívar left the group. Landívar, a restless and inconstant person, blamed not only Arias for persuading him to break with Iñigo but also some Spaniards in Rome who stated that the Ignatian group were secret Alumbrados. Arias had a yen for

money. Schurhammer, *Francis Xavier*, 1:339–40. He also seems to have been a homosexual. Schurhammer shows that the editors of the *Monumenta Historica Societatis Jesu* omitted from their edition of a letter from Landívar to Xavier the passage that indicates Arias's homosexuality. Schurhammer, *Francis Xavier*, 1: 364–65, n. 216.

69. Ibid., 1:342–44, 347–48. Diego Hozes was a Spanish priest who joined Iñigo at Venice. Iñigo probably was the one who arranged the groupings of the pilgrims. Ibid., 1:370, n. 249.

70. Ibid., 1:361–63. *MonBroet*, 489. This hermitage still exists on the road that leads into the valley of Valsugana. *FN*, 4: 362, n. 3. Pedro Ribadeneyra in his life of St. Ignatius relates that Claude Jay at this time experienced a strong temptation to give up the toil of the apostolic life for the sweetness of the contemplative life. Jay went to seek the advice of the hermit Antonio. Suddenly, astride the road, appeared an armed man with an ugly, deformed face, and with sword raised in air. Jay attempted to pass by. The stranger lunged at him. Jay turned on his heel and raced into Bassano with his assailant after him. At that moment Iñigo and Favre were in Bassano. They had come there because they had heard that Rodrigues was seriously ill. Jay in panic ran to the inn where Iñigo and Favre were staying. There Iñigo, with a smile, greeted Jay with the gentle admonition: "O you of little faith, why did you doubt? "And so ended Jay's temptation to become another Antonio of San Vito. *FN*, 4: 262–65 with n. 4 on 262–63. Ribadeneyra makes two errors: first, he attributes to Jay an experience of inconstancy that was Rodrigues's; second, Rodrigues suffered this temptation not at San Vito but at the hermitage of St. Nicolas-du-Port. Schurhammer, *Francis Xavier*, 1:362–63, n. 204. Paul Dudon uncritically accepts the story as related by Ribadeneyra. *St. Ignatius of Loyola*, 239–40.

71. Schurhammer, *Francis Xavier*, 1: 356–58.

72. Ibid., 1:358–63, 365–66.

73. Ibid., 1:369.

74. *FN*, 1:204, 2:159, 595–96. *PolChron*, 1:72–73. For a study of the significance of this title, see *ConsSJComm*, 345–49.

75. Schurhammer, *Francis Xavier*, 1: 369.

76. Ibid., 1:369–70. *MonBroet*, 491.

77. Schurhammer, *Francis Xavier*, 1:372, 393.

78. J. A. Symonds, *Sketches and Studies in Southern Europe* (New York, 1880), 1:267.

79. C. J. Blaisdell, "Politics and Heresy in Ferrara, 1534–1559," *The Sixteenth Century Journal*, 6 (1974): 70.

80. Ibid., 73–75.

81. D. Cantimore, "Italy and the Papacy," *New Cambridge Modern History* (Cambridge, 1968), 2:255–56.

82. Blaisdell, "Politics and Heresy," 70–71. Prat, *Le Jay*, 45. H. Rahner, S.J., *Saint Ignatius Loyola. Letters to Women* (New York, 1960), 490–91, n. 14.

83. Blaisdell, "Politics and Heresy," 71–73.

84. Ibid., 76. Prat, *Le Jay*, 46. Schurhammer, *Francis Xavier*, 1: 396.

85. Blaisdell, "Politics and Heresy," 77 and n. 32. Ercole by this action broke open a diplomatic hornets' nest. Strong French objection and resistance from Renée were to be expected. But papal intervention in the claim of jurisdiction over the French Protestants who had been arrested challenged Ercole's sovereignty. Tedious and prickly negotiations followed. To protect his sovereignty, Ercole sent the prisoners away from Ferrara to the French ambassador in Venice, who set them free.

86. Rahner, *Saint Ignatius*, 129–30.

87. Joseph Crehan, S.J., "Saint Ignatius and Cardinal Pole," *AHSJ*, 25(1956): 77–78.

88. Schurhammer, *Francis Xavier*, 1:397.

89. Ibid., 1:397. Prat, *Le Jay*, 48.

90. Father Cuthbert, O.S.F.C., *The Capuchins. A Contribution to the History of the Counter-Reformation*, 2 vols. (New York, 1929), 1: 121–22, 124–30.

91. Prat, *Le Jay*, 52.

92. Ibid., 48.

93. *MonBroet*, 495–96.

94. Ibid., 495–96.

95. Ibid., 496.

96. Rahner, *Saint Ignatius*, 130–32.

97. *MonBroet*, 497.

98. Ibid., 497.

99. Ibid., 497–98.

100. Ibid., 492–93.

101. *EppMixt*, 4: 717. *EppXav*, 2:117.

102. Schurhammer, *Francis Xavier*, 1:407–9.

103. Ibid. 1: 420.

104. Ibid. 1:420–21.

105. Ibid., 1:421–25, 429–30.

106. *PolChron*, 1: 69.

107. Schurhammer, *Francis Xavier*, 1: 435–37.

108. Ibid. 1:439. Bangert, *To the Other Towns*, 59.

109. *ConsSJComm*, [605] on 268. Aldama, *Repartiéndose*, 24–31.

110. FN 1:42. Bangert, *To the Other Towns*, 58–59.

111. P. Tacchi-Venturi, S.J., *Storia della Compagnia di Gesù in Italia*, 2 vols. in 4, 2nd edition, (Roma, 1950–51) 2, 1:161–69. Schurhammer, *Francis Xavier*, 1: 445.

112. *MonBroet*, 499–500.

113. Schurhammer, *Francis Xavier*, 1:446–47.

114. Ibid., 1:453, 511.

115. Ibid., 1: 454.

116. Ibid., 1:448–52. Usually historians write about ten participants in these discussions. Several reasons indicate that more than ten participated. First, on two documents signed during the discussions the name Diego de Carceres also appears. *Cons*MHSJ, 1:8, 13; second, in the minutes of the meeting, where the diversity of nationalities is mentioned, the secretary wrote of the Portuguese in the plural form—*galli, alii hispani, alii sabaudi, alii cantabrii*. *Cons*MHSJ, 1:2. Among the first ten companions Simão Rodrigues was the only Portuguese. Therefore, Bartolomeu Ferrão, the other Portuguese in the enlarged group, must have been included among the participants; third, the secretary was Francisco Strada, not one of the original ten. It is difficult to conclude that he was present but did not take part in the discussions; fourth, it is also difficult to believe that the original ten excluded the others from discussions that were designed to determine the lives of all of them.

117. Schurhammer, *Francis Xavier*, 1:454. Schurhammer contends that the editors of the MHSJ and Tacchi-Venturi erred in identifying the secretary as Jean Codure. Ibid., 1:454, n. 14.

118. Bangert, *To the Other Towns*, 63–64.

119. Ibid., 67. The only one besides the original ten companions to sign this formula was Diego de Carceres, who was a master of Paris. The others did not sign, since they were not masters of Paris. Besides, it would have been rash to receive them formally before Pope Paul ratified the *Compañía*. Schurhammer, *Francis Xavier*, 1:458.

120. J. B. Ross, "Gasparo Contarini and His Friends, "*Studies in the Renaissance*, 17 (1970):194, 232. F. Gilbert, "Religion and Politics in the Thought of Gasparo Contarini, "*Action and Contemplation in Early Modern Europe. Essays in Memory of E. H. Harbison* (Princeton, 1969), ed. Theodore K. Rabb and Jerrold E. Seigel, 115–16. On 21 May 1534, in the Great Council of Venice, it was announced that Contarini had been nominated a cardinal. Alvise Mocenigo angrily shouted, "These priests have robbed us of the best gentleman the city has." Contarini himself was stunned. "Why Cardinal? "he said. "I am a counsellor of the government of Venice." 116.

121. Ross, "Gasparo Contarini," 194. Gilbert, "Religion and Politics," 115–16.

122. Ross, "Gasparo Contarini," 232. Schurhammer, *Francis Xavier*, 1:458–65. The text of the First Sketch is translated in full in Ibid., 462–65.

123. Schurhammer, *Francis Xavier*, 1:466–68.

124. Ibid., 466, 466–70.

125. Ibid., 470–72.

126. Ibid., 472–74. *MonBroet*, 385.

127. Dudon, *St. Ignatius of Loyola*, 259–60.

128. Ignatius Loyola, *Constitutions*, 259–60.

129. Ibid., 67–72. David Knowles, *From Pachomius to Ignatius. A Study in the Constitutional History of the Religious Orders* (Oxford, 1966), 6.

130. M. Dortel-Claudot, S.J., *Le Genre de vie extérieur de la Compagnie de Jésus* (Rome, 1971), 14–16. The Theatines, despite their principle of resembling praiseworthy secular priests, seemed more like the traditional canons with their obligation to recite the divine office in choir and care that the liturgy be carried out "appropriately, with order, and becomingly" (*apte, composite et decore*). "The vocation of the Theatine is more that of canon in its character than missionary and apostolic." Ibid., 16 with n. 13.

131. Olin, *The Catholic Reformation*, 193.

132. D. Knowles, *The Religious Orders in England* (Cambridge, 1961), 3:141–56.

133. D. Knowles and D. Obolensky, *The Christian Centuries, II: The Middle Ages* (New York, 1968), 443.

134. Knowles, *From Pachomius to Ignatius*, 62.

135. H.O. Evennett, *The Spirit of the Counter-Reformation* (Cambridge, 1968), 112.

136. *MonBroet*, 265.

137. Ibid., 265–70. The editors of the MHSJ missed an earlier letter of Jay's, sent by him to Jean Codure from Bassano on 5 September 1537. See Schurhammer, *Francis Xavier*, 1:354–55.

138. Schurhammer, *Francis Xavier*, 1:259 with n. 94.

139. *PolChron*, 1:84. Tacchi-Venturi, *Storia*, 2,1:257.

140. *EppCan*, 1:359.

141. *MonBroet*, 265–67.

142. Tacchi-Venturi, *Storia* 2, 1:258.

143. *PolChron*, 1:84.

144. Tacchi-Venturi, *Storia* 2, 1:259.

145. *MonFabri*, 26.

146. Tacchi-Venturi, *Storia*, 2, 1:260.

147. *MonBroet*, 267–68.

148. Ibid., 269.

149. Dudon, *St. Ignatius of Loyola*, 262–63.

150. J. Brodrick translates parts of the ballots in *The Origin of the Jesuits* (New York, 1940), 90–92. Three of the group, Xavier, Rodrigues and Codure, chose Pierre Favre as a second choice. Bangert, *To the Other Towns*, 107–8.

151. P. de Leturia, S.J., "Conspectus chronologicus vitae Sancti Ignatii," *Estudios Ignacianos*, 1:26. *PolChron*, 1:90–91. Dudon identifies the site within St. Paul-Outside-the-Walls as the Chapel of the Crucifix. *St. Ignatius of Loyola*, 263.

152. Tacchi-Venturi, *Storia*, 2, 2: 238.

153. *MonBroet*, 269–70. *PolChron*, 1:92.

154. Tacchi-Venturi, *Storia*, 2,2:238–40. *PolChron*, 1:92.

155. H. O. Evennett, "The Counter-Reformation," in *The Reformation Crisis*, ed. J. Hurstfield (New York: Harper Torchbooks, 1965), 62.

CHAPTER II

1. Prat, *Le Jay*, 98–101. Prat made a strange mistake in identifying the bishop of Aquila. He calls him simply Berardi. The bishop was, in fact, Bernardo Sanzio.

2. Ibid., 101.

3. Ibid., 101.

4. L. von Pastor, *The History of the Popes from the Close of the Middle Ages* (St. Louis, 1891–1953), 12:131–34. *EppIgn*, 1:195. Prat, *Le Jay*, 103–4.

5. *PolChron*, 1:97. *MonFabri*, 140–41.

6. In 1550 Vauchop conducted a fruitful visitation of his entire archdiocese. A year later, he died in Paris as he was preparing to repeat his visit. His name has been spelled in a variety of ways: Wanchop, Wancop, Mancop, Wauchop. Orlandini and Agricola called him Bax. He himself signed his name Vauchop. Prat, *Le Jay*, 105. Schurhammer, *Francis Xavier*, 1:248 with n. 7.

7. Prat, *Le Jay*, 111.

8. Ibid., 107. G. Boero, S.J., *Vita del Servo di Dio P. Claudio Iaio* (Florence, 1878), 41.

9. Prat, *Le Jay*, 113. For the complete text of Morone's letter to Contarini, see Ibid., 451–54.

10. Ibid., 113–14, 455.

11. Ibid., 112. Morone informed Contarini of the assignment in his letter of May 21, 1542. Ibid., 452.

12. *PolChron*, I, 99.

13. Prat, *Le Jay*, 115.

14. Ibid., 117. P. Matheson, *Cardinal Contarini at Regensburg* (Oxford, 1972), p. 63.

15. *MonBroet*, 270.

16. Ibid., 270–71.

17. Ibid., 270–71.

18. Ibid., 272. *PolChron*, 1:99–100.

19. Prat, *Le Jay*, 121, 127. Bangert, *To the Other Towns*, 132.

20. *MonBroet*, 276.

21. Ibid., 273–76.

22. Ibid., 276.

23. Ibid., 274–75.

24. Ibid., 277.

25. Ibid., 275.

26. Ibid., 275–76.

27. Bangert, *To the Other Towns*, 130–33, 138.

28. *MonBroet*, 275–76.

29. Ibid., 274. Bangert, *To the Other Towns*, 90–91.

30. *PolChron*, 1:113.

31. Ibid., 1:113. Prat, *Le Jay*, 129.

32. *MonBroet*, 276.

33. Prat, *Le Jay*, 139.

34. Ibid., 137–39. *PolChron*, 1:113.

35. *MonBroet*, 278.

36. Ibid., 278.

37. Ibid., 278–80.

38. Ibid., 280. B. Duhr, S.J., *Geschichte der Jesuiten in den Ländern Deutscher Zunge* (Freiburg-im-Breisgau, 1907–28), 1:19.

39. Juan Polanco described the work of the first Jesuits in Germany as follows: "Those who were sent to Germany enjoyed a wide range in their work" (*Qui in Germaniam missi sunt, non uno loco versabantur*), *PolChron*, 1:99.

40. *PolChron*, 1:113.

41. *EppCan*, 1:358–59.

42. N. Orlandini, S.J., *Historiae Societatis Jesu Pars Prima* (Cologne, 1615), 108.

43. Prat, *Le Jay*, 140.

44. E. M. Buxbaum, *Petrus Canisius und die Kirchliche Erneuerung des Herzogtums Bayern 1549–1556* (Rome, 1973), 51.

45. Prat, *Le Jay*, 145–47. Boero, *Vita del Servo*, 53–54. *PolChron*, 1:113.

46. Prat, *Le Jay*, 147–48. Boero, *Vita del Servo*, 54–55.

47. G. Pfeilschifter, ed., *Acta Reformationis Catholicae Ecclesiam Germaniae Concernentia Saeculi XVI* (Regensburg, 1959–73), 4:393. Vauchop greatly admired Jay. On April 15, 1544, in a letter to the bishop of Hildescheim, he spoke of Jay as ''the companion in our work, Master Claude Jay, a very devout man, intent on the cause of Christ'' (*comes laboris nostri dns. Claudius Jayus, vir religiossimus et zelosus pro Christo*). Ibid., 4:395.

48. *PolChron*, 1:132. CT, 4:441, n. 2.

49. *PolChron*, 1:132–33.

50. Ibid., 1:133.

51. *MonFabri*, 165.

52. Prat, *Le Jay*, 151–52.

53. Ibid., 165–66. H. Jedin, *A History of the Council of Trent* (London, 1957), 1:490–544.

54. Prat, *Le Jay*, 166.

55. *PolChron*, 1:133.

56. Ibid., 1:133–34.

57. Ibid., 1:134.

58. Ibid., 1:134. Prat, *Le Jay*, 169.

59. *PolChron*, 1:134.

60. Ibid., 1:134–35.

61. Pope Paul III, realizing the importance of Truchsess's presence at Worms, dispensed him from the visit to Rome to receive the red hat, and delegated the Archbishop of Mainz to conduct this ceremony.

62. J. Gretser, S.J., ''Speculum Praesulis ex Verbis Sacrae Scripturae, Canonum et Doctorum, jam olim a R.P. Claudio Jaio,'' *Opera Omnia* (Regensburg, 1734–41), 17:141–58. In this edition of Gretser's works, the text of the *Speculum* takes thirteen and a half pages, in folio and with double columns.

63. Ibid., 17:160. Gretser saw Lippomano's work and hoped that it would be published one day. Gretser also discovered and published a work entitled *Commentariolus de Officio Episcopi*. Ibid., 17:161–78. The manuscript did not carry the name of the author, but Gretser judged it likely that Jay had done the work. The *Commentariolus*, taking seventeen and a half pages, in folio and with double columns, is basically an expanded version of the ideas of the *Speculum Praesulis*.

64. J. Lecuyer, C.S.Sp., ''Episcopat, Moyen Age et Période Moderne,'' *DS*, 4,1:col. 900–901.

65. Prat, *Le Jay*, 172–78. Jedin, *History*, 1:527–28. Pastor, *History*, 12:213–14.

66. Jedin, *History*, 1:527. The Protestants claimed that the council summoned to Trent was not what was promised them: "the Christian council in German Lands."

67. Prat, *Le Jay*, 179.

68. *MonBroet*, 293.

69. Ibid., 293.

70. J. Janssen, *Geschichte des Deutschen Volkes seit dem Ausgang der Mittelalters* (Freiburg-im-Breisgau, 1893–1901), 4:374. The translation of Seibert's critique as given in the English version of Janssen's work is awkward and inaccurate. *History of the German People at the Close of the Middle Ages* (London, 1896–1925), 8:221.

72. J. Brodrick, S.J., *Saint Peter Canisius* (London, 1936), 44–84.

73. *EppCan*, 1:159, 1.

74. Bangert, *To the Other Towns*, 147–48.

75. *EppCan*, 1:159.

76. *PolChron*, 1:154. Prat, *Le Jay*, 188–89.

77. Pastor, *History*, 12:234. Prat, *Le Jay*, 191.

78. Prat, *Le Jay*, 202.

79. *PolChron*, 1:151. *CT*, 4:440–42. Ignatius actually wanted Jay to go to Rome, but he yielded to the desire of Truchsess. *EppIgn*, 1:344–46.

80. *PolChron*, 1:154. *MonBroet*, 292–94.

81. Prat, *Le Jay*, 191–92.

82. Ibid., 193. *PolChron*, 1:154. H. Jedin comments on this religious colloquy of Regensburg that ran concurrently with the early phase of the Council of Trent: "The two theological fronts faced each other in a stiff and even hostile attitude which could at any moment turn into military fronts . . . While the theologians of both parties faced each other in an atmosphere of depression in the town-hall of Ratisbon, and finally separated without having achieved anything, the Emperor set out from the Netherlands for the Rhine, passing through Maastricht, where he received a deputation of the Protestant Estates." Then followed the emperor's bootless talks with Landgrave Philip of Hesse of the League of Schmalkalden. *History of the Council of Trent*, 2:200–202.

83. *MonBroet*, 297–300.

84. *EppIgn*, 1:343.

85. Ibid., 1:343–44.

86. *PolChron*, 1:153–54. Prat, *Le Jay*, 198.

87. *MonPaed*, 1:7*. Ladislaus Lukács, S.J., "De origine collegiorum externorum deque controversiis circa paupertatem obortis 1539–1608," *AHSJ*, 29 (1960):197–99.

88. Lukács, "De origine collegiorum externorum," 199–200. Gandía was the first place where the Jesuits taught lay students within a Jesuit college. This was in 1546. Ibid., 200. *FN*, 2:206–7. Allan P. Farrell, S.J. claims that the first place where Jesuits taught was in Goa, and this in 1543. *The Jesuit Code of Liberal Education. Development and Scope of the Ratio Studiorum* (Milwaukee, 1938), 16, 22 with n. 54. Lukács disagrees, contending that the Jesuits to whom Farrell refers only helped in counselling the Indian boys in 1543 and that not until 1548 did they assume charge of the college in Goa. "De origine collegiorum externorum," 200 with n. 55. Jerónimo Nadal clearly states that the college at Gandía was the first where Jesuits taught lay students. *FN*, 2:206–7. See also G. Ganss, S.J., "The Origins of Jesuit Colleges and the Controversies about their Poverty, 1539–1608," *WL*, 91(1962): 130. This article is a digest, in English, of the article by Lukács.

89. Lukács, "De origine collegiorum externorum," 204–6. Ganss, "The Origins of Jesuit Colleges," 131.

90. *MonBroet*, 286.

91. Ibid., 283. *PolChron*, 1:152.

92. *MonBroet*, 282–83.

93. Ibid., 282–83.

94. This letter is lost but the points made by Ignatius are known through Jay's response of 21 January 1545. *MonPaed*, 1:360 with n. 3.

95. *MonPaed*, 1:359–66. *MonBroet*, 286–91. That Jesuits be lecturers in universities was not in itself novel. Laynez, Favre, Salmerón, and indeed Jay himself already had this experience. But Jay's suggestion carried with it a note of permanence. Conditions in Germany called for a long-range commitment to the classroom, something quite different from the earlier occasional and brief assignments.

96. *MonBroet*, 287–88.

97. Ibid., 287.

98. Ibid., 288.

99. Ibid., 289.

100. Ibid., 289.

101. Ibid., 288.

102. Ibid., 289–90.

103. Ibid., 289–90.

104. Ibid., 291.

105. Ibid., 287.

106. *PolChron*, 1: 152–53.

107. *MonBroet*, 286–91.

CHAPTER III

1. Jedin, *History*, 1:576–77.

2. *CT*, 4:440–42. *PolChron*, 1:154.

3. Jedin, *History*, 2:19–20. Dom Ernest Graf translates *procurator* as *proctor*. In the United States, *proctor* connotes a supervisory function in a school. *Deputy* seems to be more accurate in the context of the council.

4. Ibid., 2:20.

5. Ibid., 2:20. Prat, *Le Jay*, 209–10.

6. Jedin, *History*, 2:20. *Dudum* was issued on 5 December 1545. This brief had unforeseen consequences. The German bishops, who generally did not favor the council, did not go to Trent; nor were they prepared to pay the expenses of deputy who had only a consultative vote. Ibid., 2:20. By 2 February 1546 Michael Helding, the auxiliary bishop of Mainz, was the only German bishop in attendance at Trent. Ibid., 2: 36. See also Prat, *Le Jay*, 211.

7. *CT*, 4:532 with n. 5. Actually another *procurator* was sent to Trent by Truchsess. He was Wolfgang Andreas Rhem von Kotz. For some reason or other he left Trent early. The only German representatives at the council's opening were Bishop Michael Helding, auxiliary of Mainz, his two companions, and Johann Armbuster, the deputy for the bishops of Würzburg and Eichstätt. Jedin, *History*, 1:529. Angelo Massarelli, the secretary of the council, consistently spelled Jay's name as Zaius. *CT*, 1:352 with n. 6.

8. *EncSym*, 363.

9. Yves M-J Congar, O.P., *Tradition and Traditions. An Historical Essay and a Theological Essay* (New York, 1967), 138, 160.

10. *CT* 1:491.

11. Jean-Pierre Massaut, *Josse Clichtove, L'Humanisme et la Réforme du Clergé* (Paris, 1968) 2:412. See 2:326 for Clichtove's influence on the early Jesuits, including Ignatius Loyola. See also James D. Tracy's book review of *Critique et tradition à la veille de la Réform en France. Étude suivie de textes inédits traduits et annotés* by Jean-Pierre Massaut in the *Catholic Historical Review*, 63 (1977): 280–81.

12. *CT* 1:491. Maurice Bévenot "*Traditiones* in the Council of Trent," *The Heythrop Journal*, 4 (1963): 337–38. Johannes Beumer, S.J., "Der Erste Jesuit aus Deutschland auf dem Trienter Konzil P. Claude Jay," *AHSJ* 39 (1970): 174–75.

13. *CO*, 639.

14. Ibid., 639.

15. *CT*, 1:524. In this intervention, Jay suggested that in the listing of the books of the Old Testament the council use the term *liber psalmorum 150* rather than *psalmi davides*, because in this way the doubts about the authorship of the various psalms could be avoided. The council did not follow Jay's proposal and used the term "The Davidic Psalter of 150 Psalms" (*Psalterium Davidicum centum quinquaginta psalmorum*). *CT*, 1:524.

16. Congar, *Tradition and Traditions*, 272–74.

17. Ibid., 272–74. *CO*, 639.

18. *CT*, 5:72–75. This particular question was discussed also the previous day, April 5.

19. Ibid., 5:79.

20. Ibid., 5:79.

21. L. Pascoe, S.J., "The Council of Trent and Bible Study: Humanism and Culture," *Catholic Historical Review*, 52 (1966): 36–37.

22. *CO*, 643–44.

23. Ibid., 746–48.

24. Ibid., 639–41.

25. J. Ratzinger, "The Transmission of Divine Revelation," *Commentary on the Documents of Vatican II*, ed. Herbert Vorgrimler (New York, 1969), 3: 181–84.

26. Jedin, *History*, 2:118. Pascoe, "The Council of Trent," 35.

27. *CT*, 5:105.

28. Ibid., 5:111.

29. Ibid., 5:112.

30. *CO*, 643.

31. *CT*, 5:106, 109–10.

32. Ibid., 5:109. J.H. Overfield, "Scholastic Opposition to Humanism in Pre-Reformation Germany," *Viator. Medieval and Renaissance Studies*, 7 (1976): 392, 419.

33. *CT*, 5:130.

34. Jedin, *History*, 2:104.

35. *CT*, 5:130.

36. Ibid., 5:130.

37. Ibid., 5:106.

38. Ibid., 5:130.

39. Ibid., 5:125.

40. Ibid., 5:130.

41. *CO*, 644.

42. *CT*, 5:151.

43. *CO*, 643–46.

44. *CT*, 5:175, 194, 222. Jedin, *History*, 2:151, 163. This decree had two distinctive traits: a grasp of the teaching of earlier councils, and an appreciation of the contemporary theological concerns of the sixteenth century. Z. Alszeghy, S.J., and M. Flick, S.J., "Il Decreto Tridentino sul Peccato Originale," *Gregorianum*, 52 (1971):595–635.

45. *CT*, 5:175, 194, 203, 222.

46. Jedin, *History*, 2:139–40 with n. 3.

47. *CO*, 643. *EncSym*, 348, 351.

48. E. Villaret, S.J., *Abridged History of the Sodalities of Our Lady* (St. Louis, 1957), 20–22. Bangert, *To the Other Towns*, 56–57.

49. Jedin, *History*, 2:166.

50. J. Wicks, S.J., "Martin Luther's Treatise on Indulgences," *TheolSt*, 28 (1967): 513 with n. 78.

51. Ibid., 513 with n. 79.

52. Jedin, *History*, 2:169.

53. D. Fenlon, *Heresy and Obedience in Tridentine Italy. Cardinal Pole and the Counter Reformation* (Cambridge, 1972), 34–35.

54. Matheson, *Cardinal Contarini*, 93.

55. Ibid., 107–09.

56. Ibid., 174–75.

57. Jedin, *History*, 2:172.

58. Fenlon, *Heresy and Obedience*, 46. Pole went to Viterbo in 1541. Juan de Valdes died in Naples in July of the same year. Some of Valdes's disciples went to Viterbo after his death. "In Viterbo Valdensianism, Lutheranism and the Reformation in general met for the first time and mingled on Italian soil." J.C. Nieto, *Juan de Valdes and the Origins of the Spanish and Italian Reformation* (Geneva, 1970), 149.

59. Fenlon, *Heresy and Obedience*, 25.

60. M. W. Anderson, "Trent and Justification (1546): A Protestant Reflection," *Scottish Journal of Theology*, 21 (1968): 387.

61. Evennett, *Spirit of the Counter-Reformation*, 29.

62. Ignatius Loyola, *The Spiritual Exercises*, 160–61.

63. Evennett, *Spirit of the Counter-Reformation*, 40. For a recent evaluation of the relations between the *spirituali* and the Jesuits, see J. O'Malley, S.J., "The Jesuits, St. Ignatius, and the Counter Reformation. Some Recent

Studies and Their Implications for Today,'' *Studies in the Spirituality of Jesuits*, 14 (1982):19–25.

64. Matheson, *Cardinal Contarini*, 153.

65. Philip McNair, *Peter Martyr in Italy. An Anatomy of Apostasy* (Oxford, 1967), 283.

66. Fenlon, *Heresy and Obedience*, 52.

67. O. M. T. Logan, "Grace and Justification: Some Italian Views of the Sixteenth and Early Seventeenth Centuries," *Journal of Ecclesiastical History*, 20 (1969):70.

68. James Kelsey McConica, *English Humanists and Reformation Politics under Henry VIII and Edward VI* (Oxford, 1965), 17–18, 26–27.

69. *CT*, 1:88, 443; 5:330.

70. Fenlon, *Heresy and Obedience*, 134–35.

71. *CT*, 5:366, 465, 484–85.

72. Ibid., 5:409.

73. Ibid., 5:330. In this intervention, Jay adopted St. Thomas's approach to the process of justification, which states that the sanctification of the soul precedes the remission of sins. This position placed him in opposition to the formidable Girolamo Seripandc, who held that God sanctifies man after he has forgiven man his sins. Hubert Jedin, *Papal Legate at the Council of Trent. Cardinal Seripando* (St. Louis, 1947), 331–32.

74. *CT*, 5:330.

75. Ibid., 5:366.

76. Jedin, *History*, 2:172–73, 253–58.

77. Ibid., 2:258–59.

78. *CT*, 5:485.

79. Jedin, *History*, 2:255–56.

80. Ibid., 256–57. In this work, Jedin changed his earlier judgment that no one at Trent did more than Laynez to achieve the defeat of the *duplex justitia* theory. *Papal Legate*, 372–73. Laynez approached the issue with Aristotelian categories and consequently found it "nearly impossible" to have grasped the Augustinian explanation of *duplex justitia*. Carl E. Maxcey, "Double Justice, Diego Laynez, and the Council of Trent," *Church History*, 48 (1979): 277–78.

81. John W. O'Malley, S.J., "Thomas More's Spirituality Compared," *Thought*, 52 (1977):321–22.

82. Jedin, *History*, 2:309.

83. Ibid.

84. *CO*, 647.

85. Evennett, *Spirit of the Counter-Reformation*, 31–32.

86. Léon Cristiani, *Histoire de L'Église*, 16: *L'Église à L'Époque du Concile de Trent*, 73.

87. Jedin, *History*, 2:345.

88. Ibid., 2:317–18 with n. 1.

89. *CT*, 5:215.

90. Jedin, *History*, 2:372–73.

91. *MonBroet*, 333. *PolChron*, 1:182.

92. Jedin, *History*, 2:370.

93. Ibid., 2:370.

94. *CT*, 5:836, 935. Beumer, "Der Erster Jesuit aus Deutschland," 175–76.

95. *CO*, 661.

96. *CT*, 5:990.

97. Jedin, *History*, 2:391.

98. *EppCan*, 1:206–7. The autograph of Jay's letter has not been found. A number of copies exist. They vary somewhat in wording, but the sense is the same. Braunsberger gives the copy made by Jakob Keller, S.J. Ibid. 1:206.

99. *MonBroet*, 386–88.

100. Ibid., 389.

101. J. Brodrick, S.J., *The Progress of the Jesuits* (New York, 1947), 39.

102. *MonBroet*, 307.

103. Ibid., 305, 307–09, 314–15, 322.

104. Ibid., 305.

105. Ibid., 311.

106. Brodrick, *Progress of the Jesuits*, 39.

107. *MonBroet*, 390–91.

108. Ibid., 391–92.

109. Ibid., 313.

110. Ibid., 312–16.

111. Ibid., 317.

112. Prat calls Trieste "a hotbed of error, indeed a bulwark of heresy" (*un foyer d'erreurs, et même un des boulevards de l'herésie*), *Le Jay*, 238.

113. Ibid., 238.

114. Ibid., 240. *MonBroet*, 106.

115. *MonBroet*, 323.

116. Ibid., 313–14.

117. Ibid., 314–15.

118. Orlandini, *Historiae Societatis Jesu Pars Prima*, 1:391.

119. *MonBroet*, 318–19, 327–29.

120. Ibid., 329–32.

121. Ibid., 326.

122. Tacchi-Venturi, *Storia*, 2, 2:92.

123. Ibid., 2, 2:95.

124. Ibid., 2, 2:95–96.

125. Ibid., 2, 2:96. Ignatius, through Jerónimo Nadal, wrote to King Ferdinand and recited basically the same arguments he presented to Pope Paul. *MonNad*, 1:50–53.

126. Tacchi-Venturi, *Storia*, 2, 2:97.

127. Rahner, *Saint Ignatius*, 75.

128. Ibid., 83–84. Tacchi-Venturi, *Storia*, 2, 2:97–99.

129. Tacchi-Venturi, *Storia*, 2, 2:98–101.

130. *MonBroet*, 392–93.

131. Ibid., 317.

132. Rahner, *Saint Ignatius*, 435.

133. *EppIgn*, 1:435.

134. *MonBroet*, 317.

135. Tacchi- Venturi, *Storia*, 2, 2:100.

136. *MonNad*, 2:3. Fr. Bartolomeu Ferrão wrote a seven-page letter to Fr. Miguel Torres on 2 March 1547, describing the steps taken by Ignatius in this affair. *EppIgn*, 1:460–67.

137. Prat, *Le Jay*, 247–49. *MonNad*, 1:51.

138. P. H. Hallett, *Catholic Reformer. A Life of St. Cajetan of Thiene* (Westminster, Md., 1959), viii.

139. Brodrick, *Saint Peter Canisius*, 85–86, 96.

140. Jedin, *History*, 2:434–35.

141. Ibid., 2:435. H. Jedin, *Ecumenical Councils of the Catholic Church* (New York, 1960), 164–65.

142. *CT*, 4:116 with n. 11. *PolChron*, 1:215.

143. *EppMixt*, 1:356–57. *PolChron*, 1:215.

144. *PolChron*, 1:215.

145. Ibid., 1:215–16. *CT*, 6:69 with n. 2; 116 with n. 11. *MonLain*, 1:55–56.

146. *PolChron*, 1:216. *MonSalm*, 1:38.

147. *MonSalm*, 1:38.

148. *MonLain*, 1:58. *PolChron*, 1:216. *CT*, 6:84 with n. 1.

149. *MonSalm*, 1:28–30. *PolChron*, 1:179.

150. *EppIgn*, 1:387.

151. Ibid., 1:386–89.

152. *CT*, 6:15.

153. Ibid., 6:116 with n. 11. *PolChron*, 1:216.

154. Jedin, *Papal Legate*, 421.

155. *CT*, 6:116–17.

156. *CO*, 731–35.

157. *CT*, 6:116–17. Jay erred in his identification of the pope who excommunicated Lothair. It was Nicholas I. When he spoke of children as an end of marriage, Jay, it seems, must have meant the education as well as the propagation of children, an end that polygamy makes abnormally difficult to attain. The terse records of the council at his point simply say "children." From the context, it is reasonable to conclude that Jay intended to include the education of children, and that indeed he so spoke in the council.

158. Ibid., 6:58–60.

159. Ibid., 6:277. Beumer, "Der Erster Jesuit aus Deutschland," 179.

160. R. E. McNally, S.J., "The Counter-Reformation Views of Sin and Penance," *Thought*, 52 (1977): 152. Fr. McNally points out that Josef Lortz held the view that theological fogginess compounded by religious ignorance was "the one cause that made the Reformation possible." Ibid., 152, n. 4. *CO*, 688.

161. *CT*, 6:336–38.

162. *EppMixt*, 1:351–52.

163. Ibid., 1:356–57.

164. Ibid., 1:393–94. Jay was loved not only in Germany. Ignatius had been briefed on how Jay had won the love of others at Trent. *EppIgn*, 1:376, 381–82.

165. Prat, *Le Jay*, 272.

166. Ibid., 273–74. *PolChron*, 1:224.

167. *PolChron*, 1:224–25.

168. *MonLain*, 1:58.

169. *MonBroet*, 395. *PolChron*, 1:224.

170. *CT*, 6:116–17 with n. 11.

171. Ibid., 6:116–117 with n. 11. *EppIgn*, 1:568–70.

172. *EppIgn*, 1:568–70. Prat, *Le Jay*, 278–79.

173. Prat, *Le Jay*, 279.

CHAPTER IV

1. *MonBroet*, 336.

2. Ibid., 336, 338 with n. 3.

3. Ibid., 336.

4. Ibid., 338 with n. 8. D. Bartoli, S.J., *Dell'istoria della Compagnia di Giesu. L'Italia* (Rome, 1673), 3: chapter 10, and J-M. Prat. S.J., in *Le Jay*, 282–83, give a picture of a cordial prince extending a warm and magnanimous welcome to the visiting Jesuit. They also tell of a pious argument between Ercole, urging Jay to live in the castello, and Jay, insisting that he take shelter in the hospital. These stories do not mesh with Jay's personal reports. *MonBroet*, 338 with n. 8. Yet Polanco reports that Jay was received by Ercole "politely" (*humaniter*). *PolChron*, 1:225.

5. *MonBroet*, 338.

6. Ibid., 339. *PolChron*, 1:278.

7. *MonBroet*, 240.

8. Tacchi-Venturi, *Storia*, 2, 2:255.

9. Ibid., 2, 2:255. *PolChron*, 1:278.

10. *PolChron*, 1:406–7 with n. 1 on 407.

11. *MonBroet*, 341 with n. 2. Rahner, *Saint Ignatius Loyola*, 188–89.

12. *MonBroet*, 341 with n. 2.

13. Ibid., 341. In several letters from Ferrara, Jay used a modified kind of hieroglyphic writing. He referred to certain persons by symbols. For example, ⟨W⟩ meant Lanfranco del Gesso; ⟩ or ⟨ meant Jay himself; ▽ meant Princess Renée. What Jay meant by ⌣ is unknown. Why he resorted to these devices is not clear. He may have been afraid that his correspondence might be intercepted by officials of Ferrara, or elsewhere. *MonBroet*, 337–38 with nn. 2–7.

14. Tacchi-Venturi, *Storia*, 2, 2:257–58. This legislation of 1549 may have been part of Ercole's duel with the Holy See on the issue of religious jurisdiction in Ferrara. The creation of the Congregation of the Inquisition in 1542 by Pope Paul III and the Vatican's determination to replace Ferrara's local inquisition with a tribunal responsible to Rome threatened Ercole's autonomy. Despite Ercole's coup against the Protestants in 1536, they continued, with his knowledge, to infiltrate the Estense domain. In some diplomatic circles, people questioned Ercole's ability to be master in his own house. This legislation conceivably was a show of force employed by Ercole to dissolve doubts about his capacity to rule and to prove that he held the reins of government. By 1553 Ercole feared Rome's intervention against the Protestants and Rome's scrutiny of his own orthodoxy. In late summer 1554 Ercole demanded that Renée abjure heresy. By the end of September, Renée confessed and attended mass. At this

point Jesuits entered deeper into the Estense story, but beyond the dates of Jay's life. Blaisdell, ''Politics and Heresy,'' 85–87.

15. *MonBroet*, 351. Polanco has a tantalizingly brief record of an incident at Ferrara. ''The duke wanted Jay to be present at the trial of a heretic then in session. The heretic was punished severely enough.'' Polanco gives not a word about Jay's reaction. *PolChron*, 1:407.

16. *PolChron*, 1:272–73.

17. *MonRib*, 1:50. Prat, *Le Jay*, 288–89.

18. *PolChron*, 1:406–07.

19. Ibid., 1:406–7.

20. Ibid., 1:278, 411. Polanco wrote: Cum de reductione Ducessae ad Catholicam religionem spes fere nulla affulgeret, non tanta spiritualis messis Ferrarae quanta in Germania ad Dei gloriam fore sperabatur. *PolChron*, 1:411.

21. See chapter two. Jay lectured in Ingolstadt from the early summer of 1543 to the spring of 1544.

22. Buxbaum, *Petrus Canisius*, 51.

23. Ibid., 50.

24. *MonBroet*, 286.

25. Buxbaum, *Petrus Canisius*, 57 with n. 134.

26. Ibid., 57 with n. 134. Jay's insistence with the bishops whom he knew was shown in chapter two.

27. Ibid., 58.

28. Ibid., 59.

29. Ibid., 60 with n. 142 on 61. Pankratius Sinzenhofer had died on June 25, 1548.

30. Ibid., 62 with n. 148. In Duke Wilhelm's correspondence on this episode, there is not a word about the Society of Jesus. Yet there can be no doubt that Schweicker introduced Jay's name. Ibid., 62 with n. 148. *PolChron* 1:410. A year and a half earlier, in late 1547 or early 1548, Truchsess wrote Ignatius and Cardinal Farnese, insisting that Jay return to Germany so that he might found a college. Truchsess's plea could not be honored immediately, since Jay was then engaged in Ferrara. *EppIgn*, 1:670.

31. *PolChron*, 1:411.

32. *CT*, 1:856 with n. 5 and n. 7, 859 with n. 2.

33. Ibid., 1:48 with n. 4. *EppIgn*, 1:685–86. *PolChron*, 1:491–92.

34. *MonSalm*, 1:85–86. *EppCan*, 1:685. *PolChron*, 1:492.

35. *EppIgn*, 1:386–89.

36. Ibid., 12:239–47.

37. Buxbaum, *Petrus Canisius*, 67.

38.   *PolChron*, 1:414. The chancellor should not be confused with the famous theologian Johannes Eck, who was dead six years.

39.   Ibid., 1:411.

40.   Buxbaum, *Petrus Canisius*, 85–86.

41.   *EppCan*, 1:307.

42.   *MonBroet*, 345–47.

43.   Ibid., 345–48.

44.   Ibid., 348.

45.   Ibid., 348–49.

46.   Buxbaum, *Petrus Canisius*, 251.

47.   Ibid., 128. About this time, Schweicker communicated to Cardinal Farnese his gratitude for the three Jesuits who were at Ingolstadt. Ibid., 255–56.

48.   Ibid., 252–53.

49.   Ibid., 128.

50.   Ibid., 86 with n. 13.

51.   Ibid., 87 with n. 16.

52.   Brodrick, *Saint Peter Canisius*, 139.

53.   *EppCan*, 1:323–27.

54.   Ibid., 1:326. The authorities of the university recognized in the lives of the three Jesuits the seal of *eruditio pia* and *pietas erudita*. They wrote an inscription that included the following phrases:

Quorum singularis in sacrosanctis

Studiis scientia tum in omnibus disciplinis

Exercitatio postrema sanctimonia vitae

Expectationem omnium eamque maximam

Non solum aequat verum etiam superat.

Prat, *Le Jay*, 487.

55.   H. O. Evennett, *The Cardinal of Lorraine and the Council of Trent* (Cambridge, 1930), 26.

56.   *MonBroet*, 351–52. *PolChron*, 2:72. Buxbaum, *Petrus Canisius*, 259 with nn. 1 and 2.

57.   *PolChron*, 2:66.

58.   Buxbaum, *Petrus Canisius*, 69 with n. 3.

59.   Ibid., 110 with n. 24. Wolf later wrote to Jay of his enduring friendship with the Society. Ibid., 111 with n. 37.

60.   *PolChron*, 2:66–67. *EppCan*, 1:331–33.

61.   *MonBroet*, 352.

62.   Brodrick, *Saint Peter Canisius*, 151.

63. *PolChron*, 2:72. Jay had the impression that the mission of Salmerón, Canisius, and himself to Ingolstadt was meant to be temporary and not of long duration. Ibid., 2:72.

64. *MonBroet*, 360–61.

65. Ibid., 360–61. Jesuits continued to be confused with the Theatines. In the records of the university for 1550–51, the following entry was made: Petrus Scorichius, Magister Artium Coloniensis studiosus theologiae theatinus. Ibid., 359 with n. 6.

66. Ibid., 364.

67. Ibid., 364.

68. Ibid., 350.

69. Rahner, *Saint Ignatius Loyola*, 188–89. In 1573 the fourth Jesuit general, Everard Mercurian, told Donna Maria of the Society's debt to her "because you have always been a mother to us." The two Jesuits whom Ignatius sent to Ferrara after Jay's departure for Germany were Frenchmen, Paschase Broët and Jean Pelletier. No doubt Ignatius had the Duchess Renée in mind. Ibid., 188–89.

70. K. Brandi, *The Emperor Charles V* (London: Jonathan Cape Paperback, 1965), 590–600.

71. Janssen, *History*, 6:428–29. Pastor, *History*, 13:83–84, 91.

72. *MonBroet*, 354–55.

73. Ibid., 354–55.

74. Ibid., 357–58. The text of this folder is lost. *MonPaed*, 1:392 with n. 2.

75. *MonBroet*, 362.

76. Ibid., 356.

77. Prat, *Le Jay*, 470.

78. Ibid., 471–72.

79. *MonBroet*, 362.

80. *EppCan*, 1:343–44.

81. *MonPaed*, 1:392–94.

82. S. Kuttner, "Papal Efforts Toward Protestant Representation at Trent," *The Review of Politics*, 10 (1948): 433. Pastor, *History*, 13:85. Brandi, *Emperor Charles V*, 596–97. Janssen, *History*, 6:432–33.

83. Kuttner, "Papal Efforts," 434. Jedin, *Ecumenical Councils*, 166–67. R. E. McNally, S.J., "The Council of Trent and the German Protestants," *TheolSt*, 25 (1964): 18–20.

84. *EppCan*, 1:359–60 with n. 4 on 360.

85. Ibid., 1:359–60. The first Jesuits opposed Luther's theology, but they did not expend their literary efforts in polemics against him. In a survey of the

literature by Luther's contemporary Catholic critics, a scholar included not a single Jesuit author. This meshes with the eirenic approach so strongly pronounced in the persons of Favre and Jay. J. P. Dolan, "Some Catholic Literary Opponents of Luther," *Journal of Ecumenical Studies*, 11 (1974): 447–65. Some later Jesuits did not follow the example of Favre and Jay. Jerónimo Nadal had some hard things to say about Luther and the Protestants.

86. *EppCan*, 1:360 with n. 4.

87. Bangert, *To the Other Towns*, 88–89.

88. *EppCan*, 1:360 with n. 4.

89. Ibid.

90. A decade earlier, Cardinal Contarini at the abortive Diet of Regensburg of 1541 admitted this situation when he spoke of the Catholic church as a beleaguered fortress that faced a long and hard struggle. Matheson, *Cardinal Contarini*, 163. See also 109.

91. *MonBroet*, 357. A week later, on September 18, Jay again wrote Ignatius of his "meagre talent." Ibid., 364.

92. *PolChron*, 2:264.

93. Ibid., 2:265.

94. Ibid.

95. Ibid.

96. Ibid., 2:266. Polanco identifies the monastery as that of Ottobeuren. The editors of MHSJ, however, note that there was no monastery of that name within a two-day radius of Augsburg. Ibid., with n. 1.

97. *MonBroet*, 352. Jay's description of Truchsess differs from that of James Brodrick, who listed the several titles that the cardinal enjoyed: Protector of the German Nation, Bishop of Augsburg, Prince of the Empire, Count Consistorial of the Emperor, Provost of the Cathedral of Würzburg and of the collegiate church of Ellwangen, Canon Cantor of the Cathedral of Speyer. "As if that were not enough, he had set his heart on being Provost of the Cathedral of Freising also. For some reason, he received in addition to his other stipends an annual pension of five thousand gold pieces from the Archdiocese of Toledo . . . . Despite the remarkable influence of Lejay and St. Peter [Canisius] himself on him, he had obviously not yet thoroughly reformed." *Saint Peter Canisius*, 356 with nn. 1 and 2.

98. *PolChron*, 2:266.

99. Ibid.

CHAPTER V

1. *PolChron*, 2:267. Janssen, *History*, 2:60–61. Enea Silvio Piccolomini, before he became Pope Pius II, wrote a vivid description of

Vienna's beauty and affluence. See J. B. Ross and M. M. McLaughlin, ed., *Portable Renaissance Reader* (New York, 1953), 208–11.

    2.   Brodrick, *Saint Peter Canisius*, 170–71. In the nearby diocese of Passau, there were 254 parishes without the mass and the sacraments. Brodrick, *Progress of the Jesuits*, 158.

    3.   *MonBroet*, 371. *PolChron*, 2:274.

    4.   Orlandini, *Historiae Societatis Jesu Pars Prima*, 1:347.

    5.   *PolChron*, 2:267. According to an earlier account of the Jesuits' arrival in Vienna, the Dominicans gave the Jesuits a cordial welcome. This was not so. See Brodrick, *Saint Peter Canisius*, 172.

    6.   *PolChron*, 2:267. Which of Ignatius's brothers died in battle against the Turks is not known.

    7.   Ibid., 2:267.

    8.   *EppIgn*, 2:401–2.

    9.   *PolChron*, 2:268–69.

    10.   Ibid., 2:269.

    11.   *MonBroet*, 371.

    12.   *PolChron*, 2:268.

    13.   Ibid., 2:268.

    14.   Ibid., 2:270.

    15.   *MonBroet*, 379–80.

    16.   Ibid., 374 with n. 5. *EppCan*, 1:380. *PolChron*, 2:568.

    17.   *MonBroet*, 374.

    18.   Ibid., 374.

    19.   *EppCan*, 1:380.

    20.   *MonBroet*, 375.

    21.   *PolChron*, 2:270.

    22.   Ibid., 2:271.

    23.   Orlandini, *Historiae Societatis Jesu Pars Prima*, 1:391.

    24.   *EppCan*, 1:407–8.

    25.   *PolChron*, 2:271.

    26.   *MonBroet*, 370.

    27.   Ibid., 370.

    28.   Ibid., 370. *PolChron*, 2:271.

    29.   *MonPaed*, 1:400–405.

    30.   Ibid., 1:404–5.

    31.   *ConsSJComm*, [623] on 275–76.

32. *MonBroet*, 378.

33. *PolChron*, 2:272–73.

34. Ibid., 2:273.

35. *EppCan*, 1:329 with n. 1.

36. *PolChron*, 2:275–76.

37. *MonBroet*, 373–74.

38. *PolChron*, 2:564.

39. *MonPaed*, 1:405–8. Prat, *Le Jay*, 375.

40. *MonBroet*, 367–68.

41. Ibid., 368–69.

42. *EppIgn*, 3:328–31.

43. Ibid., 3:328–31.

44. *MonPaed*, 1:405–8.

45. Ibid., 1:406–7.

46. *PolChron*, 2:564.

47. Ibid., 2:564.

48. Prat, *Le Jay*, 479–80.

49. *PolChron*, 2:564–65. Brodrick, *Saint Peter Canisius*, 166–67.

50. *PolChron*, 2:564.

51. Ibid., 2:564–65.

52. Brodrick, *Saint Peter Canisius*, 285. Although Jay was dead three years, he deserves to be regarded as the founder of the Jesuit college at Ingolstadt. Buxbaum, *Petrus Canisius*, 123.

53. *PolChron*, 2:565–66.

54. Ibid., 2:565–68. Brodrick, *Saint Peter Canisius*, 171.

55. *MonPaed*, 1:542.

56. Lukács, "De origine collegiorum externorum," 241.

57. *MonPaed*, 1:542 with n. 42.

58. *EppCan*, 1:415–16.

59. Ibid., 1:471. *PolChron*, 2:571. Prat, *Le Jay*, 482–83.

60. Prat, *Le Jay*, 419. *PolChron*, 2:571–72.

61. Brodrick, *Saint Peter Canisius*, 178 with n. 2.

62. Prat, *Le Jay*, 419–20.

63. Jay was then only about fifty years old.

64. *EppCan*, 1:406.

65. Farrell, *Jesuit Code*, 433.

66. L. von Ranke, *The History of the Popes, Their Church and State and Especially of Their Conflicts with Protestantism in the Sixteenth and Seventeenth Centuries* (London, 1847–48) 1:415–17. When he made this judgment, von Ranke had no intention of expressing admiration for the Society. He continued: "When any new intellectual movement has exercised its influence on mankind, this had always been effected by great and imposing personal qualities, or by the overpowering force of new ideas; but in this case the effect was accomplished without any extraordinary display of mental effort." Ibid., 417.

67. W. V. Bangert, S.J. *A History of the Society of Jesus* (St. Louis, 1972), 71.

68. S. d'Irsay, *Histoire des Universités Françaises et Etrangères* (Paris, 1933) 1:345–46.

69. *EppCan*, 1:740–41.

CHAPTER VI

1. J. Brodrick, S.J., *Saint Ignatius Loyola. The Pilgrim Years.* (London, 1956), 168–79.

2. P. Ribadeneyra, S.J., "La Vida del Padre Ignacio de Loyola," in *FN*, 4:230. G. Boero, S.J,. *Vita del Servo di Dio P. Alfonso Salmerone* (Firenze, 1880), 6. C. Gutierrez, S.J., in his *Españoles en Trento* (Valladolid, 1951) cites Bartolomé Alcázar, S.J., who wrote in his *Chronology of the Society of Jesus in the Province of Toledo* (1710) that Salmerón was twelve years old when he went to Alcalá, 55 with n. 75. Alcázar is not a reliable authority. Bangert, *A History of the Society of Jesus*, 292. Candido de Dalmases, S.J., has assured me in a personal letter that the exact year of Salmerón's enrollment remains unknown after careful research by modern scholars.

3. *MonSalm*, 1:v–vi.

4. *Cons*MHSJ, 1:cxxix and cxxxi. *FN*, 4:942. His brother Didacus entered the Society of Jesus, but he died early, in 1545. In his correspondence Alfonso never refers to Didacus. Antonio Araoz, recalling a trip he made to Spain, mentioned that he had visited Salmerón's mother and sisters. He did not, however, give the number of the sisters. *FN*, 4:942.

5. Pedro Ribadeneyra, S.J., "La Vida y Muerte del Padre Alfonso de Salmerón," *Historias de la Contrarreforma* (Madrid, 1945), 587.

6. D'Irsay, *Histoire des Universités*, 1:331–33.

7. Marcel Bataillon, *Erasme et L'Espagne, Recherches sur l'Histoire Spirituelle du XVIe Siècle* (Paris, 1937), 49. It is notable that the translator was a layman. Ibid, 49.

8. Ibid., 49. This was a revision of Santa Maria's work.

9. Ibid., 47.

10.   J.H. Elliott, *Imperial Spain 1469–1716* (Mentor Book Edition. (London, 1963), 101–2.

11.   Ibid., 101.

12.   Ibid., 102.

13.   Ibid., 126.

14.   A. Jimenez, *Seleccion y Reforma. Ensayo sobre la Universidad Renacentista Española* (Mexico City, 1944), 96.

15.   Ibid., 99–101. B. Hall, "The Trilingual College of San Ildefonso and the Making of the Complutensian Bible," *Studies in Church History*, Vol. 5, *The Church and Academic Learning*, ed. G.L. Cuming (Leiden, 1969), 121–22.

16.   Jimenez, *Seleccion y Reforma*, 101–2. Hall, "Trilingual College," 123.

17.   Jimenez, *Seleccion y Reforma*, 101, 122–23.

18.   C. M. Ajo G. y Sáinz de Zuñiga, *Historia de las Universidades Hispanicas. Orígines y desarrollo desde aparición a nuestros días* (Avila, 1958), 2:304.

19.   Jimenez, *Seleccion y Reforma*, 113–14. Hall, "Trilingual College," 134.

20.   Jimenez, *Seleccion y Reforma*, 130. Bataillon, *Erasme et L'Espagne*, 28.

21.   Bataillon, *Erasme et L'Espagne*, 77–78.

22.   Elliott, *Imperial Spain*, 158.

23.   Ibid., 158.

24.   T. O'Reilly, "Saint Ignatius and Spanish Erasmianism," *AHSJ*, 43 (1974): 301–2.

25.   Ibid., 301–2.

26.   Ribadeneyra, "La Vida y Muerte del Padre Alfonso de Salmerón," 587.

27.   Ibid., 587–88. As indicated in n. 2, above, Salmerón may have been among the first students at the Colegio Trilingüe when it opened in 1528, but the precise date of Salmerón's arrival at Alcalá is not known.

28.   Ibid., 587.

29.   *MonSalm*, 2:818.

30.   Ibid., 2:818.

31.   *FN*, 2:565.

32.   A. Salmerón, S.J., *Commentarii in evangelicam historiam, et in Acta Apostolorum: nunc primum in lucem editi* (Cologne, 1612) 1:4.

33.   Ibid., 1:6.

34. Ibid., 1:4.

35. Schurhammer, *Francis Xavier*, 1:203–4.

36. *MonSalm*, 2:734. F. Cereceda, S.J. *Diego Laínez en la Europa religiosa de su tiempo* (Madrid, 1945–46), 1:49–51.

37. Schurhammer, *Francis Xavier*, 1:204.

38. Ibid., 1:205. Pedro Ribadeneyra, "Vida del Maestro Diego Laínez," *Historias de la Contrarreforma*, 460–61. M. Scaduto, S.J., *Storia della Compagnia di Gesù in Italia*, vol. 3, *L'Epoca di Giacomo Lainez. Il Governo 1556–1565* (Rome, 1964), 126 (hereafter cited as *Storia: Lainez*).

39. Schurhammer, *Francis Xavier*, 1:155–58.

40. Ibid., 1:172 with n. 189.

41. Ibid., 1:185–87.

42. Ibid., 1:205.

43. *MonSalm*, 1:571–72. Bobadilla also received his master's degree under Francis Xavier. Schurhammer, *Francis Xavier*, 1:269 with n. 197.

44. *MonSalm*, 1:572–73.

45. Schurhammer, *Francis Xavier*, 1:254–55.

46. Salmerón, *Commentarii*, 1:330.

47. Ibid.

48. Ibid.

49. Ibid., 1:338.

50. Ibid., 1:335–36.

51. Ibid., 1:336.

52. Schurhammer, *Francis Xavier*, 1:162–63 with n. 119. Bernard-Maitre, "Calvin et Loyola," 78–79.

53. Dudon, "Sur un texte inédit de Salmerón," 416.

54. Ibid.

55. Rice, *Prefatory Epistles*, xx. Salmerón, *Commentarii*, 1:15, 329. To set off *sapientia* against *scientia* within the context of the Renaissance and the Reformation is a chancy business. It demands riding the rapids of constantly changing meanings in terminology. Through the centuries *sapientia*, for example, took on various shades of significance. For Lefèvre, *sapientia* was the Word of God. This was the essence of his theology. Rice, *Renaissance Idea of Wisdom*, 144. See also chapter one, n. 56, of the portrait of Claude Jay. Within Lefèvre's brand of theology lay a latent hostility to human reason, a hostility that John Colet made explicit: "Human reason is the enemy and opponent of grace." Rice, *Renaissance Idea of Wisdom*, 126–27. Salmerón, on the other hand, by his respect for scholastic dialectics, paid tribute to the human reason and what it can achieve, cooperating with God's grace, in the grasp of revelation. Lefèvre's *sapientia* is here aptly set off against Salmerón's *scientia*.

56. Rice, *Prefatory Epistles*, xxiii–xxiv.

57. Rouquette, "Ignace de Loyola," 25.

58. Salmerón, *Commentarii*, 13:57.

59. Ibid.

60. Ozment, *The Reformation in Medieval Perspective*, 7–8.

61. Salmerón, *Commentarii*, 13:57. Diogo de Gouvea, when he scored Erasmus's criticism of St. Jerome, used the expression: "Erasmus laid the egg; Luther hatched it. Would to God that the chicken be choked and the eggs broken." Gouvea was quoting a German Franciscan. Schurhammer, *Francis Xavier*, 1:135. Salmerón's harsh judgment on Erasmus is but one of hundreds, perhaps thousands, of opinions advanced about the Dutch humanist through four centuries. These opinions run through the gamut from censure to praise. H. de Lubac, S.J., has assembled some of the widely diverse opinions that have been aired since the middle of the nineteenth century. *Exégèse Médiévale. Les Quatre Sens de L'Écriture*. 2 vols. 2 parts in each vol. (Paris, 1959–64), 2, 2:454–87. This is not the place to sort out these opinions. But Salmerón's voice should be recognized as one in the continuing cacophony about Erasmus.

62. Salmerón, *Commentarii*, 14:215.

63. Ibid.

64. J.M. Granero, S.J., *San Ignacio de Loyola. Panoramas de su Vida* (Madrid, 1967), 244–45.

65. T. O'Reilly, "Saint Ignatius Loyola," 311.

66. Ibid., 302–3. These incidents at Barcelona and Alcalá are honeycombed with vexing historical problems. Dr. John Olin, for example, judges that Iñigo did not read the *Enchiridion* at Barcelona, and suggests that Pedro Ribadeneyra fabricated the story in his *Vita Ignatii Loyolae* in order to put Iñigo securely on the side of orthodoxy in the latter part of the sixteenth century, when Erasmus had fallen into disrepute with the Roman authorities. See his "Erasmus and St. Ignatius Loyola" in *Luther, Erasmus and the Reformation. A Catholic-Protestant Reappraisal* (New York, 1969), which he edited, 116–22. For a different interpretation of the same sources, see R. Garcia-Villoslada, S.J., *Loyola y Erasmo. Dos Almas, dos Epocas* (Madrid, 1965), 50, 244–53. T. O'Reilly in his "Saint Ignatius Loyola," indicates much of the literature on this prickly point, 303–4. More recently he pushes on with Dr. Olin's opinion that Pedro Ribadeneyra, in his life of Ignatius, doctored a number of the facts in the episode of Ignatius's rejection of Erasmus's *Enchiridion*. Dr. O'Reilly carries his study through Ignatius's Rules for Thinking with the Church to the conclusion that Ignatius was not quite so anti-Erasmian as has been traditionally assumed. He shows, for example, that Ignatius in the 1520s and 1530s moved in circles that favored Erasmus. "Erasmus, Ignatius Loyola and Orthodoxy," *Journal of Theological Studies*, 30 (1979): 118–20, 125–27. Ten years after his "Erasmus and St. Ignatius Loyola," Dr. John Olin reworked that essay and continued the

scholarly debate on Ignatius's response to Erasmus. "Erasmus and St. Ignatius Loyola" in *Six Essays on Erasmus* (New York, 1979), 76–92.

67. Garcia-Villoslada, *Loyola y Erasmo*, 51.

68. D. Knowles, *The Religious Orders in England* (Cambridge, 1950–61) 3:144–47. Eugene F. Rice, Jr., identifies Erasmus with what he calls an "ethical secularism." "Yet ethical secularism, when embodied in a revealed religion whose principal aim is salvation, remains visible only as long as the contradictions between the ethic, essentially worldly, and the metaphysic, essentially supernatural, do not become explicit. Erasmus, however, never allowed this to happen." "Erasmus and the Religious Tradition, 1495–1499," 162–63.

69. Hugo Rahner, S.J., *Ignatius the Theologian* (New York, 1968), 219. T. O'Reilly makes a detailed study of the restrained, moderate spirituality of Erasmus, which could not have appealed to Ignatius. "Saint Ignatius Loyola," 311–16. He cites J. Huizinga, who speaks of the velvet softness and the limp piety of Erasmus as being inadequate for the white heat of Loyola. Ibid., 314. Other like criticisms of the *Enchiridion* are most recently recounted in Peter Iver Kaufman's "John Colet and Erasmus' *Enchiridion*," *Church History*, 46 (1977): 309–10 with n. 65.

70. Mark Rotsaert, S.J., "Les premiers contacts de saint Ignace avec l'érasmisme espagnol," *Revue d'Histoire de la Spiritualité*, 49 (1973): 464.

71. Granero, *San Ignacio de Loyola*, 245 with n. 75.

72. Schurhammer, *Francis Xavier*, 1:168.

73. *MonSalm*, 1:577 with n. 1. Salmerón moved into his twenty-third year on 6 September 1537. He was ordained by 4 November 1537. Ibid., 1:578–79. Salmerón, however, participated with his friends in the ordination to the subdiaconate on 15 June 1537, and to the diaconate on 17 June 1537. Schurhammer, *Francis Xavier*, 1:343.

74. The places to which they dispersed were chosen by lot. Schurhammer, *Francis Xavier*, 1:348.

75. Ibid., 1:353–54.

76. Ibid., 1:355.

77. Ibid.

78. Ibid., 1:361.

79. Ibid., 1:365–66.

80. Ibid., 1:358.

81. Ibid., 1:369–70. Iñigo probably arranged the groups, mixing their ages and nationalities. He placed twenty-two year old Spanish Salmerón with thirty-seven year old French Paschase Broët.

82. It is possible to read the evidence to say that Salmerón went with Broët to the latter's place of hermitage, Verona. Ibid., 1:372–73 with n. 368.

83. Ibid.

84. Ibid., 1:401.

85. Ibid., 1:402.

86. Ibid., 1:401.

87. Ibid., 1:407.

88. Ibid., 1:496.

89. *FN*, 1:658. After Salmerón, Iñigo listed Francisco de Villanueva and Jerónimo Doménech for their competence in this work.

90. I. Iparraguirre, S.J., *Historia de los Ejercicios de San Ignacio* (Rome, 1946–73), 1:15.

91. Ibid., 1:122, 160.

92. *MonSalm*, 1:1–2.

93. Schurhammer, *Francis Xavier*, 1:205–6. Ribadeneyra, "La Vida y Muerte del Padre Alfonso de Salmerón," 596.

94. *FN*, 1:541.

95. Schurhammer, *Francis Xavier*, 1:206.

96. *PolChron*, 1:153.

97. *EppIgn*, 1:599. That Ignatius so described Salmerón is questionable. In one copy of Ignatius's letter, the words *y sin barbas* are missing; in another, they are crossed out. Yet, ten years before, in 1537, a gentleman of Siena, Lorenzo Alessandrini, described Salmerón as "a tall man with a black beard." *MonBroet*, 197.

98. *MonBroet*, 421 with n. 1.

99. R.D. Edwards, *Church and State in Tudor Ireland. A History of Penal Laws against Irish Catholics 1534–1603* (London, 1935), 20–23, 68, 117. *MonSalm*, 1:1 with n. 1.

100. Schurhammer, *Francis Xavier*, 1:551 with n. 117.

101. Ibid.

102. *MonSalm*, 1:580 with n. 2. *MonBroet*, 204–16, 421–23.

103. *MonBroet*, 206–12.

104. Ibid., 25. Beaton was assassinated in his palace at St. Andrews on 29 May 1546.

105. *MonSalm*, 1:3.

106. Ibid., 1:4–5.

107. Ibid.

108. Ibid., 1:6.

109. *MonBroet*, 25. Broët observed that this decision had been made "with no one person's urging but, as it worked out, at the prompting of the good spirit" (*nullo hominum ad id exhortante sed forte bono spiritu id suggerente*).

110. Ibid., 26. *MonSalm*, 1:10, 580.

111. E.A. D'Alton, *History of Ireland* (London, 1912) 2:529–33.

112. *MonBroet*, 26.

113. T. Corcoran, S.J., *The Clongowes Record 1814 to 1932 with Introductory Chapters on Irish Jesuit Educators 1564 to 1813* (Dublin, 1932), 5–6. Edwards, *Church and State*, 78–81, 97.

114. *MonBroet*, 28.

115. Ibid., 29.

116. *MonSalm*, 1:11.

117. Ibid., 1:13.

118. *MonBroet*, 215–16.

119. *MonSalm*, 1:581–82.

120. Ibid.

121. *PolChron*, 1:99.

122. *MonSalm*, 1:130–31.

123. *EppIgn*, 1:259.

124. *PolChron*, 1:127. Tacchi-Venturi, *Storia* 2, 2:226. Pastor, *History*, 12:85–86.

125. *EppIgn*, 1:257–59.

126. Tacchi-Venturi, *Storia*, 1, 2:154–71; 2, 2:225–35. With copious documentation Tacchi-Venturi corrects the erroneous presentations of this incident in the works of Ribadeneyra and Orlandini. Henri Bremond relates this incident as an illustration of how in the Society of Jesus, and here specifically in Salmerón, the spirit of the Catholic Reform and the spirit of Humanism with its reverence for human values merged and formed an alliance. *Histoire littéraire du sentiment religieux en France depuis la fin des guerres de religion jusqu'à nos jours* (Paris, 1924–36), 1:14–15. For background at Modena see Fenlon, *Heresy and Obedience*, 62–63.

127. As seen in the essay on Claude Jay, Morone was a member of the *spirituali*, that group of earnest Catholics who sought a more biblical, personal, and inspirational spirituality. Fenlon, *Heresy and Obedience*, 46. Nieto, *Juan de Valdes*, 149. Evennett, *Spirit of the Counter-Reformation*, 29–30.

128. Tacchi-Venturi, *Storia*, 2, 2:230–31.

129. *MonSalm*, 1:52–53. This dispute in Modena, as shall be seen, had serious repercussions for Morone under Pope Paul IV and brought embarrassment to Salmerón.

130. *EppIgn*, 1:290.

131. Ibid., 1:332.

132. Ibid., 1:306–7. Rahner, *Saint Ignatius*, 132.

133. *EppIgn*, 1:270. *EppMixt*, 1:228 with n. 2.

134. *EppIgn*, 1:289 with n. 10.

135. Tacchi-Venturi, *Storia*, 2, 2:502.

136. *PolChron*, 1:175.

137. Ibid.

138. *MonSalm*, 1:582–83.

139. Ibid., 1:582.

CHAPTER VII

1. *EppMixt*, 2:162. *PolChron* 1:175. *CT*, 2:243; 7:106; 9:1008. A. Astráin, *Historia de la Compañía de Jesús en la asistencia de España* (Madrid, 1912–25) 1:520.

2. J. C. Hughes, "Alfonso Salmerón: His Work at the Council of Trent" (Ph. D. Diss., University of Kentucky, 1973)., 60–61. André Ravier, S. J., states that Salmerón and Laynez did not go to Trent as official theologians of the pope but simply as "reformed priests." *Ignace de Loyola fonde la Compagnie de Jésus* (Paris, 1974), 138. John Hughes devotes an entire section of his dissertation to the implications of this office for Salmerón and Laynez. "Alfonso Salmerón," 60–82. The title of this section is "Salmerón as Papal Theologian at Trent: Concepts and Misconceptions." Why Pope Paul III chose papal theologians from an order only six years old rather than from an older order is a matter for speculation. Some reasons that may have prompted Pope Paul were the Jesuits' special tie of obedience to the papacy in an age when conciliarist thinking was still strong; the international character of the Society in a period of mounting nationalism; the fresh approach of the Jesuits in an age that still clung to older forms. The Jesuits had not produced an Aquinas or a Bonaventure. But neither had they produced a Savonarola or a Luther. Ibid., 48–50.

3. *MonSalm*, 1: 26.

4. E. V. Lewis, "Concepts of the Church at the First Period of the Council of Trent 1545–1547" (Ph. D. diss., Fordham University, 1970), 100–103.

5. *MonSalm*, 1:26.

6. Ibid., 1:26–27.

7. Ibid., 1:27.

8. *MonBroet*, 310–11.

9. *MonSalm*, 1:27.

10. Jedin, *History*, 2:175–76.

11. *CT*, 5:265–72. In his report of this address, Angelo Massarelli referred to Salmerón as "a reformed priest" (*presbyter reformatus*), a popular term used by many in referring to the Jesuits during their early history.

12. Ibid., 5:265 with n. 1.

13. Ibid., 5:266 with n.2. The editors of this fifth volume of *CT* observe that Salmerón's quotation of Melanchthon, compared with the edition examined by themselves, is not a literal one and is quite free. The editors note that they realize that Salmerón may have been using an edition different from the one they used. *CT*, 5:266 with n. 2.

14. *MonSalm*, 1:26.

15. Ibid., 1:26–27.

16. Ibid., 1:27. Ignatius also received evidence, independent of Salmerón's, about Jesuit efficacy at Trent. He heard that the bishop of Lucca, Felino Sandaeo, had informed officials of the Roman curia that Salmerón, Laynez, and Jay "were preeminent among the preeminent." *EppIgn* 1:412.

17. *CT*, 5:434, 437–38, 547–47.

18. Ibid., 5:266–67.

19. J. Olazaran, S.J., "En el IV centenario de uno voto tridentino del Jesuita Alfonso Salmerón sobre la doble justicia," *Estudios Eclesiasticos*, 20 (1946); 213–15. A synthesis of this intervention of Salmerón's was included in *CT*, but not the text itself. In 1913 the text was published by Stephen Ehses in "Alphons Salmerón Soc. J. Über duplex justitia inhaerens oder imputata," *Römische Quartalschrift* (1913), 129*–45*. The better text is the one edited by Olazaran and used here.

20. Ibid., 240.

21. Ibid., 237. Jedin, *Papal Legate*, 373. Jedin, *History of the Council of Trent* 2:257. Maxcey, "Double Justice, Diego Laynez, and the Council of Trent," 276–78. Salmerón's intervention became the victim of plagiarism. Giacomo Giaconnelli, bishop of Belcastro, gave his own name to a tract on justification. This tract was basically what Salmerón presented at the council on 16 October. The bishop added a brief preface of his own and dropped some of Salmerón's scriptural documentation. Giuseppe Alberigo scores Giaconnelli's action as "rancid, arrogant plagiarism" (*un plagio, acido e insolente.*) He interprets it as an attack, not only doctrinal but also personal, against Seripando. Years later, Giaconnelli led the column of accusers against Morone during the pontificate of Pope Paul IV. Giuseppe Alberigo *I Vescovi Italiani al Concilio di Trento (1545–1547)* (Firenze, 1959), 205–6, 381–82.

22. *CT*, 12:658–62.

23. Ibid., 5:372 with n. 2, 430 with n. 9, 547 with n. 1; 12:727–36.

24. Gutierrez, *Españoles en Trento*, 62.

25. Jedin, *History* 2:459–60.

26. Ibid., 2:460.

27. G. D. Mansi, *Sacrorum Conciliorum Nova et Amplissima Collectio* (Paris, 1901–27), reproduced and continued by L. Petit and J. B. Martin,

33:1118–27. The translation is the work of Robert Lawton, S.J., as part of his work in the Department of History, Fordham University, New York.

28. Ibid., 33:1120–21.

29. Ibid., 33:1122–23.

30. Ibid., 33:1126–27.

31. Gutierrez, *Españoles en Trento*, 62 with n. 90.

32. *MonSalm*, 1:46–7.

33. *EppMixt*, 1:359.

34. *MonBroet*, 332–34.

35. Jedin, *Papal Legate* 702– 3.

36. Jedin, *History* 2:370–71.

37. *CT*, 5:835–39.

38. Ibid., 5:849–50.

39. Ibid., 5:869.

40. Ibid., 5:877–78.

41. Ibid., 5:879–80.

42. *MonSalm*, 1:22–23, 32. *PolChron* 1:179.

43. *EppIgn*, 1:386–89.

44. *MonSalm*, 1:22–25.

45. *MonLain*, 1:49.

46. *MonSalm*, 1:16 with n. 5:29.

47. Ibid., 1:20–22.

48. Ibid., 1:21.

49. James Brodrick, *The Origin of the Jesuits* (London, 1940). 238–39. Astráin, *Historia* 2:14. The editors of MHSJ judge that Nadal's sharp remark is unbalanced and prejudiced. They quote Horace: Quaecumque ostendis mihi sic, incredulus odi. *MonBobad*, xv.

50. A.L. Fisher, ''A Study in Early Jesuit Government: The Nature and Origins of the Dissent of Nicolás Bobadilla,'' *Viator. Medieval and Renaissance Studies* 10 (1979):423.

51. *MonLain*, 1:55–56. *PolChron* 1:215–16.

52. *PolChron*, 1:216.

53. *MonSalm*, 1:37–39.

54. *PolChron*, 1:216.

55. *MonLain*, 1:59. *CT*, 6:84 with n. 1.

56. *CT*, 6:84–85.

57. Ibid., 6:110–12.

58. Ibid., 6:275, 278.

59. Ibid., 6:279–83.

60. Ibid., 6:375–78.

61. Ibid., 6:380–82.

62. *PolChron*, 1:218.

63. *CT*, 6:375–78.

64. Ibid., 6:279–83.

65. *PolChron*, 1:218.

66. Ibid., 1:225.

67. Ibid., 1:218.

68. *EncSym*, 363.

69. Iparraguirre, *Historia de los Ejercicios* 1:231.

70. *MonSalm*, 1:29. *MonLain*, 1:50.

71. *MonSalm*, 1:54.

72. Ibid., 1:58–59.

73. *PolChron*, 1:273–78, 408–10.

74. Ibid., 1:218, 276.

75. Ibid., 1:277. *MonSalm*, 1:70–72.

76. *PolChron*, 1:277, 408.

77. Ibid., 1:408.

78. Alberigo, *I Vescovi Italiani*, 81–82.

79. *MonSalm*, 1:76–77. *PolChron*, 1:409–10.

80. *MonSalm*, 1:74.

81. Ibid., 70–1 with n. 1.

82. Agostino Bea, S.J., "La Compagnia di Gesù e gli studi biblici," *La Compagnia di Gesù e le Scienze Sacre* (Rome), (Rome, 1942), 117.

83. Tacchi-Venturi, *Storia* 1,1:291–92. F. J. McGinness, "Preaching Ideals and Practice in Counter-Reformation Rome," *The Sixteenth Century Journal*, 11 (1980):115.

84. McGinness, "Preaching Ideals and Practice," 116–17. Fenlon, *Heresy and Obedience*, 32–3, 50–51.

85. A. Durand, "Jésuites (Travaux des) sur les Saintes Ecritures," *Dictionnaire de la Bible* (Paris , 1912–72), ed. F. Vigouroux, 3, 2: col. 1404.

86. Ibid. Ignatius, in chapter 8 of the *Constitutions*, prescribed that Jesuits be trained to deliver "sacred lectures," which included the scriptures as their subject matter. *ConsSJComm*, [402, 403, 404] with n. 2 on p. 201.

87. L. Alonso Schökel, S.J., *Understanding the Bible* (New York, 1963), 17.

88. Fenlon, *Heresy and Obedience*, 50.

89. Ibid., 33, 50.

90. Ibid., 34–35, 46–47.

91. Anderson, "Trent and Justification," 387.

92. Logan, "Grace and Justification," 77–78.

93. Ibid., 71.

94. McNair, *Peter Martyr in Italy*, 249.

95. Fenlon, *Heresy and Obedience* 52.

96. Bangert, *To the Other Towns*, 57.

97. Tacchi-Venturi, *Storia* 224–25.

98. *MonSalm*, 1:62.

99. Ibid., 67–69.

100. Ibid., 1:78–79.

101. See the essay on Claude Jay, 111–15.

102. *PolChron*, 1:414.

103. Ibid., 1:415–16.

104. H. Hurter, S.J. *Nomenclator Litterarius Theologiae Catholicae Theologos Exhibens Aetate, Natione, Disciplinis* (Innsbruck, 1903–13), 3:79.

105. Ibid., 2:72.

106. See the essay on Claude Jay, 111–15.

107. *EppCan*, 1:694. *MonSalm*, 1:88. Brodrick, *Saint Peter Canisius* 147–48.

108. *EppCan*, 1:376.

109. Ibid., 1:645.

110. Brodrick, *Saint Peter Canisius*, 146–47.

111. *PolChron*, 2:68.

112. Alberigo, *I Vercovi Italiani*, 85.

113. *EppCan*, 1:694.. *MonSalm*, 1:88.

114. *PolChron*, 2:68.

115. Ibid., 2:72. *EppCan*, 1:332.

116. Brodrick, *Saint Peter Canisius*, 151. For the details of the Jesuit presence at Ingolstadt in 1550, see the essay on Claude Jay, 111–15.

117. *MonSalm*, 1:92–3 with n.1.

118. Ibid., *Cons* MHSJ 1: lxxx

119. *ConsSJComm*, 49.

120. *Cons*MHSJ, 1:lxxvii–lxxxi.

121. Ibid., 1: lxxviii.

122. Ibid., 1:lxxx. Rodrigues did not reach Rome until 8 February 1551, by which time the conference was over. Bobadilla and Broët were detained by work in other areas of Italy. Ibid. 1: lxxviii–xxix.

123. Ignatius's original text is known as text *a*. The revised Spanish text, used at this conference, is known as Text A. For an exposition on the various texts, Spanish and Latin, of the Jesuit Constitutions , see *ConsSJComm*, 49–54.

124. *Cons*MHSJ, 1:395 with n. 22. Bobadilla later made the same criticism. Ibid., 3:xxxix.

125. Ibid., 1:391, 2:285 with n. 1.

126. Ibid., 1:391, 2:6–7. *ConsSJComm*, [3] on 77.

127. *Cons*MHSJ, 1:391, 2:30–31. *ConsSJComm*, [36] on 88.

128. *Cons*MHSH, 1:391, 2:8. *ConsSJComm*, [8] on 80.

129. *Cons*MHSJ, 1:392, 2:53–54, 3:19 with n. 10. *ConsSJComm*, [65] on 96 with n. 8.

130. *Cons*MHSJ, 1:393 with n. 15, 2:280–82. *Cons SJComm*, [162] on 130–31.

131. *Cons*MHSJ, 1: 393–94, 2:424–26. *ConsSJComm*, [367] on 192 with n. 7. For reasons why General Congregation I dropped the phrase *en quanto se pudiere*, see *Cons*MHSJ 3:XLII–XLIV. Antonio Araoz joined Salmerón and Laynez in these suggestions. Emphasis in the text is added.

132. *Coms SJComm*, 51. J. de Roeck, S.J., "La Genèse de la Congrégation Générale dans la Compagnie de Jésus," *AHSJ*, 36 (1967): 283.

133. *MonSalm*, 1:92–3 with n.1.

134. Tacchi-Venturi, *Storia*, 2:292.

135. *MonLain*, 1:104–6.

136. Farrell, *The Jesuit Code of Liberal Education*, 432–33.

137. *PolChron*, 2:167.

138. Ibid., 2:167–68. Polanco here mentions that Salmerón refuted a large number of Protestant errors that pervaded Naples. He does not identify these errors as, say, the teachings of Juan de Valdes, who died in Naples in 1541.

139. Gutierrez, *Españoles en Trento*, 58 with n. 84.

140. *PolChron*, 2:167.

141. Ibid., 2:169. *MonSalm*, 1:92–93 with n.1.

142. *MonSalm*, 1:92–93 with n. 1. *PolChron*, 2:168–69.

143. *MonSalm*, 1:92 with n. 1. *PolChron*, 2:170, 249.

144. *PolChron*, 2:249.

145. *MonLain*, 1: 192–96.

146. *CT*, 7:111–14. Pastor, *History*, 13:102.

147. *CT*, 7:114–24.

148. Ibid., 5:835 with n.3.

149. Ibid., 7:119.

150. *MonSalm*, 1:591. *PolChron*, 2:250–51.

151. *MonSalm*, 1:96.

152. Kuttner, "Papal Efforts," 433–34.

153. J. Hughes, "Alfonso Salmerón," 125–26.

154. *MonSalm*, 1:95–96.

155. *CT*, 7:233–40.

156. *PolChron*, 2:253.

157. *CT*, 7:244–47.

158. Ibid., 7:244.

159. Ibid., 7:247.

160. *CO*, 679–94.

161. *CT*, 7:375–78.

162. Ibid., 7:383–86.

163. Ibid., 7:386.

164. J. Hughes, "Alfonso Salmerón," 137–38.

165. *MonSalm*, 1:100.

166. McNally, "The Council of Trent," 19–20.

167. *MonSalm*, 1:101–2. Astráin, *Historia*, 1:558 with n.1.

168. *MonSalm*, 1:102.

169. Ibid., 1:100.

170. J. Hughes, "Alfonso Salmerón," 140.

171. *MonLain*, 1:197–98. *PolChron* 2:253–54. Astráin, Historia 1:559–60.

172. Astráin, *Historia*, 1:561.

173. *PolChron*, 2:253–54.

174. Astráin, *Historia*, 1:562–63. *MonNad*, 2:45. In his account Nadal gives the words of Cano and Laynez as quoted. This incident apparently is not recorded in the documents of the Dominican order. The late Fr. William A. Hinnebusch, O.P., learned in the history of his order, told me that he had no knowledge of the Cano-Laynez encounter. Fr. Angelus Maria Walz, O.P., in his *I Domenicani al Concilio di Trento* (Rome, 1961), records the incident but bases his account entirely on that of the Jesuit historian Pietro Tacchi-Venturi in *Storia della Compagnia di Gesù in Italia* 2, 2:531–32. Walz does not contest Tacchi-Venturi but advises his readers to remember that other new religious orders — not the Jesuits alone — have been subjected to criticism even though they had been approved by the Holy See. He goes on to point out that in recent times some Jesuits have taken on the role of "Cani" and censured new religious foundations.

175. *PolChron*, 2:468.

176. Rahner, *Saint Ignatius Loyola*, 39.

177. Ibid., 43.

178. Ibid., 42.

179. Brandi, *Emperor Charles V*, 603. At this same hunting box on the Lochau heath, Charles had scored a great victory over John Frederick of Saxony four years earlier, on 24 April 1547. Brandi sees the alliance of October 1551 as an example of poetic justice in history. Ibid., 603.

180. Ibid., 606, 611. H. Rahner, *Saint Ignatius Loyola*, 42.

181. *CO*, 697–98. Jedin, *Ecumenical Councils*, 170–71.

182. Brandi, *Emperor Charles V*, 611.

183. *PolChron*, 2:471, 513, 526. *MonSalm*, 1:103 with n. 1.

184. *MonBobad*, 173–74. Bobadilla mentions that all the scholastics, save one, were beardless. *PolChron*, 2:174,518.

185. Tacchi-Venturi, *Storia* 2,2:438. This classical scholar referred to himself as "leodiensis, germanus, peltanus." Ibid., 2, 2:438 with n. 2.

186. Fisher, "A Study in Early Jesuit Government," 428–30. Ravier *Ignace de Loyola*, 170. *PolChron*, 2: 522–23.

187. Fisher, "A Study in Early Jesuit Government," 428.

188. Ibid., 430. Ravier, *Ignace de Loyola*, 178–79. *PolChron*, 2:526.

189. Ribadeneyra, "La Vida y Muerte del Padre Alfonso de Salmerón," 590.

190. *PolChron*, 2:185–86.

191. Ibid., 3:180 with n. 1. The editors of MHSJ, who describe Fonseca as *huom dotissimo*, use as their authority Francesco Schinosi, S.J., *Istoria della Compagnia di Giesù appartenente al Regno di Napoli*, (Naples, 1706–11).

192. Ibid., 4:186.

193. *Con SJComm*, [565] on 256, [816] on 333–34.

194. *EppIgn*, 7:729–30. *PolChron*, 4:186. Alberigo, *I Vescovi Italiani*, 215–16. Polanco relates that during the previous year, 1553, Fonseca tried to obtain two Jesuits, one for the chair of Sacred Scripture, the other for lectures on the *Sentences* of Peter Lombard. To each chair was attached a honorarium of 100 gold pieces. Polanco does not mention any particular Jesuit desired by Fonseca. Most likely Salmerón was one. Ignatius refused Fonseca's offer for the same reasons as narrated above. Polanco based his information on a letter of Salmerón's. *MonSalm*, 1:110. *PolChron*, 3:180.

195. *PolChron*, 4:171.

196. *MonSalm*, 1:114–15.

197. *PolChron*, 3:171.

198. Gutierrez, *Españoles en Trento*, 59 with n. 84.

199. *MonSalm*, 1:116.

200. *PolChron*, 4:174.

201. Ibid., 4:175. Donna Bellota Spinola also gave her home to the Society, and then took up a life of poverty and austerity. Her son Geronimo entered the Society in 1555. Ibid., 4:175. *EppIgn*, 8:303. Geronimo persevered hardly a year. After his mother died in 1556, he and the Society became entangled in a nasty legal engagement about the ownership of the house. Years later, in 1568, when Salmerón was provincial of Naples, the Society sold the house for 2600 ducats for the benefit of the college. Rahner, *Saint Ignatius Loyola*, 224, 519–20 with n. 66.

202. *PolChron*, 4:179–80.

203. Ibid., 4:189–90. *MonSalm*, 1:117–19.

204. *PolChron*, 4:174. E. Villaret, S.J., "Les Premières origines des Congrégations mariales dans la Compagnie de Jésus," *AHSJ*, 6 (1937), 34–35. M. Scaduto, S.J., *Storia de la Compagnia di Gesù in Italia*, vol. IV *L'Azzione 1556–1565* (Rome, 1974), 626 (hereafter cited as *Storia: Lainez*).

205. Villaret, "Les premières origines," 35.

206. *MonSalm*, 1:18–19.

207. Ibid., 1:124 with n. 1. *PolChron*, 5:176–77.

208. Ibid., 1:126 with n. 1.

209. P. Dudon, S.J., "Le 'Libellus' du P. Bobadilla sur la communion fréquent et quotidienne," *AHSJ*, 2 (1933): 259–61. Nicolás Bobadilla anticipated Ignatius by four years in his attention to writing about frequent holy communion. He approached the subject from a different angle. An archpriest of Luna, Virgilio Zinquino, asked Bobadilla for his opinion on this question: can a bishop set the ceiling on the number of times a person may receive holy communion in his diocese? Bobadilla's answer affirmed frequent, even daily, reception of the Holy Eucharist. This view he presented in *A Booklet on the Praiseworthy and Fruitful, Frequent or Daily, Reception of the Holy Eucharist* (*Libellus de laudabili et fructuosa, frequenti aut quotidiana sacrosanctae Eucharistiae sumptione*). This work was not published until Dudon did so in this article. Ibid., 261–64. De Guibert, *The Jesuits*, pp. 376–77.

210. L. Gonçalves da Câmara, *Mémorial 1555* ed. Roger Tandonnet, S.J. Collection Christus No. 20. *Textus* (Paris, 1966), p. 248. St. Thomas and St. Bonaventure, and others held that a confessor might, for proper reasons, use knowledge acquired in confession so long as there was no danger of revealing the confession. Pope Clement VIII, in a decree to all religious superiors, 26 May 1594, forbade this practice. The Society of Jesus anticipated this decree by four years. In 1590 Father General Claudio Acquaviva ruled out such use by Jesuits of confessional matter. Ibid., 248 with n. 5.

211. Ibid., 152 with n. 1. Another group of Jesuits who received invitations to dine alone with Ignatius were those about to leave Rome and those

who had just arrived in Rome. This was a device used by Ignatius to spread a spirit of mutual charity. Ignatius intended to give legislative authority to this practice by including it in the *Constitutions*. However, he did not get around to editing and polishing the text of the intended legislation. General Congregation I (1558) voted on the question whether a proviso for dining alone by the general and all superiors with a community of more than thirty should be inserted in the *Constitutions* or in the rules of superiors. In the 76th decree the congregation voted to include this practice among the rules of superiors. General Congregation III (1573), in the 38th decree, reversed this decree without, however, prejudicing "that old custom" (*antiquam illam consuetudinem*) enjoyed by the general and those who might be dispensed by the general. *InstSJ* 2:227.

212. Alberigo, *I Vescovi Italiani*, 75 with n. 2.

213. *MonNad*, 2:37.

214. *EppCan*, 1:553–54. *PolChron*, 5:274–75. Bangert, *To the Other Towns*, 109–10.

215. Pastor, *History*, 14:327, 340.

216. *PolChron*, 6:356–57.

217. Ibid., 6:357. *MonSalm*, 1:130 with n.1.

218. Brodrick, *Saint Peter Canisius*, 375–76. A. C. Dickens calls Sigismund II and Stephen Báthory highly liberal Catholics who, correctly interpreting the independent temper of the Poles, "made their country the most tolerant in Europe." *Reformation and Society in Sixteenth Century Europe* (London, 1966), 176.

219. *MonSalm*, 1:130–31.

220. Ibid., 1:133. *PolChron*, 6:358–60.

221. *MonSalm*, 1:133. *PolChron* 6:358–60.

222. *MonSalm*, 1:133–34.

223. Ibid., 1:135. *PolChron*, VI, 360.

224. *EppCan*, 2:322.

225. *PolChron*, 6:21–22. *MonSalm*, I, xiv.

226. Pastor, *History*, XIV, 114–19.

227. Scaduto, *Storia: Lainez*, 3:14.

228. Ibid., 3:14.

229. Pastor, *History of the Popes*, 14:117–19, 140 with n.2.

230. F. Sacchini, *Historiae Societatis Jesu pars secunda sive Lainius* (Antwerp, 1620), 6.

231. Astraín, *Historia*, 1:563–66.

232. C. J. McNaspy, S.J., and T. D. Culley, S.J., "The Fine Arts in the Old Society: A Preliminary Investigation," *AHSJ*, 40 (1971): 218.

233. Scaduto, *Storia: Lainez*, 3:7–8 with n. 40.

234.   C. J. McNaspy, S.J., "Art in Jesuit Life," *Studies in the Spirituality of Jesuits*, 5 (No. 3., 1973), 95.

235.   A. des Freux, S.J., *Epigrammata in Haereticos*, (Douai, 1956), 1.

> Cum peteres versus, me scribere posse negavi;
> Non petis, en scribo: ne lege, et ultus eris.
> Inconstans videor? non te latet esse Poëtis
> Hunc morem, vates ut Venusinus ait.
> Causa tamen non deest: facit indignatio versum.
> Quis visa haereseôn peste tacere queat?
> Mutus ut ante puer vocem prorupit in altam,
> Dum Croesum patrem cerneret ense peti:
> Sic mihi nunc linguae franguntur vincla coacte,
> Dum matrem aspicio poene perire meam.

236.   Ibid., 6.

> Cur monach' fratres et claustra relinquis Erasme.
> Non misera factum hoc ambitione caret.
> Namq. latens illic velut in scrobe, vilis eras mus;
> In lucem, ut videas et videare, salis.
> Ridiculum at murem mons paturisse videatur,
> Theologum dum te rhetor inepte facis.
> Quin etiam temere scrinia sacra vagantem
> Muscipulam haereseos subsisse ferunt.
> Dum strepis et rodis sanctorum dogmata patrum,
> Tartarei saevo felis ab ungue cave.

Ignatius must have known of these epigrams. He spoke of des Freux's "most generous muse." What he thought of the Frenchman's lampoon against Luther he did not commit to paper. It is better left in the original.

> Dum stomachans loqueris, merda est tibi semper in ore:
> Merda sit ac utinam semper in ore tuo.
> Os ea si loquitur, quibus et cor abundat (ut auctor
> Certus ait) cor erit quanta latrina tuum.
>
> Ibid., 26.

237.   Ibid., *3.

238.   Sacchini, *Historiae*, 6.

239.   *MonSalm*, 1:140.

240.   *ConsSJComm*, [4] on 68.

CHAPTER VIII

1.   *MonSalm*, 1:142, 147, 182.

2.   Ibid., 1:182.

3.   Ibid., 1:149.

4. Ibid., 1:177.

5. Ibid., 1:147.

6. Ibid., 1:192.

7. Ibid., 1:xv. *EppCan*, 2:175 with n. 2. Scaduto, *Storia: Lainez*, 3:79.

8. Scaduto, *Storia: Lainez*, 3:78–79.

9. *MonSalm*, 1:220 with n. 7.

10. Brodrick, *Saint Peter Canisius*, 385–421.

11. Ibid., 393.

12. *MonSalm*, 1:214–15.

13. Brodrick, *Saint Peter Canisius*, 393. Ever since the Interim of Augsburg (1548), the Philippists (followers of Melanchthon) and the Flacians (followers of Flacius Illyricus) engaged in bitter controversy. Ibid., 130.

14. *MonSalm*, 1:215.

15. Ibid., 1:216.

16. Ibid., 1:216.

17. Brodrick, *Saint Peter Canisius*, 419.

18. *EppCan*, 2:178–79.

19. Scaduto, *Storia: Lainez*, 3:79.

20. Rahner, *Saint Ignatius Loyola*, 43.

21. Brandi, *Emperor Charles V*, 633–34.

22. J.-M. Prat, S.J., *Histoire du Père Ribadeneyra, Disciple de Saint Ignace* (Paris, 1862), 100–101.

23. Rahner, *Saint Ignatius Loyola*, 43.

24. Ibid., 43–44.

25. *MonSalm*, 1:221.

26. Ibid., 1:220.

27. Ibid., 1:230.

28. Ibid., 1:220.

29. Ibid., 1:220–22.

30. Scaduto, *Storia: Lainez*, 3:83.

31. *PolChron*, 4:180.

32. *MonSalm*, 1:229.

33. Ibid., 1:233–34.

34. Ibid., 2:11.

35. Ibid., 1:230.

36. Ibid., 1:235.

37. Ibid., 1:235.

38. Tacchi-Venturi, *Storia*, 1, 2:154–71. Scaduto suggests that a reason Paul IV selected Salmerón as a member of his nephew's mission to Philip II was to express his gratitude for the testimony he gave in the proceedings against Cardinal Morone. Ibid., 3:79.

39. Ibid., 2, 2:230.

40. *MonSalm*, 1:235 with n. 20.

41. Scaduto, *Storia: Lainez*, 3:469.

42. *MonSalm*, 1:354.

43. Scaduto, *Storia: Lainez*, 3:469.

44. Tacchi-Venturi, *Storia*, 1, 2: 174–75.

45. Ibid., 2, 2:234 with n. 2.

46. *MonSalm*, 1:122.

47. Ibid., 137. Pedro Ribadeneyra joined the ambassadorial mission of Conde de Feria to the court of Queen Mary of England. Mary died at St. James's Palace at eight in the morning of 17 November 1558. Eight hours later, Cardinal Reginald Pole died in Lambeth Castle, across the Thames. The Conde de Feria advised Pope Paul to excommunicate the new queen, Elizabeth. Ribadeneyra urged dampening the fires of hatred (*enfin non est addendum oleum igni*). Very probably this advice of Ribadeneyra's was decisive in shaping Paul's policy. J. H. Fichter, S.J., *James Laynez, Jesuit* (St. Louis, 1944), 179 with n. 13.

48. *MonSalm*, 1:276.

49. Ibid., 1:xv–xvi. *PolChron*, 2:624.

50. F. J. Egaña, S.J., *Origenes de la Congregación General en la Compañía de Jesús* (Rome, 1972), 216–17.

51. Ibid., 217. Brodrick, *Progress of the Jesuits*, 26. The cardinal protector of the Society, Rodolfo Pio di Carpi, was absent from Rome. Pope Paul designated Cardinal Pedro Pacheco as vice-protector.

52. Ibid., 217–18.

53. Ibid., 255–56, 348.

54. Ibid., 256–57.

55. Astráin, *Historia*, 2:27.

56. Ibid., 2:33. Astráin errs in saying that Paul IV also requested consideration of choir at this particular moment.

57. *InstSJ*, 2:167.

58. Astráin, *Historia*, 2:34.

59. Ibid., 2:34–35.

60. Scaduto, *Storia: Lainez*, 3:116. Pope Paul's additions (*additamenta paulina*) appeared in the *editio princeps* of the *Constitutions*. Ibid., 3:116.

61. Ibid., 3:250.

62. Iparraguirre, *Historia de los Ejercicios*, 2:289.

63. Ibid., 2:419 with n. 6.

64. Ibid., 2:16.

65. *MonSalm*, 1:250.

66. Scaduto, *Storia: Lainez*, 3:211.

67. Ibid., 3:211–12.

68. Ibid., 3:213 with n. 18.

69. *MonSalm*, 1:447.

70. Scaduto, *Storia: Lainez*, 3:213–14.

71. Ibid., 3:215.

72. J. Reites, S.J. "St. Ignatius of Loyola and the Jews," *Studies in the Spirituality of Jesuits*, 13 (No. 4, 1981): 19–20.

73. Ibid., 21–23.

74. *MonRib* 2:250.

75. Ibid., 2:251–53.

76. Reites, "St. Ignatius of Loyola and the Jews," 29–30. *InstSJ*, 2:278–79. The decrees were numbers 52 and 53. In January 1608 Pedro Ribadeneyra, then seventy-two years old, wrote to Fr. General Acquaviva, urging him to use his influence to rescind the racial legislation of General Congregation V. He marshalled statements of Ignatius, Laynez, and Salmerón to support his plea. *MonRib* 2:247–54. In 1608 General Congregation VI did not cancel those decrees of the previous congregation, but it did modify them considerably. In the twenty-eighth decree it stipulated that those whose Christianity could be established back through five generations should be considered free of "the impediment of origin." There was no need to go back further in ancestry to determine the presence or non presence of Jewish or Moorish ancestry. *InstSJ*, 2:302–3.

77. *Colld*, 235. Reites, "St. Ignatius of Loyola and the Jews," 31, 46 and n. 140.

78. Elliott, *Imperial Spain*, 225–26.

79. F. Cereceda, S.J. "Laínez y Salmerón y el Catecismo de Carranza," *Razon y Fe*, 100 (1932): 212.

80. Ibid., 215. *MonSalm*, 1:252.

81. Cereceda, "Laínez y Salmerón," 218–20.

82. *MonSalm*, 1:275.

83. Ibid., 1:258.

84. Ibid., 1:256–57.

85. *MonRib*, 1:319.

86. *MonSalm*, 1:271.

87. Ibid., 1:272.

88. Ibid., 1:276.

89. Astráin, *Historia*, 2:43.

90. Scaduto, *Storia: Lainez*, 4:27 with n. 27.

91. Ibid., 4:27–28. M. Scaduto, S.J., "Lainez e l'Indice del 1559. Lullo, Sabunde, Savonarola, Erasmo," *AHSJ*, 24 (1955), 13.

92. Scaduto, "Lainez e l'Indice," 17–19.

93. Scaduto, *Storia: Lainez*, 4:27. Bataillon, *Érasme et L'Espagne*, 760.

94. Garcia-Villoslada, *Loyola y Erasmo*, 238.

95. Ibid., 248–51.

96. Scaduto, "Lainez e l'Indice," 23.

97. *MonSalm*, 1:415.

98. Scaduto, "Lainez e l'Indice," 23–27.

99. *MonSalm*, 1:415.

100. Scaduto, "Lainez e l'Indice," 25–27.

101. Ibid., 22.

102. Ibid., 21–22.

103. Ibid., 28. Scaduto, *Storia: Lainez*, 4:34 with n. 64.

104. Scaduto, "Lainez e l'Indice," 28–30.

105. Garcia-Villoslada, *Loyola y Erasmo*, 257 with n. 49.

106. *MonSalm*, 1:548.

107. Ibid., 1:259.

108. Ibid., 1:269.

109. Ibid., 1:278.

110. Ibid., 1:263.

111. Ibid., 1:367.

112. Ibid., 1:300.

113. Scaduto, *Storia: Lainez*, 4:361–62.

114. *MonSalm*, 1:247.

115. Ibid., 1:300–305.

116. Scaduto, *Storia: Lainez*, 3:306–7.

117. *MonSalm*, 1:355.

118. Ibid., 1:355–56.

119. Ibid., 1:402–3. Cristóbal Sánchez de Madrid, often referred to in Jesuit correspondence simply as Madrid, was born in 1503 in Daimiel, near Toledo, went to Rome in 1540 as theological advisor to Cardinal Giovanni Domenico de Cupis, entered the Society in 1550. At General Congregation I in

1558, he was elected the assistant for the provinces of Italy and Sicily. Scaduto, *Storia: Lainez*, 3:166–67.

120. *MonSalm*, 1:400.

121. Ibid., 1:401–2.

122. Ibid., 1:414.

123. Ibid. 1:415.

124. Ibid., 1:422–23.

125. Ibid., 1:420–26.

126. Ibid., 1:462–64.

127. Scaduto, *Storia: Lainez*, 3:341.

128. *MonSalm*, 1:465.

129. Ibid., 1:469–70.

130. Ibid., 1:473.

131. Ibid., 1:478.

132. Ibid., 1:487, 490.

133. Scaduto, *Storia: Lainez*, 3:341–42.

134. *EppCan*, 3:224.

135. Ibid., 3:253.

136. Ibid., 3:270.

137. Ibid., 3:205. Vitoria appears prominently in Brodrick, *Saint Peter Canisius*.

138. *EppCan*, 3:214.

139. Ibid., 3:259–60.

140. Ibid., 3:303.

141. Ibid., 3:323.

142. Ibid., 3:418.

143. Ibid., 3:461.

144. Ibid., 3:461.

145. Scaduto, *Storia: Lainez*, 3:124 with n. 7.

146. *MonLain*, 1:177.

147. Scaduto, *Storia: Lainez*, 3:124 with n. 7.

148. Fichter, *James Laynez*, 178.

149. Ibid., 178.

150. *EppCan*, 3:302–3. For the sequel to this story of Peltan's manuscript, a story that illumines the trials of scholars, see Brodrick, *Saint Peter Canisius*, 400–62.

151. *MonSalm*, 2:742.

152. Ibid., 2:743. *EppCan*, 3:333–34.

153. *EppCan*, 3:341–42. The project of the Cologne Jesuits did not materialize. Their Carthusian friend, Lawrence Surius, brought out an edition of this council in four volumes in 1567. Ibid., 3:241, 343.

154. Ibid., 3:344.

155. *MonSalm*, 1:374–75.

156. Ibid., 1:376.

157. Scaduto, *Storia: Lainez*, 4:61. Actually Morone was not made a president at the beginning of this third period of the council. Later, in March of the following year, Pope Pius IV appointed him to that post. The editors of MHSJ identify Cardinal Seripando as the man Salmerón was reluctant to work with. Scaduto's later researches point to Morone as the man.

158. Ibid., 4:43–44. *MonSalm*, 1:350–57. *EppCan*, 3:425 with n. 4. Laynez also participated in the council as the general of a religious order.

159. Jedin, *Papal Legate*, 600.

160. Ibid., 593.

161. Ibid., 593.

162. Ibid., 593.

163. Scaduto, *Storia: Lainez*, 3:576 with n. 7.

164. *EppCan*, 3:447–48. Canisius possibly refers to a *tractatus* that Salmerón had composed. Bishop Carlo Visconti of Ventimiglia reported that Salmerón had carried with him *un trattatello*. Ibid., 3:448 with n. 1.

165. Ibid., 3:438. Astráin, *Historia*, 2:164–65.

166. *CT*, 8:537–38 with n. 3.

167. Ibid., 7:537–38.

168. Ibid., 7:540.

169. Astráin, *Historia*, 2:167.

170. *EppCan*, 3:532.

171. Ibid., 3:532. Brodrick, *Saint Peter Canisius*, 490 with n. 2. In the twenty-first session of 16 July 1563, the council left the practical question of granting or denying the chalice to the laity to the pope. Pius IV, on 16 April 1564, allowed several bishops in the empire to make the decision in their own dioceses. The result was generally poor. Gregory XIII revoked this concession by Pius IV. Even Georg Drascovics regretted his stand at Trent. Astráin, *Historia*, 2:172–73. Brodrick, *Saint Peter Canisius*, 602, 607–8.

172. *EppCan*, 3:461 with n. 6.

173. Ibid., 3:461–62.

174. *CT*, 3:369–370, 8:696. Jedin, *Papal Legate*, 639–40. Salmerón and Torres wanted changes in chapter one of the draft. They cited the sentence that began *Nam etsi Christus Dominus*. After the word *traditio*, they wanted the

addition: *ita ad omnes Christi fideles extenditur ut*; and after the final word of this same sentence, *astringantur*, they wanted the addition *sed ad eos tantum, quibus dictum est: Hoc facite in meam commemorationem hoc est, quibus conficiendi et offerendi corporis et sanguinis sui potestatem tradidit. CT*, 3: 369–70.

175. *CT*, 3:370, 8:696 with n. 1.

176. Ibid., 3:372.

177. Ibid., 8:719–720, 722

178. Ibid., 8:722 with n. 3. *EppCan*, 3:476 with n. 1 Astráin, *Historia*, 2:168.

179. Dudon, "Sur un texte inédit," 414–15.

180. *EppCan*, 3:476 with n. 1. Jedin, *Papal Legate*, 631.

181. Astráin, *Historia*, 2:168–69. Four days after his protracted and exasperating intervention of 21 July, Salmerón preached what seems to have been his first sermon at the common liturgy during the third period of the council. This was the feast of St. James the Apostle. He gave other sermons on 20 December 1562, 29 March 1563, 9 May 1563, and 21 November 1563. Gutierrez, *Españoles en Trento*, 62–63 with n. 92.

182. *CO*, 708–13.

183. *CT*, 4:7–9 Astráin, *Historia*, 2:173–74.

184. J. Ratzinger, "Announcements and Prefatory Notes of Explanation," *Commentary on the Documents of Vatican II*, (New York, 1968), 1:300.

185. Evennett, *Spirit of the Counter-Reformation*, 97.

186. Ibid., 99–100.

187. Lecuyer, "Episcopat," *DS* 4, 1:901–902.

188. *CO* 657.

189. Astráin, *Historia*, 2:175.

190. Ibid., 2:176.

191. Carl J. Peter, "Dimensions of Jus Divinum in Roman Catholic Theology," *TheolSt*, 34 (1973), 242.

192. Ibid., 242–43.

193. John Bossy, "Editor's Postscript" in the *The Spirit of the Counter-Reformation*, 135.

194. Astráin, *Historia*, 2:178.

195. Ibid., 2:178–79. *CT*, 3:499–500. Peter, "Dimensions of Jus Divinum," 242–43.

196. Astráin, *Historia*, 2:180–81.

197. *MonSalm*, 1:508–9. The solution to the theological and juridical dimensions of these episcopal problems did not monopolize all of Laynez's

energies. The pastoral and spiritual dimensions also absorbed him. During this period, he wrote two tracts that expressed this preoccupation: *De beneficiis ecclesiasticis instructio ad usum confessariorum* (*An Instruction for Confessors on the Question of Ecclesiastical Benefices*), and *De muneribus episcopalibus rite obeundis instructiones diversae* (*Various Guidelines for the Proper Performance of Episcopal Obligations*). Regardless of how the theological and juridical issues would be resolved, Laynez embraced a wider vision: a body of personally reformed, devout, zealous, hardworking bishops. Philip J. Scarcella, "James Laynez: Christian Humanist and Catholic Reformer During the Tridentine Period, 1545–1563" (Ph. D. diss. New York University, 1974), 493–95.

198. Scaduto, *Storia: Lainez*, 4:192–93. Evennett, *Cardinal of Lorraine*, 463–64.

199. Scaduto, *Storia: Lainez*, 4:193–94.

200. Ibid., 4:194–95. *CT*, 3:495.

201. *MonSalm*, 1:668.

202. *CT*, 3:516 with n. 2.

203. Scaduto, *Storia: Lainez*, 4:195. *PolChron*, 1:357 with n. 42.

204. *MonLain*, 6:635 –36.

205. *EppCan*, 4:109. Fichter, *James Laynez*, 228.

206. Jedin, *Papal Legate*, 702–3.

207. Scaduto, *Storia: Lainez*, 4:217.

208. Gentian Hervet, "Litterae Gentiani Herveti ad Salmeronem soc. Jesu theologum, de residentia episcoporum," in *Monumentorum ad Historiam Concilii Tridentini potissimum illustrandam spectantium amplissima collectio*, ed. Judocus Le Plat (Louvain, 1781–87), 5:778–79.

209. Ibid., 787.

210. *CT*, 3:614.

211. *MonSalm*, 1:674–75.

212. *CT*, 3:613–14.

213. *MonLain*, 6:610–11.

214. H. Jedin, *Crisis and Closure of the Council of Trent* (London: Sheed & Ward Stagbooks, 1967), 97–98.

215. Ibid., 103, 121–22.

216. *MonSalm*, 1:515–16.

217. *CT*, 9:587–90, 3:665–66.

218. Scaduto, *Storia: Lainez*, 4:220.

219. *MonSalm*, 1:680.

220. Scaduto, *Storia: Lainez*, 4:220. Jedin, *Crisis and Closure*, 108.

221. Jedin, *Crisis and Closure*, 102–3.

222. Scaduto, *Storia: Lainez*, 4:209–10, 222.

223. Ibid., 4:222–223. *CO*, 720–22. Polanco kept Canisius informed on how the popularity of Salmerón and Laynez rose and fell during the changing moods of the council through the tense months of June and July. *EppCan*, 3:216, 267, 285, 292.

224. Scaduto, *Storia: Lainez*, 4:188–89.

225. Salmerón, *Commentarii*, 12:532–46. The editors of *MonSalm* and Hartmann Grisar, S.J., the editor of *Jacobi Lainez Disputationes Tridentinae* (Innsbruck, 1886) disagree on whether Salmerón is the author of this treatise on episcopal residence. Grisar judges that the pages in the *Commentarii* are an edited version of an essay by Laynez on the relationship between the pope and the hierarchy. An inscription on an old codex in the Jesuit Roman archives, as well as corrections in Laynez's handwriting, indicate this. Grisar thinks that Salmerón's editor, Bartolomé Pérez de Nueros, possibly found a copy of Laynez's work among Salmerón's notes, concluded wrongly that it had been composed by Salmerón, and then exercised his talent at clipping (*suam detruncationis artem*) with unhappy results. Grisar also judges that the pages as they appear in the *Commentarii* have the appearance of a huge purple patch, so out of style are they with the rest of the work. *Jacobi Lainez Disputationes Tridentinae*, 1:52*–61*. The editors of *MonSalm* think that this work as it appears in the *Commentarii* is really Salmerón's. They concede the possibility that in its original form it may have been the joint work of Salmerón and Laynez, or that it may have been composed entirely by Salmerón and then corrected by Laynez. The two men had collaborated very closely at the council of Trent. *MonSalm* 1:xxx–xxxiii.

226. Bossy, "Editor's Postscript," 135–36. Cardinal Manning is among the worst of authorities to whom to make appeal for an objective judgment of the Society of Jesus. He once defined the Society as "the continual thwarting of the English clergy." To him the Jesuits incarnated "a mysterious permission of God for the chastisement of England." Bangert, *History of the Society of Jesus*, 469.

227. Peter, "Dimensions of Jus Divinum," 242 with n. 45.

228. *CT*, IX, 79. *Alio modo est gradus eminens in ecclesia Dei; et sacerdotium a diaconatu, et presbyterium ab episcopatu distringuitur*. Ibid., 9:7.

229. Scaduto, *Storia: Lainez*, 3:496–533. In 1837 Fr. Peter Verhaegen, superior of the Jesuit Missouri mission, went to the Third Provincial Council of Baltimore. Jan Roothaan, General of the Society, wrote Verhaegen: "I say nothing of the manner of dealing with the chief pastors of America, or of the humility and reverence with which our own men should conduct themselves on such occasions. Your Reverence knows how Fathers Laynez and Salmerón bore themselves." G. J. Garraghan, S.J., *The Jesuits of the Middle United States* (New York, 1938), 1:487–88.

230. Astráin, *Historia*, 2:188–89 with n. 2.

231. Ibid.

232. *MonLain*, 7:156.

233. *MonNad*, 2:313.

234. *CT*, 3:567–8, 9:382–85.

235. Ibid., 9:384–85.

236. Astráin, *Historia*, 2:192.

237. Ibid., 2:192. *EppCan*, 3:326–27.

238. Scaduto, *Storia: Lainez*, 4:233–34.

239. *MonLain*, 7:248.

240. *CT*, 2:696. G. Grabka, O.F.M. Conv., "Cardinal Hosius and the Council of Trent," *TheolSt*, 7 (1946), 573–74. In his estimation of Hosius, Grabka judges that "there is perhaps no greater name in the history of the Counter-Reformation.," Ibid., 558.

241. Cereceda, *Diego Lainez*, 2:255–56.

242. Scaduto, *Storia: Lainez*, 4:237.

243. *CO*, 731–35.

244. Scaduto, *Storia: Lainez*, 4:238.

245. Jedin, *Crisis and Closure*, 148–49.

246. *MonLain* 7:216. See also 319 and 399 for the feelings of Laynez about ambiguous language in some of the decrees.

247. M. Scaduto, S.J., "Concilio di Trento e Reforma Cattolica," *AHSJ*, 38 (1969): 504.

248. Scaduto, *Storia: Lainez*, 4:256–59.

249. Ibid., 4:266 with n. 52.

250. Jedin, *Crisis and Closure*, 155–56.

251. *MonSalm*, 2:74, 579, 736.

252. G. Alberigo, "The Council of Trent: New Views on the Occasion of Its Fourth Centenary," *Concilium* (New York, 1965), 7:77.

253. Scaduto, *Storia: Lainez*, 4:580.

254. Ibid., 4:580. *MonSalm*, 1:517–19.

255. Scaduto, *Storia: Lainez*, 4:580.

256. *MonSalm*, 1:518–19.

257. Ibid., 1:523 with n. 1.

258. Ibid., Scaduto, *Storia: Lainez*, 4:580.

259. P. Pirri, S.J., *Giovanni Tristano e i Primordi della Architettura Gesuitica* (Rome, 1955), 16–18.

260. Ibid., v–vi. Frequently Giacomo Vignola and his Gesù in Rome are thought of as the entry of Jesuit Baroque onto the European scene.

261. Ibid., 19.

262. Ibid., 20.

263. Scaduto, *Storia: Lainez*, 4:791.

264. Ibid., 4:791.

265. *MonSalm*, 1:xxix. Salmerón refers to the fable of Aesop in which Zeus determined to appoint a king of birds, Zeus set a day on which all birds were to present themselves before him. A jackdaw, filled with ambition, collected feathers that fell from other birds. With these feathers he plumed himself in gorgeous array. On the day of assembly before Zeus, the other birds detected the jackdaw's plan to make a grand impression, set upon him, and stripped him of the feathers. The jackdaw stood before Zeus nothing more than just a jackdaw.

266. Scaduto, *Storia: Lainez*, 4:793.

267. Bossy, "Editor's Postscript," 133.

268. Jedin, *Ecumenical Councils*, 186. Almost a year after the council, on 22 September 1564, Belgian Jesuit Frans DeCostere had dinner with Bishop Nicolas Psaulme, O. Praem., of Verdun. Psaulme, who saw Salmerón's performance at the third period of the council, singled him and Canisius out for praise, "men whom he described as great and admirable" (*quos viros magnos et egregios nominabat*). *EppCan* 3:1047.

269. This seems to be the judgment of A. Dupont and H. O. Evennett. *Spirit of the Counter-Reformation*, 133–34.

270. Alberigo, "The Council of Trent," 7:76–77.

271. Ribadeneyra, "Vida y Muerte del P. Alfonso de Salmerón," 497.

272. McGinness, "Preaching Ideals and Practice," 109. Scaduto, *Storia: Lainez*, 4:511–13.

CHAPTER IX

1. *MonSalm*, 2:10.

2. Ibid., 2:15.

3. Ibid., 2:15–16.

4. Ibid., 2:21 with n. 3.

5. Ibid., 2:22.

6. P. Leturia, S.J., "La hora matutina de meditación en la Compañía naciente [1540–1590]," *AHSJ*, 3 (1934): 71.

7. B. Schneider, S.J., "Der Konflikt zwischen Claudius Acquaviva und Paulus Hoffaeus, " *AHSJ*, 26 (1957): 11–12.

8. *ConsSJComm*, 582 on p. 259–60.

9. Leturia, "La hora matutina," 63–64, 70–71. J. W. Padberg, S.J., "The General Congregations of the Society of Jesus," *Studies in the Spirituality of Jesuits*, 6 (Nos. 1 and 2, 1974): 10.

10. Leturia, "La hora matutina," 72. Borgia has his defenders. They see him making a scrupulous effort to depart as little as possible from Ignatius's spirit and law, and at the same time effectively checking the exaggerations in Spain and Italy. Pedro Leturia is a leading spokesman for this benign interpretation. Ibid., 72–73. Paul Dudon, S.J., however criticizes Leturia's efforts to trace back to Ignatius's generalate the justification for such a program of prayer as decreed by Borgia. He does this by a careful and critical study of the documents used by Leturia to justify his own position. "Saint Ignace et l'oraison dans la Compagnie de Jésus, "*RAM*, 15 (1934): 245–57. Leturia in turn answered Dudon in "De 'Constitutionibus collegiorum' P. Joannis de Polanco ac de earum influxu in Constitutiones S. I.," *AHSJ*, 7 (1936): 1–30.

11. It is also surprising to note that Nadal was among those who favored a legislated quantity of prayer, since Ignatius had personally chided him on this precise issue. But Nadal changed with the tide. He seems to have been strongly influenced by Borgia and others who shared Borgia's view. M. A. Fiorito, S.J., "Ignatius' Own Legislation on Prayer. Ignatian and Post-Ignatian Concepts," *WL*, 97 (1968), 166–67, 171. That Nadal allowed himself to be so influenced by Borgia is odd, since he [Nadal] had some unhappy memories of Borgia's imperial manners, including the occasion when he carried to Francis, then in Spain, Ignatius's admonition about moderation in prayer and penance. He entered Borgia's heated response in his *Journal*: "Between the two of you, you will drive me off to the Carthusians." *MonNad*, 2:43.

12. T. H. Clancy, S.J., *An Introduction to Jesuit Life* (St. Louis, 1976), 142.

13. Lukács, "De origine collegiorum," 241. Actually, a few of the colleges designed for Jesuit scholastics could not open their classes to the public because of difficulties with the universities at which they were located. These were Alcalá, Salamanca, Valencia, Paris, Louvain, and Cologne. Ibid., 241.

14. *MonPaed*, 2:10*–11*.

15. Ibid., 2:9*.

16. *InstSJ*, 2:195–96.

17. *MonPaed*, 2:16* with n. 38.

18. Ibid., 2:11*–14*. Scaduto, *Storia: Lainez*, 4:363.

19. *MonPaed*, 2:14*.

20. Ibid., 2:660.

21. Ibid., 2:444–45

22. Ibid., 3:293.

23. *InstSJ*, 2:197–98.

24. *EppIgn*, I, 603. Ignatius was careful about the influences on the novices. One day he noticed a Jesuit priest talking with a novice. He asked the priest the subject of their conversation. The priest replied that he had been telling the novice about the Spanish Franciscan Juan de Tejeda, whose magnetism had been attracting some Jesuits from their apostolic spirit and toward a contemplative form of life. Ignatius reprimanded the priest and forbade him to have anything to do with the novices. De Guibert, *The Jesuits*, p. 104–5.

25. *InstiSJ*, 2:197.

26. *ConsSJComm*, 588 on 262–63.

27. *MonPaed*, 2:12*–13*.

28. *InstSJ*, 2:197.

29. Ibid., 2:128–29.

30. *ConSJComm*, 555 on 253.

31. Ibid., 5 on 69. When Ignatius uses the term "professed," he means priests who have pronounced solemn vows.

32. Ibid., on p. 79, 392 on pp. 198–99.

33. *MonPaed*, 2:16*. *ConsSJComm*, 815 on 333.

34. *MonPaed*, 2:16*. Other statistics show how history ran ahead of Ignatius's plans. When he died in 1556, he had admitted only fifty priests to final vows, forty-six professed and four spiritual coadjutors. This was but 4% of the Society.

35. *ConsSJComm*, 166 with n. 19.

36. *MonPaed*, 2:16*. One of Ignatius's pieces of unfinished business was the up-dating of the legislation on poverty, *ConsSJComm*, 166 with n. 19. The legislation he left had several ambiguities that occasioned disputes throughout Jesuit history about the correct interpretation. In 1571, for the first time, a question was raised about the juridical status of those colleges which enrolled only lay students and had no Jesuits in studies. Only in 1608 was the issue settled. Lukács, "De origine collegiorum," 19.

37. *MonPaed*, 3:362.

37. Brodrick, *Progress of the Jesuits*, 53–58.

39. *ConsSJComm*, 167 with n. 1.

40. *InstSJ*, 2:195–96.

41. Iparraguirre, S.J. et al., "Jésuites," *DSpir*, 8:978. Mario Scaduto gives the Latin form. Mercurian used to say, "Societatem magis forma quam reformatione egere quandoquidem nondum ad plenissimum actum erat deducta in suo instituto." *Storia: Lainez*, 3:264 with n. 17.

42. T. V. Cohen, "Why the Jesuits Joined. 1540–1600," *Historical Papers 1974 Communications Historiques* (A supplement to vol. 55 of *The Canadian Historical Review*), 251. Scaduto, *Storia: Lainez*, 3:254–55.

43. Cohen, "Why the Jesuits Joined," 251. *MonPaed*, 2:40*; 3:224–25.

44. Scaduto, *Storia: Lainez*, 3: 257, 259.

45. Ibid., 3:259. Iparraguirre, "Jésuites," *DSpir* 8:974–75.

46. Scaduto, *Storia: Lainez*, 3:262.

47. Ibid.

48. Ibid., 3:262–63.

49. Ibid., 3:263.

50. Ibid., 3:262. Ignatius estimated that only a third of those who entered the Society would persevere. Ibid., 3:261.

51. M. Scaduto, S.J., "Il 'Libretto consolatorio' di Bobadilla a Domenech sulle vocazioni mancate (1570)," *AHSJ*, 43(1974): 93–101.

52. Scaduto, *Storia: Lainez*, 3:262.

53. Ibid., 3:264.

54. Ibid., 257, 264. Many secular priests who became novices found it impossible to submit to what was in fact a second formation. Ibid. 3:262.

55. Ibid., 3:264. Iparraguirre, "Jésuites," *DSpir*, 8:974.

56. Scaduto, *Storia: Lainez* 3:265.

57. Iparraguirre, "Jésuites," *DSpir*, 8:974–79. Some novices did their novitiate without having the most basic experience of Jesuit formation, making the Spiritual Exercises through the period of a month. Of 1205 Jesuits who gave unambiguous answers to a questionnaire submitted by Nadal, 195 said that they had not made the Exercises through a month. Iparraguirre judges that this total does not give a true picture of the situation. He removes from those 195 the ninety-three temporal coadjutors, who normally at that time did not make the Exercises, and the fifty-six who were admitted into the Society in Cologne, where unusual circumstances removed the opportunity to make the Exercises. The total, therefore, of those who did not make the Exercises through a month was really only 46. Iparraguirre, *Historia de los Ejercicios*, 2:267–72.

58. *MonSalm*, 2:29. Boero, *Vita...Alfonso Salmerone*, 122–23. Scaduto, *Storia: Lainez*, 3:231.

60. *MonBob*, 401–2.

61. Scaduto, *Storia: Lainez*, 3:429–30.

62. Ibid., 4:368.

63. Ibid., 3:430–31.

64. Ibid., 4:367–68.

65. *MonBob*, 434–35.

66. *MonSalm*, 2:106–7.

67. Ibid., 2:73.

68. Ibid., 2:xx–xxi, 107 with n. 6, 148. Information about this transfer from one province to another is hazy. In November, 1567, Salmerón recommended to the Italian assistant, Benedetto Palmio, that the transfer be a modified one, with some kind of shared responsibility between the Neapolitan provincial and the Sicilian provincial. Ibid., 2:149.

69. Ibid., 2:193 with n. 1, 195.

70. Ibid., 2:215.

71. *MonBob*, 443–44.

72. *MonSalm*, 2:41.

73. Ibid., 2:72.

74. Ibid., 2:42.

75. Ibid., 2:27–28.

76. Ibid., 2:75–76.

77. Ibid., 2:67–68.

78. Ibid., 2:329–30 with n. 6.

79. *MonBob*, 443–44. Gaspar Cervantes was, in turn, archbishop of Messina, Salerno, and Tarragona, where he built a Jesuit college, in which he was buried. *MonSalm*, 2:108–9 with n. 3.

80. *MonSalm*, 2:130–31. This tiny San Severino is not to be confused with the slightly larger San Severino in the March of Ancona. The San Severino of Gaspar Cervantes was a diminutive town located forty-five Roman miles from Naples. Ibid., 2:142 with n. 3.

81. Ibid., 2:142.

82. Ibid., 2:73.

83. *MonPaed*, 3:393–94.

84. *MonSalm*, 2:40.

85. Ibid., 2:123. The college at Nola was opened in late December 1568, one of Laynez's first actions as general in regard to the schools. Scaduto, *Storia: Lainez*, 3:415–16. The boarding facilities were opened in 1563. *MonPaed*, 3:398.

86. *MonPaed*, 3:399.

87. *MonSalm*, 2:133 with n. 2, 141 with n. 2. The foundress, Maria Sanseverino, Countess of Nola, died in February 1565. *MonPaed*, 3:403 with n. 16.

88. *MonSalm*, 2:189.

89. Pirri, *Giovanni Tristano*, 20–21. The last phase of the project to be done was the dining room, which was formally opened 11 June 1578. The rector, Giuseppe Biono, wrote Mercurian that the whole plant formed ''una grande isola.'' Another famous Jesuit architect entered the picture later, when

discussions about expansion were underway. In 1582 Giuseppe Valeriano went to Naples to give advice on the feasibility of purchasing the Palazzo Gravina or the Palazzo Salerno, or some other piece of real estate. Salmerón was no longer superior at that time. P. Pirri, *Giuseppe Valeriano, S.J. Architetto e Pittore (1542–1596)*. (Rome, 1970), 85–86.

90. *MonSalm*, 2:11.

91. Ibid., 2:176–77.

92. This reference to a restriction on the ordination of Jesuits refers to the decree of Pope Pius V, according to which a religious might not be ordained until he pronounced his final vows. According to the Society's constitutions, Jesuits are ordained before their final vows. Ibid., 2:176 with n. 3.

93. Ibid., 2:176–77. In 1574 Salmerón again took up, this time with Mercurian, the problem of Jesuits bypassing the provincial and communicating directly with the general. Salmerón felt that this practice was eroding the provincials' authority. Ibid., 2:414 with n. 3.

94. Ibid., 2:178.

95. Ibid., 2:47, 50, 53.

96. Ibid., 2:177.

97. Ibid., 2:555.

98. Ibid., 2:146.

99. Astráin, *Historia*, 2:550.

100. *MonSalm*, 2:441.

101. Ibid., 2:519.

102. Ibid., 2:427.

103. Ibid., 2:430.

104. Ibid., 2:472.

105. Ibid., 2:484.

106. Ibid., 2:490–91.

107. Ibid., 2:496–97 with n. 4. This proverb is ascribed to the Roman politician Marcus Lucinius Crassus (115?–53 B.C.) on an occasion when he saw a donkey eating thistles. It means that like attracts like. For a brief curriculum vitae of Bravo, see Scaduto, *Storia: Lainez*, 4:96–97 with n. 30.

108. *MonNad*, 1:553, 666, 678, 708.

109. *MonSalm*, 2:52.

110. Ibid.

111. Ibid., 2:50.

112. Scaduto, *Storia: Lainez*, 3:124 with n. 7.

113. *MonSalm*, 2:42, 46.

114. Scaduto, *Storia: Lainez*, 3:298. F. Sweeney, S.J., *Bernardine Realino. Renaissance Man* (New York, 1951), 59–63.

115. Sweeney, *Bernardine Realino*, 163.

116. *MonSalm*, 2:837–38 with n. 1.

117. Ibid., 2:820 with n. 2.

118. Ibid., 2:474.

119. Ibid.

120. Ibid., 2:497.

121. Ibid., 2:596.

122. Ibid., 59–60 with n. 8; 96.

123. Scaduto, *Storia: Lainez*, 3:568.

124. *MonSalm*, 2:96.

125. Ibid., 2:67. *InstSJ*, 2:209.

126. *MonSalm*, 2:70.

127. Ibid., 2:29.

128. Ibid., 2:244.

129. Ibid., 2:250.

130. Ibid., 2:303.

131. Ibid., 2:72.

132. Ibid., 2:182–83.

133. Ibid., 2:819. McGinness, "Preaching Ideals and Practice," 112–18. McGinness points out that Ludwig von Pastor made the same mistake as did Erasmus in judging the Renaissance preachers at the Vatican. During this article McGinness frequently cites the prize winning *Praise and Blame in Renaissance Rome: Rhetoric, Doctrine, and Reform in the Sacred Orators of the Papal Court, c. 1450–1521* by John W. O'Malley, S.J., (Durham, N.C., 1979).

134. *MonSalm*, 2:184.

135. SMV, 8:481–82.

136. Gutierrez, *Españoles en Trento*, 58–59.

137. S. Leite, S.J., in a review of Vieira's *Defesa perante o Tribuna do Santo Officio*, ed. Hernâni Cidade (Bahia, 1957) in *AHSJ*, 27 (1958): 381–84.

138. Vatican Library Microfilm (Biblioteca Vaticana, 1961), 152. This is available at the Fordham University Library.

139. Ibid., 327–36.

140. Vatican Library Microfilm (Bilioteca Vaticana, 1961), 126. This is available at the Fordham University Library.

141. M. Scaduto, S.J., "La Ginevra di Teodore Beza nei ricordi di un Gesuita Lucano Luca Pinelli (1542–1607)," *AHSJ*, 20 (1951): 135–36. There

may have been a further implication in Pinelli's and Caracciolo's play on the words *illuminatio* and *lume*. They may have been subtly alluding to the Illuminism that some people associated with the biblical enthusiasts of the Mediterranean countries.

142. *MonSalm*, 2:187.

143. Ibid., 2:191 with n. 3, 282–85.

144. Ibid., 2:202.

145. Ibid., 2:317–18. In his last sentence, Salmerón refers to the *Historia Naturalis* of Pliny. Otto Braunsberger, who also edits this letter, advises his readers with scholarly gravity that bears do not, as Pliny thought, lick their young in order to give them shape. Rather, they do so to cleanse them. *EppCan*, 7:45 with n. 2.

146. Salmerón, *Commentarii*, 1:4. *MonSalm* 1:xxvii.

147. Astráin, *Historia*, 3:10.

148. Ibid., 3:15 with n. 3.

149. Ibid., 3:18.

150. Ibid., 3:19. Salmerón also served the congregation in another role. To facilitate the formulation of decrees in clear and succinct language for review by the delegates, the congregation appointed six men, called *definitores*. Salmerón was one. Ibid., 3:21.

151. *EppCan*, 7:653.

152. *MonSalm*, 2:642 with n. 3.

153. Ibid., 2:640.

154. Ibid., 2:72.

155. Ibid., 2:642–43 with n. 5.

156. Ibid., 2:644–46, 650 with n. 2.

CHAPTER X

1. *MonSalm*, 2:651. Salmerón sent this letter on 13 April 1576.

2. Ibid., 2:651 with n. 2.

3. Ibid., 1:46–47.

4. Salmerón, *Commentarii*, 1:4.

5. *MonSalm*, 2:684.

6. Ibid., 2:684 with n. 1.

7. Ibid., 2:836.

8. Ibid., 2:808.

9. Ibid., 2:697.

10. Ibid., 2:808.

11. Ibid., 2:720–21.

12. Ibid., 2:720–21.

13. Ibid., 2:705–08.

14. Ibid., 1:xxv with n. 61. Acquaviva informed Salmerón of the appointment on 18 February 1584.

15. Ibid., 2:726–27.

16. Ibid., 1:xxvi.

17. Ibid., 1:xxv.

18. Ibid., 1:xxvi–xxvii.

19. R. E. Brown, S.S., J. A. Fitzmyer, S.J., R.E. Murphy, O. Carm., ed., *The Jerome Biblical Commentary* (Englewood Cliffs, N.J., 1968).

20. Salmerón, *Commentarii*, 6:66–75, 7:41–45. *Jerome Biblical Commentary*, 2:26, 31, 77, 87, 132, 147.

21. *Jerome Biblical Commentary*, 2:31, 87.

22. Salmerón, *Commentarii*, 7:41. *Jerome Biblical Commentary*, remarks: "nor is the tree (more properly a shrub, which grows to a height of 10–12 ft.) remarkably tall." 2:87.

23. *Jerome Biblical Commentary*, 2:31, 87.

24. Salmerón, *Commentarii*, 7:42.

25. *Jerome Biblical Commentary*, 2:26.

26. Salmerón, *Commentarii*, 6:69.

27. *Jerome Biblical Commentary*, 2:77.

28. Salmerón, *Commentarii*, 6:67.

29. Ibid.

30. Ibid., 6:68.

31. Gutierrez, *Españoles en Trento*, 58–59.

32. Brodrick, *Progress of the Jesuits*, 112.

33. Salmerón, *Commentarii*, 1:5.

34. Ibid., 1:90–227.

35. *EppCan*, 3:476 with n. 1. *CT*, 8:722 with n. 3. Jedin, *Papal Legate*, 631.

36. F. de Lanversin, "Salmeron (Alphonse)," *DTC* 14, 1:1041.

37. J. W. Aldridge, *The Hermeneutic of Erasmus* (Richmond, Va., 1966), 30.

38. Ibid., 30–31, 99–103.

39. Salmerón, *Commentarii*, 1:69. Salmerón's criticism of what he called Erasmus's imbalance toward the pursuit of the literal sense of Holy Scripture was

but one flame in the general conflagration about the methods of exegesis in the sixteenth century. Salmerón also took on the Protestants. For the latter, there was but one norm for the allegorical interpretation of Scripture: that given by Scripture itself. No tradition, even when embodied in the writings of the fathers of the church, could be normative. Salmerón opposed that position. He saw in it a sign that the Holy Spirit, "who penetrates the very marrow of the Scriptures," was not present among the Protestants. Before Salmerón, Dominican Francisco Vitoria reproached the Protestant opinion as "impious and sacrilegious." On their side, the Protestants scolded "the pope's men" (*Pontifici, Papicolae*) for their "lavish free-wheeling use of allegory" (*prodigam allegorizandi libertatem*). De Lubac, *Exégèse Médiévale 2*, 2:70.

40.   Salmerón's quotation can give the impression that Erasmus had little esteem for the fathers of the Church. Actually, Erasmus respected the church fathers, but for their ability to increase *eruditio*, that learning on which Erasmus was so intent. He regarded them as coworkers in the search for learning in order to illumine the literal meaning of Holy Scripture. Aldridge, *Hermeneutic of Erasmus*, 86–94.

41.   Salmerón, *Commentarii*, 13:8.

42.   Ibid, 3:64.

43.   Bea, "La Compagnia di Gesù e gli studi biblici," 119.

44.   Ibid., 129.

45.   L. Alonso Schökel, S.J., *Understanding the Bible* (New York, 1963), 12, 27.

46.   *MonSalm*, 2:314–15, 318. Earlier, Salmerón had aided and encouraged Canisius to press on with the publication of his *Catechism*. *EppCan* 7:122, 275, 579, 779–780.

47.   *EppCan*, 7:45.

48.   Iparraguirre, *Historia de los Ejercicios* 2:21, 309. Despite Bobadilla's concern for the Exercises, he himself rarely did any retreat work. His impetuous and inconstant character made him unsuitable for that apostolate. Bobadilla admits, rather ingenuously, that he spent his last years going from college to college in Italy without finding gratification in any of them. Ibid., 2:435.

49.   Ibid., 2:21.

50.   Ibid., 2:309. For a more ample treatment of this movement, see Ibid., 2:292–320.

51.   *InstSJ*, 2:302–3. This movement and this decree were developments of Ignatius's original legislation. The General Examen requires that before vows, first and final, the Jesuit should spend a week making "some of the former Exercises or some others." *ConsSJComm*, [98] on 106–07. De Guibert, *The Jesuits*, 237. Iparraguirre, *Historia de los Ejercicios*, 2:319–20. G. Ganss, S.J., "The Authentic Spiritual Exercises of St. Ignatius," *Studies in the Spirituality of Jesuits* 1 (1969), 14.

52. Astráin, *Historia*, 3:209–10.

53. Ibid., 2:211. Acquaviva had the longest generalate in the history of the Society, from 19 February 1581, to 31 January 1615, a term of thirty-three years and eleven months. During the congregation, Cardinal Carlo Borromeo requested Pope Gregory XIII to intervene with a view to bringing about the election of either Francesco Adorno or Benedetto Palmio. Ibid., 3:215 with n. 1.

54. *Mon Salm*, 2:715–16.

55. Ibid., 2:716.

56. Ibid., 2.

57. *ConsSJComm*, [464–70] on 219–20.

58. *MonSalm*, 2:710.

59. Ibid., 2:711.

60. Ibid., 2:714.

61. Ibid.

62. Ibid., 2:715.

63. *MonPaed*, 3:383–85. Borgia's document reads as follows:

DECRETUM R. P. N. GENERALIS PRAEPOSITI FRANCISCI
BORGIAE IN MENSE NOVEMBRI 1565

1. Nihil defendatur vel doceatur quod adversetur vel deroget vel minus fidei faveat tam in philosophia quam in theolgia.

2. Nihil defendatur quod sit contra axiomata recepta philosophorum; qualia sunt : tantum sunt quatuor genera causarum; tantum sunt quatuor elementa, et tria principia rerum naturalium. Ignis est calidus et siccus, aër humidus et calidus etc.

3. Nihil defendatur contra communissimam philosophorum aut theologorum sententiam, ut quod agentia naturalia agant sine medio, etc.

4. Nulla opinio defendatur contra communem, inconsulto superiore aut praefecto.

5. Nulla nova opinio in philosophia aut theologia introducatur, inconsulto superiore aut praefecto.

OPINIONES SUSTINENDAE A NOSTRISQUE
DOCENDAE UT VERAE AC TENENDAE

De Deo—1. Deus est infinitae virtutis intensive, et agens liberum secundum veram philosophiam.

2. Deus habet providentiam omnium inferiorum etiam singularium et humanarum rerum, et cognoscit omnia: praeterita, praesentia et futura, secundum veram philosophiam.

De angelis—3. Angeli ponuntur vere in praedicamento, et non sunt purus actus secundum veram philosophiam.

4. Angeli sunt in loco et moventur localiter, ita ut non sit asserendum, in nullo loco esse aut non moveri, ita ut substantia sit

praesens, modo aliquo uni, postea alteri loco.

5. Anima intellectiva non est assistens, sed vere forma informans secundum Aristotelem et veram philosophiam.

6. Anima intellectiva non est una numero in omnibus hominibus, sed in singulis hominibus distincta et propria secundum Aristotelem et veram philosophiam.

7. Anima intellectiva est immortalis secundum Aristotelem et veram philosophiam.

8. Non sunt plures animae in homine : intellectiva, sensitiva et vegetativa, secundum Aristotelem et veram philosophiam.

9. Anima in homine aut in bruto non est pilis aut capillis.

10. Potentiae sensitivae et vegetativae in homine aut in bruto non subiectantur in materia prima immediate.

11. Humores aliquo modo sunt partes hominis seu animalis.

12. Tota quidditas substantiae compositae non est sola forma sed materia et forma.

13. Praedicabilia sunt tantum quinque.

14. Essentia divina non habet unam subsistentiam communem tribus personis, sed tantum tres subsistentias personales.

15. Peccatum et malum formaliter est privatio et non positivum quid.

16. Praedestinationis non datur causa ex parte nostra.

Hic ordo praescriptus a praeceptoribus nostris omnino servetur, neque contra propositiones hic scriptas, neque publice neque privatim ullo modo loquantur, neque pietatis neque veritatis neque alterina rei praetextu aliter doceant quam constitutum et definitum est. Haec enim docenda a nostris non solum admonemus sed etiam statuimus.

64. Ibid. 2:46*–47*, 3:385 with n. 3. Some scholars interpret Borgia's catalog as a partial response to the acute need in the Jesuit schools of that age: a *Ratio Studiorum*. One of the early Society's more influential educators, Diego Ledesma, who for eighteen years was associated with the Roman College, as professor of theology (1557–62), and as prefect of studies (1563–75) advocated a systemization of the Jesuit educational enterprise. ''Let a book be written with a complete plan of studies, clearly spelled out step by step'' (*Scribatur liber, in quo distincte et particulatim contineatur totus ordo studiorum*). X. Le Bachelet, S.J., et al., ''Jesuites (La Théologie dans l'ordre des),'' *DTC* 8, 1:1016–17.

65. H. Quillet, ''Congruisme,'' *DTC* 3, 1:1132–33. This decree led to confusion among Jesuits about its precise meaning. Muzio Vitelleschi, Acquaviva's successor, tried to clarify this issue in a letter of 7 January 1616. Ibid., 3, 1:1133.

66. Astráin, *Historia*, 5:284.

67. Ibid., 7:13–15. *InstSJ*, 2:382, 413, 432.

68. *MonSalm*, 2:811–19.

A RECAPITULATION

1. André Ravier, S.J., attempts to construct personality portraits of the first ten Jesuits from their correspondence, their writings, and their penmanship. He incorporates the conclusions of an expert in handwriting, Pierre Coulet, who made graphological studies of the founders of the Society of Jesus. Ravier portrays Jay as a man who had need of warm personal relations with others; who did not conceive the world and men in a cold, abstract way; who, because of a pronounced aesthetic sense and a lively affective sensibility, understood people the better; who had an extreme concern for authenticity; whose dynamic forces of action were somewhat disoriented and agitated. André Ravier, S.J., *Les Chroniques. Saint Ignace de Loyola* (Paris, 1973), 305.

2. Scaduto, *Storia: Lainez* 3:307. Ravier, again using Pierre Coulet's graphological studies, describes Salmerón as a strong, resolute, intransigent man of ideas, a debater set on the conquest of his opponents with proofs; who was inclined to cling too closely to the letter lest he be guilty of treason to the spirit; whose occasional outbursts showed the state of tension in which he lived; from whom at times a tenderness, owing nothing to logic, broke forth. Ravier, *Les Chroniques*, 315.

3. G. Codina Mir, S.J., *Aux Sources de la Pédagogie des Jésuites. Le "Modus Parisiensis."* (Rome. 1968), 284.

4. P. Hughes, *A History of the Church. An Introductory Study.* Revised Edition (New York, 1947–49), 3:224.

5. Y. M-J Congar, O. P., *A History of Theology* (Garden City, 1968), 148–49. See also 163.

6. R. R. Bolgar, *The Classical Heritage and its Beneficiaries* (New York: Harper Torchbook edition, 1964), 333–34.

7. F. de Dainville, S.J., "Saint Ignatius and Humanism," *The Jesuit Educational Quarterly*, 21(1958–59): 200–201.

8. L. Cognet, *Post-Reformation Spirituality* (New York, 1959), 24–25.

9. Poncelet, *Histoire de la Compagnie de Jésus*, 2:584, 587.

10. Fenlon, *Heresy and Obedience*, 32, 45, 50.

11. Durand, "Jésuites (Travaux des) sur les Saintes Ecritures," 3-2:1404.

12. J. Leclercq, O.S.B., *The Love of Learning and the Desire for God* (New York: A Rose Hill Book, 1974), 5–7.

13. Iparraguirre, *Historia de los Ejercicios*, 1:267–96. Fr. Iparraguire made a statistical study of the number of persons, not including Jesuits, who made the Exercises during Ignatius's lifetime. He approached the total of at least 1295. This figure can be only approximate, since the sources in some instances use phrases such as "some youths," "three or four at a time," "two priests," "several Dominican nuns." 267–96.

14. L. Cognet, *Histoire de la Spiritualité Chrétienne. 1. L'essor: 1500–1650* (Paris, 1966): 25.

15. Cognet, *Post-Reformation Spirituality*, 13.

16. *ConsSJComm*, 270, number 615.

17. *MonNad*, 5:195.

18. M. O'Connell, *The Counter Reformation 1559–1610* (New York, 1974), 108.

19. *CT*, 5:812–15.

20. McNally, "Counter-Reformation Views on Sin and Penance," 153.

BIBLIOGRAPHY

PRIMARY SOURCES: MHSJ

The volumes in the *Monumenta Historica Societatis Jesu* that are referred to. This historical series, which began in 1894, now numbers more than 110 volumes.

Bobadillae Monumenta. Edited by D. Restrepo, S.J. 1 vol. Madrid, 1913.

Chronicon Societatis Iesu, auctore Joanne Alphonso de Polanco, S.J. Edited by J.M. Velez, S.J. and V. Agusti, S.J. 6 vols. Madrid, 1894–98.

Constitutiones et Regulae Societatis Iesu. Edited by A. Codina, S.J. and D. Fernández Zapico, S.J. 4 vols. Rome, 1934–48.

Epistolae et Monumenta P. Hieronymi Nadal. Edited by F. Cervós, S.J. and M. Nicolau, S.J. 6 vols. Vol. 1–4, Madrid, 1898–1905. Vols. 5–6, Rome, 1962–64.

Epistolae Mixtae ex variis Europae locis, 1537–1556. Edited by V. Agusti, S.J. 5 vols. Madrid, 1898–1901.

Epistolae P. Alphonsi Salmeronis. Edited by R. Vidurre, S.J. and F. Cervós, S.J. 2 vols. Madrid, 1906–7.

Epistolae PP. Paschasii Broet, Claudii Jaji, Joannis Codurii et Simonis Rodericii S.J.. Edited by F. Cervós, S.J. 1 vol. Madrid, 1903.

Epistolae S. Francisci Xaverii. Edited by G. Schurhammer, S.J. and J. Wicki, S.J. 2 vols. Rome, 1944–45.

Fabri Monumenta. Edited by F. Lirola, S.J. 1 vol. Madrid, 1914.

Fontes narrativi de S. Ignatio de Loyola et de Societatis Iesu initiis. Edited by D. Fernández Zapico, S.J., C. de Dalmases, S.J., and P. Leturia, S.J. 4 vols. Rome, 1943–60.

Lainii Monumenta. Edited by E. Astudillo, S.J. 8 vols. Madrid, 1912–17.

Litterae Quadrimestres. Edited by M. Lecina, S.J. and D. Fernández Zapico, S.J. 7 vols. Madrid and Rome, 1894–1932.

Monumenta paedigogica Societatis Iesu (1540–1556). Edited by L. Lukács, S.J. 3 vols. Rome, 1965–75.

Patris Petri de Ribadeneira Confessiones. Epistolae aliaque scripta inedita. Edited by D. Restrepo, S.J. and J. Vilar, S.J. 2 vols. Madrid, 1920–23.

Polanci Complementa. Edited by D. Restrepo, S.J. and D. Fernández Zapico, S.J. 2 vols. Madrid, 1916–17.

CLAUDE JAY AND ALFONSO SALMERÓN

Sancti Ignatii de Loyola Societatis Jesu Fundatoris Epistolae et Instructiones. Edited by M. Lecina, S.J., V. Agusti, S.J. and D. Restrepo, S.J. 12 vols. Madrid, 1903–11.

Sanctus Franciscus Borgia. Edited by I. Rodriguez, S.J., V. Agusti, S.J. and F. Cervós, S.J. 5 vols. Madrid, 1894–1911.

OTHER PRIMARY SOURCES

Acta Reformationis Catholicae Ecclesiam Germaniae Concernentia Saeculi XVI. Edited by Georg Pfeilschifter. 5 vols. Regensburg, 1959–73.

Bobadilla, Nicolás, S.J. *Libellus de Laudabili et Fructuosa, Frequenti, aut Quotidiana, Sacrosanctae Eucharistiae Sumptione.* In Paul Dudon, S.J. "Le *Libellus* de P. Bobadilla sur la communion fréquent et quotidienne." *Archivum Historicum Societatis Jesu* 2 (1933): 258–79.

Câmara, Luis Gonçalves da, S.J. *Mémorial.* Edited and translated by Roger Tandonnet, S.J. Collection Christus, No. 20, *Textes.* Paris, 1966.

Canisius, Peter, S.J. *Beati Petri Canisii Societatis Jesu epistulae et acta.* Edited by Otto Braunsberger, S.J. 8 vols. Freiburg-im-Breisgau, 1896–1923.

Collectio Decretorum Congregationum Generalium Societatis Jesu a Congregatione XXVII approbata et a Congregationibus Generalibus XXVIII, XXIX, et XXX retractata. Rome, 1961.

Conciliorum Oecumenicorum Decreta. Edited by Joseph Alberigo et al. Basle, 1962.

Concilium Tridentinum. Diariorum, Actorum, Epistularum, Tractatuum nova collectio. Edited by Stephen Ehses and Görres Gesellschaft. 13 vols. Freiburg-im-Breisgau, 1901–61.

Decreta, Canones, Censurae et Praecepta Congregationum Generalium Societatis Jesu, cum Formulis, et Quorundam Officiorum Regulis. 3 vols. Avignon, 1830.

Enchiridion Symbolorum Definitionum et Declarationum de Rebus Fidei et Morum, 33rd edition. Edited by Heinrich Denzinger and Adolf Schönmetzer, S.J. Freiburg-im-Breisgau, 1965.

Erasmus, Desiderius. *Opus Epistolarum Desiderii Erasmi Roterodami; denuo recognitum et auctum.* Edited by Percy S. and Helen M. Allen. 12 vols. Oxford, 1906–58.

Favre, Pierre. *Mémorial.* Edited and translated by Michel de Certeau, S.J. Collection Christus, No. 4, *Textes.* Paris, 1939.

Freux, André des, S.J. *Epigrammata in Haereticos.* Douai, 1596.

Gretzer, Jakob, S.J. *Jacobi Gretseri Societatis Jesu Theologi Opera Omnia . . . ad certos titulos revocata.* 17 vols. Regensburg, 1734–41.

Hervet, Gentian. "Litterae Gentiani Herveti ad Salmeronum Soc. Jesu theologum, de residentia episcoporum." *Monumentorum ad Historiam Concilii Tridentini potissimum illustrandam spectantium amplissima collectio* 5:777–89. Edited by Judocus Le Plat. Louvain, 1785.

Institutum Societatis Jesu. I: *Bullarium et Compendium Privilegiorum.* II: *Examen et Constitutiones, Decreta et Canones Congregationum Generalium.* III: *Regulae, Ratio Studiorum, Ordinationes.* 3 vols. Florence, 1892–93.

Jay, Claude, S.J. "Commentariolus de Officio." Jakob Gretzer, S.J. *Jacobi Gretseri Opera Omnia.* 17:160–78. Regensburg, 1734–41.

_____. "Speculum Praesulis ex verbis Sacrae Scripturae, Canonum, et Doctorum, jam olim a R.P. Claudio Jaio." Jakob Gretzer, S.J. *Jacobi Gretseri Opera Omnia* 17:141–58. Regensburg, 1734–41.

Laynez, Diego, S.J. *Jacobi Laínez Disputationes Tridentinae.* Edited by Hartmann Grisar, S.J. 2 vols. Innsbruck 1886.

Lefèvre d'Etaples, Jacques. *The Prefatory Epistles of Jacques Lefèvre d'Etaples and Related Texts.* Edited by Eugene F. Rice, Jr. New York, 1972.

Le Plat, Judocus, editor. *Monumentorum ad Historiam Concilii Tridentini potissimum illustrandam spectantium amplissima collectio.* 8 vols. Louvain, 1781-87.

Loyola, Ignatius, S.J. *The Constitutions of the Society of Jesus.* Translated with an introduction and commentary, by George E. Ganss, S.J. St. Louis, 1970.

The Spiritual Exercises of St. Ignatius. Translated by Louis J. Puhl, S.J. Westminister, Md., 1951.

Portable Renaissance Reader. Edited by J.B. Ross and M.M. McLaughlin. New York, 1953.

Ribadeneyra, Pedro, S.J. *De Ratione Instituti Societatis Jesu ex Hispano in Latinum Conversa a P. Laurentio Carli ex eadem Societate.* Rome, 1864.

_____. *Historias de la Contrarreforma.* Edited by Eusebio Rey, S.J. Madrid, 1945.

Sacrorum Conciliorum Nova et Amplissima Collectio. Edited by Giovanni Domenico Mansi. Reproduced and continued by L. Petit and J.B. Martin. 53 vols. in 60. Paris, 1901–27.

Salmerón, Alfonso, S.J. *Alfonsi Salmeronis Toletani e Societate Jesu theologi praeclarissimi, Commentarii in evangelicam historiam, et in Acta Apostolorum: nunc primum in lucem editi.* 16 vols. Cologne, 1612.

_____. *Alphonsi Salmeronis Doctoris Toletani atque in Concilio Tridentino Theologi Doctrina de Jurisdictionis Episcopalis Origine ac Ratione.* Edited by J.B. Andries. Mainz, 1871.

_____. *De Imputativa Justitia.* In "En el IV centenario de uno voto tridentino del Jesuita Alfonso Salmerón sobre la doble justicia." *Estudios Eclesiasticos* 20 (1946): 211–40. Edited by Jesús Olazaran, S.J.

OTHER WORKS

Ajo González y Sáinz de Zuniga, Candido Maria. *Historia de las Universidades Hispanicas. Orígenes y desarrollo desde su aparición a nuestros diás.* 9 vols. Avila. 1957– .

Alberigo, Giuseppe. "The Council of Trent: New Views on the Occasion of Its Fourth Centenary." *Concilium* 7 (1965): 69–87.

———. *I Vescovi Italiani al Concilio de Trento (1545–1547).* Florence, 1959.

Aldama, Antonio de, S.J. *Repartiendose en la viña de Cristo. Comentario a la séptima parte de las Constituciones de la Compañia de Jesús.* Rome, 1973.

Aldridge, John W. *The Hermeneutic of Erasmus.* Richmond, Va., 1966.

Alonso Schökel, Luis, S.J. *Understanding the Bible.* Translated by Peter J. McCord, S.J. New York, 1963.

Alszeghy, Zoltan, S.J., and Maurizio Flick, S.J. "Il Decreto Tridentino sul peccato originale." *Gregorianum* 52 (1971): 595–635.

Anderson, Marvin W. "Trent and Justification (1546): A Protestant Reflection." *Scottish Journal of Theology* 21 (1968): 385–406.

Astráin, Antonio, S.J. *Historia de la Compañía de Jesús en la Asistencia de España.* 7 vols. Madrid, 1912–25.

Bangert, William V., S.J. *A History of the Society of Jesus.* St. Louis, 1972.

———. *To the Other Towns. A Life of Blessed Peter Favre.* Westminster, Md., 1959.

Bartoli, Daniello, S.J. *Dell'istoria della Compagnia di Gesù. L'Italia.* Rome, 1673.

Bataillon, Marcel. *Erasme et l'Espagne. Recherches sur l'Histoire Spirituelle du XVIe siècle.* Paris, 1937.

Bea, Agostino, S.J. "La Compagnia di Gesù e gli studi biblici." *La Compagnia di Gesù e le Scienze Sacre,* 115–43. Editor not given. Rome, 1942.

Bernard-Maitre, Henri, S.J. "Calvin et Loyola." *Bulletin de l'Association Guillaume Budé,* Troisième Série, numéro 2 (June 1953): 74–85.

———. "Les Fondateurs de la Compagnie de Jésus et l'Humanisme Parisien de la Renaissance (1525–1536)." *Nouvelle Revue Théologique* 72 (1950): 811–33.

Beumer, Johannes, S.J. "Der erste Jesuit aus Deutschland auf dem Trienter Konzil P. Claude Jay." *Archivum Historicum Societatis Jesu* 39 (1970): 1681–82.

Bévenot, Maurice, S.J. "*Traditiones* in the council of Trent." *The Heythrop Journal* 4 (1963): 333–47.

Blaisdell, Charmarie Jenkins. "Politics and Heresy in Ferrara, 1534–1559." *The Sixteenth Century Journal 6 (1975): 67–83.*

Boero, Giuseppe, S.J. *Vita del Servo di Dio P. Alfonso Salmerone*. Florence, 1880.

_____. *Vita de Servo di Dio P. Claudio Iaia*. Florence, 1878.

Bolgar, R.R. *The Classical Heritage and Its Beneficiaries*. New York: Harper Torchbook Edition, 1964.

Bossy, John. "Editor's Postscript." *The Spirit of the Counter-Reformation* by H. Outram Evennett, 126–45. Cambridge, 1968.

Bouwsma, William J. "Postel and the Significance of Renaissance Cabalism." *Renaissance Essays*, 252–66. Edited by Paul Kristeller and Philip P. Wiener. New York, 1968.

Brandi, Karl. *The Emperor Charles V*. Translated by C.V. Wedgwood. London: Jonathan Cape Paperback Edition, 1965.

Bremond, Henri. *Histoire littéraire du sentiment religieux en France depuis la fin des guerres de religion jusqu'à nos jours*. 12 vols. Paris, 1924–36.

Brodrick, James, S.J. *The Origin of the Jesuits*. New York, 1940.

_____. *The Progress of the Jesuits (1556–1579)*. London, 1946.

_____. *Saint Ignatius Loyola. The Pilgrim Years*. London, 1956.

_____. *Saint Peter Canisius*. London, 1935.

Brown, Raymond, S.S., Joseph Fitzmyer, S.J. et al., editors, *Jerome Biblical Commentary*. Englewood Cliffs, N.J., 1968.

Buxbaum, Englebert Maximilian. *Petrus Canisius und die Kirchliche Erneuerung des Herzogotums Bayern 1549–1556*. Rome, 1973.

Cantimori, Delio, "Italy and the Papacy." *New Cambridge Modern History*. 3:251–74. Cambridge, 1968.

Cereceda, Feliciano, S.J. *Diego Laínez en la Europa religiosa de su tiempo 1512–1565*. 2 vols. Madrid, 1945–46.

_____. "Laínez y Salmerón y el proceso del Catecismo de Carranza." *Razon y Fe* 100 (1932): 212–26.

Certeau, Michel de, S.J. *See* Dalmases, Candido de, S.J., Ignacio Iparraguirre, S.J., and Michel de Certeau, S.J.

Clancy, Thomas H., S.J. *An Introduction to Jesuit Life*. St. Louis, 1976.

Codina Mir, Gabriel, S.J. *Aux Sources de la Pédagogie des Jésuites. Le "Modus Parisiensis."* Rome, 1968.

Cognet, Louis. *Histoire de la Spiritualité Chrétienne*. Paris, 1966.

_____. *Post-Reformation Spirituality*. Translated by P. Hepburne Scott. New York, 1959.

Cohen, Thomas V. "Why the Jesuits Joined: 1540–1600." *Historical Papers 1974 Communications Historiques* (Supplement to vol. 55 of *The Canadian Historical Review*).

Concilium: Theology in the Age of Renewal. New York, 1965–.

Congar, Yves M.-J., O.P. "'The Cross of Jesus' by Fr. Louis de Chardon, O.P." *The Revelation of God*, 116–28. Translated by A. Manson and L.C. Sheppard. New York, 1968.

——. A *History of Theology.* Translated and edited by Hunter Guthrie, S.J. Garden City, 1968.

——. *Tradition and Traditions. An Historical Essay and a Theological Essay.* Translated by Michael Naseby and Thomas Rainborough. New York. 1967.

Corcoran, Timothy, S.J. *The Clongowes Record 1814 to 1932 with Introductory Chapters on Irish Jesuit Educators 1564–1813.* Dublin, 1932.

Crehan, Joseph, S.J. "Saint Ignatius and Cardinal Pole." *Archivum Historicum Societatis Jesu* 25 (1956): 72–98.

Cristiani, Léon. *L'Eglise à L'Epoque du Concile de Trent.* Vol. 17 of *Histoire de l'Eglise*, edited by A. Fliche and V. Martin. Paris, 1948.

Culley, Thomas D., S.J. *See* McNaspy, C.J., S.J. and Thomas D. Culley, S.J.

Cuthbert, O., S.F.C. *The Capuchins. A Contribution to the History of the Counter-Reformation.* 2 vols. New York and Toronto, 1929.

Dainville, François de, S.J. "Saint Ignatius and Humanism." Translated by J. Robert Barth, S.J. and John M. Culkin, S.J. *Jesuit Educational Quarterly* 21 (1958–59): 189–208.

Dalmases, Candido de, S.J., Ignacio Iparraguirre, S.J., and Michel de Certeau, S.J. "Jésuites." *Dictionnaire de Spiritualité* 8:958–1065.

D'Alton, E.A. *History of Ireland.* 3 vols. in 6. London, 1912.

Dickens, Arthur G. *The Counter-Reformation.* London, 1969.

——. *Reformation and Society in Sixteenth-Century Europe.* London, 1966.

Dictionnaire de la Bible. Edited by F. Vigouroux. 8 vols. Paris, 1912–72.

Dictionnaire de Spiritualité. Ascetique et Mystique. Doctrine et Histoire. Edited by Marcel Viller, S.J. Paris, 1932– .

Dictionnaire de Théologie Catholique. Edited by Jean M. A. Vacant. 15 vols. Paris, 1903–47.

Dolan, John P. "Some Catholic Literary Opponents of Luther." *Journal of Ecumenical Studies* 11 (1974): 447–65.

Dortel-Claudot, Michel, S.J. *Le genre de vie extérieur de la Compagnie de Jésus.* Rome, 1971.

Dudon, Paul, S.J. *St. Ignatius of Loyola.* Translated by William J. Young, S.J. Milwaukee, 1949.

——. "Le 'Libellus' du P. Bobadilla sur la communion fréquent et quotidienne." *Archivum Historicum Societatis Jesu* 2 (1933): 258–79.

——"Saint Ignace et l'oraison dans la Compagnie de Jésus." *Revue d'Ascetique et de Mystique* 15 (1934): 245–57.

_____. "Sur un texte inédit de Salmeron (1562)." *Gregorianum* 11 (1930): 410–17.

Duhr, Bernard, S.J. *Geschichte der Jesuiten in den Ländern Deutscher Zunge.* 4 vols. in 6 parts. Munich-Regensburg, 1907–28.

Dumeige, Gervais, S.J. "Ignace de Loyola. II. Expérience et doctrine." *Dictionnaire de Spiritualité* 7:1277–1306.

Durand, A., S.J., "Jésuites (Travaux des): sur les Saintes Ecritures." *Dictionnaire de la Bible* 3,1:1403–21.

Edwards, Robert Dudley. *Church and State in Tudor Ireland. A History of Penal Laws against the Irish Catholics 1534–1603.* London, 1935.

Egaña, Francisco Javier, S.J. *Origines de la Congregación General en la Compañia de Jesús.* Rome, 1972.

Elliott, J.H. *Imperial Spain 1469–1716.* New York: Mentor Book Edition, 1966.

Evennett, H. Outram. *The Cardinal of Lorraine and the Council of Trent. A Study in the Counter-Reformation.* Cambridge, 1930.

_____. "The Counter-Reformation." *The Reformation Crisis*, 58–71. Edited by Joel Hurstfield. New York: Harper Torchbooks, 1965.

_____. *The Spirit of the Counter-Reformation.* Cambridge, 1968.

Farrell, Allan P., S.J. *The Jesuit Code of Liberal Education. Development and Scope of the Ratio Studiorum.* Milwaukee, 1938.

Fenlon, Dermot. *Heresy and Obedience in Tridentine Italy. Cardinal Pole and the Counter Reformation.* Cambridge, 1972.

Fichter, Joseph H., S.J. *James Laynez, Jesuit.* St. Louis, 1944.

Fiorito, Miguel A., S.J. "Ignatius' Own Legislation on Prayer." Edited and translated by Aloysius A. Jacobsmeyer, S.J. with the assistance of George E. Ganss, S.J. and John R. Kelly, S.J. *Woodstock Letters* 97 (1968): 149–224.

Fisher, Arthur L. "A Study in Early Jesuit Government: The Nature and Origins of the Dissent of Nicolás Bobadilla." *Viator. Medieval and Renaissance Studies*, 10 (1979): 397–431.

Fitzmyer, Joseph S.J. *See* Brown, Raymond, S.S., Joseph Fitzmyer, S.J. et al., editors.

Flick, Maurizio, S.J. *See* Alszeghy, Zoltan, S.J., and Maurizio Flick, S.J.

Ganss, George E., S.J. "The Authentic Spiritual Exercises of St. Ignatius." *Studies in the Spirituality of Jesuits* 1 (1969): 1–36.

_____. "The Origin of Jesuit Colleges for Externs and the Controversies about their Poverty, 1539–1605." *Woodstock Letters* 91 (1962): 123-66.

Garcia-Villoslada, Ricardo, S.J. *Loyola y Erasmo. Dos Almas, dos Epocas.* Madrid, 1965.

Garraghan, Gilbert J., S.J. *The Jesuits of the Middle United States.* 3 vols. New York, 1938.

Gilbert, Felix. "Religion and Politics in the Thought of Gasparo Contarini," 90–116. *Action and Conviction in Early Modern Europe. Essays in Memory of E.H. Harbison.* Edited by Theodore K. Rabb and Jerrold E. Seigel. Princeton, 1969.

Grabka, Gregory, O.F.M. Conv. "Cardinal Hosius and the Council of Trent." *Theological Studies* 7 (1946): 558–75.

Granero, Jésus M., S.J. *San Ignacio de Loyola. Panoramas de su Vida.* Madrid, 1967.

Guibert, Joseph de, S.J. *The Jesuits. Their Spiritual Doctrine and Practice.* Translated by William J. Young, S.J. Chicago, 1964.

Gutierrez, Constancio, S.J. *Españoles en Trento.* Valladolid, 1951.

Hall, Basil. "The Trilingual College of San Ildefonso and the Making of the Complutensian Bible." 114–46 *Studies in Church History.* Vol. 5 *The Church and Academic Learning.* Edited by G. L. Cuming. Leiden, 1969.

Hallet, Paul H. *Catholic Reformer. A Life of St. Cajetan of Thiene.* Westminster, Md., 1959.

Herman, J.B., S.J. *La Pédagogie des Jésuites au XVIe siècle. Ses sources, ses caractéristiques.* Louvain, 1914.

Horne, P.R. "Reformation and Counter-Reformation at Ferrara." *Italian Studies* 13 (1958): 62–82.

Hughes, John C. "Alfonso Salmerón: His Work at the Council of Trent." Ph.D. dissertation, University of Kentucky, 1974.

Hughes, Philip. *A History of the Church. An Introductory Study.* Revised edition. 3 vols. New York, 1947–49.

Hurstfield, Joel, editor. *The Reformation Crisis.* New York, 1965.

Hurter, Hugo von, S.J. *Nomenclator Literarius Theologiae Catholicae Theologos Exhibens Aetate, Natione, Disciplinis.* Innsbruck, 1871–86.

Iparraguirre, Ignacio, S.J. *Historia de los Ejercicios de San Ignacio.* 3 vols. Rome, 1946–73.

———. "Para la historia de la oración en el Colegio Romano durante la segunda mitad del siglo XVI." *Archivum Historicum Societatis Jesu* 14 (1946): 77–126.

———, editor. *Estudios Ignacianos.* Vol. 1: *Estudios Biograficos.* Vol. 2: *Estudios Espirituales.* Rome, 1957.

———. *See also* Dalmases, Candido de, S.J., Ignacio Iparraguirre, S.J., and Michel de Certeau, S.J.

Irsay, Stephen d'. *Histoire des Universités Françaises et Etrangères des Origines à nos Jours.* 2 vols. Paris, 1933.

Janssen, Johannes. *Geschichte des deutschen Volkes seit dem Ausgang der Mittlealters.* 8 vols. Freiburg-im-Breisgau, 1893–1901.

Jedin, Hubert, *Crisis and Closure of the Council of Trent*. Translated by N. D. Smith. London: Sheed and Ward Stagbooks, 1967.

———. *Ecumenical Councils of the Catholic Church*. Translated by Ernest Graf, O.S.B. New York, 1960.

———. *A History of the Council of Trent*. Translated by Ernest Graf, O.S.B. 2 vols. London, 1957–61.

———. *Papal Legate at the Council of Trent. Cardinal Seripando*. Translated by Frederic C. Eckhoff. St. Louis, 1947.

Jimenez, Alberto. *Seleccion y Reforma. Ensayo sobre la Universidad Renancentista Española*. Mexico City, 1944.

Kaufman, Peter Iver. "John Colet and Erasmus' *Enchiridion*." *Church History* 46 (1977): 296–312.

Knowles, David. *From Pachomius to Ignatius. A Study in the Constitutional History of the Religious Orders*. Oxford, 1966.

———. *The Religious Orders in England*. Vol. 3: *The Tudor Age*. Cambridge, 1959.

——— and Dimitri Obolensky. *The Christian Centuries*. Vol. 2: *The Middle Ages*. New York, 1968.

Kristeller, Paul O., and Philip P. Wiener, editors. *Renaissance Essays*. New York, 1968.

Kuttner, Stephan. "Papal Efforts toward Protestant Representation at Trent." *The Review of Politics* 10 (1948): 427–36.

Lanversin, Fernand de, S.J. "Salmerón (Alphonse)," *Dictionnaire de Théologie Catholique* 14,1:1040–47.

Le Bachelet, Xavier, S.J. et al. "Jésuites (La Théologie dans l'ordre des)," *Dictionnaire de Théologie Catholique* 8,1: 1012–1107.

Leclercq, Jean, O.S.B. *The Love of Learning and the Desire for God*. Revised edition. Translated by Catherine Misrahi. New York, 1974.

———. "St. Ignatius at Monserrat." 295–307. *Aspects of Monasticism*. Translated by Mary Dodd. Kalamazoo, Michigan, 1978.

Lécuyer, Joseph, C.S.Sp. "Episcopat. Moyen Age et Pèriod Moderne." *Dictionnaire de Spiritualité* 4,1:879–907.

Leite, Serafim, S.J. Book review of *Defesa perante o Tribuna do Santo Officio* by Antonio Vierira, S.J. *Archivum Historicum Societatis Jesu* 27 (1958): 381–84.

Leturia, Pedro de, S.J. "Conspectus Chronologicus Vitae Sancti Ignatii." *Estudios Ignacianos* 1:189–260. Rome, 1957.

———. "De 'Constitutionibus collegiorum' P. Joannis de Polanco ac de earum influxu in Constitutiones S.I." *Archivum Historicum Societatis Jesu* 7 (1936): 1–30.

———. "Génesis de los ejercicios de San Ignacio y su influjo en la fundación de la Compañía de Jesús (1521–1540)," *Estudios Ignacianos* 2:3–55.

———. "La hora matutina de meditación en la Compañía naciente." *Archivum Historicum Societatis Jesu* 3 (1934): 47–86.

———. "Problemas Historicos en torno a las Reglas para Sentir con Iglesia." *Estudios Ignacianos* 2:175–86.

———. "Sentido verdadero en la Iglesia Militante." *Estudios Ignacianos* 2:149–74.

———. "Un documento de 1558 sobre las misiones." *Archivum Historicum Societatis Jesu* 8 (1939): 102–17.

———. "Why the Society of Jesus Became a Teaching Order." Translated by Victor R. Yanitelli, S.J. *Jesuit Educational Quarterly* 4 (1941): 31–54.

Lewis, Eleanor V. "Concepts of the Church at the First Period of the Council of Trent 1545–47." Ph.D. dissertation, Fordham University, 1970.

Linder, Robert D. "Calvinism and Humanism. The First Generation." *Church History* 44 (1975): 167–81.

Logan, O. M. T. "Grace and Justification: Some Italian Views of the Sixteenth and Early Seventeenth Centuries." *Journal of Ecclesiastical History* 20 (1969): 67–78.

Lubac, Henri de, S.J. *Exégèse Médiévale. Les Quatre Sens de L'Ecriture.* 2 vols., 2 parts in each vol. Paris, 1959–64.

Lukács, Ladislaus. S.J. "De origine collegiorum externorum deque controversiis circa eorum pauperatatem obortis 1539–1608." *Archivum Historicum Societatis Jesus* 19 (1960): 189–245; 30 (1961): 3–69.

McConica, James Kelsey. *English Humanists and Reformation Politics under Henry VIII and Edward VI.* Oxford, 1965.

McGinness, Frederick J. "Preaching Ideals and Practice in Counter-Reformation Rome." *The Sixteenth Century Journal* 11 (1980): 109-27.

McNair, Philip. *Peter Martyr in Italy. An Anatomy of Apostasy.* Oxford, 1967.

McNally, Robert E., S.J., "The Council of Trent and the German Protestants." *Theological Studies* 25 (1964): 1–22.

———. "The Counter-Reformation Views of Sin and Penance." *Thought* 52 (1977): 151–66.

McNaspy, C.J., S.J. "Art in Jesuit Life." *Studies in the Spirituality of Jesuits* 5, No. 3 (1973): 93–109.

McNaspy, C.J., S.J. and Thomas D. Culley, S.J. "The Fine Arts in the Old Society of Jesus: A Preliminary Investigation." *Archivum Historicum Societatis Jesu* 40 (1971): 213–45.

Massaut, Jean-Pierre. *Josse Clichtove, L'Humanisme et la Rèform du Clergé.* 2 vols. Paris, 1968.

Matheson, Peter. *Cardinal Contarini at Regensburg*. Oxford, 1972.

Maxcey, Carl E. "Double Justice, Diego Laynez, and the Council of Trent." *Church History* 48 (1979): 269–78.

Nieto, Jose C. *Juan de Valdes and the Origins of the Spanish and Italian Reformation*. Geneva, 1970.

Obolensky, Dimitri. *See* Knowles, David and Dimitri Obolensky.

O'Connell, Marvin. *The Counter-Reformation 1559–1610*. New York, 1974.

Olazaran, Jesús, S.J. "En el IV centenario de uno voto tridentino del Jesuita Alfonso Salmerón sobre la doble justicia." *Estudios Eclesiasticos* 20 (1946): 211–40.

Olin, John C. "Erasmus and St. Ignatius of Loyola." *Luther, Erasmus and the Reformation. A Catholic- Protestant Reappraisal*, 114–33. Edited by John C. Olin. New York, 1969.

——, editor. *The Catholic Reformation: Savonarola to Ignatius Loyola*. New York, 1969.

——, editor. *Luther, Erasmus and the Reformation. A Catholic-Protestant Reappraisal*. New York, 1969.

O'Malley, John W., S.J. *Giles of Viterbo on Church and Reform. A Study in Renaissance Thought*. Leiden, 1968.

——. "The Jesuits, St. Ignatius, and the Counter Reformation. Some Recent Studies and Their Implications for Today." *Studies in the Spirituality of Jesuits* 14 (1982).

——. "Thomas More's Spirituality Compared." *Thought* 52 (1977): 319–23.

O'Reilly, Terence. "Erasmus, Ignatius Loyola and Orthodoxy" *Journal of Theological Studies* 30 (1979): 115-27.

——. Saint Ignatius Loyola and Spanish Erasmianism." *Archivum Historicum Societatis Jesu* 43 (1974): 301–21.

Orlandini, Nicolaus, S.J. *Historiae Societatis Jesu Pars Prima*. Cologne, 1615.

Overfield, James H. "Scholastic Opposition to Humanism in Pre-Reformation Germany." *Viator. Medieval and Renaissance Studies* 7 (1976): 391–420.

Ozment, Steven, editor. *The Reformation in Medieval Perspective*. Chicago: Quadrangle Books, 1971.

Padberg, John W., S.J. "The General Congregations of the Society of Jesus: A Brief Survey of Their History." *Studies in the Spirituality of the Jesuits* 6, Nos. 1 and 2 (1974).

Pascoe, Louis, S.J. "The Council of Trent and Bible Study. Humanism and Culture." *Catholic Historical Review* 52 (1966): 18–38.

Pastor, Ludwig von. *The History of the Popes from the Close of the Middle Ages*. Translated by Ralph E. Kerr, E. F. Peeler and Ernest Graf, O.S.B. 40 vols. St. Louis. 1891–1953.

Peter, Carl J. "Dimensions of *Jus Divinum* in Roman Catholic Theology." *Theological Studies* 34 (1973): 227–50.

Pierri, Pietro, S.J. *Giovanni Tristano e i Primordi della Architettura Gesuitica.* Rome, 1955.

———. *Giuseppe Valeriano, S.J. Architetto e Pittore (1542–1596).* Rome, 1970.

Poncelet, Alfred, S.J. *Histoire de la Compagnie de Jésus dans les anciens Pays-Bas.* 2 vols. Brussels, 1927.

Prat, Jean-M., S.J. *Histoire du Père Ribadeneyra Disciple de Saint Ignace.* Paris, 1862.

———. *Le Père Claude Le Jay Un des premiers compagnons de S. Ignace de Loyola.* Lyon, 1874.

Prosperi, Adriano. *Tra Evangelismo e Controriforma. G. M. Giberti (1495–1543).* Rome, 1969.

Quilliet, H. "Congruisme." *Dictionnaire de Théologie Catholique* 3,1:1120–33.

Rahner, Hugo, S.J. *Ignatius the Theologian.* Translated by Michael Barry. New York, 1968.

———. *St. Ignatius of Loyola. Letters to Women.* Translated by Kathleen Pond and S.A.H. Weetman. New York, 1960.

———. *The Spirituality of St. Ignatius of Loyola. An Account of Its Historical Development.* Translated by Francis J. Smith, S.J. Westminster, Md., 1953.

Ranke, Leopold von. *The History of the Popes, Their Church and State and especially of Their Conflicts with Protestantism in the Sixteenth and Seventeenth Centuries.* Translated by E. Foster. 3 vols. London, 1847–48.

Ratzinger, Joseph. "Announcements and Prefatory Notes of Explanation." *Commentary on the Documents of Vatican II.* 1:297–305. Edited by Herbert Vorgrimler. New York, 1967.

———. "The Transmission of Divine Revelation." *Commentary on the Documents of Vatican II.* 3:181–98. Edited by Herbert Vorgrimler. New York, 1969.

Ravier, André, S.J. *Ignace de Loyola fonde la Compagnie de Jésus.* Paris, 1974.

———. *Les Chroniques. Saint Ignace de Loyola.* Paris, 1973.

Rayez, André, S.J. "The Golden Age of Medieval Devotion: The Fourteenth and Fifteenth Centuries." *Jesus in Christian Devotion and Contemplation,* 44–85. Edited by Edward Malatesta, S.J. Translated by Paul J. Oligny, O.F.M. St. Meinrad, 1974.

Reites, James W., S.J. "St. Ignatius of Loyola and the Jews." *Studies in the Spirituality of Jesuits* 13, No. 4 (1981).

Rice, Eugene F., Jr. "Erasmus and the Religious Tradition, 1494–99." *Renaissance Essays,* 162–86. Edited by Paul O. Kristeller and Philip P. Wiener. New York, 1968.

_____. "Humanist Aristotelianism in France: Jacques Lefèvre d'Etaples and His Circle." *Humanism in France at the End of the Middle Ages and in the Early Renaissance*,132–49. Edited by Anthony H.T. Levi. New York, 1970.

_____. "Jacques Lefèvre d'Etaples and the Medieval Christian Mystics." *Florilegium Historiale. Essays presented to Wallace K. Ferguson*, 89–124. Edited by J.G. Rowe and W.H. Stockdale. Toronto, 1971.

_____. *The Renaissance Idea of Wisdom*. Cambridge, Mass., 1958.

_____, editor. *The Prefatory Epistles of Jacques Lefèvre d'Etaples and Related Texts* New York, 1972.

Roeck, Jozef de, S.J. "La Genèse de la Congrégation Générale dans la Compagnie de Jésus." *Archivum Historicum Societatis Jesu* 36 (1967): 267–90.

Ross, James Bruce. "Gasparo Contarini and His Friends." *Studies in the Renaissance* 17 (1970): 192–232.

Rotsaert, Mark, S.J. "Les premiers contacts de saint Ignace avec l'érasmisme espagnol." *Revue d'Histoire de la Spiritualité* 49 (1973): 443–64.

Rouquette, Robert, S.J. "Ignace de Loyola dans le Paris intellectuel du XVIe siécle." *Etudes* 290 (1956): 18–40.

Sacchini, Francesco, S.J. *Historiae Societatis Jesu pars secunda sive Lainius*. Antwerp, 1620.

Scaduto, Mario, S.J. "Concilio di Trento e Riforma Cattolica." *Archivum Historicum Societatis Jesu* 38 (1969): 501–31.

_____ "'Il 'Libretto consolatorio' di Bobadilla a Domenech sulle vocazione mancate (1570)." *Archivum Historicum Societatis Jesu* 43 (1974): 85–102.

_____. "La Ginevra di Teodore Beza nei ricordi di un Gesuita Lucano Luca Pinelli (1542–1607)." *Archivum Historicum Societatis Jesu* 20 (1951): 117-42.

_____. "Laínez e l'Indice del 1559. Lullo, Sabunde, Savonarola, Erasmo." *Archivum Historicum Societatis Jesu* 24 (1955): 1–82.

_____. *Storia della Compagnia di Gesù in Italia*. Vol. 3: *L'Epoca di Giacomo Lainez. Il Governo 1556–65*. Vol. 4: *L'Epoca di Giacomo Lainez. L'Azzione 1556–65*. Rome, 1974.

Scarcella, Phillip J. "James Laynez: Christian Humanist and Catholic Reformer During the Tridentine Period, 1545–1563." Ph.D. dissertation, New York University, 1974.

Schenk, Wilhelm. *Reginald Pole. Cardinal of England*. New York. 1950.

Schneider, Burkhard., S.J. "Der Konflikt zwischen Claudius Aquaviva und Paulus Hoffaeus." *Archivum Historicum Societatis Jesu* 26 (1957).

Schurhammer, Georg, S.J. *Francis Xavier. His Life, His Times*. Vol. 1. Translated by M. Joseph Costelloe, S.J. Rome, 1973. This is a translation of the first of four volumes in German.

Sommervogel, Carlos, S.J. *Bibliothèque de la Compagnie de Jésus* Première partie: *Bibliographie* par les PP. Augustin et Aloys Backer, S.J. Seconde partie: *Histoire*, par A. Carayon, S.J. *Tables*. . . par P. Bliard, S.J. 12 vols. Brussels and Paris, 1890–1932. Reprinted Héverlé-Louvain, 1960.

Southern, Richard W. *The Pelican History of the Church*, Vol. 2: *Western Society and the Church in the Middle Ages*. Baltimore: Pelican Books, 1970.

Sweeney, Francis, S.J. *Bernardine Realino: Renaissance Man*. New York. 1951.

Symonds, J.A. *Sketches and Studies in Southern Europe*. 2 vols. New York, 1880.

Tacchi-Venturi, Pietro, S.J. *Storia della Compagnia di Gesù in Italia*. 2 vols. in 4 parts. Secunda edizione. Rome, 1950.

Tavernier, H. "Le P. Claude Jay, sa patrie et sa famille." *Revue Savoisienne* 35 (1894): 79–84.

Tracy, James D. Book review of *Critique et tradition à la veille de la Réforme en France, Etude suivie de textes inédits traduits et annotés* by Jean- Pierre Massaut. *Catholic Historical Review* 63 (1977): 280–81.

Trinkaus, Charles. *In Our Image and Likeness. Humanity and Divinity in Italian Humanist Thought*. 2 vols. Chicago, 1970.

_____, editor. *The Pursuit of Holiness in Late Medieval and Renaissance Religion*. Brill, 1975.

Villaret, Emile, S.J. *Abridged History of the Sodalities of Our Lady*. Translated by William J. Young, S.J. St. Louis, 1957.

_____. "Les premières origines des Congrégations mariales dans la Compagnie de Jésus." *Archivum Historicum Societatis Jesu* 6 (1937): 25–57.

Vorgrimler, Herbert, editor. *Commentary on the Documents of Vatican II*. 3 vols. New York, 1967–69.

Walz, Angelus Maria, O.P. *I Domenicani al Concilio di Trento*. Rome, 1961.

Wicks, Jared, S.J. "Martin Luther's Treatise on Indulgences." *Theological Studies* 28 (1967): 481–518.

Zaccaria, Francesco A., S.J. *Excursus litterarii per Italiam ab anno MDCCXLII ad annum MDCCLII. Volumen I*. A Vatican Library Microfilm. Biblioteca Vaticana, 1961. Available at Fordham University.

_____. *Iter Litterarium per Italiam ab anno MDCCXLIII ad MDCCLVII*. A Vatican Library Microfilm. Biblioteca Vaticana, 1961. Available at Fordham University.

INDEX

Achille, Paolo, 188, 335
Acquaviva, Claudio: appointment as provincial, 331–32; elected General, 346; on racial purity, 247–48
Acquaviva, Rodolfo, 307
Act of Supremacy (1534), 167
Adorno, Francesco, 245; commission to investigate election, 331
Adriaenssens, Adriaan, 307
Agarenes, 62
Agricola, Johann, 203
Albrecht V, Duke of Upper Bavaria, opinion of Jesuit college, 115, 202
Alcalá, University of, Salmerón enrolled at, 154
Alcalá Polyglot Bible, 151, 152
Alexander VI, Pope, authorization of college at Alcalá, 151
Alfonso, Alvaro, 47
Alfonso I, Duke of Ferrara, 254
Altieri, Baldasarre, 21
Ambrose, Saint, 99
Anabaptists, 45
Apostolate, intellectual, 109–11
Appianus, Philip, 50
Aragon, Juan de, 47
Araldo, Giovanni Francesco, 221, 255, 318
Araoz, Antonio, 28, 188, 247
Artes Praedicandi, 198
Art of Good Living, The, 137
Attrition, 100
Auer, Lambert von, 133
Augsburg Confession, 235
Augsburg, Diet of, 15, 98, 119–20
Avalas, Ferrante de, 22
Avalos y Aquino, Alfonso, 60
Avila, Luis de, 165
Ayala, Martin de, 288

Badia, Tommaso, 32
Bagnacavallus, Christopher, 193

Bagnorea (Italy), 36-38
Baptism, and original sin, 76
Barnabites, 9, 35
Bayern, Ernst Von, 50, 63; and Synod of Salzburg, 53–54
Beaton, David, 168
Beda, Noel, 11, 158; censure of Erasmus, 162
Bellarmine, Robert, St., 307, 335, 336
Benedictines, 28, 33
Benefice, 83
Bernal Diaz de Luco, Juan, 178
Bertano, Pietro, 73
Beza, Theodore, 328
Bible, Alcalá polyglot, 151
Bible, Vulgate edition of, 72
Biblia Polyglota Complutenese, 152
Biblical languages, study of, 206
Biblical scholarship, 152
Bishop's Image, A (Jay), 54
Bishops: divine right of, 273; formation of, 73; jurisdictional powers of, 272–76
Blado, Antonio: *Index of Forbidden Books*, 250; *Moderatio Indicis*, 252
Bobadilla, Nicolás, 8, 352, assigned to Germany, 43–44; assigned to Verona, 17; at Council at Trent, 191–92, and de Oviedo, disagreements, 218; on departures from the order, 306; in Ferrara, 24; on Jesuit colleges, 308; ordained, 162; in Rome, 165–66; and Sant' Angelo college, 311–13; supervisor of Naples school, 218; vote for General Superior, 39; at Worms, 58
"Bobadillian colleges," 311–13
Bologna, Council of Trent at, 95–96, 193–94
Boncuore, Giovanni Battista, 318
Bonomo, Pietro, 88
Booklet on the Frequent Reception of the Holy Eucharist, A, 224
Borghese, Marcantonio, 240
Borgia, Francis, 62, 246, 249, 298;

451